A Dictionary for the
Modern Trumpet Player

DICTIONARIES FOR THE MODERN MUSICIAN

Series Editor: David Daniels

Contributions to **Dictionaries for the Modern Musician** offer both the novice and the advanced artist lists of key terms designed to fully cover the field of study and performance for major instruments and classes of instruments, as well as the workings of musicians in areas from conducting to composing. Focusing primarily on the knowledge required by the *contemporary* musical student and teacher, performer, and professional, each dictionary is a must-have for any musician's personal library!

A Dictionary for the Modern Singer by Matthew Hoch, 2014
A Dictionary for the Modern Clarinetist by Jane Ellsworth, 2014
A Dictionary for the Modern Trumpet Player by Elisa Koehler, 2015

A Dictionary for the Modern Trumpet Player

Elisa Koehler

ROWMAN & LITTLEFIELD
Lanham • Boulder • New York • London

Published by Rowman & Littlefield
A wholly owned subsidiary of The Rowman & Littlefield Publishing Group, Inc.
4501 Forbes Boulevard, Suite 200, Lanham, Maryland 20706
www.rowman.com

Unit A, Whitacre Mews, 26-34 Stannary Street, London SE11 4AB

British Library Cataloguing in Publication Information Available

Library of Congress Cataloging-in-Publication Data
Koehler, Elisa.
A dictionary for the modern trumpet player / Elisa Koehler.
    pages cm. — (Dictionaries for the modern musician)
Includes bibliographical references.
ISBN 978-0-8108-8657-5 (hardcover : alk. paper) — ISBN 978-0-8108-8658-2 (ebook)
1. Trumpet—Dictionaries.   I. Title.
ML102.T78K64 2015
788.9'219303—dc23   2014038772

Printed in the United States of America

In Memoriam
Walter Louis Koehler
(August 23, 1919–October 19, 2000)

Contents

List of Illustrations

Acknowledgments

I would like to take a moment to thank several colleagues who provided assistance or inspiration to make this work possible: Barry Bauguess, Raymond Burkhart, Tom Crown, Stanley Curtis, Bruce Dickey, David Hickman, Friedemann Immer, Joe Kaminsky, Sabine Klaus, H. M. Lewis, Henry Meredith, Gary Mortenson, Jeff Nussbaum, Mark Ponzo, Brian Shaw, Jim Sherry, Crispian Steele-Perkins, Edward Tarr, Kiri Tollaksen, Dutch Uithoven, and Jari Villanueva. I especially want to thank Bennett Graff at Rowman & Littlefield for inviting me to write this volume in the *Dictionaries for the Modern Musician Series* and for his visionary leadership in creating a much-needed new reference tool. Working with series editor David Daniels has been an immense privilege and a distinct pleasure; his encyclopedic knowledge of all things musical (and more) borders on the supernatural. Any errors that may appear in this volume are my responsibility alone. Finally, I am especially grateful to the wonderful artist whose illustrations appear throughout this volume, Todd Larsen.

Introduction

When Georg Frideric Handel composed the obbligato aria "The Trumpet Shall Sound" for his oratorio *Messiah* in 1741, he probably never dreamed that more than a dozen different trumpets would be pressed into service to perform it over the next three centuries. From the natural trumpet, the English slide trumpet, the "Bach trumpet," and the cornet to modern trumpets with piston or rotary valves in B-flat, C, or D, the modern Baroque trumpet with vent holes, and the piccolo trumpet in B-flat or A, the steady march of trumpet history presents a bewildering catalog of change.

This book's title is especially fitting because the "modern" trumpet pictured on its cover has been standard only since the 1930s. Before then, the simple term *trumpet* meant different things in different eras. For example, for nearly two hundred years (1600–1800), a "trumpet" was an eight-foot-long natural trumpet in C. In Victorian England, it meant the six-foot-long English slide trumpet in F or its successor, the "long F" trumpet with piston valves. In German-speaking countries, it still means a rotary valve trumpet.

But that is only part of the story. There are many other branches on the trumpet's family tree. The cornet, bugle, flugelhorn, posthorn, and cornetto are certainly not trumpets, but trumpet players play them or at least the music written for them. There are also trumpets or trumpet-like instruments from antiquity and non-Western countries, of which the rowdy vuvuzela is perhaps the most recognizable modern representative. While organologists rightly distinguish cylindrical and conical bore brasses as belonging to "the trumpet family" and "the bugle family," respectively, I prefer to put them all under one roof for the purposes of this dictionary because they are all played by trumpet players.

By definition, a trumpet is a lip-vibrated aerophone with a cylindrical bore. There are two primary categories of trumpets: natural trumpets and chromatic trumpets. Natural trumpets produce notes of the harmonic overtone series with an unmodified tube, and chromatic trumpets produce all of the notes of the chromatic scale through modifications such as valves, keys, vent holes, and slides. Trumpets were primarily military signal instruments until the seventeenth century, when players developed the clarino range and began to venture into the realm of concert music. The golden age of Baroque trumpet music that followed elevated the artistic status of the trumpet to new heights and led the best composers of the age to bestow upon the instrument the repertoire that still defines it today.

As styles changed in the late eighteenth century and high-register playing fell out of fashion, the art of clarino playing on natural trumpets died out. Ironically, the Age of Enlightenment was the lowest point in the trumpet's history, from an artistic standpoint. The Industrial Revolution spurred mechanical experiments such as vent holes, keys, slides, and valves that enabled trumpets to play chromatically in the lower register. Despite the efforts of Haydn and Hummel to compose concerti for the keyed trumpet, it took a long time for new inventions to gain traction with audiences who were accustomed to the traditional military role of the trumpet. Hearing trumpets perform lyrical melodies in the low register simply struck many conservative concert patrons as "unnatural."

While the keyed trumpet had a short lifespan, its conical cousin, the keyed bugle, revolutionized brass virtuosity and played a leading role in the development of the wind band. Keyed bugle virtuosos became bandleaders and chamber musicians who redefined the artistic possibilities of high brass instruments amid a new democratic landscape. With the invention of the valve and the development of the cornet in the nineteenth century, the tide began to turn and never receded. Cornet virtuosos dazzled audiences, became conservatory professors, and even found their way into the orchestra. Mass production techniques made cornets affordable for amateur musicians and fueled the brass band movement, which later played a role in the development of jazz.

By the early twentieth century, changes in the design of the cornet (stretching out the bell and adding a fixed leadpipe) made it more trumpet-like to such an extent that it eventually evolved into the modern B-flat trumpet, which is the standard instrument today (see figure 1).

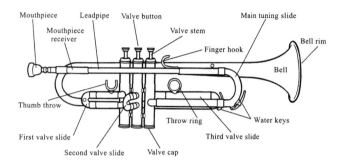

Figure 1. A modern B-flat trumpet with parts identified. *Drawing by T. M. Larsen.*

In the years surrounding the Second World War, jazz redefined trumpet virtuosity while enterprising classical trumpeters made inroads as soloists and chamber musicians. The advent of the piccolo trumpet and the early music revival brought trumpet history full circle by resurrecting the popularity of Baroque trumpet music in the 1960s. At the same time, the development of professional brass quintets elevated the artistic status of brass musicians as never before. Now, in the twenty-first century, trumpeters play leading roles in all musical genres and enjoy career options that were unimaginable just sixty years ago.

This whirlwind tour of trumpet history and development has a common theme: change. The colorful menagerie that is the trumpet family can be obscure, but this dictionary is designed to help in several ways. Entries listed include instruments, musicians, and technical terms, as well as explanations of playing techniques. Terms appear in several languages along with obscure indications from orchestral parts that resulted from attempts to create new labels for unfamiliar instruments, mutes, and playing techniques. An extensive bibliography appears in the back listing the latest scholarship divided into several categories for easy access. Four appendices are also included to provide helpful information and context. The first appendix includes a timeline of trumpet history to present a chronological perspective, the second presents illustrations of the many different valve mechanisms applied to trumpets and cornets since 1814, the third appendix provides a classification system for the different varieties of mutes, and the fourth one lists the major trumpet audition excerpts for orchestras and opera companies.

LIST OF COMMON ABBREVIATIONS

abbr.	abbreviation	ITG	International Trumpet Guild
app.	appendix		
b.	born	instr.	instrument
ca.	circa	It.	Italian
cm	centimeter	Lat.	Latin
d.	died	m	meter
ed.	edition	mm	millimeter
Eng.	English	op.	opus
fl.	flourished	pl.	plural
Fr.	French	Pol.	Polish
Ger.	German	trans.	translator, translation
HBS	Historic Brass Society		
Hz	Hertz (cycles per second)	v.	verb
in.	inches		

THE DICTIONARY

A

Abblasen. (Ger.) To blow off or to call off (cancel). 1. A type of brilliant **fanfare**. 2. The title of a fanfare attributed to **Gottfried Reiche** that appears on a sheet of paper held by Reiche in the 1726 portrait painted by Elias Gottlob Haussmann (1695–1774). This fanfare is well known in the United States as the theme of the television news program *CBS News Sunday Morning*, which has broadcast recordings of the work by **Don Smithers** (on **natural trumpet**), **Doc Severinsen**, and **Wynton Marsalis**.

abẹn. An ivory **side-blown trumpet** played by the Asante in Ghana (Western Africa) made from an elephant tusk. In the Asante Twi language, the term translates as "animal horn," but it literally means "tooth" because that is the true nature of an elephant's tusk: it protrudes from the mouth, not the head, and is two-thirds hollow. When a tusk is prepared to be played as an instrument, a rectangular hole is cut into the side, where the player's vibrating lips create the sound, and a small hole is cut into the tip, which is manipulated by a finger to adjust pitch. When the hole is opened, the pitch of the abẹn raises approximately one whole step; when it is closed, the entire length of the tusk resonates (not just the length from the lip hole), which lowers the pitch.

abẹntia. A shorter, higher pitched version of the **abẹn**. (See figure 38 under **natural trumpet**.)

absolute pitch, perfect pitch. A vivid memory for pitch. In musicians it takes the form of the ability to identify the name of an isolated note without any surrounding context of a given key or related pitches. In nonmusicians without the musical vocabulary to express the experience, it is harder to recognize, though such cases do exist. Often it is associated with a particular instrument or timbre (e.g., a clarinetist recognizes tones when played on the clarinet but not when played on the violin, synthesizer, or tuning fork), but some subjects can recognize the pitch of nonmusical sounds—the squeak of a floor board or the buzz of an electrical machine—and express them as musical notes ("a little below A-flat"). The possessor of this ability is able to recognize and follow complex key changes and modulations when listening.

Despite the term *absolute* pitch, the phenomenon is found in varying degrees in various individuals. Also, as the body ages, the perception tends to rise, perhaps due to the age-related shrinkage of the cochlea (an anatomical structure within the ear): thus a piece in D major might be perceived by the elderly trained musician as being in E-flat, E, or F major. This can be very disturbing to a musician who has relied on the exactitude of his/her aural perceptions for decades.

acoustics. The branch of science that studies the physical properties of sound and how they relate to auditory perception (psychoacoustics), rooms (especially spaces for performing and recording), and sound generation.

Adams, John (b. 1947). American composer and conductor. After beginning his musical studies on the clarinet, Adams studied composition at Harvard University with Leon Kirchner, Roger Sessions, Harold Shapero, and David Del Tredici. Between 1972 and 1982 he taught composition at the San Francisco Conservatory; he served as composer-in-residence at the San Francisco Symphony between 1982 and 1985, achieving notice for his symphonic compositions *Harmonium* and *Harmonielehre*, written for the orchestra during that time in a tonal style featuring elements of minimalism and neoromanticism. Adams composed several operas on contemporary themes including *Nixon in China* (1987), *The Death of Klinghoffer* (1991), and *Doctor Atomic* (2005). He earned the Pulitzer Prize in 2003 for his orchestral 9/11 tribute, *On the Transmigration of Souls.*

Adams's writing for the trumpet favors the trumpet in C and the piccolo trumpet with sweeping lyricism as well as demanding passages in terms of range, endurance, and technical facility. A notable piccolo trumpet solo appears in his symphonic work *The Wound Dresser* (1989). Other works that feature the trumpet include *Tromba Lontana* (1985), *Short Ride in a Fast Machine* (1986), and *Doctor Atomic Symphony* (2007).

Adelstein, Bernard (b. 1928). American trumpeter. He began playing the trumpet at the age of eight on the advice of his doctor, who recommended that it might be good therapy for his asthma. He began lessons with Louis Davidson at the age of ten, and later studied with **Harry Glantz** and **Georges Mager**. In 1944 he joined the Pittsburgh Symphony as second trumpet and became the principal trumpet of the Dallas Symphony four years later in 1948. Between 1950 and 1960 he served as principal trumpeter of the Minneapolis Symphony Orchestra, moving on to the position of principal trumpet of the Cleveland Orchestra in 1960 and remaining there for the next twenty-eight years until his retirement in 1988. In addition to performing, Adelstein also taught at the University of Minnesota, the Cleveland Institute of Music, and Indiana University.

Aebersold, Wilton Jameson "Jamey" (b. 1939). American saxophonist, publisher, and jazz educator. He began performing professionally at the age of fifteen and went on to earn bachelor's and master's degrees from Indiana University. In addition to performing, Aebersold taught music education at Indiana University Southeast (1969–1967) and classical saxophone at the University of Louisville (1970–1972). In the early 1970s he began leading week-long "jazz camps" in the summer that expanded into an educational project that included international workshops and numerous publications. His multi-volume series, *A New Approach to Jazz Improvisation*, was begun in 1967 and includes books on jazz styles and theory as well jazz standards and transcriptions of solos by influential jazz artists, including many trumpet players. The series of play-along recordings that accompany the books has impacted the practice routines of jazz musicians around the world by allowing students to practice skills with tracks recorded by experienced jazz musicians. The series is a classic in jazz education and contains nearly 130 volumes (as of 2013). Aebersold was inducted into the International Association of Jazz Educators Hall of Fame in 1989, and he was awarded an honorary doctorate by Indiana University in 1992. Aebersold also plays piano, bass, and banjo, in addition to the saxophone.

aerophone. Term devised by Erich Moritz von Hornbostel and Curt Sachs to classify musical instruments that gen-erate sound through a vibrating air column as opposed to other means (strings are chordophones). This category includes brass instruments as well as woodwinds and was created in 1914 for ethnomusicologists to describe musical instruments from nonwestern traditions. The other categories in this system include idiophones (metallic or wooden percussion), membranophones (drums), and more recently electrophones.

Aida trumpet. A long, straight trumpet similar to a **herald trumpet** that was originally designed to play the "Triumphal March" in the second act of Giuseppe Verdi's opera, *Aida* (1871). Various incarnations of this instrument have included one or more piston valves.

airstream. The flow of breath through the tubing of a trumpet.

Allen, Joseph Lathrop (1815–c. 1905). American brass instrument manufacturer. He began making **keyed bugles** in the 1830s and built his first valved instrument in Boston in 1842, a B-flat trumpet with **Vienna valves**. Some of his instruments are made with the system featuring a half-step slide for the first valve, known as the **"Catholic" fingering**. In 1845, Allen made an **over-the-shoulder cornet** in A with five **rotary valves** for **Harvey Dodworth**, which he used for over forty years as leader of the Dodworth Band of New York City. In Boston, Allen made valved **posthorns**, valved trumpets, trombones, **ophicleides**, and **bugles**. Around 1850, he designed a new rotary valve with string linkage known as the **Allen valve** that was smaller in diameter and longer than the usual rotaries.

Between 1852 and 1857, he was partners with Benjamin F. Richardson (1823–1894), and the company was known as "Allen & Richardson." Around 1855, Allen made an over-the-shoulder cornet in A-flat with five Allen rotary valves. The right hand played three valves while the left hand could lower the instrument to F or E-flat by pressing the fourth or fifth valve respectively. Between 1861 and 1863, Allen's partnership with David C. Hall was known as "Allen & Hall." In 1865, David C. Hall and Benjamin F. Quinby bought the tools and stock of the company and with George Quinby became known as "Hall & Quinby" until 1869.

Allen valve. A type of **rotary valve** attributed to Boston instrument maker **Joseph Lathrop Allen**. Produced sometime after 1853, the mechanism was designed for faster, more efficient valve function with longer and thinner rotors, oval-shaped valve ports, and flatter tubing entering and exiting the valve chamber than similar components on conventional rotary valves. The smaller diameter of the rotors and the top action valve levers resulted in fluid movement that was especially popular with instruments used by American brass bands in the nineteenth century. (See figure A6 in appendix 2.)

Alpenhorn. (Ger). **alphorn**.

Alpert, Herb (b. 1935). American trumpeter, composer, and recording industry executive. Following service in the U.S. Army performing at military ceremonies and two years at the University of Southern California playing with the Trojan Marching Band, Alpert embarked on a career in Hollywood as an actor and as a musician in the field of popular music in the 1950s. He wrote or co-wrote several top-twenty hits for other artists, including "Baby Talk" (Jan and Dean) and "Wonderful World" (Sam Cooke). He made recordings as a vocalist himself, starting in 1960, and started his own record label with business partner Jerry Moss, known as A&M Records. Alpert and Moss sold A&M to PolyGram Records in 1987 and continued to manage the label until 1993.

As a trumpeter, Alpert is best known for his work as the leader of the Tijuana Brass. Inspired by hearing **mariachi** musicians at a bullfight on a trip to Tijuana, Mexico, Alpert released the single "The Lonely Bull" in 1962, overdubbing all of the trumpet parts himself. Its tremendous popularity led to the formation of the Tijuana Brass in 1964 and a string of successful hits. While the band performed Latin-flavored music, none of the musicians were Hispanic themselves. The group won six Grammy awards, fifteen gold records, and fourteen platinum discs with hits including "Spanish Flea" and "Tijuana Taxi." Alpert's only number-one single with the group was his vocal rendition of "This Guy's in Love with You" in 1968. The Tijuana Brass disbanded in 1969 and Alpert pursued a solo career, scoring a number-one hit with "Rise" in 1979 and performing at high-profile events like the 1984 Summer Olympic Games in Los Angeles and Super Bowl XXII in San Diego.

alpha angle. Term coined by American **mouthpiece** maker Gary Radke to describe the angle of the **bite** radius inside the **cup** of a trumpet mouthpiece, which determines how much a player's lips extend inside the mouthpiece. This measurement is also known as the "undercut" of a mouthpiece **rim**.

alphorn. *Cor des alpes* (Fr.), *Alpenhorn* (Ger.). A long, wooden trumpet with an upturned **bell** indigenous to the Swiss Alps and similar alpine regions. Made from the solid wood of a spruce, pine, or poplar tree, an alphorn measures approximately six feet (185 cm) in its most common form. The wood is carved into halves from a tree, hollowed out, and bound together with bark, roots, or gut. The cup-shaped **mouthpiece** is usually carved from a removable piece of hardwood or plastic. Alphorns vary in size from nearly four feet (120 cm) to

seventeen feet (518 cm) in length. Instruments tuned in F or G range between eleven and twelve feet long (340–360 cm).

Alphorns originated in the Middle Ages as a signal instrument for herding livestock and for sounding alarms for the local population in times of war. As a natural instrument made from a single tube, the alphorn sounds notes of the **harmonic overtone series.** Traditional alphorn music often goes as high as the twelfth partial; such tunes inspired the horn solo in the finale of **Brahms**'s First Symphony after the composer heard an alphorn while vacationing in Switzerland in 1868. Several twentieth-century composers favored the alphorn with concert repertoire including Jean Daetwyler (1907–1994), Ferenc Farkas (1905–2000), and Etienne Isoz (1905–1987).

alta cappella. The earliest type of wind band in Europe. It originated in the fourteenth century and was comprised of two shawms and a bombardon, and later, a **slide trumpet** or trombone. The ensemble primarily played dance music and dinner music, and was staffed by minstrels, also known as *Stadtpfeifer*, piffari (pipers), or **town waits**.

Altenburg, Johann Caspar (1689–1761). Father of **Johann Ernst Altenburg** and an eminent court trumpeter in **Weissenfels**, Germany, between 1711 and 1746. His official rank was that of chamber, court, and field trumpeter, also court chamber and traveling quartermaster. At the age of eighteen he traveled to Weissenfels to become an apprentice to the court trumpeter Röbock. According to his son's treatise—which includes a drawing of his mouthpiece as the only illustration in the original edition—he was especially adept at playing in the high register, performing ornaments (*Manieren*), and in delicate, expressive clarino playing in works by **Telemann**, **Fasch**, and others. His travels to several German courts in the 1730s resulted in "considerable applause" and "lavish gifts" as well as job offers and a substantial raise in his salary at Weissenfels. His two eldest sons, Johann Rudolph Altenburg and Johann Christoph Altenburg, achieved the rank of "Princely Saxon Court and Field Trumpeter."

Altenburg, Johann Ernst (1734–1801). German trumpeter and organist who wrote an important treatise on Baroque trumpet playing. His father, **Johann Casper Altenburg**, the duke's trumpeter at **Weissenfels**, committed him to a trumpet apprenticeship when he was only two years old. He achieved professional status by the age of eighteen, but unlike his two older brothers, Johann Rudolph Altenburg and Johann Christoph Altenburg, he was not able to secure a court position because of the decline in demand for trumpeters amid the changing social order. He pursued studies in organ and composition with Johann Theodor Römhild in Merseburg until 1757 and also briefly studied with Johann Christoph Altnickol (J. S. Bach's son-in-law) in Naumburg. He joined the French army as a field trumpeter in 1757 and participated in the Seven Year's War before returning to Weissenfels in 1766. Altenburg spent the rest of his life as an organist, first in Landsberg, and after 1769 in the small town of Bitterfeld.

Altenburg's treatise, *Versuch einer Anleitung zur heroisch-musikalischen Trompeter- und Pauker-Kunst [Essay on an Introduction to the Heroic and Musical Trumpeters' and Kettledrummers' Art]*, was completed in manuscript and offered on a subscription basis by Johann Adam Hiller in his *Musikalische Nachrichten* in 1770 before it was published in Halle twenty-five years later in 1795. Providing valuable insights into Baroque trumpet technique, the *Versuch* detailed explanations of expressive **articulation** (unequal **tonguing**), **clarino** playing, **lipping** out-of-tune partials, **huffing**, military field trumpet **signals**, and instruments of the time.

He may not have written the *Concerto a VII Clarini con Tymp* published in the back of his treatise, but Altenburg did compose six piano sonatas published in 1780 and 1781. Altenburg was only twelve years old when the Weissenfels court ceased to exist following the death of Duke Johann Adolph in 1746, but the profession of his father and two older brothers was forever memorialized in his *Versuch*, the most important primary source on the trumpet from the late Baroque era.

alternate fingering. A **valve combination** that is used as a second choice to produce a given note in order to facilitate the performance of **trills**, to simplify awkward **fingering** patterns, or to provide different options for intonation or tone color. (See figure 2.) Such combinations usually do not produce optimal purity of tone or **intonation**. On a trumpet with three **valves**, for example, the third valve can be used as a substitute for the combination of the first two valves because both fingerings (3 or 1+2) engage nearly identical lengths of appended tubing (**valve slides**), though the pitch produced by the alternate fingering is slightly sharp. Alternate fingerings can also be used to perform special effects like **valve tremolo** and **lip slurs**.

Figure 2. Alternate fingerings. *Elisa Koehler.*

altissimo playing. Extreme high register trumpet playing, especially in jazz.

alto e basso. The middle range (G3 to C4) of the **natural trumpet** ensemble in the sixteenth century, as described by **Bendinelli** and **Fantini**.

Amado water key. See **water key**.

American Brass Quintet. One of the pioneer ensembles in the history of brass chamber music. Formed in 1960, the quintet gave its first performance at the 92nd Street Y in New York City and debuted at Carnegie Hall in 1962. Dedicated to expanding the repertoire and exposure of serious chamber music for brass, the quintet commissioned substantial works from several notable composers including Samuel Adler (b. 1928), Daniel Asia (b. 1953), Jan Bach (b. 1937), Robert Beaser (b. 1954), William Bolcom (b. 1938), Elliott Carter (1908–2012), Jacob Druckman (1928–1996), **Eric Ewazen** (b. 1954), **Anthony Plog** (b. 1947), David Sampson (b. 1951), Gunther Schuller (b. 1925), William Schuman (1910–1992), Joan Tower (b. 1938), Melinda Wagner (b. 1957), and Charles Whittenberg (1927–1984). Known for their virtuosity, precision, and artistry, the quintet is responsible for premiering a sizable percentage of the serious brass quintet repertoire.

Unlike the **New York Brass Quintet**, the instrumentation of the American Brass Quintet included a bass trombone instead of a tuba. The current members of the group are trumpeters Kevin Cobb (since 1998) and Louis Hanzlik (since 2013), David Wakefield on horn, Michael Powell on trombone, and John Rojak on bass trombone. In addition to performing and touring, members of the quintet serve on the faculty at the Juilliard School as well as the Aspen Music Festival. Past American Brass Quintet trumpeters have included Theodore Weis, Robert Heinrich, Ronald Anderson, Allan Dean, John Eckert, **Gerard Schwarz**, Louis Ranger, John Aley, **Chris Gekker**, and **Raymond Mase**.

anchor tonguing. A technique designed to aid high-register playing by placing (anchoring) the tip of the tongue behind the bottom teeth and lifting the back of the tongue near the roof of the mouth. Variations of this technique of **tongue placement** are also known as **dorsal tonguing** or "snake" tonguing. **Claude Gordon** refers to it as "K Tongue Modified" (KTM) because the raised position of the back of the tongue is similar to that used for the secondary syllable in **multiple tonguing**.

Anderson, Joseph G. (ca. 1816–1873). American cornetist and bandmaster. Based in Philadelphia, Anderson was a performer on several instruments including the cornet, the flute, and the violin. He was the cornet soloist with the brass band led by keyed bugle virtuoso **Francis Johnson** and assumed the leadership of the band when Johnson died in 1844. His bands toured extensively in the

1850s and he was asked to train the bands of the African American regiments during the American Civil War.

Anderson, William Alonzo "Cat" (1916– 1981). American jazz trumpeter noted for his mastery of the extreme high register. Anderson lost both of his parents at the age of four and grew up at the Jenkins Orphanage in Charleston, South Carolina. He earned his nickname, "Cat," for his unique style of fighting as a boy. Anderson's first instrument was the trombone, but he switched to trumpet in 1929 at the age of thirteen and learned music theory in the school band. He left school in 1932 and formed a band called the Carolina Cotton Pickers with some of his friends. In 1935 he left that group to play with many other jazz artists including Claude Hopkins, Doc Wheeler, and Lionel Hampton.

Anderson achieved fame with Duke Ellington's band in 1944 and played with the group off and on until 1971, working with other groups from 1947 to 1950 and 1959 to 1960. His five-octave range and colossal sound along with the unrivaled power of his stratospheric **altissimo playing** set new standards for jazz trumpet players. More than just a high-note specialist, Anderson was an expressive artist who knew how to ride a musical climax to new heights and excelled at **plunger mute** playing as well as subtle **half-valve** effects. After leaving Duke Elllington's band in 1971, Anderson moved to Los Angeles and spent the rest of his life doing studio work and playing in big bands led by Bill Berry and Louis Bellson.

André, Maurice (1933–2012). French trumpet soloist and recording artist. André's first teacher was his father (also named Maurice), who was a miner by trade, but also a gifted amateur trumpeter known for his powers of endurance. He progressed quickly and joined a local military band in order to receive free tuition to attend the Paris Conservatory, where he began studies in 1951 with Raymond Sabarich (1909–1966). André earned the top prize (*premier prix*) in both trumpet and **cornet** at the end of his first and second years of study and soon after embarked on an orchestral career, performing with the Lamoureux Orchestra (1953–1960), the Radio France Philharmonic (1953–1962), and the Opéra-Comique (1962–1967). He succeeded his teacher Sabarich at the Paris Conservatory in 1967 and taught there until 1978.

André's success at international competitions launched his solo career, which was unprecedented in the classical music field at the time. He won first prize at both the 1955 Geneva International Music Competition and the 1963 ARD International Competition in Munich. With his brilliant technique, soulful lyricism, extraordinary range, and peerless stamina, André single-handedly elevated the status of the trumpet as a classical solo instrument in the twentieth century. A major factor in his success was his mastery of the newly minted **piccolo trumpet**, which coincided with a revival in public interest in Baroque music as well as the growth of the recording industry.

André made over three hundred recordings during his career, covering the entire trumpet solo repertoire. Several composers wrote new works for him, including **André Jolivet**, **Henri Tomasi**, Boris Blacher (1903–1975), Charles Chaynes (b. 1925), Jean Langlais (1907–1991), and Antoine Tisné (b. 1932). In addition to new works and classical literature, many Baroque works for flute, oboe, and violin were transcribed for André's creamy piccolo trumpet. His brother, Raymond André (b. 1941), was also a trumpeter who performed and recorded with Maurice and his children, Nicholas (trumpet) and Beatrice (oboe).

anfār (also *anafir*). The long, straight trumpet of the medieval Arabs, who were known at the time as the Saracens. When western musicians encountered the instrument during the crusades in the Middle Ages, its name evolved into the word, **fanfare**.

angularity. Term used to describe melodic lines with a preponderance of large intervals, often intervals of a fifth or more. Such passages occur frequently in twentieth-century music featuring octave displacement; the challenge for trumpeters in performance is to maintain an efficient **embouchure** and produce a centered tone when shifting **registers**.

Ansatz. (Ger.) **Embouchure**.

Antonsen, Ole Edvard (b. 1962). Norwegian trumpeter, composer, and conductor. Growing up in a musical family, his father was a music teacher and bandleader who played the clarinet and saxophone. He began his musical studies on the **cornet** and progressed rapidly. His international breakthrough came in 1987 when he won first prize at the Geneva International Music Competition, after which he made several solo recordings. A uniquely versatile artist, Antonsen has performed as a soloist internationally with major orchestras including the Berlin Philharmonic Orchestra, London Symphony Orchestra, BBC Philharmonic Orchestra, Atlanta Symphony Orchestra, Tokyo Philharmonic Orchestra, Sao Paulo Symphony Orchestra, and Australian Chamber Orchestra, as well as with pop and rock musicians like John Miles, Level 42's Mark King, Lisa Stansfield, Ute Lemper, and Secret Garden. He has also performed with jazz groups like the Metropole Orchestra (Holland) and Willem Breuker Kollektief, as well as his own band.

As a conductor, Antonsen has led orchestras and ensembles like the Stavanger Symphony Orchestra, Bergen Philharmonic Orchestra, Gothenburg Symphony Orchestra, and Sao Paulo Symphony Orchestra. In

2006 Antonsen became the chief conductor and artistic director of the Royal Norwegian Airforce Band, and in 2010 he assumed a similar position with the Norwegian Wind Orchestra. He was appointed commander of the Royal Norwegian Order of St. Olav by His Majesty King Harald of Norway in August 2007 for his formidable contribution to Norwegian music both in Norway and abroad. In addition to his more than sixty recordings in classical, jazz, and popular styles, Antonsen recorded the official Olympic Fanfare for the Winter Olympics in Lillehammer in 1994.

aperture. The place in the center of the **embouchure** where the lips vibrate to generate sound on a brass instrument.

Arban, Joseph Jean-Baptiste Laurent (1824–1889). French cornetist, pedagogue, composer, and conductor. The most influential French cornet soloist of his time and the author of the world's best-known brass **method book**, *Grande méthode complète pour cornet à pistons et de saxhorn*, Arban entered the Paris Conservatory at the age of sixteen in 1841 to study with **François Dauverné** until 1845, when he won the first prize for cornet. In 1852, Arban appeared as soloist with Jullien's orchestra, and in 1856, he began to develop a significant reputation as a conductor of salon orchestras and the Paris Opera Orchestra. Arban became the professor of saxhorn at the École Militaire in 1857, and in 1869, he established the first cornet class at the Paris Conservatory, after an unsuccessful attempt seven years earlier. **Cerclier** succeeded Dauverné and took over the trumpet class at the conservatory.

Because of his extensive touring, especially his annual performances in St. Petersburg, Arban resigned his post at the conservatory in 1874. Arban's success as a Frenchman in Russia was unique, considering that the music scene was previously monopolized by German musicians. Follow several successful seasons in St. Petersburg and Pavlovsk, Arban returned to the conservatory in 1880 when a position became vacant.

Arban's cornet playing was marked by a brighter, more brilliant sound than other soloists because he used a shallower **mouthpiece**, which exerted a wide influence through his virtuosic performances. Although **multiple tonguing** was not an innovation to brass technique in the nineteenth century, Arban was the first to apply double and triple tonguing to melodic figuration rather than streams of repeated notes, which required more complex coordination between fingering and articulation. Arban's many solo performances helped to establish the cornet as the premier high brass solo instrument in the late nineteenth century. His *Grande méthode complète* (known in English as his *Complete Conservatory Method*) presented a systematic approach to all aspects of technique and has been used by brass players worldwide for nearly 150 years. Toward the end of his life, Arban worked with the engineer L. Bouvet in 1885 to develop a **compensating valve** system for the cornet. Although a newspaper in Finland reported that Arban recorded a "Fanfare d' Edison" on an early Edison cylinder in 1890, no copies of the recordings have survived. He received many honors during his life including that of officer of the Academie and knight of the Order of Leopold of Belgium, of Christ of Portugal, of Isabella the Catholic, and of the Cross of Russia.

Arbuckle, Matthew (1828–1883). Scottish-American cornet soloist and bandmaster. Born in Scotland, Arbuckle began his musical career at the age of thirteen in the Twenty-Sixth Regiment of the British Army. He gradually rose in the ranks as a **cornet** soloist and also served as a drum major and bagpiper. After serving in China and India, he served with the Royal Scottish Regiment of Canada, and eventually left the army to join the Troy Brass Band of Troy, New York. Arbuckle first came to the United States in 1853 to perform with Louis Antoine Jullien's elaborate concert programs; he also studied cornet with **Hermann Koenig**, another Jullien cornetist, at that time. **Isaac Fiske** later persuaded him to join Fiske's Cornet Band in Worcester, Massachusetts, as cornet soloist, and Arbuckle performed on Fiske's instruments and endorsed them as well. He joined Gilmore's Band in 1860. During the American Civil War Arbuckle performed with the Twenty-Fourth Massachusetts Volunteer Regiment Band of the Union Army, and after the war appeared as a cornet soloist with **Patrick Gilmore**'s Boston Brigade Band.

Arbuckle also appeared as cornet soloist in two massive festivals in Boston organized by Gilmore: the National Peace Jubilee of 1869 (organized to benefit the widows and orphans of American Civil War soldiers) and the World Peace Jubilee of 1872 (celebrating the end of the Franco-Prussian War). He joined Gilmore's New York Twenty-Second Regiment Band in 1873 as cornet soloist and was subjected to a public rivalry with Gilmore's other cornet soloist, **Jules Levy**, who was promoted as "the greatest cornet player living," while Arbuckle was touted as "the great favorite American cornet player." The rivalry devolved into a feud and eventually came to blows in Madison Square Garden during the band's opening concert of the 1879 season. Arbuckle left the acrimony behind the following year to become the conductor of D. L. Dowling's Ninth Regiment Band in 1880; he became the cornet soloist of Carlo A. Cappa's Seventh Regiment Band in 1881. He organized his own band in 1883, but died before the band made its public debut.

As a cornet player, Arbuckle was known for his passionate artistry and warm tone, as well as technical brilliance: especially his sparkling **triple tonguing**. Several composers wrote solo works for him including **John**

Hartmann's *Arbucklenian Polka, Grand Concert Valse*, and *West Brighton Polka*, and F. M. Steinhauser's *Culver Polka, Surf Polka*, and *Fantasie on le Desir*. During his career Arbuckle played cornets by Richardson & Bailey, Fiske (a rotary valve model), and **Courtois** (with a medium **bore** and a large Koenig bell).

Archias from Yvla (ca. 396 BC). Champion of the trumpet-blowing contests at the Ancient Greek Olympic Games according to Pollux the Historian. He is reported to have won the event three times and had a column erected in his honor. The type of instrument he played was the **salpinx**. He also won honors in the Pythian Games, where a portrait of him was created complete with a laudatory epigram.

Armstrong, Louis (1901–1971). American jazz trumpeter, singer, and bandleader. Armstrong was raised in poverty in New Orleans. His formative musical experiences involved singing in church and absorbing the musical atmosphere of the saloons and dance halls near his home. He first learned the cornet at the Colored Waif's Home from staff member Peter Davis. As a teenager, he benefitted from the mentorship of jazz cornetist **Joe "King" Oliver**, who gave him his first cornet and went on to give Armstrong many professional performance opportunities. In 1918, he even replaced Oliver in Kid Ory's band, and by 1922 Armstrong was playing in the Creole Jazz Band at Lincoln Gardens in Chicago, on Oliver's recommendation. Known by his nickname, **Satchmo**, in 1924 he joined Fletcher Henderson's band in New York, but returned to Chicago in 1925 and began recording. Armstrong's originality as an improviser and the power and beauty of his ideas, as revealed in these remarkable early recordings, established his international reputation as the greatest and most creative jazz musician of the day.

Although he started out on the cornet, Armstrong had switched to the trumpet by the late 1920s. He performed with groups of various sizes from small combos to big bands, playing with groups of five to seven players earlier in his career. Some of Armstrong's notable early recordings include "Big Butter and Egg Man" (1926, OK), "Potato Head Blues" (1927, OK), and "Struttin' with Some Barbecue" (1927, OK). The audacious virtuosity on his recording of "West End Blues" set a new standard in trumpet technique with expanded high range and a bold new sound. His improvisational style exhibited less innovation during his big band years in the 1930s, but his command of nuanced artistry never diminished. Hallmarks of Armstrong's style included soulful lyricism, a wide variety of expressive articulation, creative melodic innovation tempered by sophisticated harmonic awareness, an ability to play with and against the prevailing rhythmic pulse with varying levels of tension, and a deft control of formal architecture.

Armstrong appeared in several films including *Pennies from Heaven* (1936), *High Society* (1956), and *Hello Dolly* (1969). Also an accomplished vocal stylist with a distinctive, gravelly voice, Armstrong is best known for his performances of "Mack the Knife" (1955), "Hello Dolly" (1964, for which he won a Grammy Award for "Best Male Vocal Performance"), and "What a Wonderful World" (1970). Later in his life he toured with a six-piece group known as the All Stars. Armstrong died in 1971 and was honored with a Grammy Lifetime Achievement Award in 1972.

Arnold, Malcolm (1921–2006). English composer and trumpeter. Following composition lessons as a boy, Arnold was inspired to learn the trumpet at the age of twelve after hearing a live performance of **Louis Armstrong** in Bournemouth. He won a scholarship at the age of sixteen to the Royal College of Music, where he studied composition with Patrick Hadley and Gordon Jacob, and trumpet with **Ernest Hall**. Arnold performed with the London Philharmonic Orchestra between 1941–1942 as second trumpet and as principal trumpet in 1943. Unhappy serving in the army during the Second World War, he shot himself in the foot, literally, in order to be discharged. Thereafter he served as principal trumpet of the BBC Symphony in 1945 and returned to the London Philharmonic Orchestra in 1946. Arnold won the Mendelssohn Scholarship from the Royal College of Music in 1948, which gave him the confidence to pursue a full-time composing career.

Writing for both the concert stage and for films, Arnold produced an extensive creative output in an eclectic, accessible style. He composed nine symphonies, four operas, five ballets, numerous instrumental concerti, vocal works, and chamber pieces as well as over one hundred film scores. Arnold won an Academy Award in 1957 for his score for David Lean's film, *Bridge over the River Kwai*. He also composed educational works for young musicians, brass band music, and humorous works for the Hoffnung Festival such as *A Grand, Grand Overture, Op. 57* (1956) for vacuum cleaner, floor polisher, four rifles, and orchestra. Arnold received numerous honors throughout his career including a knighthood in 1993.

Arnold's works for brass are staples of the repertoire written in a melodic, idiomatic style. His solo works for trumpet include "Fanfare for Louis" (for two trumpets), "Fantasy for Trumpet, Op. 100," and "Trumpet Concerto, Op. 125," which was premiered by **John Wallace** in 1983. His "Quintet for Brass, Op. 73" (1961), written for the **New York Brass Quintet**, is a classic of the genre. Other works include "Symphony for Brass Instruments, Op. 123," two "Little Suites" for brass band, and "Quintet No. 2 for Brass, Op. 132." His trumpet ensemble composition, "A Hoffnung Fanfare" (1960), for 12 trumpets (or 36, with three players on a part) was written for the memorial service in honor of the multitalented musician and humorist Gerard Hoffnung (1925–1959).

articulation. The degree to which notes are separated or connected during performance. Brass instrument articulations include tonguing, slurring, and breath attacks (called "poo" attacks by **James Stamp**) to achieve a wide variety of staccato and legato effects. Nuanced articulation is achieved through a variety of tonguing syllables from soft ("nah" or "dah") to hard ("tah") as well as **multiple tonguing** that employs the rebounding effect of the back of the tongue using the "kah" or "gah" syllable in **double tonguing** (tah kah tah kah) or **triple tonguing** (tah tah kah—or—tah kah tah). The vowel that accompanies the consonant plays a role in controlling the **tongue placement** as an aid to playing in different ranges from low ("toe" or "tah") to high ("tee"). Trumpet pedagogical methods in France often expressed articulations using the vowel *u*, as in "tu ku" because in French pronunciation it encouraged the pucker formation of a brass embouchure. Other forms of articulation used in jazz and avant-garde music include **doodle tonguing** and **flutter tonguing.**

Articulation in early wind music was decidedly unequal. For example, rather than playing "ta ta ta" when single tonguing beats in triple meter, "ta da la" might be used to reflect metric stress (strong and weak beats in a measure) as well as phrasing. Syllables were generally softer and more vocal, overall, and reflected a hierarchy of accentuation. Most important was bringing out differences between melodic high points and passing notes. For example, "le re le re" was highly favored for performing florid virtuosic passages (*passaggi*) and lines of sparkling ornamentation in seventeenth-century repertoire (especially for the **cornett**) because it imitated the sound of coloratura vocal writing (usually melismas, or streams of fast notes sung on open vowel like "ah"). This technique was often referred to as *lingua reversa.* **Girolamo Fantini** included an entire section on tonguing in his method (1638), titled *Modo di battere la lingua puntata in diversi modi [Method of Tonguing with a Pointed Tongue in Different Ways]*, which demonstrated several different options for articulating melodic passages.

Arutiunian, Aleksandr Grigori (1920–2012). Armenian composer and pianist. Known for his lyrical Romantic style and expressive harmonic palette, Arutiunian wrote one of the most famous and widely performed trumpet concertos in the twentieth century. Composed in 1950 for trumpeter Haykaz Mesiayan, the *Concerto for Trumpet and Orchestra* is a single-movement work in three contrasting sections. Arutiunian also composed a *Concert Scherzo* (1954) and *Theme and Variations* (1972) for trumpet and orchestra, *Aria and Scherzo* (1983) for trumpet and piano, and a brass quintet, *Armenian Scenes* (1984).

ascending valve. A mechanism that cuts out a section of the main tube of a brass instrument, rather than appending additional tubing to its length, consequently raising the pitch. Such valves were added to trumpets by **Jerome Thibouville-Lamy** and used by **Roger Voisin** and **Armando Ghitalla.**

auf der Bühne. (Ger.) On stage, as opposed to being in the orchestra pit.

Aufführungspraxis. (Ger.) **Performance practice.**

Aufzug. (Ger.) "Procession" or "cortege." A processional **fanfare** for **trumpet ensemble** similar to an **intrada** or a **toccata** that originated in the late sixteenth century. It typically featured the **clarino** part performing an active melody above a supporting harmonic or drone-like accompaniment in the lower parts of the ensemble. It endured as a genre of trumpet ensemble composition until the middle of the nineteenth century.

avant-garde. (Fr.) advance guard or vanguard. A term borrowed from the French military to described leaders of modernism in the arts. The term connotes associations with risk-taking, exploring new territory, pushing boundaries, and fearless leadership. Music composed with experimental tonalities, extended techniques like **multiphonics**, and extreme **angularity** and **range** is often described by this term.

ax. Slang term used by jazz musicians to describe their instruments. Originally referred to a saxophone in the 1950s, but was later applied to any instrument.

B. In German "B" alone stands for B-flat. The German "H" is reserved for B-natural. Hence "Trompete in B" is "Trumpet in B-flat." The reason for this practice traces back to early music notation in the Middle Ages when the "soft b" represented a B-flat and a "hard b" represented a B-natural. The lower case *b* and *h* resemble the symbols for flats and naturals used in music notation today.

Bach trumpet. A late-nineteenth-century trumpet employed to perform music from the Baroque era. The most popular form of this instrument was a four-foot-long trumpet pitched in A with two **piston valves**. The long, unwrapped version of the instrument caused audiences to mistakenly believe that it resembled a long, eighteenth-century **natural trumpet**, hence the name. The first instrument of this type was developed in 1870 for **Julius Kosleck** in Berlin. After performing concerts with Kosleck in London, **Walter Morrow** had a similar instrument made for him by Silvani & Smith. Later the term was loosely applied to a variety of smaller **high-pitched trumpets** used to play the music of J. S. Bach before the adoption of the modern **piccolo trumpet**. (See figure 3.)

Figure 3. A Bach trumpet from the late nineteenth century. *Drawing by T. M. Larsen.*

Bach, Johann Ambrosius (1645–1695). German court musician and violinist. The father of **Johann Sebastian Bach**, he started his career as a *Stadtpfeifer* and played the trumpet and the violin, although the organ was his main instrument. A copy by Max Martini (1907) of a portrait of Ambrosius Bach by Johann David

Herlicius (ca. 1685) hangs in the Bachhaus Museum in Eisenach, Germany, with the following inscription on the identification plate, "The portrait shows Ambrosius as the master of his craft. The open shirt was the sign of a trumpet player." E. G. Haussmann's famous portrait of **Gottfried Reiche** (1727) also depicts Reiche with an open shirt collar.

Bach, Johann Sebastian (1685–1750). German composer. Considered the greatest composer of the late Baroque era, Bach favored the trumpet with some of the most demanding and artistically satisfying music in its repertoire. He primarily scored for the **natural trumpet**, but also wrote for the **slide trumpet** (*tromba da tirarsi* or *Zugtrompete*), the **cornett**, the **horn** (*corno da caccia*), and an unusual instrument that no other composer wrote for, the *corno da tirarsi.* Although Bach did not write solo concerti for the trumpet, he lavished the instrument with prominent solo parts in many of his works, especially the ***Brandenburg Concerto No. 2***, a concerto grosso where the *tromba* in F shares the spotlight in the solo group with flute (recorder), oboe, and violin, and plays some of the highest most demanding parts in the literature. Bach's large choral works with trumpet include the *Mass in B Minor* (BWV 232), the *Magnificat* (BWV 243), the *Christmas Oratorio* (BWV 248), the *Easter Oratorio* (BWV 249), and the *Ascension Oratorio* (BWV 11). In particular the first trumpet part of the *Mass in B Minor* is legendary for its demands on stamina and virtuosity, especially the opening solo of the *Credo (Symbolum Nicenum: Patrem omnipotentem)*, the *Osanna*, and the final *Dona Nobis Pacem*. Of Bach's orchestral compositions, the *Orchestral Suites No. 3* and *No. 4* (BWV 1068 and 1069) contain parts for three trumpets in D.

The largest amount of solo trumpet writing in Bach's music appears in many of the church cantatas, especially in the florid obbligato solo trumpet part in the cantata *Jauchzet Gott in allen Landen* (BWV 51). Of the seventy surviving cantatas that include trumpet parts, twenty-one feature major solo obbligato trumpet parts in aria movements. There are cantatas that include a festive orchestra with three trumpets (sometimes two or four) and timpani as well as those scored for a single trumpet with reduced forces. The majority of these cantatas (sixty-two) are sacred, while only eight are secular cantatas (designated as "Dramma per Musica"). On average, trumpets participate primarily in the outer movements of cantatas (especially opening choruses and closing chorales), and occasionally accompany solo arias and other choral movements.

Most of the trumpet parts in Bach's cantatas are labeled "*Tromba*" and were intended to be performed on the natural trumpet. Only rarely did he refer to the instruments as *clarino* or *principale*. According to published editions currently available, Bach usually wrote for trumpets pitched in C before assuming the position as Thomaskantor in Leipzig in 1723. Thereafter, most of his trumpet parts are pitched in D. However it is possible that the same instrument, a trumpet in C, was used and the key designations merely reflect changes in **pitch standards** from Weimar to Leipzig. Bach writes for a trumpet in B-flat only in three solo obbligato arias (BWV 5, 46, and 90).

During the nineteenth and early twentieth centuries, the performance of Bach's trumpet parts was a subject of great controversy as developments in instrument manufacture and playing techniques regained the lost art of clarino playing. Before the **period instrument** revival and the development of the **piccolo trumpet**, Bach's trumpet parts were sometimes given to clarinets or a so-called **Bach trumpet**. Some performances of *Brandenburg Concerto No. 2* were even given with a soprano saxophone playing the solo trumpet part in the early twentieth century.

Bach, Vincent [born Vincenz Schrottenbach] (1890–1976). Austrian-American trumpeter and brass instrument manufacturer. His first instrument was the violin, but he went on to study trumpet and **cornet** with Josef Weiss and Georg Stellwagen. Because his family did not support his desire for a musical career, he earned a degree in mechanical engineering at the Maschinenbauschule in Wiener Neustadt at the age of twenty. During compulsory military service in the Austro-Hungarian Imperial Navy he played in the Austrian Marine Band. Determined to pursue a musical career, Schrottenbach studied cornet with Fritz Werner in Wiesbaden and subsequently toured as a cornet virtuoso in Germany, Denmark, Sweden, Russia, Poland, and England. At the start of the First World War he encountered political troubles as an enemy alien while touring in England, so he changed his name

to Vincent Bach and fled to the United States. After arriving in New York in the autumn of 1914, he served as assistant principal trumpet of the Boston Symphony Orchestra for one season and performed as first trumpet with Diaghilev's ballet orchestra at the Metropolitan Opera House between 1915 and 1916. He served in the United States Army as the bandmaster of the 306th Field Artillery Regiment between 1916 and 1918, and became an American citizen in 1925.

Following his release from the military in 1918, Bach began experimenting with **mouthpieces** and started his own business in the back of the **Selmer** music store in New York. He expanded his work to include the production of trumpets and cornets in 1924, adding the "Stradivarius" name for marketing purposes. He relocated to a Bronx factory in 1928 and added trombones to his product line. The company survived the depression and by 1953 moved to Mount Vernon, New York. Collaborating with **Georges Mager**, during the Second World War, Bach developed the large bore C trumpet that would become the standard of symphonic trumpeters in America in the late twentieth century. In 1961, at seventy-one years of age, Bach sold his company to the Conn-Selmer Corporation even though some of the other thirteen bids were higher. After the sale of the business, he stayed on as a researcher until 1974.

The combination of his engineering training with his musical artistry empowered Bach to establish exacting standards of brass instrument design and construction. He modeled his trumpets after the French **Besson** B-flat trumpet and strove to give his instruments a secure "feel" for each note in the scale. Bach was also the first to set up a system for the precise duplication of mouthpieces, which helped to define standards for the dimensions and measurements of brass mouthpieces throughout the industry. The rich sound and reliable quality of his instruments made them popular with professional brass players worldwide.

Bach, Wilhelm Friedemann (1710–1784). German composer. The eldest son of **Johann Sebastian Bach**, he added parts for three trumpets in D to his father's cantata, *Ein feste Burg ist unser Gott* (BWV 80), around the time of his father's death.

back pressure. Excessive resistance experienced by musicians when playing brass instruments and mutes.

backbeat. The accentuation of the second and fourth beats in 4/4 or 12/8 time, common in rock music and some jazz styles.

backbore. The internal dimensions of a mouthpiece shank, usually conical in design from the **throat** to the end of the shank.

Bagley, Ezra (1853–1886). American cornetist. Bagley grew up in a large musical family in Vermont and began his musical career as a boy soprano with Leavitt's Concert Company at the age of thirteen. His first instrument was the alto horn; he studied cornet with L. S. Batchelder of Boston. By the age of seventeen he was a cornetist with the Germania Band of Boston and a member of D. C. Hall's Band. Known for his brilliant sight-reading and facile articulation, Bagley performed as first chair cornet with Gilmore's European Tour Band of 1878. He served as the principal trumpeter of the Boston Symphony Orchestra between 1880 and 1884. Bagley composed several marches, but it was his brother Edwin who wrote the famous "National Emblem March."

Baker, Chesney Henry "Chet" (1929–1988). American jazz trumpeter and singer. His father was a professional guitarist, and he began his musical career singing in a church choir. Baker's first instrument was the trombone, but he switched to the trumpet because he found its smaller size to be more suitable. At the age of sixteen he joined the U.S. Army in 1946. He was posted to Berlin, where he joined the 298th Army Band. Leaving the army in 1948, Baker studied theory and harmony at El Camino College in Los Angeles, but later dropped out to pursue a professional performing career. Moving between the army and professional life for the next few years, he was finally discharged in 1951 and devoted his time exclusively to performing in his uniquely understated style. Baker exerted a seminal influence on West Coast Jazz with his subdued stylings at softer dynamic levels with a clear tone and a narrow melodic range (usually less than an octave).

In 1952 he played briefly with Charlie Parker before beginning an important association with Gerry Mulligan in his distinctive quartet known for not including a piano. Baker's performances with the group, particularly his ballad rendition of "My Funny Valentine," brought him instant fame. His career became erratic in the 1960s due to battles with drug addiction. Between 1964 and 1970 Baker played the flugelhorn when his trumpet was stolen, but he resumed playing the trumpet regularly in the 1970s, and by the mid-1980s he was again much in demand for club performances and recording dates. Baker was the subject of Bruce Weber's celebrated film documentary *Let's Get Lost* (1988).

ball. On a **natural trumpet**, the bulbous metal ornament that covers the seam that connects the bell section, often used as a hand grip. It was also called a **boss** or a **knop**.

ballad horn. A tenor brass instrument pitched in C and built in circular shape with three piston valves and a bell pointing down toward the floor. It employed a funnel-shaped mouthpiece and was used to play along with vocal and piano music (without needing to transpose) for home entertainment in the nineteenth century. Similar in tone to the **mellophone** and in use to the **C cornet**, the ballad horn was introduced by **Henry Distin** in 1856 and flourished until the 1920s. Models made with the bell pointing forward were made by the firm of Rudall, Carte & Company called the "vocal horn."

Ballerina's Dance. A trumpet solo from Igor Stravinksky's ballet, *Petrouchka*. Originally written for a B-flat **cornet** in the 1911 version, the composer rescored it for B-flat trumpet in the 1947 revised edition. It is considered one of the most popular and demanding excerpts on orchestral trumpet audition repertoire lists.

Balsom, Alison (b. 1978). British trumpet soloist and recording artist. Following studies at the Guildhall School of Music and Drama, the Royal Scottish Academy of Music and Drama, and the Paris Conservatory, Balsom also studied privately with **Håkan Hardenberger**. She released her debut recording in 2002 and has earned several Classical BRIT awards (2006, 2009, and 2011). In addition to an international performing career she serves as visiting professor of trumpet at the Guildhall School of Music and Drama. Balsom performs primarily on modern trumpets, but she has also performed and recorded on a **Baroque trumpet** with **vent holes.**

banda. (It.) band. Refers to an extra group of instruments separate from the pit orchestra in an opera or other stage work. These may be off stage, or fully costumed on stage. Often (but not always) a military band or some subset thereof, the *banda* music is often written in the score on two staves, like a piano reduction, with the expectation that the in-house bandmaster would score the music for whatever instruments happen to be available. The *banda* is prevalent especially in nineteenth-century Italian opera. Also referred to as "stageband," even if it is just a single instrument, like the famous off-stage trumpet **call** in **Beethoven**'s *Fidelio*.

The off-stage brass band parts appear occasionally in nineteenth-century Italian opera. Notable *banda* parts appear in Verdi's *Rigoletto* and Puccini's *Turandot*.

banderole. A leather strap or cord attached to the **bows** of a **natural trumpet** used for carrying the instrument over the shoulder.

Baptist, Rick (b. 1948). American trumpeter and composer. Baptist began playing the trumpet for therapeutic purposes on the suggestion of his doctor following a near-fatal childhood accident in which his left lung collapsed. He performed with a band for the first time at the age of twelve and made such rapid progress that he was playing professionally by the age of fifteen with the San Francisco and Oakland symphonies. His career progressed into the world of studio and commercial music in Reno, Las Vegas, and Hollywood. As one of the world's most recorded studio trumpeters, Baptist has performed on soundtracks for over 4,000 cartoons, numerous television shows, and more than 1,200 movies. He has also performed as the first trumpeter for the Academy Awards show for twenty-nine years and for the Emmy Awards show for twenty-three years in addition to working with such artists as Ray Charles, Frank Sinatra, Michael Jackson, and Josh Groban.

Barber, Samuel (1910–1981). American composer. One of the most widely performed of all American composers, Barber wrote music in an accessible tonal language marked by heartfelt lyricism and a command of traditional formal structures. He entered the Curtis Institute at the age of fourteen and eventually taught piano there between 1931 and 1933. A talented baritone vocalist, himself, Barber composed many art songs (nearly 70 percent of his output) and infused his instrumental works with flowing melodies, especially his *Adagio for Strings* (an orchestral version of a movement from his *String Quartet in B Minor*) and *Violin Concerto*. He composed at least one work in every genre, and most of his pieces were written on commission for prominent artists and ensembles including "Knoxville: Summer of 1915" for soprano Eleanor Steber and the ballet *Medea* (1946) for Martha Graham. He wrote two operas, *Vanessa* (1958) and *Antony and Cleopatra* (1966).

Barber's orchestral works with prominent trumpet parts include *Overture to "The School for Scandal,"* his two symphonies and three essays for orchestra, as well as *Die natali, Chorale Preludes for Christmas* (1960). The finale of his *Violin Concerto* includes an awkward solo for the first trumpet requiring challenging **articulation**, and an important muted passage for the second trumpet appears in the second movement, which interacts with the solo violin line. Barber's writing for the trumpet favors the B-flat trumpet and the C trumpet and often calls for a **straight mute**. Although he never wrote any solo concerti or chamber music for the trumpet, he included the trumpet as one of the three solo instruments in his *Capricorn Concerto* (1944) along with a flute and an oboe. The work is scored for a C trumpet, but a B-flat trumpet is required at the end of the second movement to perform the *E*s below the staff (E3) that would be **pedal tones** on a C trumpet, but are playable low F-sharps (F-sharp3) on a B-flat trumpet.

barillet. (Fr.) rotary, cylinder. A quick-change **rotary valve** on some late-nineteenth-century **cornets** that lowered the pitch of the instrument from C to A. Some of these valves were made with integrated levers that lengthened the first and second **valve slides** accordingly.

Baroque mute. A wooden **mute** that fits inside the bell of a trumpet and acts as a **transposing mute** to raise the pitch of the trumpet either a half step or a whole step depending on the size of the **bell**. If the bell had a wider flare, like a so-called Renaissance bell found on many seventeenth-century trumpets, the mute went in farther and served to shorten the length of the vibrating air column for the trumpet at the point of contact to raise the pitch one whole step. Later Baroque bell designs admitted the mute only a short distance into the bell, and raised the pitch one half step. A mute of this type is pictured in Marin Mersenne's *Harmonie Universelle* (1636). The mute does not have any cork on the top and is made with an ornamental stem at the end, which serves as a handle for manipulating the mute. The center of the mute includes a hollow tube through which the sound escapes. (See figure 4 and appendix 3.)

Figure 4. A wooden Baroque mute. *Drawing by T. M. Larsen.*

Baroque pitch. A **pitch standard** of A4 = 415 Hz often employed by modern **period instrument** ensembles for performances of repertoire from the Baroque era (approximately 1600–1750). Actual pitch standards during the seventeenth and eighteenth centuries varied greatly according to geographical location, time period, instruments (especially keyboards), and performance circumstances under consideration. For example, the pitch A4 on late-seventeenth-century organs in France ranged between 388 and 396 Hz while organs in Germany of the same period rendered A4 around 466 Hz. Various pitch standards were assigned names, such as **Chorton, Cornet-ton, Kammerton,** and **French theatre pitch.**

These various standards impacted the **nominal pitches** of trumpets because, for example, a trumpet pitched in C at Chorton (A4 at approximately 466 Hz) would be in D at Kammerton (A4 at approximately 415 Hz).

Baroque trumpet. A twentieth-century instrument of similar dimensions to the eighteenth-century **natural trumpet** designed with **vent holes** for the performance of Baroque repertoire as part of the modern **period instrument** revival. Around 1960 **Otto Steinkopf** devised a system of three vent holes for a natural trumpet built by the German maker **Helmut Finke** that rendered the fickle eleventh and thirteenth partials of the harmonic overtone series in tune by the standards of equal **temperament**. The Steinkopf-Finke trumpet was a coiled instrument patterned after the *Jägertrompete* held by **Gottfried Reiche** in his famous portrait painted by E. G. Haussmann. It was not the first trumpet to employ vent holes, however. The earliest known trumpet with vent holes was made by the British craftsman William Shaw in 1787. It was discovered in the vaults of St. James Palace in London in 1959. The three-hole system developed by Steinkopf and Finke was later modified by **Walter Holy** in Cologne on a trumpet of more conventional shape with an extra folded section that made the instrument slightly shorter than the traditional natural trumpet.

Later, the British trumpeter **Michael Laird** devised a four-hole system that increased the stability of many pitches and offered additional solutions to intonation problems. Although vent holes made the natural trumpet safer to play, they altered the sound slightly. The resulting compromise instruments would certainly not have been used by trumpeters three hundred years ago and could hardly be called "natural." In an attempt to clarify terms for these instruments, **Edward Tarr** has recommended that trumpets without holes be referred to as genuine *natural trumpets* while vented instruments should be called *Baroque trumpets*. Trumpets with

vent holes have also been called **vented trumpets.** Some Baroque trumpets include tapered **leadpipes** and smaller **mouthpieces** from twentieth-century trumpets that conspire to produce a sound much closer to that of a **modern trumpet** than a genuine natural trumpet. Such instruments have fallen into disuse as vented trumpets with internal dimensions closer to those of eighteenth-century trumpets have become available and are preferred by trumpeters in period instrument ensembles. Makers of Baroque trumpets include **Rainer Egger**, **Frank Tomes**, and Andrew Naumann. (See figure 5.)

bass trumpet. A valved trombone folded into trumpet shape with a narrow **bore** pitched in eight-foot C or nine-foot B-flat. It is played with a trombone mouthpiece and built with either **piston** or **rotary valves**. There are three varieties of the instrument. The first is Richard Wagner's original conception, which is pitched in C with rotary valves; its bore profile and **bell** dimensions are closer to those of the trumpet. The second is an American version pitched in B-flat with piston valves; it sounds more like a valve trombone and is a popular instrument with jazz musicians. The third type is a German band instrument pitched in B-flat with a wider bore and a larger bell than the orchestral bass trumpet. Leonhard Paul, a trombonist with **Mnozil Brass,** often plays a bass trumpet made by **Schagerl** during performances.

basse de trompette. (Fr.) bass [range] of the trumpet. A term used by **Marin Mersenne** to describe an eight-foot-long trumpet that performed the lowest notes (often the fundamental) in French Baroque trumpet ensembles. The term was also used (with the same meaning) by André Danican Philidor l'Aîné (ca. 1652–1730), the royal oboist and music librarian for King Louis XIV.

basso. The lowest part (usually a drone on C3) of the **natural trumpet** ensemble in the sixteenth century, as described by **Bendinelli** and **Fantini**. The part was also labeled "grob" in some works. Occasionally an even lower part, labeled "fladdergrob," would be added to sound the **fundamental** (C2).

battaglia. (It.) battle. A genre of musical composition popular between the sixteenth and seventeenth centuries, either vocal or instrumental, that imitates the sounds of a battle including shouts, **fanfares** (especially triadic figures), drum rolls, and canon or musket fire. Ironically, trumpets usually do not participate in these works, but were imitated by other instruments or voices. One of the earliest examples of the genre was Clément Janequin's chanson, *La Guerre* (1528), which was composed to commemorate the French victory at the Battle of Marignano in 1515. Adriano Banchieri's madrigal, *La battaglia* (1596), includes passages that imitate trumpet fanfares

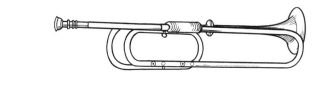

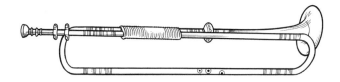

Figure 5. Two modern Baroque trumpets with vent holes. One with three holes (top) and another with four (bottom). *Drawing by T. M. Larsen.*

with the text "Ta ra ra tun ta ra," which is similar to the iambic "**tarantara**" of later literature. Instrumental *battaglias* included Andrea Gabrieli's *Battaglia à 8* (1590); William Byrd's keyboard work, *The Battle* (1591); and **Heinrich Biber**'s *Battaglia* (1673) for nine-part strings and continuo. Later orchestral compositions such as Beethoven's *Wellington's Victory* (1813) and Kodály's *Háry János Suite* (1927) also depicted battles, but should not be considered examples of the earlier genre.

Bebop, Bop. A style of jazz popular in the 1940s and 1950s that featured elaborate harmonic structures and technical virtuosity often performed at a fast tempo. Prominent Bebop artists include the saxophonist Charlie Parker, pianist Thelonious Monk, and trumpeter **Dizzy Gillespie**.

Beethoven, Ludwig van (1770–1827). German composer. One of the iconic composers of classical music, Beethoven's major works include nine symphonies, five piano concerti, sixteen string quartets, thirty-two piano sonatas, and numerous chamber pieces as well as his vocal works and theatrical music. He was one of the first composers who consciously wrote for posterity as well as for his contemporary audience. Born in Bonn, his father, Johann (ca. 1740–1792), was a professional tenor vocalist, and his grandfather, also named Ludwig (1712–1773), was a Kappellmeister to the court of the elector of Cologne at Bonn. He began his musical training with his father and Christian Gottlob Neefe in Bonn, and went on to study with **Haydn**, Salieri, and Albrechtsberger in Vienna. Beethoven began his career as a virtuoso pianist who astonished audiences with his compositions marked by innovative forms and passionate emotional power as well his dazzling improvisations. By the age of thirty he began to lose his hearing and eventually went completely deaf. Incredibly, Beethoven could only hear many of his late works, including the Ninth Symphony, in his imagination. He wrote a famous letter to his brothers in 1802 (it was never sent, but discovered after his death) known as the "Heiligenstadt Testament," in which he poured out his despair over his deafness and resolved not to commit suicide in order to continue composing.

Beethoven's music and career are often divided into three style periods. The first period, from his youth up till 1802, includes music of more conventional classical influences, forms, and genres. In the second period, from 1802 until about 1815, Beethoven's music features more expansive forms, experimental structures, and intensified emotional drama as he grapples with his increasing deafness and resolves to include more personal expression in his music. The third period, from about 1815 until his death in 1827, is marked by increased harmonic and formal complexity as well as deeply profound musical thought.

Like **Mozart**, Beethoven also favored the **horn** with soloistic brass writing, including the heroic trio of the Third Symphony ("Eroica") and the triumphant passages in the first movement of the Seventh Symphony. He even studied the horn as a student in Bonn. With the exception of the offstage **calls** from *Leonore Overture No. 3* (and occasionally *No. 2*), Beethoven's trumpet parts are not known for exposed solo passages, technical difficulty, or demanding endurance or range. Writing exclusively for pairs of **natural trumpets** usually scored in octaves, Beethoven restricted their range to the lower octaves of the **harmonic overtone series** and the subordinate role of emphasizing tonic and dominant key centers in orchestral compositions. While he included the horn in several chamber works of mixed instrumentation, he never scored for trumpets outside of the orchestra.

The orderly flow of trumpet octaves in Beethoven's orchestral writing occasionally encounters disruptions when a note comes along that a natural trumpet could not physically produce in the lower register, such as D4 or F4. Trumpeters performing Beethoven symphonies with valved trumpets today have the power to easily fix this problem, but every single D5 or F5 written in the second trumpet part should not be played down an octave, as a reflex. It is important to consult the surrounding evidence and strive to serve the musical context of the passage in question. **Period instrument** performances using natural trumpets obviously do not make any changes to the octave disruptions.

Beiderbecke, Leon Bismark "Bix" (1903–1931). American jazz cornetist. He began his musical studies on the piano at a young age and taught himself to play the **cornet**. He developed an unorthodox **fingering** technique by playing along with early recordings by ear without any formal instruction. In 1921 his family sent him to the Lake Forest Academy to discourage his interest in jazz, but Beiderbecke missed so many classes in order to visit jazz clubs in nearby Chicago that he was eventually expelled. After working for his father for a number of years, he moved to Chicago to start his musical career. His playing attracted attention when he began recording with a band called the Wolverines in 1924. In the same year he began a long association with Frankie Trumbauer, recording with him in New York in a group called the Sioux City Six. Beiderbecke's association with Trumbauer broadened his musical experience and helped him improve his music-reading ability, but he never developed complete fluency. In late 1926 he and Trumbauer joined Jean Goldkette, and were prominent members of his group in New York until it disbanded in September 1927. They then joined Paul Whiteman's band, with which, and with various groups under their own names, they made a series of influential recordings, notably "Singin' the Blues" and "Riverboat Shuffle" (both 1927, Okeh Records).

Beiderbecke's alcoholism caused his health to deteriorate and frequently caused him to miss performances. He left the Whiteman band in September 1929 and worked in New York, in a radio series, with the Dorsey Brothers a few times, with the Casa Loma Orchestra, and with Benny Goodman. The demands of relentless touring and recording along with his persistent problems with alcohol led to his untimely death at the age of twenty-eight in 1931. Beiderbecke's originality made him one of the first white jazz musicians to be admired by black performers such as **Louis Armstrong**, who recognized him as a kindred spirit. Known for warm tone and melodic invention, Beiderbecke's understated style emphasized harmonic sophistication and tone color rather than technical pyrotechnics in the high register. Throughout his career he played cornets by **Conn** (especially the Victor 80a with a 0.484 **bore**), **Holton**, and **Vincent Bach**. Although he was largely unknown to the general public at the time of his death, he acquired an almost legendary aura among jazz musicians and enthusiasts. Because of such popularized accounts as Dorothy Baker's novel *Young Man with a Horn* (Boston, 1938), based very loosely on his life and career, he soon came to symbolize the "Roaring Twenties" in the popular imagination.

bell. The end of the trumpet from which the sound is released. Both the shape of the bell and the thickness of the metal influence the tone quality and playing experience of the instrument. Trumpet bell shapes changed over the years from simply flaring the end of the tube on a **mandrel** to increasing dimensions of width and flare. (See figure 6.)

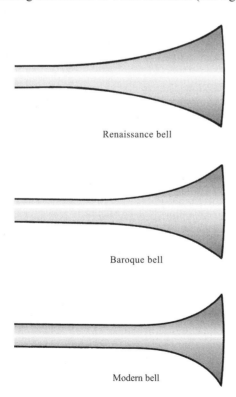

Renaissance bell

Baroque bell

Modern bell

Figure 6. Three different trumpet bell sizes from three different centuries. *Drawing by T. M. Larsen.*

bell bow, bell crook. The curved tubing directly below the mouthpiece on most trumpets and cornets that connects the bell to the rest of the instrument. On a **natural trumpet**, this is also known as the second bow because the first bow connects the first **branch** of tubing (including the **mouthpiece receiver**) to the second branch, or **yard**.

bell rim. The piece of metal wire placed on the end of the bell to reinforce the strength of the metal and protect the bell from damage. Additional reinforcement is sometimes provided by a **garland** around the bell.

bell throat. The part of the **bell** that begins to widen from the preceding tubing and leads to the bell flare.

Bellstedt, Hermann (1858–1926). German-American cornetist, bandmaster, and composer. Bellstedt came to the United States in 1867 at the age of nine, and his family settled in Cincinnati in 1872. He studied cornet with his father and Mylius Weigand and was promoted as a "boy wonder" when he made his debut on May 10, 1873. Following stints as solo cornetist with the orchestra at Arctic Gardens and the Cincinnati Reed Band, he became the cornet soloist with the Red Hussar Band on Manhattan Beach in 1879. In the years that followed, Bellstedt performed with several of the leading bands of the time: **Gilmore**'s Band (1889–1892), Sousa's Band (1904–1906), and Frederick N. Innes's Band (1906–1909), where he was billed as "Germany's greatest cornet soloist." In the years between his tenures with Gilmore and Sousa (1892–1904), he performed as first trumpeter in orchestras conducted by Theodore Thomas (founder of the Chicago Symphony), Van der Stucken, and Schradieck. Bellstedt was known for his wide range and facile **tonguing** on the cornet.

As a conductor, Bellstedt founded the Bellstedt-Ballenger Band in 1892 and directed the Denver Municipal Band between 1909 and 1912. He became a professor of wind instruments at the Cincinnati Conservatory in 1913 and later conducted the Syrian Temple Shrine Band between 1919 and 1920. As a composer, Bellstedt wrote for band, orchestra, piano, violin, and cornet. Some of his best known cornet solos include *Napoli*, *Fantasia No. 1*, *La Coquette*, *Capriccio Brilliante*, *La Mandolinata*, and *Variations on the Carnival of Venice*. His compositions for band include *Indian War Dance*, *Pettibone's Compliments*, *Joke on Bodelia*, *The Everett*, *The Zoo*, *Royal Arcanum*, *Victory Day*, *The Elk's Reunion*, *Los Angeles Pilgrimage*, and *Chelton Hills*.

Bendinelli, Cesare (ca. 1542–1617). Italian trumpeter and author of the first published method for trumpet playing, *Tutta l'arte della Trombetta* in 1614. Originally from Verona, Bendinelli worked as a trombonist at the court of Schwerin from 1562 to 1564 and later served as a trumpeter at the Imperial court of Vienna between 1567 and 1577. From 1580 until his death in 1617 he worked at the court of Munich first as an "instrumentalist," then "musikus," and later "obrister trommeter" ("chief court trumpeter"), before rising to the rank of "komponist" ("composer"). Bendinelli's 1614 **method** includes the first published works for the trumpet in the high *clarino* register as well as five-part trumpet ensembles and **articulation** syllables for tonguing. His unique pretzel-shaped trumpet made by Anton Schnitzer in 1585 was donated by Bendinelli to the Accademia Filarmonica in Verona in 1614 along with a copy of his trumpet **method** and survives there today. A painting from 1582 depicts Bendinelli praying in a boat on the Danube that was imperiled by a broken rudder. According to the inscription below the painting, the damaged boat was drawn into a whirlpool and headed for certain destruction on nearby rocks when disaster was averted by a miraculous appearance of the Virgin Mary of Aufkirchen. Bendinelli donated the votive painting to the Pilgrimage Church in Aufkirchen near Stamberg (Bavaria), where it still resides today.

Benge, Elden (1904–1960). American trumpeter and brass instrument manufacturer. He began studies on the cornet with Walter Eby and later studied with **Vladimir Drucker** and Harold Mitchell. While a student, Benge corresponded with **Herbert L. Clarke** to seek advice, and received a famous letter from Clarke dated January 13, 1921, in which he urged the teenaged Benge not to switch from the cornet to the trumpet. Benge did switch to the trumpet and performed in several dance bands, variety shows, and studio orchestras before becoming principal trumpet of the Detroit Symphony Orchestra in 1928 at the age of twenty-four. In 1933 he replaced Edward Llewellyn as principal trumpet of the Chicago Symphony Orchestra (CSO). After befriending fellow CSO trumpeter **Renold Schilke**, Benge began experimenting with designing trumpets modeled after his **Besson** B-flat trumpet in Schilke's home workshop. He built his first trumpet (from spare parts) in 1935 and produced his own new instrument in 1937. In 1939 he left the Chicago Symphony and began the Benge Company.

Between 1940 and 1952 Benge performed as principal trumpet with the WGN Radio Orchestra in Chicago and continued to build trumpets in his home workshop. In 1953 he moved to Burbank, California and began manufacturing and marketing his trumpets in Los Angeles. He died in a car accident in 1960, and his son, Donald, then took over the business. The company changed hands in the 1970s and is currently owned by the Conn-Selmer Company. In the late 1960s, the Benge Company advertised a full array of models including B-flat trumpets (ranging in bore from 0.458 inches to 0.468 inches), C trumpets, D and E-flat trumpets, a **pocket cornet**, a **pocket trumpet**, and a **flugelhorn**.

Bent, Benjamin (1847–1898). English-American cornetist. Bent's father was a fine cornetist who got him started on the instrument. At the age of ten, Bent ran away from home to join a traveling circus band. Later, at the age of twenty, he became the cornet soloist with the Royal Artillery Band and a special soloist with Howe's Great London Circus Band in 1871. The following year he traveled to the United States to join Harvey Dodworth's Thirteenth Regiment Band of New York as well as Dodworth's Ninth Regiment Band. Between 1875 and 1891 he played with Gilmore's Twenty-Second Regiment Band, and later joined the Innes Band in 1891. He retired from public performance in 1894 and devoted the remaining years of his life to teaching.

Bent's cornet playing was marked by impressive artistry, a singing tone, clean technique, and a serious work ethic, which greatly impressed **Herbert L. Clarke.** Bent played with false teeth for many years with no noticeable impact on his playing. His three brothers—Arthur, Fred, and Tom—were also fine cornet players, and together they formed the Bent Brothers Military Band. Ben and Arthur played together in the Gilmore Band and were frequently featured in cornet duets, most notably Ben's own composition, *Variations on the Swiss Boy.* As a result of wise financial investments, Bent died a wealthy man.

Berger, Anna Teresa (1853–1925). American cornetist. One of the first female cornet soloists, she was born in Baltimore and learned to play both the cornet and the violin. She toured as a child with the Carter Zouave Troupe in 1862, which may have been one of the first all-female brass bands. She originally belonged to the Berger Family's Ladies' Orchestra and performed in concert at New York's leading theaters, such as the Olympic, Booth's, the Academy of Music, and Union Square Theatre. Berger studied with **Matthew Arbuckle** in 1875 and toured Europe in 1889, performing at Covent Garden and London's Promenade concerts as well as in France, Germany, and Russia. She also studied with **Jules Levy** and performed several of his solos in concert. Berger married Leigh Lynch, who also served as her concert manager; she had five children and ultimately retired from professional performing.

Berlin valve. A type of **piston valve** distinguished by its short and stout appearance that was developed in Berlin first by Heinrich Stölzel (1777–1844) in 1827 and later (independently) by Wilhelm Wieprecht (1802–1872) in 1833. Originally called the *Stecherbüchsen-Ventil* by Wieprecht, the Berlin valve featured **valve slide** tubing that entered the piston on opposite sides, while the main tubing the brass instrument pierced the center. (See appendix 2, figure A1.)

Berliner Pumpen. (Ger.) **Berlin valves**.

B.E.R.P. Buzz Extension Resistance Piece. **Practice aid** invented by Maurio Guaneri to develop **embouchure** strength and efficiency. The item plugs into the **leadpipe** and features a separate receiver for the **mouthpiece** that allows the player to perform mouthpiece **buzzing** exercises while holding the trumpet in the normal playing position. A movable sleeve allows the player to adjust the level of resistance.

Bersag horn. A valved bugle used in early **drum and bugle corps.** It was pitched in B-flat and E-flat with a single **piston valve** that lowered the pitch by a fourth. Bersag horns were patterned after the *tromba alla berseglari* and were known for their ease of response and sonorous ensemble music.

beryllium bronze. An alloy developed for use in space exploration that was used for trumpet **bell**s built by the **Schilke** company in the late twentieth century because its properties of sound refraction were deemed to be more efficient than brass.

Besson. French and English brass instrument-manufacturing company, founded in Paris by Gustave Auguste Besson (1820–1874) in 1837. He produced his first cornet in 1838 and went on to become a leader in cornet manufacture and design. Besson opened a factory in London in 1851 on the occasion of the Great Exhibition. He revolutionized brass instrument manufacturing by developing the prototype system of mandrels in 1856, which standardized the sizes of **bells** and **leadpipes** as well as other instrumental components to facilitate the exact duplication of instruments. Besson also improved the design of the **Périnet piston valve** and worked to continually improve valve mechanisms. He left Paris for London in 1858 and opened another factory in the wake of unsuccessful litigation against **Adophe Sax.**

Besson continued to operate factories in both Paris and London, and distributed instruments to warehouses in Brussels, Charleroi, Madrid, and Barcelona in the nineteenth century. When Besson died in 1874, his widow, Florentine, assumed management of the London firm. Florentine Besson died three years later in 1877, and the company then passed to her daughter, Marthe Josephine Besson (ca. 1852–1908), an astute businesswoman who had trained with her father and took over both the French and English firms. When Marthe married Adolphe Fontaine in 1880, she kept her maiden name of Besson and became an equal owner of the company, which was renamed Fontaine-Besson (instruments were often stamped "F. Besson").

Under the leadership of Marthe Besson, the company designed numerous instruments, including a cornet (1882) with two extra transposing **rotary valves** designed to eliminate the need for removable mouthpipes; a trumpet

in F-sharp (1884) with crooks to lower the pitch down to C; the first **piccolo trumpet** in G (with a long, straight bell and crooks down to F and E-flat) that was used by **Xavier-Napoléon Teste** for performances of Bach's *Magnificat* in 1885; and other **high-pitched trumpets** in F, E-flat, D, C, B-flat, and A (often convertible to two neighboring keys, such as F/E-flat and E-flat/D). Other instruments produced included a **bass trumpet** in C (primarily for works by Wagner) and a family of cornophones, featuring large-bore conical tubing and played with a funnel-shaped mouthpiece.

Marital problems and subsequent litigation between Marthe Besson and Adolphe Fontaine resulted in two different companies after 1895: Fontaine-Besson in France and Besson & Company in England, one of the largest suppliers of British brass bands. The F. Besson B-flat trumpet, called the "Meha" model, was the first modern B-flat trumpet; it provided the model for the trumpets made by **Vincent Bach** and **Elden Benge** in the early twentieth century. When the Paris factory was destroyed in the Second World War, several American trumpet makers strove to copy the Besson "Meha" B-flat trumpet including **Renold Schilke**, **F. E. Olds**, and **Dominic Calicchio**. In 1948, Boosey & Hawkes acquired the Besson London brand. In addition to the "Meha" B-flat trumpet, other model names used by Besson included "Brevetée," "Desideratum," and "Etoile."

bezel. An alternate term for the **rim** of a brass **mouthpiece**.

Biber, Heinrich Ignaz Franz von (1644–1704). Bohemian-Austrian composer and violinist. He began his career as a composer and musician at the court of Kroměříž (Kremsier) in Moravia (now the Czech Republic) between 1666 and 1670, where there was an exceptionally fine trumpet corps led by **Pavel Vejvanovský**. In 1673 he received an official appointment to work at the archbishop's court in Salzburg, becoming vice musical director in 1679 and chief musical director (*kappelmeister*) in 1684. Best known for his compositions for solo violin, especially the virtuosic *Mystery Sonatas* that employ scordatura, Biber also wrote several important works for the trumpet including the *Sonata a 7* (1668) for six trumpets and the *Sonata Sancti Polycarpi* (1673) for eight trumpets—both with timpani and basso continuo—as well as a series of twelve duets. Biber's solo works for trumpet include several sonatas and balletti, notably *Sonata IV in C Major*. He also included prominent trumpet ensemble parts in several of his sacred compositions such as the motet, *Plaudite tympana*. In 1682 he composed the colossal *Missa Salisburgensis*, which was composed in 1682 to celebrate the 1,100th anniversary of the ecclesiastical status of Salzburg in the Holy Roman Empire. This lavish work is scored in grand polychoral style with fifty-three parts in six groups including two trumpet choirs each with four trumpets and timpani.

Biber, Karl Heinrich (1681–1749). Austrian composer. The son of **Heinrich Ignaz Franz von Biber**, he began his career in Salzburg, following in his father's footsteps. He joined the court musical establishment in 1704, was promoted to deputy kappelmeister in 1714, and eventually became kappelmeister in 1743. Composing exclusively for the church, Biber wrote several solo works for trumpet and orchestra including *Sonata Paschalis* (1729) as well as sonatas for ensembles of up to nine trumpets.

bicycle bugle. A compact triple-folded bugle used by those who rode high-wheeled bicycles in the late nineteenth century as a device to alert pedestrians on the street. They often featured a flatter, oval-shaped bell to allow them to easily fit into the pocket of a jacket.

Billingsgate trumpet. A long, straight medieval trumpet (**buisine**) built circa 1375 that was discovered in a bog in the Billingsgate area of London in 1984. Next to the two Egyptian trumpets (**šnb**) discovered in 1922 in the tomb of King Tutankhamun (ca. 1323 BC), it is the second oldest surviving trumpet in the world and the oldest surviving trumpet from Europe. The next oldest surviving trumpet (from 1442) is the **Guitbert trumpet**.

bit. A small piece of tubing inserted into the **leadpipe** of a trumpet built before the middle of the nineteenth century as a way to adjust tuning. Tuning bits preceded **tuning slides** and adjustable leadpipes. Sometimes more than one bit was used (telescoping into each other) when pitch needed to be lowered more than the length of a single bit.

bite. Term used to describe how the **rim** of a **mouthpiece** feels on the lips of a trumpet player; a fit that influences clarity of attack and pitch control. Mouthpieces with a sharp bite generally facilitate the production of accurate, stable pitch and a rich tone. A bite that is too sharp impairs lip control and flexibility. A sharp bite can also be painful on the lips and reduce endurance. On the other hand, a round, soft bite may be comfortable to play, but might produce a blurred attack and poorly defined pitch.

Bitsch, Marcel (1921–2011). French composer and theorist. He studied at the Paris Conservatory and later became a professor of counterpoint there. His compositions for trumpet include *Quatre variations sur un thème de D. Scarlatti* for **cornet** and piano, *Fantasietta* for trumpet and piano, and *20 Etudes* for trumpet in C or B-flat. Bitsch also wrote solo works for horn, flute, oboe, and bassoon.

Blackburn, Clifford (b. 1947). American trumpeter and brass instrument maker. He began playing the trumpet at the age of nine and went on to earn a bachelor's degree in music from Tennessee Technological University as a student of Patrick McGuffey and George Bitzer. He also studied with Leon Rapier at the University of Louisville. Blackburn performed with the Nashville Symphony, the Louisville Orchestra, and the Louisville Bach Society. He began making **leadpipes**, known as "Louisville Leadpipes," in 1974 and later marketed them professionally through his own company, Blackburn Music Services. After working with noted trumpet acoustician **William Cardwell**, he built his first C trumpet in 1983. The sales of his trumpets increased to the point that Blackburn resigned from the Louisville Orchestra in 1987 and moved to Decatur, Tennessee, to work full time in his own workshop building custom trumpets and leadpipes. Blackburn Trumpets are all personally handcrafted by Blackburn with the help of his assistant, Tina Erickson.

Blanchard, Terrence (b. 1962). American jazz trumpeter, bandleader, and composer. Born in New Orleans, he began playing the piano at the age of five and the trumpet at the age of eight. In high school he studied at the New Orleans Center for Creative Arts with Roger Dickerson and Ellis Marsalis Jr. From 1980 to 1982, Blanchard studied with jazz saxophonist Paul Jeffrey and trumpeter Bill Fielder at Rutgers University, while touring with the Lionel Hampton Orchestra. He replaced his childhood friend, **Wynton Marsalis**, in Art Blakey's Jazz Messengers in 1982 and served as the band's trumpeter and bandleader until 1986.

Blanchard became involved with film music after performing on the soundtracks for Spike Lee's movies *Do the Right Thing* and *Mo' Better Blues* (where he coached Denzel Washington on effective trumpet-playing posture). Lee invited Blanchard to compose the score for their next collaboration, *Jungle Fever*. He has written the score for every Spike Lee film since then including, *Malcolm X*, *Clockers*, *Summer of Sam*, *25th Hour*, and *Inside Man*. In 2006, he composed the score for Spike Lee's four-hour HBO documentary on Hurricane Katrina, *When the Levees Broke: A Requiem in Four Acts*. Blanchard has composed over forty film scores to date and continues to perform on the trumpet and teach. He was named artistic director of the Thelonious Monk Institute of Jazz at the University of Southern California in 2000. In 2008 he won his first Grammy Award as a bandleader for *A Tale of God's Will (A Requiem for Katrina)* in the category of Best Large Jazz Ensemble Album.

Blechbläser. (Ger.) Brass instruments.

Blühmel, Friedrich (d. before 1845). German musician and co-inventor of the valve along with Heinrich Stölzel (1777–1844). Blühmel played trumpet and horn as well as the violin and a variety of woodwind instruments. Growing up as a coal miner, he got the idea for applying a valve mechanism to brass instruments between 1810 and 1813 by observing the ventilating pipes and faucets of Silesian blast furnaces. In July 1814 he invented with Stölzel the first valve mechanism. Two years later he developed the **box valve** in 1816 and, together with Stölzel, jointly secured a patent for the valve on April 12, 1818. Stölzel purchased exclusive rights to the patent from Blühmel soon afterward. In 1819 Blühmel applied a **rotary valve** to a trumpet. He and Stölzel both applied for separate patents for their rotary valve designs in 1828, but were denied because only the idea of the valve mechanism for brass instruments could be patented at the time, not individual design variations on the same principle.

Böhme, Max William "Willi" (1861–1928). German trumpeter and composer. The older brother of **Oskar Böhme**, Willi (as he was known) played principal trumpet at the Royal Hungarian Opera House in Budapest between 1889 and 1908. Böhme was a member of the Bayreuth Festival Orchestra between 1891 and 1901, and was singled out by the conductor Hans Richter for his performance of *Parsifal* as principal trumpet. Between 1897 and 1908 he served as the first professor of trumpet at the National Hungarian Royal Music Academy (the precursor of the Franz Liszt Music Academy). He returned to his hometown of Potschappel, Germany (near Dresden), in 1908 to open his own music school and stayed there for the rest of his life. In addition to performing and teaching, Willi Böhme also composed several light works and study material for the trumpet including *Die schönste Blume*, *Ungarisches Lied*, *Große ausführliche Schule für B-Trompete oder Cornet à Pistons oder Althorn* (1910), and *Kleine Trompetenschule mit 20 instrumentalen Übungen nebst Fanfaren* (1910).

Böhme, Oskar (1870–ca. 1938). German cornetist and composer. His father, Heinrich Wilhelm Böhme (1843–?), was a wind instrument player in a miner's band in Potschappel (near Dresden), and his mother, Juliane Henriette Böhme *née* Kästner, was originally from Neudöhlen. His older brother, **Willi Böhme**, was a trumpeter, but Oskar played the cornet. As Edward Tarr points out in his book *East Meets West* (Pendragon Press, 2004), Böhme may have played the cornet and later emigrated to Russia in an effort to strike out on his own and seek new opportunities. Böhme toured as a cornet soloist beginning in 1885 and played in the Royal Hungarian Opera House Orchestra in Budapest from 1894 until 1896, when he enrolled in the Leipzig Conservatory to study composition with Salomon Jadassohn (1831–1902). Although he later dedicated his *Concerto in E Minor for Trumpet and Orchestra, Op. 18* to **Ferdinand Weinschenck**, the trumpet professor in Leipzig, there is no evidence that Böhme studied trumpet with Weinschenck during his short time at the conservatory (November 1896—December 1897).

Böhme moved to St. Petersburg in 1897 and remained in Russia for the rest of his life, where he was known as a cornetist, not as a trumpeter. He played in the Mariinsky Theater orchestra from 1897 to 1921 and taught at a music school on Vasilevsky Island from 1921 until 1930. Böhme then played in the orchestra of the Leningrad Drama Theater from 1930 until 1934. Although he apparently did not suffer from anti-German sentiments during the First World War or the Russian Revolution, Böhme was swept up by Stalin's purge of artists and scientists known as the "Great Terror" in 1936 and banished to Chkalov, a remote town at the foot of the Ural Mountains, where he taught at a music school. He is reported to have died two years later, but no records exist; a worker claims to have seen him at a hard labor camp in the Turkmenian Channel in 1941.

Böhme's compositions include the only trumpet concerto from the Romantic era, the aforementioned *Concerto in E Minor for Trumpet and Orchestra, Op. 18* (1899), the *Trompetensextett in E-flat minor, Op. 30* (1907), and the popular cornet solos *La Napolitaine: Tarantelle, Op. 25* (1903) and *Ballet Scene, Op. 31* (1907). His collection of etudes, *24 melodische Übungen in allen Dur—und Moll—Tonarten, Op. 20*, is a staple of the repertoire. Böhme's *Concerto, Op. 18* was originally written for a trumpet in A (or cornet in A as a second choice) in the key of E Minor, but appears in several modern editions transposed up one half step to the key of F Minor to facilitate performance on a B-flat trumpet. Franz Herbst created the first edition in F Minor in 1941.

Bolden, Charles Joseph "Buddy" (1877–1931). American jazz cornetist and bandleader. Often cited as one of the pioneers of jazz brass playing, Bolden did not begin playing the **cornet** until he had finished school in New Orleans around 1894. He was noted for his unique style and powerful sound that commanded attention and inspired imitators. He started his own six-piece group in 1901 consisting of cornet, clarinet, valve trombone, guitar, double bass, and drums. Bolden reached the peak of his fame in 1905, performing in parks, dance halls, and neighboring towns. The following year his mental health deteriorated as a result of alcoholism, and by 1907 he was admitted to a mental institution in Jackson, Louisiana, where he spent the remaining twenty-four years of his life. Bolden's short career had a lasting impact and he is credited with creating a new, more aggressive style of playing that influenced other New Orleans cornetists like **King Oliver** and **Louis Armstrong**. Some of the titles for which he is best known include *Make Me a Pallet on the Floor, Bucket's Got a Hole in It,* and *Buddy Bolden Blues.*

Boos, Louis F. (1858–1935). American cornetist, bandmaster, and composer. His first musical experiences took place in his church, where his father was the choir director and Boos played both piano and pipe organ. At the age of sixteen he joined **Patrick Gilmore**'s Twenty-Second Regiment Band as a cornetist. He eventually settled in Jackson, Michigan, where he reorganized Jackson's Central City Band and called it Boos' First Infantry Band. He also directed the Knights of Pythias Cornet Band and the Citizen Patriot Newspaper Boys Band. Boos frequently toured the country as a cornet soloist, often performing duets with **Anna Teresa Berger** Lynch, and taught cornet to many outstanding students including Hale VanderCook, Bert Brown, and Frank Hoffman. Boos composed several cornet solos including *The Charmer*, *Mildred: Grand Fantasie with Variations*, several polkas, and a duet, *The Two Roses*.

bore. The interior dimensions of the tubing of a wind or brass instrument. The measurements of a tube's interior, known as its bore profile, determines the distribution of the vibrating air column inside the instrument, while its length determines the lowest note it can play. The lowest note, or **fundamental**, of a prescribed length of tubing generates the **harmonic overtone series** for the tubing and is known as the instrument's **nominal pitch**. It may not be possible to sound the fundamental on an instrument with a narrow bore and higher harmonics may be difficult to sound on wider bore instruments. Trumpets and trombones have a high percentage of **cylindrical bore** tubing, while for cornets, bugles, and flugelhorns generally a larger portion of the bore is **conical**. Dents or other irregularities in the bore can negatively impact an instrument's **intonation** and sound quality.

borija. A wooden trumpet made from the bark of a willow or ash tree approximately one and a half feet in length that is played in Bosnia, Croatia, Serbia, and Slovenia.

boss. An alternate term for the **ball** on a **natural trumpet**, also known as the **knob**, **knop**, or **pommel**.

Boston Musical Instrument Manufactory. Instrument-making firm that flourished in Boston, Massachusetts, between 1869 and 1919. The company was formed when two instrument manufacturers combined forces in 1869: Graves & Company and E. G. Wright. During the late nineteenth century Boston produced a wide variety of different cornets with **Périnet piston valves** as well **rotary valves** with both side- and top-action mechanisms. Best known was their "Three Star Cornet," one of the premier cornet models at the turn of the twentieth century; Boston also made **echo bell cornets** and **over-the-shoulder cornets** in both E-flat and B-flat. The company was acquired by the Cundy-Bettoney Company in 1919.

Botti, Chris (b. 1962). American jazz trumpeter and composer. Before starting to play the trumpet at the age of nine, Botti's first musical influences came from his mother, a classically trained pianist. His dedication to the trumpet intensified at the age of twelve when he heard **Miles Davis**'s recording of *My Funny Valentine*. In high school, Botti was selected for the McDonald's All American High School Jazz Band in 1983, took classes at Mount Hood Community College, and began playing in clubs in his hometown of Portland, Oregon. Following studies with Bill Adam and David Baker at Indiana University, Botti earned two grants from the National Endowment of the Arts to pursue studies with **Woody Shaw** and saxophonist George Coleman during summer breaks. He left the university to tour with Frank Sinatra and Buddy Rich, and moved to New York in 1985 to embark on a career in studio playing.

Botti performed with many singers and pop artists in the 1990s including Paul Simon, Aretha Franklin, Natalie Cole, Joni Mitchell, and Sting. He released his debut album, *First Wish*, in 1995. Known for his affinity for smooth jazz, Botti has been nominated for several Grammy Awards in 2007 and 2009 including Best Pop Instrumental Album and Best Long Form Video. Known for his preference for vintage equipment, Botti's instrument of choice is a **Martin Committee** large bore Handcraft trumpet made in 1939, which he plays with a Bach No. 3 **mouthpiece**. His preferred mute is a Leblanc Vacchiano Harmon mute made in the 1950s.

bouché. (Fr.) Blocked or stopped. This term appears in some French repertoire (Milhaud's *Le boeuf sur le toit*, Op. 58) to indicate that a hand in the bell or a mute should be used to simulate early jazz styles.

bow. The curved segment of a trumpet's tubing that connects the straight tubing and/or bell of the instrument. This term is most often used to describe parts of a single-folded **natural trumpet**, where the specific bows (bends) in the tubing are numbered according to their relation to the mouthpiece. For example, the bow closest to the bell is the first bow because it is the first bend encountered by the airstream as it flows through the instrument, and the bow closest to the mouthpiece is the second.

bow knob. A small button or piece of metal attached to the side of the end of a tuning slide on a trumpet or cornet to facilitate a firm grip for removal of the slide. Commonly found on the inner curve of the second valve slide on most trumpets, older instruments sometimes included two bow knobs on the ends of other valve slides as well.

box trumpet. A compact **natural trumpet** designed by Adam Buchschwinder (d. 1743/1745) of Ellwangen, Germany, in the 1730s. The trumpet featured seven feet of tubing pitched in D tightly wrapped in spiral form around a short bell pointing downward. Aside from the horizontal mouthpiece and receiver, the entire instrument was covered by a metal barrel or box, hence the name. (See figure 7.) The instrument's reduced size facilitated **hand-stopping** as well as the performance of military field signals on horseback. The design of the box trumpet no doubt influenced the compact hunting horn known as the **Trompe de Lorraine** in the late nineteenth century.

Figure 7. A box trumpet with and without its covering. *Drawing by T. M. Larsen.*

box valve. The earliest type of valve applied to a brass instrument. **Charles Clagget** developed the first box valve in 1788 for his **Cromatic** [*sic*] **Trumpet**, which simply toggled between two conjoined natural trumpets in D and E-flat. **Friedrich Blühmel** invented a box valve mechanism that was applied to a trumpet and a horn with two valves in 1816 and later to a trombone with three in 1818. (See appendix 2, figure A2.) **Friedrich Wilhelm Schuster** of Karlsruhe produced brass instruments with Blühmel's box valves up until 1833.

Bozza, Eugène (1905–1991). French composer, conductor, and pedagogue. Bozza studied at the Paris Conservatoire, where he earned first prizes in violin (1924), conducting (1930), and composition (1934) as well as the Prix de Rome for his cantata, *La légende de Roukmāni* (1934). He conducted at the Opéra-Comique in Paris from 1938 to 1948 and served as the director of the Ecole Nationale de Musique, Valenciennes from 1951 to 1975. Bozza composed ballets, operas, oratorios, cantatas, concerti, and symphonies along with numerous works for chorus, orchestra, and band; however, he is best known for his many solo and chamber compositions for wind and brass instruments.

Bozza's twelve solo works for the trumpet are *Caprice [No. 1], Op. 47* for trumpet and piano (1943), *Concertino* for trumpet and chamber orchestra (1949), *Badinage* for trumpet and piano (1950), *16 Etudes* (1950), *Dialogue* for two trumpets (1954), *Rustiques* for trumpet and piano (1955), *Rapsodie* for trumpet and piano (1957), *Cornettina* for cornet or trumpet and piano (1965), *Frigariana* for trumpet and piano (1967), *11 Etudes sur des modes karnatiques* (1972), *Lied* for trumpet and piano (1976),

and *Caprice No. 2* for trumpet and piano (1978). Bozza composed several works for brass ensemble including one quartet and six quintets, especially the popular *Sonatine* for brass quintet (1951).

brace. Part of the construction of a brass instrument that supports the position of various sections of tubing and the bell to prevent undesired movement or collision of parts and to support the structure of the instrument and enhance the playing position. On early single folded trumpets, the brace was a simple block of wood between branches of tubing wrapped in yarn or cord, and on later instruments braces were made out of metal. In the late twentieth century, extra metal was added to the bracing structure of a valved trumpet to dampen the overall vibration of the instrument and darken the sound.

braces. A dental appliance designed to straighten the position of crooked teeth. Trumpet players who wear braces experience challenges with playing the instrument because the braces distort the feeling of playing, and adjustments must be made. Many trumpeters choose to apply a protective wax fitting over the braces to prevent injury or discomfort while playing.

Brahms, Johannes (1833–1897). German composer. His father, Johann Jakob, played the **keyed bugle** in the brass band of the Hamburg town militia. Although he wrote prominent solo passages for the horn in his symphonic and chamber works, Brahms did not write any substantial music for high brass instruments. He preferred to write for the **natural trumpet** with **crooks** to different keys, and eschewed the valved trumpet and the **cornet** altogether. The prominent trumpet parts in his symphonic works include the opening of the *Academic Festival Overture*, and the finale of his *Symphony No. 2 in D Major.*

branch. The straight segment of tubing on a **natural trumpet** or **slide**.

Brandenburg Concerto No. 2. Composition by **Johann Sebastian Bach** with a famously high solo trumpet part. Written in 1721, the work is a concerto grosso for trumpet in F, violin, oboe, and recorder (*flauto a bec* or beaked flute, sometimes played on a modern flute) with string orchestra. The unusually high **range** of the trumpet part along with the delicacy required to blend with the woodwinds and violin in the solo group made the work a benchmark for trumpet virtuosi over the past three hundred years. Its unique **endurance** requirements (long stretches above **high C** with little respite) were an additional test. **Theo Charlier** was the first trumpeter in the modern era to play the Brandenburg at the original high pitch. In the early music revival, several trumpeters including **Walter Holy** and **Friedemann Immer** played the work on **vented Baroque trumpets**. French trumpeter **Jean-François Madeuf** was the first to record the Brandenburg on a **natural trumpet** with no modern compromises in 2009.

Brandi, Giovanni Pellegrino (fl. 1675–1700). Italian trumpeter. He was the leading trumpeter at the Basilica of San Petronio in Bologna during the tenure of **Giuseppe Torelli** and performed nearly one hundred solo trumpet works by composers of the Bologna School. Musician rosters at San Petronio show that he was employed there between 1679 and 1699.

Brandt, Willy [Vasily Georgiyevich] (1869–1923). German trumpeter active in Russia at the turn of the twentieth century. Following four years of study with Carl Zimmermann, he graduated from the Coburg School of Music in Germany in 1887 and performed with a spa orchestra at Bad Oeynhausen near Hanover during the summers of 1887 and 1888. Brandt served as solo trumpeter of the Orchestral Society in Helsinki (now the Helsinki Philharmonic) between 1887 and 1890, and moved to Moscow in 1890 to become principal trumpet with the Bolshoi Theater Orchestra. His career blossomed in Moscow, where he was an influential teacher and soloist, and performed in a **brass quartet** with **Mikhail Tabakov**. He joined the faculty of a new conservatory in Saratov in 1912, where he taught trumpet and cornet, and conducted the conservatory orchestra. Considered the father of the Russian trumpet and cornet school, Brandt taught several notable trumpeters including **Vladimir Drucker**, Sergei Teriomin, and Tabakov. Brandt composed several pedagogical and solo works for the trumpet that remain staples of the repertoire, including *Concert Piece Nos. 1 and 2*, *Concert Polka*, *Wiegenlied*, *34 Orchestral Etudes*, and *23 Last Studies*. He died from poisoning caused by a vaccination in 1923.

Brass Bulletin. Brass instrument periodical. Published quarterly by the Swiss firm of Editions BIM (*Bureau d'Information Musicale*) between 1971 and 2003, the *Brass Bulletin* provided readers around the world with news and current research concerning brass history, **performance practice, period instruments**, repertoire, and performers. The self-described "International Magazine for Brass Players" was edited by **Jean-Pierre Mathez** and published in English, French, and German (later Italian and Spanish as well). It was the leading source of brass news and scholarship for more than thirty years.

Brass Herald. Brass instrument periodical. Launched in August 2003, the magazine is published in February, May, August, October, and December each year. Edited by Philip Biggs (b. 1954), the periodical includes news, historical information, and interviews with leading figures from all musical genres, including classical, jazz, brass bands, concert bands, and military bands.

brass quartet. Brass chamber ensemble usually consisting of two trumpets and two trombones or two trumpets with one horn and one trombone. Brass quartets flourished from the middle of the nineteenth century until the early twentieth century. Prominent musicians who performed in professional brass quartets include **Julius Kosleck**, **Edna White**, and **Robert King**.

brass quintet. Brass chamber ensemble with two trumpets, a horn, and a trombone with either tuba or bass trombone playing the lowest part. Brass quintets became the most important medium of brass chamber music in the second half of the twentieth century through the pioneering work of the **New York Brass Quintet**, the **American Brass Quintet**, the **Philip Jones** Brass Ensemble, and the global celebrity of the **Canadian Brass**.

Breath Builder. A **practice aid** designed by American bassoonist Harold Hansen to improve lung capacity and stamina by helping the player experience the sensation of inhaling and exhaling with increased intensity. It is a tube of plastic approximately six inches tall with a ping-pong ball inside. The bottom is sealed and three holes are drilled on the top to vary the resistance. One or more of the holes may be stopped to vary the resistance. Fourteen ounces of pressure are required to hold the ping-pong ball at the top of the column, which is the goal of practicing with the device. Whether inhaling or exhaling, regular practice with the Breath Builder facilitates smooth breath control similar to the motion of a professional string player's bow moving slowly from frog to tip.

breath mark. A symbol written in printed music to indicate points at which a musician should inhale. Common breath mark symbols include a comma, a *V* (like the string marking for "upbow"), or a simple vertical line. Such marks may also indicate suggested lifts or slight pauses in musical phrasing rather than a physical need to breathe. Marks to indicate deliberate exhalation (such as an *X*) are also used occasionally, especially in music for the piccolo trumpet, where relief from excessive reserves of air (sometimes called stale air or stacked air) is beneficial.

breathing. The modification of inhalation and exhalation when playing a brass instrument to achieve artistic performance and efficient physical control. Several aspects of trumpet playing require careful attention to breathing technique, especially high-register playing (**altissimo playing**), **piccolo trumpet** playing, and performing at extremely loud volumes or soft volumes for extended periods of time. Efficient breath control plays a vital role in the production of a smooth and full-bodied tone. Several muscles and anatomical regions are involved in breathing technique on a brass instrument including the lungs, **diaphragm, intercostal muscles**, trachea, nasal and oral cavities, and the muscles of the neck (scalene and sternomastoid), which moderate tension. (See figure 8.) When all physical factors of breathing technique work in harmony, stress is reduced on the **embouchure**, and a brass musician is able to maximize artistic performance with secure control. Many **practice aids** are used to develop efficient breath control including the **Breath Builder**, the **spirometer**, and the **Voldyne**. See also, **breath mark, circular breathing**.

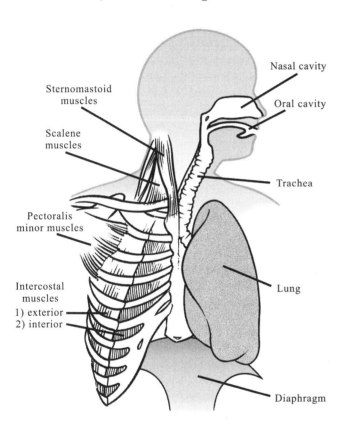

Figure 8. Anatomy involved in proper breathing for trumpet playing. *Drawing by T. M. Larsen.*

Brecker, Randy (b. 1945). American jazz trumpeter and composer. The brother of saxophonist Michael Brecker, Randy studied classical trumpet in Philadelphia before attending Indiana University (IU), where he studied jazz theory with Dave Baker. During a European tour with the IU Jazz Band, he decided to leave school and remained abroad for several months. Brecker later moved to New York, where he joined Blood, Sweat and Tears and played in Horace Silver's quintet. He also worked with several big bands, including those led by Clark

Terry, Duke Pearson, Thad Jones and Mel Lewis, Joe Henderson, and Frank Foster. In the 1970s he played in a popular group led by his brother, Michael, known as the Brecker Brothers, and later played with the Mingus Dynasty and the Mingus Big Band. He has also performed with many other artists including Jaco Pastorius, the Carnegie Hall Jazz Band, and numerous other groups as a freelancer.

Broiles, Melvyn (1929–2003). American trumpeter. Best known as the longtime principal trumpeter of the Metropolitan Opera Orchestra in New York, Broiles began playing the trumpet in the second grade in Salinas, Kansas; by high school his family had moved to Hollywood, California, where he played with various concert bands and dance bands. He began studies with **William Vacchiano** at the Juilliard School in 1950 and was drafted into military service the following year. Between 1951 and 1954 Broiles served as a member of the West Point Academy Band. He joined the National Broadcasting Company's (NBC) Symphony of the Air in 1954 and performed on numerous radio broadcasts. Broiles became principal trumpeter of the Metropolitan Opera Orchestra in 1955 and left the follow year to become principal trumpeter of the Philadelphia Orchestra. After one season in Philadelphia, Broiles returned to the Met and remained as principal until his retirement in 2001.

Known for his distinctive sense of humor and penchant for playing practical jokes, Broiles was a fine teacher who served on the faculty of the Juilliard School for thirty years between 1971 and 2001. He also taught at the Manhattan School of Music and the Mannes School of Music. Broiles composed music and pedagogical works for his students including four books of *Etudes and Duets,* two books of *Trumpet Baroque,* and *Transpositions for Orchestral Trumpeters.* He also wrote *Baroque Duets*, *Grand Opera Classics*, *Tower Calls* (solo trumpet), and the virtuoso concerto for trumpet and wind ensemble, *Vernal Equinox.* For trumpet ensemble, he composed *Fanfare* and *Blazing Trumpets.* His music library now resides at the University of Georgia.

Brown, Clifford (1930–1956). American jazz trumpeter. He began to study the trumpet at the age of thirteen and rapidly developed impressive technical prowess. While studying mathematics at Delaware State College and music at Maryland State College, his performances with the school jazz bands attracted attention along with his brief appearances in Philadelphia with such leading jazz musicians as Fats Navarro, Dizzy Gillespie, and Charlie Parker. Navarro's style exerted a strong influence on Brown, and the two men formed a close friendship. A car accident landed Brown in the hospital in June 1950, and it took him a year to recuperate. He made his first recording in March 1952 with Chris Powell's Blue Flames, and joined Tadd Dameron's band for a recording session and other appearances the following year. Brown later toured Europe with Lionel Hampton's big band and recorded with American and European jazz musicians, including Art Blakey. He formed the Brown-Roach Quintet with Max Roach in 1954 and played with the group until his untimely death in a car accident at the age of twenty-five. Known for his melodically inventive improvisations, brilliant technique, and rich tone throughout all registers of the trumpet, Brown was a leading figure in hard bop and influenced many trumpeters in the 1960s and 1970s, especially **Lee Morgan** and **Freddie Hubbard**.

Bryant, Clora (b. 1927). American jazz trumpeter. She began playing the trumpet at the age of fifteen and progressed so rapidly that she won scholarships to Oberlin College and Bennett College, but she chose to attend Prairie View College (now Prairie View A&M University) in her home state of Texas. When her family moved to California in 1945, she attended UCLA, but dropped out to tour with the Sweethearts of Rhythm. She played on Central Avenue in Los Angeles during the 1940s, performing alongside Dexter Gordon, Wardell Gray, Frank Morgan, and **Art Farmer**, and performing in backup bands for Billie Holiday and Josephine Baker. In 1949 Bryant married the bass player Joe Stone, with whom she had two sons. During the early 1950s she lived and worked in New York and Canada. After returning to Los Angeles in 1956, she met **Dizzy Gillespie**, who became a lifelong friend and mentor. She recorded her only album as a leader, "Gal with a Horn" for the Mode label in 1957. She continued to tour and freelance after the 1960s, often appearing as a singer. In 2002 she received the Mary Lou Williams Women in Jazz Award at the Kennedy Center.

bubble mute. A type of **Harmon mute** or **Wah Wah mute** made by the **Jo-Ral** company that featured a cavity shaped like a sphere rather than a barrel. It protruded from the end of the bell like a bubble, hence the name. The mute's unique shape enhanced intonation and projection in the lower register. (See appendix 3 and figure 25 under "Harmon mute.")

buburé. A wooden trumpet of the Amazonian rain forest made from tree trunks, some as long as seventeen feet.

buccina. Ancient Roman brass instrument. Evidence of the buccina, both literary and pictorial, is scarce and vague. It is sometimes confused with the **cornu**. The instrument was revived by **Ottorino Respighi** in his orchestral works *Pines of Rome* and *Roman Festivals* in the 1920s, but the use of term *buccina* was more symbolic and nostalgic than practical: the parts were performed by modern brass instruments.

buccinator muscles. Facial muscles at the corners of the mouth that assist in regulating the size of the **aperture** of the lips in the formation of a proper **embouchure** as well as the strength and flatness of the cheeks. (See figure 17 under **embouchure**.)

bucinatore. (Lat.) A **buccina** player.

bucinum. A short, straight trumpet played by Romanian shepherds in Eastern Europe to herd their flocks. The tradition survives to this day, and the instrument may be a vestige of the ancient **buccina**.

bucket mute. A straight-sided cup (a small bucket) filled with absorbent material; the **mute** is clipped on to the **bell** of a trumpet to create a warm, covered sound. The idea originated with early jazz trumpeters who held empty lard cans in front of the bell. The first mute consisting of a small bucket clipped to the **bell rim** was made by William McArthur in 1922. A model made by **Jo-Ral** fits inside the bell and features a large chamber stuffed with cotton perforated with large holes on the side. (See appendix 3.)

bugle. A trumpet-like instrument without **valves** and with a **conical bore** profile used as a military **signal** instrument. Its name comes from the Latin *buculus,* which means "bullock," or a young bull, from which the horn was taken. The medieval **oliphant** was this kind of early bugle. Metal bugle-horns were made to imitate animal horns and grew in size from a simple cone to a longer crescent-shaped horn known as the *Halbmond* (German for "half moon") or the **Hanoverian bugle**. Around 1800 the sickle-shaped Halbmond transformed into the familiar single-folded bugle, with its **bell** pointing to the front. British trumpet maker **William Shaw** may have been responsible for this fundamental change in bugle design. It was this single-folded instrument that was adapted with **vent holes** and keys to become the **keyed bugle** in the early nineteenth century.

Later bugles were made more compact and portable through a double-fold design. Copper was often used for bugles because it was deemed to enhance the instrument's ability to project sound over long distances. The single-folded bugle differed from the **cavalry trumpet** in terms of **bore** profile (the proportion of conical to cylindrical tubing) and key. The bugle was pitched in B-flat or C, while the cavalry trumpet was in E-flat. Aside from slight variations in design, bore profile, and bell size, the bugle without valves, as a signal instrument, has not changed radically in more than two hundred years. (See figure 9.) By the 1880s, bugles in North America became more **cylindrical** and were sometimes referred to as trumpets. Around the same time, smaller triple-folded bugles called **bicycle bugles**, or **buglets**, became popular with those who rode high-wheel bicycles as a device to alert pedestrians on the street. Bugles with valves, such as **Bersag horns**, later developed into instruments used in modern **drum and bugle corps**.

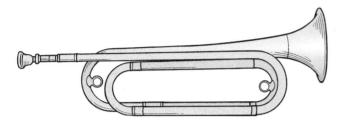

Figure 9. A U.S. regulation bugle. *Drawing by T. M. Larsen.*

bugle à clefs. (Fr.) **Keyed bugle**.

bugle call. A brief **fanfare** or **signal** played by a **bugle** usually for military purposes, such as "**Reveille**" or "**Taps**."

bugle horn. Alternate term for a *Halbmond*, or early hunting horn.

buglet. Another name for a **bicycle bugle**.

Buhl, Joseph-David (1781–1860). French trumpeter and teacher. One of the most respected trumpeters of his era, Buhl's strongest contribution was to French military music, especially his standardization of regimental trumpet calls for the French army, *Ordonnance de trompette pour les troupes à cheval*, many of which are still in use today. A seminal figure in the French trumpet school, Buhl's influence carried on through his nephew, **François Dauverné**, who became the first trumpet teacher at the Paris Conservatoire, and Dauverné's pupil, **Jean-Baptiste Arban**, the first professor of cornet at the same institution. Buhl's 1825 *Méthode de trompette* circulated widely throughout Europe and was plagiarized in 1830 by José de Juan Martinez (fl. 1825–1885) in Madrid.

Although he was born in France, Buhl's family was German. His talent developed quickly, and by the age of eleven he was a highly capable trumpeter. After serving in the military during his teens and twenties, Buhl was appointed professor of trumpet at the cavalry school at Versailles in 1805 at the age of twenty-four, a position he would hold for the rest of his life teaching more than 600 trumpeters. He earned the *Légion d'honneur* in 1814 and was also appointed head of music and major of the Gardes du Corps du Roi Louis XVIII. In addition to his military duties, Buhl served as the principal trumpet of the Paris Opéra and at the Théâtre Italien between 1816 and 1825.

Buhl lived through periods of transformation in both French politics and trumpet manufacture. Working just before the valve era, Buhl played the **natural trumpet**, occasionally used **hand-stopping** technique, and taught most of his students to play the French **cavalry trumpet** in E-flat. He developed an interest in trumpet design after 1829 and developed his own version of a **slide trumpet** in 1833 that unfortunately suffered from a slow, resistant slide mechanism and poor construction. Toward the end of his career Buhl left Paris and settled into a less demanding schedule of teaching in the winter and performing concerts in the summer. His greatest legacy remains his contributions to French military music. Buhl's standardized trumpet and bugle calls, including **Reveille**, were adopted by the United States military in the nineteenth century. His most enduring composition is the stirring trumpet ensemble fanfare *L'Etendard*, which became the theme of television broadcasts of the Olympic Games in the United States.

Bühnenmusik. (Ger.) Stage music. Music that is played on stage as part of an opera or a play. Wagner uses the term in *Lohengrin* (1850) for the onstage **herald trumpets**, which he calls ***Königstrompeten***.

buisine. (Old French.) A long, straight **herald trumpet** used in the Middle Ages, similar to the Arabian ***bûq al-nafîr***. Iconographical evidence reveals that it ranged in size between one and three meters, and was made of tubes of brass or silver with **balls** covering the joints. Heraldic banners were often suspended from its tubing. Its name resembles that of the Ancient Roman **buccina**, and other variations (busine, buzine, buyize) eventually led to *busaun*, which became, **Posaune**, the German word for "trombone." The *Chanson du Roland* (ca. 1100) mentions the instrument by name.

Bull, William (1650–1712). English trumpeter and instrument maker. Following an apprenticeship to the Haberdashers Company London in 1664, Bull was appointed "trumpeter in extraordinary" to Charles II at the age of sixteen. He continued in service as royal trumpeter while learning the trade of instrument making and repair. In 1700 he retired as a king's trumpeter and advertised his services as "trumpet master to his majesty," able to produce trumpets, horns, and kettledrums as well as ear trumpets for the deaf and powder horns for firearms. Bull crafted instruments of exceptional quality, several of which survive. John Baptist Grano (ca. 1692–1748) praised "an excellent trumpet of old Bull's making" in 1728, and organologist Eric Halfpenny wrote that Bull was "the most celebrated brasswind maker of Restoration London." A feature of Bull's **natural trumpets** that distinguishes them from contemporary German instruments is the size and purpose of the **ball** (or **knop**), which is larger and serves to connect the bell to the top **branch** of the trumpet.

Buono, Vincent C. (1875–1959). American trumpeter and cornet soloist. Buono began his career playing in theaters and with several bands and orchestras. He was one of the first musicians hired by the Columbia Phonograph Company in 1901 and spent over twenty years playing for recordings. Buono was an adept sight-reader and an expressive musician with a warm tone and clean technique who played solo cornet with Charles Prince's Band and Salvatore Minichini's Band. In 1922 Buono became first trumpeter with Walter Damrosch's Symphony Orchestra in New York and played with the group for several seasons. **Herbert L. Clarke** considered Buono to be one of the best first-chair cornetists in the field. As the golden age of bands declined in the 1930s, Buono played for theater productions and vaudeville shows. He made many recordings for Columbia and Edison over the years and enjoyed a long career, performing late into his sixties.

bûq al-nafîr. A long, straight trumpet of Arabian origin used for military signals as well as a vehicle for sonic aggression.

Burney, Charles (1726–1814). English music historian whose criticism of **John Sarjant**'s performance of Handel arias in 1784 led to developments in the use of **vent holes** and the **English slide trumpet**.

Burns, Stephen (b. 1959). American trumpeter, composer, and conductor. Originally from Wellesley Hills, Massachusetts, Burns studied with **Armando Ghitalla**, **Gerard Schwarz**, **Pierre Thibaud**, and **Arnold Jacobs** at the Juilliard School and Tanglewood Music Center and also pursued postgraduate studies in Paris and Chicago. He won several prestigious awards including the 1981 Young Concert Artists International Auditions, the 1982 Avery Fisher Career Grant, the 1983 National Endowment for the Arts Recitalist Grant, the Naumburg Scholarship at Juilliard, and "Outstanding Brass Player" at Tanglewood. Burns took first prize at the Maurice André International Competition for Trumpet in France in 1988. He has appeared as a soloist with major orchestras and ensembles throughout the world including the Atlanta Symphony, the Los Angeles Chamber Orchestra, the Ensemble Orchestral de Paris, the Arturo Toscanini Orchestra, the Leipzig Kammerorchester, the Japan National Philharmonic, and the Seattle Symphony. A former faculty member at the Jacobs School of Music of Indiana University, the State University of New York at Purchase, and the Manhattan School of Music, he is currently teaching at the Center for Advanced Musical Studies at Chosen Vale. Burns also serves as the artistic director of the Fulcrum Point New Music Project and the American Concerto Orchestra in Chicago.

busking. Performing in a public location (street, park, subway) for tips.

Butler, Barbara (b. 1952). American trumpeter and pedagogue. She first studied the piano and then switched to the cornet in high school. Butler studied with Vincent Cichowicz and **Adolph Herseth** in Chicago and earned her undergraduate degree in music from Northwestern University. She is a former member of Eastman Brass, Eastman Virtuosi, and the Vancouver and Grant Park Symphony Orchestras. She has performed, recorded, and appeared in broadcasts with the St. Louis, Chicago, and Houston Symphony Orchestras and the New York Philharmonic. Butler has appeared as a soloist with many major orchestras and festivals and presented recitals and master classes worldwide. She appears on recordings and international broadcasts with the Eastman Brass, Music of the Baroque, Chicago Chamber Musicians, and CBC Radio. She and her husband, **Charles Geyer**, have forged an extremely effective teaching partnership for more than thirty years, and many of their students have gone on to successful positions with major orchestras and other professional appointments. Butler and Geyer taught at the Eastman School of Music for eighteen years and at the Bienen School of Music at Northwestern University for fifteen years. They began teaching at the Shepherd School of Music at Rice University in July 2013.

Butler [Young], Helen May (1867–1957). American conductor and cornetist. A multitalented musician, Butler studied the violin with Bernard Listerman (concertmaster of the Boston Symphony at the time) as well as the **cornet**. She formed the Talma Ladies Orchestra in 1891 and the U.S. Talma Ladies Military Band in 1898. The band toured the United States for twelve years at the beginning of the twentieth century under various names, of which "Helen May Butler's Ladies Military Band" was the most popular. Known as "the Female Sousa," Butler enjoyed a friendship with Sousa, and he once allowed her to conduct his band in concert. Butler's band performed at many major venues including the Pan-American Exposition in Buffalo, New York (1901), the Women's Exposition at Madison Square Garden (1902), and the St. Louis World's Fair (1904). The C. G. **Conn** Company hired her and her soloists to promote their instruments and supplied her entire band with instruments. Her march, *Cosmopolitan America*, became the Republican Party's official march during Theodore Roosevelt's presidential campaign in 1904. After touring, she married James H. Young and worked as a music teacher and cornet soloist. In 1936, she ran unsuccessfully for the U.S. Senate. Her scrapbooks, papers, and photographs now reside in the Smithsonian Institution under her married name, Helen May Butler Young.

buzz. Colloquial term for the vibration of a trumpet player's lip in the **embouchure**.

buzzing. Practicing with the **mouthpiece** alone as well as without the mouthpiece to develop **embouchure** strength and efficiency.

Buzz-Wow mute. A variation on a **cup mute** made by **Humes & Berg** with vibrating membranes, like those on a kazoo, added to the bottom to create a distorted buzzing sound in performance. (See appendix 3.)

Cacciamani, Raniero (1818–1885). Italian trumpeter. He became a member of the Duke of Parma's orchestra in 1835 (promoted to principal in 1839) and was appointed professor of trumpet at the Royal Conservatory of Parma in 1859. Cacciamani published a **method book** for the early valved trumpet, *Metodo d'istruzione per tromba a macchina*, in 1853. Like **Dauverne**'s *Méthode* (1857), a large number of studies for the **natural trumpet** (called the "simple trumpet") comprise one third of the book. Cacciamani also published some arrangements of operatic selections for valved trumpet and piano between 1853 and 1855.

Calicchio, Dominic (1901–1979). Italian-American brass instrument designer and manufacturer. Known as the "Michelangelo of Brass," Calicchio was born in Rome and began working in Marchiondi's orphanage workshop in Milan at the age of thirteen. He later moved to the United States and worked with Rudy Mück for five months. In 1925 Calicchio opened his own shop in New York City, working in brass instrument repair for the first two years and producing his own trumpets and cornets thereafter. Like **Vincent Bach** and **Elden Benge**, he strove to reproduce the **Besson** B-flat trumpet, and developed his own high-quality instruments. Calicchio left New York after 1947 and moved to California. In 1978 he was commissioned by the MGM film studio to build two heart-shaped trumpets for use as props in the film *Sgt. Pepper's Lonely Hearts Club Band*. One of the instruments is currently on display at the National Music Museum in Vermillion, South Dakota. **Freddie Hubbard** served as an adviser to Calicchio.

call. A brief **fanfare** or **signal** played by a **bugle, posthorn,** or trumpet for military purposes or in a piece of concert music to represent military associations, as in the **Leonore Call.**

Callet, Jerome (b. 1930). Trumpeter, teacher, and designer of brass instruments. Following studies with James Morrow, Guy Borrelli, and Nathan Prager, Callet developed an acute interest in **embouchure** formation and optimization as well as **mouthpiece** and instrument design. His technique of the **tongue-controlled embouchure** was discussed in his book *Trumpet Secrets, Vol. 1* (2002), written with his student, Robert "Bahb" Civiletti. Callet's other publications include *Trumpet Yoga* (1971), *Brass Power and Endurance* (1974), and *Superchops* (1987).

Cammerton. See *Kammerton*.

Canadian Brass. Pioneer ensemble of brass chamber music. When the group was formed in 1970 the original members were trumpeters Bill Phillips and Stuart Laughton, Graeme Page on horn, Gene Watts on trombone, and Chuck Daellenbach on tuba. By 1972 Ronald Romm and Fred Mills had replaced Phillips and Laughton on trumpet, and the Canadian Brass embarked on a successful career of performing, touring, and recording that would have been unheard of for a brass ensemble just twenty years earlier. They excelled at performing medleys of popular music and classical favorites with an emphasis on entertainment, often including audience interaction and comedy in their performances. Musically, the frequent use of **high-pitched trumpets**, especially the piccolo and E-flat, expanded the quintet's palette of instrumental color just as their embrace of early jazz styles and the concurrent rise in popularity of Baroque music attracted a new audience to brass chamber music. The current members of the Canadian Brass are tubist (and founder) Chuck Daellenbach, trombonist Achilles Liarmakopoulos, Eric Reed on horn, and trumpeters Chris Coletti and Caleb Hudson.

Cannonball. American musical instrument manufacturer. Founded in 1996 by Tevis and Sheryl Laukat, Cannonball makes trumpets, saxophones, clarinets, and flutes. Trumpeter Ryan Laukat plays and acoustically customizes all Cannonball trumpets. Also a professional artist, Ryan Laukat engraves the bells of Cannonball saxophones and trumpets by hand. The company is based in Salt Lake City, Utah, and also runs two factories in Taiwan. Cannonball trumpet models include the 42 Artist Series (in B-flat and C) as well as a variety of B-flat trumpets including the 725, the 789RL (with reverse leadpipe), and the Lynx. Known for producing trumpets with a larger-than-normal bell size (BigBell©), Cannonball also makes a model 779 **flugelhorn**.

capistrum. A leather or fabric strap worn across the face to restrain movement of the cheeks while playing a wind instrument used in antiquity. The device was most often used by players of the aulos (an early woodwind), but was sometimes employed by players of the **tuba** in ancient Rome and the **salpinx** in ancient Greece (where it was known as the **phorbeia**) to support the embouchure and prevent cheeks puffing out while playing extremely loud signals.

Cardwell, William (1917–2012). American trumpet designer and acoustician. Cardwell started playing the trumpet when he was nine and studied trumpets throughout his life. He earned a master's degree in chemical engineering from the California Institute of Technology and worked as a chemical engineer and research scientist for Standard Oil of California (later known as the Chevron Corporation) for more than forty years. Cardwell created an extensive professional lab in his home to study trumpet acoustics and was a noted authority on all facets of trumpet design, especially **leadpipe** and **bell** tapers. He was instrumental in the design of **Olds** trumpets during the 1970s and took out a patent on one of his designs (U.S. Patent #3,507,181, of April 21, 1970). Cardwell is widely considered the father of the modern trumpet leadpipe and served as a consultant for several makers, especially **Clifford Blackburn**.

carnyx. A trumpet-like instrument of the ancient Celts from the Late Bronze Age. A complete version of the instrument has not survived, but iconographical evidence is plentiful, especially Roman coins and victory monuments, such as Trajan's Column. The carnyx is usually pictured as a vertical tube, like a periscope, with a fierce animal head like that of a boar (featuring an open mouth) at the top in place of a bell. Its shape, like a letter "J," was similar to the Roman **lituus**, from which it may have developed. The carnyx was an instrument of sonic aggression in times of war rather than a musical instrument. Rows of blaring carnyx players marching with the Celtic army were described by Polybius (ca. 203–120 BC) as creating a "dreadful din."

Caruso, Carmine (1904–1987). American brass pedagogue. Although he played the saxophone, not the trumpet, Caruso was a highly sought-after teacher in New York City known for his insights into the physical aspects of trumpet playing. He began his musical studies on the piano at the age of three with his father, Paul, who discovered that Carmine had perfect pitch at the age of four. After making remarkable progress, he abandoned the piano for the violin at the age of eight and studied with his older brother, Jimmy. At the age of seventeen he switched to the saxophone, studying again with his father, and soon embarked on a professional career performing with big bands led by Vincent Lopez, Emil Coleman, Lester Lanin, Meyer Davis, and Russ Morgan. In 1941 he concentrated on freelance playing and full-time teaching. His students were primarily woodwind players and violinists at first, but after 1942 he began teaching trumpeters when one of his saxophone colleagues from the Lopez band, Armand Camgros, discovered that Caruso's methods were applicable to brass players.

Caruso developed a reputation for being able to teach all levels of players and solve vexing problems, especially for jazz players who suffered **embouchure** damage and excessive tension from overuse. His teaching methods were outlined in his book, *Musical Calisthenics for Brass* (1979), which emphasized breath attacks, muscle coordination through conditioned reflex, and balance. His "Four Rules" were: "1) Tap your foot, 2) Keep the **mouthpiece** in contact with the lips, 3) Keep the blow steady, and 4) Breathe through your nose." Also known for his personal humility and fatherly concern for his students, Caruso summed up his teaching philosophy as "giving with love, giving in a positive manner." Caruso's ideas were passed down by his students and exerted a strong influence on brass pedagogy in the twentieth century. Some of the trumpeters who studied with him were **Herb Alpert**, **Randy Brecker**, Pat Harbison, Marvin Stamm, **Markus Stockhausen**, and **James Thompson**. His teaching methods are carried on today by another one of his students, **Laurie Frink**.

cassis. A helmut-shaped **shell trumpet** blown from the end as opposed to the side (*cassis cornuta*, or helmut shell). Shell trumpets are used in Oceania and Polynesia.

Cassone, Gabriele (b. 1959). Italian trumpeter. Known for his virtuosity and astonishing versatility, he earned his conservatory diploma in trumpet, following studies with Mario Catena as well as studies in composition with Luciano Chailly. In addition to his work as a contemporary trumpet soloist, Cassone is also a noted **period instru-**

ment specialist performing on **Baroque trumpet**, **keyed trumpet**, **rotary valve trumpet**, and **cornet**. Cassone is a professor at the Conservatory of Novara in Italy, and gives international master classes as a guest professor at the Academy of St. Cecilia in Rome. He is frequently featured as guest lecturer and teacher at master classes throughout Europe and in the United States, and is a regular jury member at prestigious international competitions throughout the world. His book, *La Tromba* (Zecchini, 2002), was translated into English by Tom Dambly and released in a second edition in 2009.

"Catholic" fingering. A system that reverses the order of the first and second valves so that the first valve lowers the tubing of the trumpet or cornet by one half step and the second valve by one whole step. The practice most likely stemmed from the evolution of the **keyed bugle** to the valved **flugelhorn**. Instruments with this configuration were manufactured from the 1820s to the 1920s in Europe and the United States. The term *catholic* became connected to these instruments because many of them originated from Bavaria, a predominantly Catholic region. The term was also used by Protestant regions of Germany to label objects that were deemed to be strange or exotic, as opposed to "evangelical," which was determined to have a more positive connotation. Some of the makers who produced such instruments were the **Boston Musical Instrument Manufactory,** John Augustus **Köhler**, Michael Saurle (1772–1845), and **Friedrich Wilhelm Schuster.**

cavalry trumpet. A **natural trumpet** pitched in E-flat that was used primarily by the French military in the nineteenth century, where it was known as the ***trompette d'ordonnance.***

Cazzati, Maurizio (1616–1678). Italian composer who wrote the first sonatas for trumpet. An ordained priest, Cazzati is best known for his work as *maestro di cappella* at the Church of San Petronio in Bologna (1657–1671), where he initiated the school of solo trumpet writing later continued by **Giuseppe Torelli.** Cazzati published three trumpet sonatas (Op. 35) that employed the clarino range (from A4 to A5). He was also the first Bolognese composer to publish solo violin sonatas (Op. 55).

Cerclier, Jules-Henri-Louis (1823–1897). French trumpeter. As a classmate of **Jean-Baptiste Arban** at the Paris Conservatory, he studied with **François Dauverné** between 1842 and 1845. Cerclier succeeded his teacher as trumpet professor at the Paris Conservatory from 1869 to 1894. Little is known about Cerclier's career, but he did write *30 Marches pour Trompettes D'ordonnance à 4 Parties avec Timbales (Ad. Lib.)*, a collection published by G. Hartmann in Paris (ca. 1891). The title page

indicates that Cerclier was a Chevalier de la Légion d'Honneur at the time of publication.

cha chiao. A trumpet made of brass from Tibet approximately three feet in length; it features a **bell** that points toward the musician playing the instrument.

Chambers, William Paris (1854–1913). American cornetist, bandmaster, and composer. Following early cornet studies as a boy, he became the **cornet** soloist and conductor of the Keystone Cornet Band, and at twenty-five he became director of the Capitol City Band of Harrisburg. In 1888 he was appointed director of the Great Southern Band of Baltimore; when he led the band on a trip to Denver in 1892, his feat of performing a cornet solo at the summit of Pike's Peak was widely reported. Moving to New York, Chambers joined Francesco Fanciulli's Seventy-First Regiment Band as cornet soloist. Around 1900 he also became manager of the C. G. **Conn** retail store in New York, and continued to perform and teach; he toured Europe and Africa in 1903 and 1905. Chambers wrote a number of cornet solos, overtures, waltzes, polkas, and other dances, but he is remembered principally as a composer of marches, of which *Chicago Tribune*, *Boys of the Old Brigade*, and *Hostrauser's March* are the most popular.

Charlier, Théophile (Théo) (1868–1944). Belgian trumpeter and composer. At the age of twelve he entered the **cornet** class of Dieudonné Gérardy at the Liège Royal Conservatory in 1880, subsequently winning first prizes in both cornet (1885) and trumpet (1886), and later appointed as a teaching assistant. When Gérardy died in 1901, Charlier was appointed professor at the conservatory. He served as the principal trumpet of the Concerts of the Palace of Arts and Commerce in Antwerp as well as the Royal French Opera between 1886 and 1895. He left the position in Antwerp in 1895 to become principal trumpet of the Royal Theater of the Monnaie in Brussels, where he performed until 1904, when he assumed the leadership of the Mariemont Bascoup Colliery Band and its School of Music.

A versatile musician, educator, and composer, Charlier founded and directed the Scola musicae in Brussels in 1905, where he taught voice as well as the trumpet. It was during this time that he composed his well-known *36 Transcendental Etudes* along with several vocal works; the etudes were not published until 1946 by Alphonse Leduc. An additional thirty-seventh etude was later discovered and published by Editions BIM in 1995. Charlier composed several solos for trumpet and piano including two *Solos de Concours* along with a *Method for Horn in F*. Outside of his pedagogical and solo works for brass, Charlier also composed a two-act opera-ballet, *Djamilch*, which was premiered at the Antwerp Royal Theater in 1897.

As an influential teacher and performer, Charlier was involved in setting trends and in instrumental design. He was one of the first to favor the B-flat trumpet over the cornet, and by 1908 had removed study of the cornet from the curriculum at the Liège Conservatory. He worked with **Mahillon** to develop a B-flat **piston valve** trumpet as well as a **piccolo trumpet** in G, on which he was the first to perform **J. S. Bach's** *Brandenburg Concerto No. 2* in the original octave (1898 in Liège and 1902 in Paris). He was also involved in the patent of the screw-rim **mouthpiece** in 1909. Charlier was one of the first in the modern era to regularly perform the works of Bach on a D trumpet and he performed frequently as a soloist throughout France and Belgium. Charlier received many honors in his native Belgium including the Order of the French Academy (1904), Knight of the Order of Leopold (1920), Officer of the Order of the Crown (1926), the Centennial Commemorative Medal (1931), and Officer of the Order of Leopold (1933).

Chase, Bill [William Chiaiese] (1935–1974). American trumpeter and bandleader. He studied with Herb Pomeroy at the Berklee College of Music and made his first recording there with a big band in 1957. Chase made two albums the following year as **Maynard Ferguson's** lead trumpeter, and in 1959, he recorded in New York with Stan Kenton and performed at the Monterey Jazz Festival with Woody Herman. Chase worked with Herman until August 1967, contributing arrangements, appearing as a featured soloist on the television show *Woody Herman and the Swingin' Herd* (1963), and touring Europe and Africa (1966). Although he was primarily known for his powerful high-**register** playing and for helping to bring elements of rock music into Herman's band, he was also an accomplished ballad player, as documented on *I Can't Get Started*, on the album *Encore: 1963*. He later formed a nine-piece jazz-rock fusion group called "Chase" with four trumpets, a rhythm section, and a singer. In March 1969 he rejoined Woody Herman's band for a six-month European tour, after which he reorganized his own group; its first album, *Chase* (1971), was well received, but later recordings were less successful. He died at the age of thirty-nine in a plane crash along with three other band members when he took the album on tour in 1974 in an attempt to revive its popularity.

chatzotzrah (or *chazozrah, hatzozrah;* pl. *hatzozroth*). A long, straight trumpet made of silver used in Ancient Israel for religious ceremonies as well as military signals. It was approximately one and one half feet long (45.72 cm, or one "ell," according to ancient historian Flavius Josephus) and primarily played in pairs by priests. Although not labeled by name, this trumpet was referenced in the Hebrew Bible in the books of Numbers (10:9–10) and Chronicles (5:13).

chiamata. (It.) **Call.** A trumpet **signal** used as an alarm. Musically, the passage featured a rising and falling triad followed by a rapidly repeated note at the end or a trill on the final note. **Bendinelli** and **Fantini** both included military *chiamati* in their seventeenth-century methods, and the figure appeared in concert music as well. **Heinrich Biber** included a *chiamata* in the first movement of his *Trombet undt musicalischer Taffeldienst* (1668), and **J. S. Bach** quoted the call in several of his works, most notably in the solo trumpet part for the aria "Grosser Herr, O starker König" from the *Christmas Oratorio.*

chiave. (It.) Key or clef. The term was also used in nineteenth-century Italy to describe the **valve.**

chops. Slang term for a trumpeter's embouchure, which refers to the player's lips as two pieces of meat, like lamb chops. The term can also be used to refer to the prowess of any musician, as in "that pianist really has chops!"

Chop-Sticks. A **practice aid** designed to strengthen the facial muscles that support a trumpeter's **embouchure.** Similar in function to the **pencil exercise,** the Chop-Sticks are a collection of metal rods of varying length and thickness used for simple isometric exercises away from the trumpet to develop embouchure strength. One end of each rod is coated with plastic and is designed to be supported by the lip muscles without the aid of the teeth. Resistance is added to the exercise by using increasingly heavier rods.

Chorton. (Ger.) Choir pitch, A4 = approximately 466 Hz. A term used in Germany and the Hapsburg Empire during the eighteenth century to indicate a **pitch standard** that was commonly used in churches at the time. Many different pitch levels have been associated with the term in different locations and time periods. Chorton was a higher pitch standard than **Kammerton,** which was generally one whole step lower and used for secular music. It came to be associated in the eighteenth century with organs, brass instruments, and *cornetti* pitched at A4 = 465 Hz, a pitch standard known as **Cornet-Ton.** The various pitch standards affected the **nominal pitches** of trumpets as well. The German theorist Johann Mattheson (1681–1764) wrote in his *Das neu-eröffnete Orchestre* (1713) that "all trumpets are in *Chorton*"; therefore, compositions written in *Kammerton* with trumpet parts "must always be set in *D*, since *D* in *Kammerton* is *C* in *Chorton.*"

chromatic brass instrument. An instrument with a slide, keys, or valves that is capable of playing notes outside the confines of the **harmonic overtone series.**

cilindro rotativo. (It.) **Rotary valves.**

circular breathing. A technique that allows a wind instrumentalist to play continuously without having to pause to breathe. In a manner similar to the way a bagpipe functions, a player allows his or her cheeks to puff out while playing and takes in air through the nose by sniffing. As the air is expelled while playing, more air is taken in through the nose to replenish the store of air in the cheeks. Circular breathing on the trumpet requires less air, but more air pressure than other wind instruments. Because of this, the deliberate exhalation of accumulated "stale air" through the nose is occasionally necessary during circular breathing to remediate oxygen depletion while playing. Trumpeters known for circular breathing include Freddie Hubbard and **Wynton Marsalis**. Circular breathing is also a necessary component of playing the **didjeridu**.

Clagget, Charles (1740–ca. 1795). Irish violinist and inventor who developed a "**Cromatic** [*sic*] **Trumpet**" in 1788. Although the instrument was not a success, it was the first time a **valve** mechanism (a **box valve**) had been applied to the trumpet.

clapper shake key. A key applied to some early **cornopeans** to improve the performance of trills (also known as **shakes**). The device consisted of a long lever on the left side of the valve section that operated a key on the **bell bow** of the instrument in a manner that added a **vent hole** like that of a **keyed bugle** to a **Stölzel valved** cornopean. It was patented by English keyed bugle and **cornet** player **George Macfarlane** in France in 1845, and was often known by his name. Similar keys appeared on other cornopeans as early as circa 1830.

claret-piece. Term used in several fifteenth- and sixteenth-century sources to describe the moveable **mouthpipe** that operated as the slide on a Renaissance **slide trumpet**.

clareta. Term used by Sebastian Virdung in his *Musica getutscht* (1511) to label a thin **natural trumpet** that was presumably intended for **clarino** playing.

clarinet. A woodwind instrument with a single reed that developed from the *chalumeau* in the eighteenth century. Its name refers to the instrument's clear tone and resembles the term *clarino*. The clarinet was often used as a substitute for the trumpet in performances of Baroque repertoire in the nineteenth century when the art of clarino playing on **natural trumpets** had declined and the use of **high-pitched trumpets**, especially the **piccolo trumpet**, had not yet developed. Felix Mendelssohn adapted the high trumpet parts in **J. S. Bach**'s *Orchestral Suite No. 3* for clarinets, and Franz published an edition of Bach's *B Minor Mass* in the middle of the nineteenth century that also scored the majority of the high trumpet passages for clarinets.

Clarinhorn. A high brass instrument developed by **Franz Streitwieser** in 1977 that was similar in dimensions to the modern **corno da caccia** or **piccolo horn**, and a **posthorn** with **rotary valves**.

clarino. The high range (C5 to C6) of the **natural trumpet** ensemble in the sixteenth century, as described by **Bendinelli** and **Fantini**. The term literally means "clear" in Italian and was sometimes used as a descriptive term for the instrument itself.

clarion. (Fr.) **Bugle**. This term was used for the military signal bugle, while the word *bugle*, in French, was used to describe the **flugelhorn**.

Clarke, Herbert Lincoln (1867–1945). American cornetist, bandmaster, and composer. Considered the greatest cornet soloist of his generation, if not all time, Clarke was born into a musical family in Woburn, Massachusetts. His father, William Horatio Clarke, was an organist, composer, and teacher, and his brothers Edwin and Ernest performed professionally on the cornet and trombone, respectively. Herbert's early training was on the violin, but he developed a fascination with the cornet at the age of thirteen, and began playing his brother Edwin's instrument. When the Clarke family moved to Indianapolis in 1885, Herbert befriended the cornetist **Walter Rogers**, who was two years older and a more experienced musician. Clarke studied informally with Rogers and performed with him in a **brass quartet**; the two were close associates throughout their lives. In 1886 he won his first cornet solo competition playing **Jules Levy's** *Whirlwind Polka* and decided to embark on a solo career. Clarke earned a solo cornet position the following year with the Citizen's Band of Toronto and later, at the age of twenty-three, joined the faculty of the Toronto Conservatory, where he taught violin, viola, cornet, and other brass instruments.

Clarke went on to become the cornet soloist with **Gilmore**'s Band in 1892, where his brother Ernest played trombone. Following Gilmore's death the same year, Clarke became cornet soloist of John Philip Sousa's band and remained with the band from 1893 until 1917. During this time Clarke also substituted as second trumpet (on cornet) with the New York Philharmonic Orchestra in December 1898 and held the chair of first trumpet (on trumpet) with the Metropolitan Opera Orchestra in the 1899 season. He served as a cornet-tester for the C. G. **Conn** Company between 1913 and 1915, and later developed his own Holton-Clarke cornet in 1916, in partnership with Sousa Band trombonist Frank **Holton**. Clarke later turned to conducting and directed the Anglo-Canadian Leather Company Band in Huntsville, Ontario, (1918–1923) and the Long Beach Municipal Band in California (1923–1943).

Clarke made many recordings during his long career, which featured over seven thousand live solo performances. He composed several cornet solo pieces, including *Bride of the Waves, Southern Cross, Twilight Dreams, From the Shores of the Mighty Pacific, The Debutante, Sounds of the Hudson, Stars in a Velvety Sky,* and *Variations on The Carnival of Venice.* His pedagogical works, still in use today, include *Elementary Studies, Technical Studies, Characteristic Studies,* and *Setting-Up Drills.* He published his autobiography, *A Cornet-Playing Pilgrim's Progress,* as a series of articles in *Jacobs' Band and Orchestra Monthly* between 1927 and 1930. Clarke's personal papers and cornets now reside in the John Philip Sousa Library at the University of Illinois.

Clarke, Jeremiah (1674–1707). English composer and organist. He was the leading composer in England in the generation of **Henry Purcell.** Primarily a church musician, Clarke composed church music, odes, songs, and incidental music for the theater, and harpsichord pieces. One of his odes, *Come, Come Along for a Dance and a Song,* was written in memory of Henry Purcell and first performed at Drury Lane Theatre early in 1696. A movement from the ode is scored for trumpets, drums, recorders, and strings titled "Mr. Purcell's Farewell," and features notes outside the **harmonic overtone series** available on seventeenth-century **natural trumpets.** Clarke is best known for his so-called *Trumpet Voluntary,* which owes its popularity to an arrangement for trumpet, organ, and drums made by English conductor Sir Henry Wood (1869–1944) and misattributed by him to Purcell. This is now known to have been a harpsichord piece, *The Prince of Denmark's March,* which Clarke contributed to *A Choice Collection of Ayres.* Unlike other harpsichord pieces written to imitate trumpet style, it may have actually been originally scored for trumpet and wind ensemble. Clarke's short life ended in his early thirties when, disconsolate over an unhappy love affair with a lady above his station, he committed suicide by shooting himself. He is buried in the crypt of St. Paul's Cathedral in London.

Classical pitch. A **pitch standard** of A4 = 430 Hz often employed by modern **period instrument** ensembles for performances of repertoire from the Classical era (approximately 1750–1820). Actual pitch standards during the eighteenth and early nineteenth centuries varied according to geographical location, time period, instruments (especially keyboards), and performance circumstances under consideration.

classicum. 1. The name of the **signal** sounded by the Ancient Roman **cornu** to announce the presence of the emperor or another personage of elevated stature in order to assemble "the classes," or the people. The tradition carried on into the Middle Ages when the term came to represent a field or battle signal played by military trumpeters.

2. The instrument that played the classicum fanfare, usually a **cornu** or a **lituus.**

clavicor. An early tenor brass instrument invented by H. Danays in Paris in 1837 and produced by the French firm of Guichard in 1838. It was designed to take the place of the French **horn** in marching band instrumentation. Sometimes known as the "althorn," the clavicor had **piston valves** (two for the right hand and one for the left) and an upright bell. Its **bore** profile and vertical shape resembled the later **saxhorns.** The clavicor appeared in some British brass bands in the 1840s and 1850s. Although it disappeared from use after the 1850s, E-flat tenor horn parts in Italian band instrumentation continued to be labeled *clavicorno;* alto **flugelhorns** (*flicorni*) or saxhorns were then used to play the parts.

Clear Tone mute. A type of **open tube mute** made by **Humes & Berg.** The name "**Solotone**" was trademarked by **Shastock.** (See appendix 3.)

coach horn. A **posthorn** built in straight form, like a **herald trumpet** or a medieval **buisine.** Such instruments were played by coachmen as a signal instrument in the nineteenth century. Many coach horns were made of copper and built in two main parts that fit inside of each other, telescopically, for easier transport. A commentary published in 1907 by **Köhler** & Son of London titled *The Coach Horn: What to Blow and How to Blow It, by an Old Guard* recommends that a coach horn should not exceed thirty-six inches in length and should have a funnel-shaped bell and a silver **mouthpiece.**

Colin, Charles (1913–2000). American trumpeter and music publisher. Raised in Salem, Massachusetts, he began playing the trumpet at the age of eleven and went on to study with Louis Kloepfel at the New England Conservatory of Music. After moving to New York in the 1930s, he performed with the WMCA [Radio] Orchestra and Charlie Barnet Band and later opened a teaching studio and began publishing a series of pedagogical books including *Charles Colin's Lip Flexibility Studies* and *100 Original Warmups.* In 1941 he founded Charles Colin Music Publishing, and in 1973, Colin founded the New York Brass Conference for Scholarships, a nonprofit organization that presents an annual three-day festival that features every genre of brass music from classical to jazz in order to raise funds and draw attention to the need for scholarships for young musicians.

comeback player. A trumpeter who resumes playing the instrument after a lengthy hiatus of several years. Such musicians usually give up the instrument because of an injury or to pursue a nonmusical career after participating in school music programs. Many comeback players pick up the trumpet after establishing a career or during retirement to perform with amateur community bands and orchestras.

compensating valve. A **valve** designed to correct **intonation** deficiencies inherent in the use of two or more valves simultaneously by automatically adding auxiliary tubing when certain valves were used in combination. Compensating systems were applied to the cornet by **J. B. Arban** with the engineer L. Bouvet in 1885 and by **Thibouville-Lamy** in the early twentieth century.

concert pitch. 1. The international **pitch standard** of A4 = 440 Hz, which was agreed upon in 1939.

2. Term used to describe a common pitch standard between musicians performing on **transposing** instruments; the objective pitch standard used as a reference. For example, when a B-flat trumpet sounds the printed note *C*, musicians refer to the resultant pitch as B-flat "concert," in order to avoid the need for multiple transpositions for various instruments pitched in different keys (like alto saxophone in E-flat, French horn in F, and instruments in C, such as the flute and the violin).

conch shell trumpet. A trumpet fashioned from a large sea shell and used for signaling. It is more correct to refer to the shell trumpets by their more distinctive shapes—**cassis**, **fusus**, **triton**, and **strombus**—than merely as conch shells, or the more generic "marine-shell trumpet." (See figure 10.) Several ancient and nonwestern cultures featured a form of conch shell trumpet, like the Greek **salpinx thalassia**, which was played by the mythological sea god **Triton**. In India the **sankh** was associated with the Hindu god Vishnu, Lord of the Waters, in Japan the conch shell trumpet was known as the **horagi**, and in Tibet, the **hai lo** was used by boatmen.

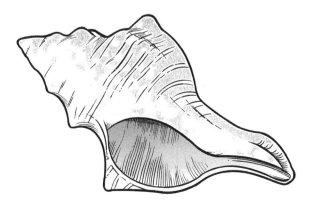

Figure 10. A conch shell. *Drawing by T. M. Larsen.*

conical bore. Tubing that gradually widens, like a cone.

Conn. American musical instrument manufacturer. The company was founded by Charles Gerard Conn (1844–1931), a cornetist who studied with **Theodore Hoch** and served in the Twenty-First Regiment Band during the American Civil War. He made a cornet **mouthpiece** with a rubber rim in 1874 after suffering a split lip in a bar brawl, and began marketing it commercially in 1875. Conn partnered with Eugene Dupont (1832–1881), who had worked with **Henry Distin**, to produce **cornets** under the name Conn & Dupont in 1876, especially a "Four-in-One" model that featured **crooks** and **slides** to play in E-flat, C, B-flat, and A. Their partnership lasted for three years before Conn became sole owner of the company based in Elkhart, Indiana. Production was slowed by a factory fire in 1883. When **Isaac Fiske** retired in 1887, Conn purchased Fiske's facilities and opened a subsidiary plant in Worcester, Massachusetts. Woodwind instruments were added to the Conn product line in the late 1880s, a new store was opened in New York City in 1897, and production at the Worcester plant was phased out in 1898, the same year the company produced the first "raincatcher" sousaphone (its upturned **bell** pointed up, like a bucket to collect rain, rather than facing forward).

The factory in Elkhart was destroyed by another fire in 1910 and a new, larger facility was built the following year. Conn retired in 1915 and sold the business to Carl Greenleaf (1876–1959), who changed the company name to C. G. Conn Ltd. and expanded production. The company established an experimental laboratory in 1928 that produced several innovations, including the "Vocabell" (1932) for brass instruments (its lack of a **bell rim** aimed to optimize resonance), the seamless "Coprion bell" (1934), short action valves (1934), and the "Stroboconn" electronic tuner (1936). Prior to the Second World War, C. G. Conn was the largest musical instrument firm in the United States, but like its industry competitors, it ceased production during the war and retooled its factories to manufacture products to support the war effort. Conn's Division of Research, Development, and Design flourished after the war under the direction of **Earle Kent** and produced numerous innovations, including the Connstellation line of brass instruments and the fiberglass-bell sousaphone.

After 1960, C. G. Conn acquired additional subsidiary companies and grew into an international corporation. The business was sold to the Crowell-Collier MacMillan Company in 1969 and the corporate headquarters moved from Elkhart, Indiana, to Oak Brook, Illinois. Daniel Henkin purchased the company in 1980 and acquired **King Musical Instruments** in 1985 before selling the company to the Swedish conglomerate of Skäne Gripen, which later became part of United Musical Instruments

(UMI). UMI merged with **Selmer** in 2002 to create the new international firm of Conn-Selmer.

Since 1875, numerous musicians have endorsed Conn brass instruments, including **Herman Bellstedt**, **W. Paris Chambers**, **Theodore Hoch**, **Jules Levy**, **Alessandro Liberati**, **Walter Rogers**, and John Philip Sousa. Conn-Selmer currently supplies instruments for the **Canadian Brass**. At the turn of the twentieth century, Conn produced several models of cornets such as the Wonder, the New York Wonder, the Conn-queror, the Wonderphone, the New Creation, the Victor, and the Director. The Conn Company Archive and more than five hundred Conn instruments currently reside at the National Music Museum at the University of South Dakota in Vermillion.

coquilles. (Fr.) French term for **intervalve tubing** on a trumpet or cornet that literally means "shells."

cor à clefs. (Fr.) **Keyed bugle**.

cor des alpes. (Fr.) **Alphorn**.

Corelli, Arcangelo (1653–1713). Italian composer and violinist. He studied in Bologna and spent his career in Rome, where he published collections of sonatas and concertos that influenced generations of composers throughout Europe. An influential composer of mostly string music—solo sonatas, trio sonatas, and concertos—Corelli published a sonata in D major for trumpet and strings in 1704. It may have been composed for the English trumpeter "Mr. **Twiselton**," who made that claim on an advertisement for a London performance in 1713.

cornet. *Cornet à pistons* (Fr.), *kornett* (Ger.), *cornetta* (It.), *cornetin* (Sp.). A high brass instrument with valves commonly pitched in B-flat generally with a higher percentage of **conical bore** tubing than a trumpet (not always the case), and a **mouthpiece** featuring a deep cup or funnel. The classic cornet of the late nineteenth century with **Périnet valves** is often considered to be the definitive form of the instrument, such as those made by **Courtois** and **Besson**. (See figure 11.) The cornet first appeared in Paris around 1825 and evolved through a wide variety in design and manufacture over the next hundred years. Cornets were commonly built in four different keys: E-flat, B-flat, C, and A, although the cornet in A was not a separate instrument, but usually a B-flat cornet with an alternative **tuning slide** and/or **shank** to lower the pitch one half step. Some cornets were supplied with extra tuning shanks or **crooks** for B-flat, C, and A.

Although the cornet in B-flat is prevalent today, the E-flat cornet was the dominant high brass instrument in bands in the United States until the 1880s; it was considered the "soprano" cornet while the B-flat was viewed as an "alto." The cornet in C was primarily used for playing in church or for parlor music because players could read out of a hymn book or piano score without the need to transpose. It was not intended for use in the orchestra, as it is sometimes today. The cornet in A—a sharp key more suitable for strings—was intended for orchestral use, not the cornet in C. Composers who wrote orchestral parts for the cornet in A include Berlioz, Stravinsky, and Tchaikovsky.

Although several patents were taken out for various valve designs in the nineteenth century, no brass instrument maker ever patented the cornet. However, both **Joseph Forestier** and **François Dauverné** credit the French brass instrument manufacturing firm **Halary** (Asté) with applying **Stölzel valves** to the **posthorn** to create the cornet around 1831. Early cornets were known as **cornopeans** and were made with two Stölzel valves at first. Cornopean mouthpieces have narrow rims and deep conical cups like horn mouthpieces, and the instruments were built in B-flat with **crooks** down to lower keys. In Paris, **horn** players, not trumpeters, took up the cornet at first. One of the first musicians to write a solo for cornet and piano, Joseph Forestier, played horn at the Paris Opera before switching to cornet and, later, trumpet. Early cornets with **Périnet valves** made by **Courtois** and Gautrot experimented with positioning the **bell** on the right or the left of the valve section. The wrapping of the valve tubing was also subject to variation as makers strived to avoid collisions between the bell and the third **valve slide**. Most of these cornets did not include **water keys** and none of them had moveable valve slides with **throw rings** or **triggers** (which were added in the early twentieth century).

In the second half of the nineteenth century **Jean-Baptiste Arban** created a sensation with a cornet in B-flat with a shallower mouthpiece, a brighter sound with a sharper attack, and astonishing virtuosity. His *Grande méthode complète pour cornet à pistons et de saxhorn* (1864) revolutionized brass pedagogy and he was the first cornetist to be appointed as a conservatory professor when he assumed his position at the Paris Conservatory in 1869.

The cornet became the primary solo brass instrument in the late nineteenth century, especially with wind bands, and many fine soloists enjoyed brilliant careers including **Herbert L. Clarke**, **Jules Levy**, **Matthew Arbuckle**, **Alessandro Liberati**, **Hermann Bellstedt**, **Herman Koenig**, and **Bohumir Kryl**, among many others. Nineteenth-century cornets, being smaller than trumpets of the time, were easier to play, more flexible, and more secure in the high register. Virtuoso cornet soloists exploited the instrument's facility with feats of **multiple tonguing**, fast passagework, **lip slurs**, **pedal tones**, and extended work in the high register. These skills impacted the way composers wrote for the trumpet as well.

After 1900, cornets became noticeably more similar to trumpets. The **shepherd's crook** (the large, curved **bell bow** on the back of the cornet) disappeared, and the bells became longer as a result. Fixed **leadpipes** replaced removable shanks and tuning slides moved from the center of the instrument to the front, next to the bell. At the same time, experiments in cornet design accelerated rapidly. Between 1888 and 1925, the C. G. **Conn** Company in the United States produced an amazing array of new cornet models with variations in bore size (ranging between 0.410 and 0.470 inches), tuning slide configurations, **windway** patterns, and **wrap** designs. **Long-bell cornets** began to resemble trumpets in sound as well as in appearance and evolved into the trumpets that eventually usurped the role of the cornet in bands. The proportion of conical versus cylindrical tubing in cornets and trumpets has long been cited as a major difference between the two high brass instruments, but the internal dimensions of the mouthpiece play a vital role in the sound of the cornet. It has often been claimed that the **bore** of the cornet was two-thirds conical and one-third cylindrical while that of the trumpet was the opposite, but in reality, they are quite similar.

Cornets gradually evolved into the modern B-flat trumpet and declined in prominence in the United States, but that was not the case in England, where classic short-model cornets continued to flourish in British brass bands. In the 1970s attention turned once again back to the classic shepherd's crook design of the old Victorian cornet. Prominent makers like **Vincent Bach**, **Yamaha**, and **Getzen** began to market instruments featuring older designs and interest was revived in finding a more authentic nineteenth-century cornet sound.

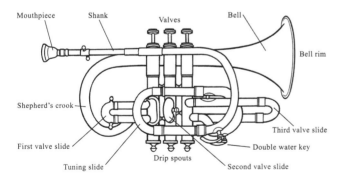

Figure 11. A cornet from the late nineteenth century with parts identified. *Drawing by T. M. Larsen.*

cornet à bouquin. (Fr.) **Cornett** or *cornetto* (woodwind instrument, not to be confused with the **cornet**; see p. 40).

cornet à pistons. (Fr.) **Cornet** with **piston valves**.

cornet de poste. (Fr.) **Posthorn**.

corneta. (Sp.) **Cornett** or *cornetto* (woodwind instrument; see p. 42), not to be confused with *cornetin*.

cornetin. (Sp.) **Cornet**.

cornett. *Cornet à bouquin* (Fr.), *zink* (Ger.), *cornetto* (It.), *corneta* (Sp.). A woodwind instrument with **finger holes** and a cup-shaped **mouthpiece** played with a brass **embouchure** (vibrating lips). It was the premier virtuoso wind instrument of the Renaissance and flourished between 1500 and 1650. The mouthpiece for the instrument features a narrow rim, is significantly smaller than that used on the trumpet, and is often called an "acorn" mouthpiece. The English name for the instrument was originally "cornet," but the English scholar and instrument collector Francis William Galpin (1858–1945) suggested the current spelling with two T's to avoid confusion with the valved **cornet** in print.

Because the old and new English terms have identical pronunciation when spoken (cornet and cornett), the Italian term for the instrument, ***cornetto***, has gained wide use due to its unique identity in both spoken and written language. Inconsistencies are encountered when discussing players of the instrument in English (cornettist) versus Italian (*cornettista,* or *cornetto* player), as well as the valved cornet (cornetist, or cornet player). Scholarship concerning the instrument in the English language favors Galpin's spelling, but the Italian term, *cornetto*, is used interchangeably. As the popularity of the cornett has grown as part of the **early music** revival in the twentieth century, the inconsistencies in nomenclature have increased. This dictionary will identify those who play the cornett as "*cornetto* players" and those who play the valved cornet as "cornetists," and will draw distinctions between the two instruments wherever necessary.

The cornett is made in a variety of different sizes and **nominal pitches**. The most common is the curved cornett pitched in G (see figure 12), which is made from two halves of carved wood (usually boxwood or various fruitwoods) glued together and covered with black leather. Other cornetts include the **straight cornett** (same as the curved instrument, but bored out of a single piece of wood with a detachable mouthpiece and no leather covering), the **mute cornett** (similar to the straight cornett, the mouthpiece is carved into the body of the instrument, which contributes to its warm tone), the ***cornettino*** (a smaller curved cornett pitched in E), and larger alto and tenor cornetts.

During its heyday, the cornett was strictly an instrument for professional musicians. *Cornetto* players were trained through rigorous apprenticeships. While the cornett was briefly mentioned in sixteenth-century theoretical treatises, few detailed instruction manuals were written for the instrument. Some of the theoretical treatises that mention the cornett are Aurelio Virgiliano's *Il dolcimelo* (ca. 1590), **Michael Praetorius**'s *Syntagma Musicum* (in three volumes, 1615–1619), and **Mersenne**'s *Harmonie universelle* (1635). The most extensive instructions on playing the cornett appear in Bistmantova's *Compendium musicale* (1677). Often used in the eighteenth century to double the soprano parts in choral works, while alto, tenor, and bass trombones doubled the remaining voices, the cornett appears in **J. S. Bach**'s cantata *Christ lag in Todesbanden*, BWV 4.

The cornett was revived in the twentieth century by **Christopher Monk**, who devised a way to manufacture inexpensive modern reproductions made of resin that enabled musicians all over the world to learn the instrument. Artists who took up the cornett professionally in the twentieth century include Michael Collver, **Bruce Dickey**, William Dongolis, Jean Tubéry, and **Jeremy West**.

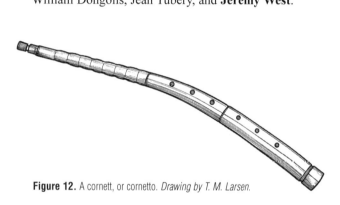

Figure 12. A cornett, or cornetto. *Drawing by T. M. Larsen.*

cornetta. (It.) **Cornet.** The term was also used in Italy in the early twentieth century to indicate a **rotary valve trumpet** in B-flat.

cornetta a chiavi. (It.) **Keyed bugle.**

cornetta di postiglione. (It.) **Posthorn.**

cornettino. (It.) Small **cornett.** Similar in shape and design to the treble cornett in G, the cornettino is pitched in E and smaller in size. Because the fingering position on the treble cornett is difficult to learn, some musicians have started to play on the smaller cornettino because the **finger holes** are closer together. The popularity of the cornettino in the twentieth-century early music revival for its perceived pedagogical utility did not match the repertoire for the instrument, which is rather small.

cornetto. (It.) **Cornett,** a woodwind instrument, not to be confused with the valved **cornet.**

cornetto alto. (It.) Loud **cornett.** The term was used to distinguish the common treble cornett from the **mute cornett**, or ***cornetto muto***, which had a softer sound because its mouthpiece was carved into the wooden body of the instrument, all in one piece.

cornetto curvo. (It.) Curved **cornett.**

cornetto diritto. (It.) **Straight cornett.**

cornetto muto. (It.) **Mute cornett.**

cornetto nero. (It.) Black **cornett.** An alternate term for the curved treble cornett that, like the German term ***schwarzer zink***, refers to the black leather casing of the instrument.

Cornet-Ton. A **pitch standard** of approximately A4 = 465 Hz that was derived from the pitch of the **cornett**, or ***cornetto***. Because the instrument was made in a fixed length of wood that remained fairly consistent for more than two centuries, the *cornetto* was used as a reliable reference pitch **frequency** in Italy, Germany, and throughout the Hapsburg Empire in the seventeenth and early eighteenth centuries; **Praetorious** referred to the standard as "Cornettenthon" in 1618. By the eighteenth century, Cornet-Ton had become associated with **Chorton** in Germany.

cornicines. (Lat.) Horn players. Musicians who played the Roman **cornu.**

corno da caccia. (It.) Hunting horn. 1. A natural **horn** that first appeared in orchestral music in the eighteenth century. **J. S. Bach** wrote solo material for the instrument in his *Brandenburg Concerto No. 1 in F, BWV 1046* (which features two *corni da caccia*) and the "Quoniam" from the B Minor Mass.

2. A modern brass instrument that combines properties of a **flugelhorn** with those of a modern French horn. Championed by German trumpeters **Ludwig Güttler** and **Franz Streitwieser** (who called it the **Clarinhorn**) in the late 1970s, the instrument resembles a **posthorn** with **rotary valves**, but with a larger bell and a **bore** profile similar to that of a **mellophone.** It may have developed from the **Kuhlohorn.** Sometimes called a "piccolo horn," the modern *corno da caccia* is pitched in B-flat or A, positions the rotary valves on the right side, and covers the same range as the modern trumpet. The **mouthpiece** is closer to that of a French horn with a strict funnel design, rather than a cup. Smaller than a descant horn in B-flat or a mellophone, yet slightly larger than a flugelhorn, the modern *corno da caccia* is not considered a member of the horn family. It is often used by trumpeters to perform the high horn parts by Baroque composers like **J. S. Bach** and **Telemann** with modern orchestras because it sounds

more horn-like than a flugelhorn, and is more secure in the upper register. It has also been used to perform the posthorn solo from Gustav Mahler's Third Symphony. The unique sound of the instrument is also influenced by the fact that the player's right hand operates the valves and is therefore not inside the bell.

corno da tirarsi. (It.) Horn that is drawn or pulled. Although no copies of this unique instrument survive, recent research by Oliver Picon suggests that the instrument was played exclusively by Gottfried Reiche and was actually a variation of a coiled natural trumpet (***tromba da caccia*** or ***jägertrompete***) with a crook featuring a double slide attached to the **mouthpiece receiver** (**leadpipe**) in the center of the instrument. A modern reproduction of the instrument has been built by Rainer **Egger** in collaboration with Gerd Friedel, Mike Diprose, and Oliver Picon. Gisela and Jozseph Csiba have performed research that suggests that some coiled trumpets during Bach's time may have been equipped with small slides (shorter than the sliding leadpipe of the Baroque slide trumpet) that might have enabled trumpeters to correct intonation without "lipping."

cornopean. An early nineteenth-century **cornet** with **Stölzel valves.** The term originally referred to early cornets equipped with a **MacFarlane clapper key**, but as the term *cornet* became exclusively connected to instruments with **Périnet valves**, this distinct term for Stölzel valve cornets came into use. (See figure 13.) Stölzel valves were narrower than the later Périnet valves because the internal diameter of the valve casing had to match the bore size of the tubing, which directed the airflow through the bottom of the valves. Consequently, Stölzel valves earned a reputation for leaking when squeezed too hard. Many contemporary illustrations show players holding the cornopean with the left hand positioned

Figure 13. A cornopean from the early nineteenth century with two Stölzel valves. *Drawing by T. M. Larsen.*

lower, near the valve tubing (perhaps to reduce pressure on the valves), rather than higher, under the bell, like modern trumpets. When a third valve was added, the second valve was sometimes aligned offset to the left of the first and third. Cornopeans with only two valves were unable to play the notes G-sharp (A-flat) and C-sharp (D-flat). Cornopean mouthpieces have narrow rims and deep conical cups like horn mouthpieces, and the instruments were commonly built in B-flat with crooks down to lower keys.

cornu. Ancient Roman brass instrument. Made of a long brass tube in the shape of the letter *G*, the cornu included a detachable **mouthpiece** in the center and a flared **bell** section on the top. A wooden bar ran diagonally from top to bottom to serve as both a **brace** as well as a hand grip for the instrument. It was probably Etruscan in origin, like the **lituus**, and may have been a modification of the **tuba**, the long, straight Roman trumpet. Its curved shape may have been influenced by the **buccina**. Pictorial evidence shows that the **cornu** participated in musical ensembles with the **lituus** and the **tuba** for civic processions, especially state funerals, and served as a military instrument.

coronet. Incorrect (misspelled) term for **cornet** or **cornett** that occasionally appears in nineteenth-century publications. This word specifically denotes a small crown or jeweled headband (hence the term *coronation*).

Couesnon. French musical instrument manufacturer. The company was founded in 1827 by Auguste Guichard (fl. 1827–1845) in Paris. It merged with the company run by Guichard's brother-in-law, Pierre Louis Gautrot (d. 1882), in 1845 and operated under Gautrot's name. Other name changes followed: Gautrot aîné & Cie. (1869) and Gautrot aîné-Durand & Cie. (1877). Gautrot's son-in-law, Amédée August Couesnon (1850–1951), assumed direction of the firm in 1882 when the company's name changed to Couesnon, Gautrot & Cie.; it was later known as Couesnon & Cie. (1888) and Couesnon S. A. (1931). The company grew in size at the turn of the twentieth century by absorbing several other firms including Triébert, Lecomte, and Massin & Thibouville. Between 1911 and 1925 Couesnon was the largest instrument-manufacturing company in the world with eleven factories that employed over one thousand workers. The company's fortunes declined after 1927 and its main factory in Château Thierry was badly damaged by fire in 1969, which destroyed its archives. In 1999, the French drum maker P.G.M. purchased the company and it became known as P.G.M. Cousenon. The firm currently produces brass band instruments, military bugles, hunting horns (***trompe de chasse***), and percussion instruments.

coulisse. (Fr.) **Slide**.

Courtois, Antoine (1770–1855). French brass instrument manufacturer. His father opened an instrument-making shop in Paris in 1789, and Courtois opened his own shop, known as "Courtois Frères," in 1803. He produced instruments such as curved **natural trumpets** (like the **demilune trumpet**, for use with **hand-stopping** technique), trombones, **keyed bugles**, **horns**, and **ophicleides**. Courtois also made **bugles** for the Garde Républicaine Band, and produced a **cornet** in C with two valves in 1830. His son, Denis Antoine Courtois (1800–1880), took over the business in 1844 and concentrated most of his efforts on developing a line of cornets that was prized by many of the great virtuosos of the nineteenth century including **Jean-Baptiste Arban, Matthew Arbuckle, Walter Emerson, Hermann Koenig**, and **Jules Levy**.

Couturier, Ernest Albert (1869–1950). American cornetist. Born in Poughkeepsie, New York, Couturier's father was French and his mother was from Brazil. His first instrument was the piano and he began playing the violin at the age of eleven. Couturier took up the **cornet** at the age of fourteen and studied briefly at the New England Conservatory of Music in Boston. After hearing **Theodore Hoch** perform in New York City's Central Park in 1885, Couturier sought lessons from Hoch and developed impressive **range** and technical skill. He made his solo debut at the age of seventeen in a performance of **Arban**'s *Variations on the Carnival of Venice*. Couturier performed with various minstrel shows, circuses, and bands in the late 1880s. He formed his own band in 1892 and performed at the St. Louis Exposition. He later joined the Innes Band and performed as cornet soloist with the recreated **Gilmore** Band under the direction of Victor Herbert. Couturier assumed leadership of the new Gilmore Band when Herbert resigned. When the band dissolved, Gilmore's widow gave the entire band library to Couturier, who later published reduced scores of the music through the P. S. Gilmore Band Library Company in St. Louis.

Couturier toured Europe as a cornet soloist in 1906 and was offered the cornet soloist position with the Sousa Band the following year, which he declined in order to perform as soloist with many other bands throughout the United States and Canada. He continued touring as a soloist for ten years and endorsed cornets for the **Holton** Corporation between 1908 and 1912. Holton produced a large **bore** Couturier Model cornet in 1910. Couturier designed his own "Conical Bore Cornet" in 1918 and had it manufactured by the York Company. He acquired the rights to the cornet design and later established his own manufacturing company in La Porte, Indiana. He sold the company in 1923 to Lyon & Healy, who produced Couturier cornets until 1929. Couturier did not record as much

as his contemporaries because he disliked the limited recording time of 78 rpm discs. He did record four solos for Edison: *Schubert's Serenade, Endearing Young Charms, A Dream*, and *The Rosary*. His solo compositions, which remain unpublished, include *Carnival of Venice, Waltz in D-Flat, Moonlight, Saturn, Mercury, Venus, Jupiter*, and *Uranus*.

Creatore, Giuseppe (1871–1952). Italian-American bandmaster and impresario. Creatore studied trumpet and cornet at the Naples Conservatory with Nicola d'Arienzo and Camillo de Nardis, and came to the United States in 1900 to start his own band. One of the most successful and flamboyant Italian band conductors in the United States, Creatore toured with his band throughout the United States and Canada, and was active professionally until the age of seventy-five.

Cromatic [*sic*] **Trumpet.** An instrument patented by **Charles Clagget** in 1788 that featured two conjoined **natural trumpets** in D and E-flat and a simple **box valve** operated by a lever near that mouthpiece that enabled the player to switch the **airstream** from one to the other during performance. It was most likely the first use of a **valve** on a trumpet of any kind. The patent, dated September 15, 1788, claimed that the trumpet produced notes that were always "in the natural tone" and capable of "regular Harmony and fine Tune, in all keys, MINOR as well as MAJOR" and that it did not require **crooks** to change key. Patented just four years after **Charles Burney**'s public criticism of **John Sarjant**'s inability to correct out-of-tune notes in Handel obbligato arias on the **natural trumpet**, it was one of the first attempts to create a **chromatic brass instrument** that did not use a slide.

crook. A curved (or crooked) length of tubing inserted into the leadpipe of a trumpet or cornet to lower the nominal pitch of the instrument. Crooks were usually designed in the shape of the loop, but on an *inventionstrompete*, crooks were large U-shaped slides inserted into the middle of the instrument. Originally conceived as devices to put **natural trumpets** into different (lower) keys, crooks were used on chromatic brass instruments as well, including the **English slide trumpet**, the **long F trumpet**, and some early valved trumpets and cornets. (See figure 16 under "F trumpet.")

Cross-grain slur. An awkward slur between two adjacent notes with markedly different lengths of tubing created by certain **valve combinations**. For example, a slur from C5 to D5 forces a trumpeter to go higher while making the instrument physically longer through the addition of the first **valve slide**. Such a slur often results in an acoustic bump in the sound that must be corrected by blowing a faster **airstream** to make a smoother connection. Other cross-grain slurs on the trumpet can be facilitated through **alternate fingerings**, such as G4 to A4 (fingering the A4 with the third valve alone instead of the first and second together). Trombonists encounter cross-grain slurs when switching between certain slide positions, such as between F3 (first position) and G3 (fourth position).

crossover. A term used to describe performers and composers who work in a musical genre different from that with which he or she is usually associated; it can also refer to a fusion of styles. The term is commonly applied to trumpeters adept in both jazz and classical styles, such as **Jens Lindemann, Wynton Marsalis, Ronald Romm,** and **Allen Vizzutti.**

Crown, Tom (b. 1929). American trumpeter and **mute** manufacturer. Growing up in Chicago, his first instrument was the tuba (the school's choice, not his), but he longed to play the trumpet. He was able to switch at the age of fourteen and later studied with **Renold Schilke, Adolph Herseth,** and Arnold Jacobs. He graduated from Roosevelt University–Chicago Musical College with bachelor's and master's degrees in music education and embarked on a professional career. He began his playing career at the age of nineteen as a member of the Grant Park Symphony Orchestra. After being drafted into the U.S. Army, he served in the Seventh Army Symphony Orchestra stationed in Vaihingen, Germany, near Stuttgart for eight months including tours to Italy, England, and France. Crown later became a member of the WGN Broadcast Studio Orchestra and the Lyric Opera Orchestra of Chicago. In 1969 he started his mute manufacturing company in a quest to copy a distinctive mute that Adolph Herseth used for the D trumpet. What started with a production of ten mutes grew into a full line of mutes for trumpet, **piccolo trumpet**, trombone, and **horn** that are now used worldwide.

cuivres. (Fr.) Brass instruments.

cup. The initial opening of a **mouthpiece** into which a player's lips vibrate. The diameter, shape, and depth of the cup play a large role in the sound of a brass instrument. Most trumpet mouthpieces feature a U-shaped cup, while mouthpieces for the **cornet** and **flugelhorn** feature a deeper funnel or V-shaped cup.

cup mute. A **straight mute** with a cup attached to the bottom that reflects the sound from the **bell** back into the instrument to create a haunting, subdued sound. Some cup mutes are made with adjustable cups that can be moved closer to the bell to create a variety of different tone colors. The first patent for a cup mute was by C. J. Kiefer dated April 25, 1899. (See figure 14 and appendix 3.)

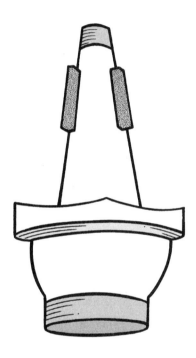

Figure 14. Cup mute. *Drawing by T. M. Larsen.*

cylindre rotatif. (Fr.) **Rotary valve.**

cylindrical bore. Tubing that maintains a consistent width throughout its length, like a cylinder.

Dagnelies, Dieudonné (1825–1894). Belgian bandmaster, composer, and cornetist. One of pioneers of Belgian band music, he began **cornet** studies as a child and made rapid progress, playing with local bands by the age of twelve. In 1847 he became the conductor of the Harmonie des Verreries Mariemont and studied conducting with Jean-Valentin Bender, the conductor of the Symphonic Band of the Belgian Guards. In 1854 Bender appointed Dagnelies as the assistant conductor of the Harmony Saint Marie d'Oignies, and Dagnelies took over as director when Bender died in 1873. Dagnelies toured with the band in Liege, Amsterdam, and Paris, and also conducted twenty-eight other brass bands in the area of Charleroi and in the north of France. As a composer, Dagnelies wrote several works for band including *Grande Fantaisie Militaire*, *Grande Marche Triomphale*, and a transcription of Verdi's *I Masnadieri Overture*. He also wrote a cornet method and a trumpet method as well as a solo for cornet and band, *Original Air Varie* (1885), which was also set for solo baritone horn or alto clarinet.

Dämpfer. (Ger.) **Mute**.

Dämpfer ab, Dämpfer weg. (Ger.) **Mute** off, mute away.

daudytë. A wooden trumpet used in regions of Lithuania ranging in size between five and seven feet long. The instrument is crafted from different types of wood that is carved out, joined with putty and tar, wrapped with twine, and covered with birch bark, which creates an airtight seal.

Dauverné, François Georges Auguste (1799–1874). French trumpeter. He was the first trumpet professor at the Paris Conservatory, where he taught **Jean-Baptiste Arban, Louis-Antonie Saint Jacome,** and **Jules Cerclier,** and introduced the early valved trumpet into the curriculum. Dauverné studied with his uncle, **Joseph-**

David Buhl, a professional trumpeter and teacher, and joined the band of the Gardes du Corps du Roi (directed by Buhl) in 1814. He became the principal trumpet of the Paris Opera Orchestra in 1820 (serving until 1851) and joined the faculty of the Paris Conservatory in 1833. He was also principal trumpet of the Orchestra of the Academie Royale de Musique and a founding member of the Société des Concerts du Conservatoire. Dauverné was one of the first to grasp the potential of trumpets and cornets with **Stölzel valves** and encouraged composers to write for these instruments. His efforts influenced the parts for valve trumpets in Chelard's *Macbeth* (1827), **Berlioz**'s concert overture, *Waverley* (1827), and Rossini's *Guillaume Tell* (1829). He also encouraged **Halary** to build valved trumpets in 1828. Dauverné experimented with his own design of a French **slide trumpet** that was not widely adopted; it differed from the **English slide trumpet** in that the slide mechanism was positioned in the front of the instrument rather than the center.

Dauverné's career spanned the dynamic years of change that impacted brass instruments in the first half of the nineteenth century, the creation of new repertoire, musical styles, and teaching methods. He published several method books, the most important being *Méthode pour la trompette* (1857). His earlier, shorter books were *Théorie ou tabulature de la trompette à pistons* (1828), *Méthode de trompette à pistons* (1835), and *Méthode théorique & pratique de cornet à pistons ou à cylindres* (ca. 1846). His comprehensive 1857 *Méthode* devoted more than 75 percent of its pages to material for the **natural trumpet**. Dauverné retired from the Paris Conservatory in 1869, when his former student, Arban, became the institution's first professor of cornet. Another student, Cerclier, succeeded Dauverné as professor of trumpet. Trumpet and cornet were taught in two separate classes at the Paris Conservatory until the tenure of **Merri Franquin** (1894–1925).

Davis, Miles Dewey (1926–1991). American jazz trumpeter and composer. One of the most influential jazz musicians of all time, Davis pioneered several styles including hard bop, cool jazz, free jazz, and jazz-rock fusion. Born in Alton, Illinois, Davis grew up in East St. Louis, Missouri. His father was a wealthy dentist who gave him a trumpet at the age of thirteen. His first teacher, Elwood Buchanan, taught Davis to play without vibrato, which later became a hallmark of his playing style. He later studied with Joseph Gustat, played in the band at Lincoln High School (directed by Buchanan), and began performing professionally at the age of sixteen. Davis moved to New York City in September 1944 to study with **William Vacchiano** at the Institute of Musical Art (later to become the Juilliard School), but left after only a few months when he began performing as a regular musician at two of Harlem's jazz clubs, Milton's Playhouse and Monroe's.

Davis replaced **Dizzy Gillespie** in Charlie Parker's quintet around 1945 and also performed with big bands led by Benny Carter and Billy Eckstine. He began leading his own bebop groups in 1948 and later collaborated with the arranger Gil Evans as well as Gerry Mulligan, John Lewis, and Johnny Carisi in a series of nonet recordings (later reissued as *The Birth of the Cool*) that helped inspire the "cool jazz" movement. In 1949 Davis began performing with Sonny Rollins, Art Blakey, and Tad Dameron until a bout with drug addiction interrupted his career for a period of more than three years. After beating his drug habit in 1954, he began performing with a stemless **Harmon mute**, which became a hallmark of his later style. Davis reignited his career with a notable performance at the 1955 Newport Jazz Festival and went on to form a quintet featuring John Coltrane. He made a series of influential solo recordings with trumpet and **flugelhorn** in the late 1950s featuring innovative arrangements by Gil Evans.

Davis turned to slow tempo modal jazz in several recordings between 1958 and 1959 including *Miles Ahead*, *Porgy and Bess*, *Sketches of Spain*, and *Kind of Blue*, an extraordinarily influential jazz album. In the 1960s and early 1970s, Davis experimented with a variety of musical styles influenced by rock, funk, and avant-garde as well as electronic music. Some of his recordings from the time include *Nefertiti* (1967), *In a Silent Way* (1969), and *Bitches Brew* (1969). Toward the end of his career, Davis also incorporated rock and rap into his music. A series of health problems caused him to retire from live performing in 1975, but he continued to record until complications from a stroke ended his life at the age of sixty-five.

Miles Davis earned numerous awards during his long and influential career. He was the winner of Downbeat's Poll for Best Jazz Trumpet Player in 1955, 1957, and 1961, and won a series of Grammy Awards between 1960 and 1993. The New England Conservatory gave him an Honorary Doctorate in 1986 and he received a posthumous star on the Hollywood Walk of Fame in 1998. He was knighted by the Legion of Honor in Paris in 1991 and inducted into the Rock and Roll Hall of Fame in 2006.

demilune trumpet. A natural trumpet curved in the shape of a crescent, which was designed to facilitate **hand-stopping**. The instrument's name comes from the French term for "half moon" (or crescent) and is distinct from the **Halbmond** (German for "half moon"), which was a type of early hunting horn. A hand-stopping trumpet was also known as an *inventionstrompete* in Germany at the turn of the nineteenth century. (See figure 15.)

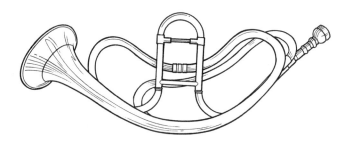

Figure 15. A demilune trumpet used for hand-stopping. *Drawing by T. M. Larsen.*

derby mute. A bowler hat made of felt or metal (stone-lined) that is held over the **bell** by the left hand. The hat can also be mounted on a stand so that a trumpeter can simply aim the bell into the hat. Gershwin's *An American in Paris* (1928) calls for a trumpet solo to be played "in felt crown" and Stravinsky asks for the trumpet to play with "hat over bell" in his *Ebony Concerto* (1945). Trumpeters often attach a piece of felt or thick cloth, known as a **felt mute**, over the bell to create this effect rather than using an actual hat. (See appendix 3.)

diaphragm. The large, dome-shaped muscle located beneath the lungs that plays a vital role in efficient **breathing** technique on a brass instrument. (See figure 8, under "breathing.") The diaphragm works with the support of the abdominal **intercostal muscles** to maximize steady airflow for players of all wind and brass instruments as well as singers. Its role is so important that the process is sometimes referred to as diaphragmatic breathing.

Dickey, Bruce (b. 1949). American *cornetto* player and leading figure in the **period instrument** revival. Beginning his musical studies on the trumpet, Dickey earned an undergraduate degree in the humanities from Michigan State University, where he studied with Byron Autrey; he earned a master's degree in musicology from Indiana University, where he studied with William Adam. Dickey then pursued studies with **Edward Tarr** at the **Schola Cantorum Basiliensis** in Basel, Switzerland, where he began to study the **cornett**, and soon developed such mastery of the instrument that he joined the faculty of the institution and has taught there for more than thirty years. Many of his students have gone on to elevate the status of the cornett and spread its influence worldwide.

As a performer, Dickey has appeared as a soloist, recording artist, ensemble player, and director with leading period instrument groups and recording labels throughout the world. He has worked with the seminal pioneers of **historically informed performance**, Gustav Leonhardt, Frans Brüggen, and Nikolaus Harnoncourt, as well as Jordi Savall's ensemble Hesperion XX, Ton Koopman, Monica Huggett, Philippe Herreweghe, and many others. He has enjoyed a longtime friendship and collaboration with Andrew Parrott, and in more recent years with Konrad Junghänel. He formed his own ensemble, Concerto Palatino, in Bologna, Italy.

As a teacher and scholar, Dickey has made important contributions to the fields of cornett technique and seventeenth-century performance practice in general. In addition to the Schola Cantorum in Basel, he has taught at the Royal Conservatory in the Hague, the Accademia Chigiana in Siena, and the Early Music Institute at Indiana University, as well as master classes in the United States, Canada, Europe, and Japan. His publications include *A Catalog of Music for the Cornett* (Indiana University Press, 1996) with Michael Collver, and *Articulation in Early Wind Music: A Source Book with Commentary* (Amadeus Verlag, 2007) with Edward Tarr. In 1997, together with his wife, Candace Smith, he founded Artemisia Editions, a small publishing house that produces editions of music from seventeenth-century Italian convents. Dickey was awarded the **Christopher Monk** Award by the **Historic Brass Society** in 2000 for his achievements and in 2007 he was honored by British conductor and musicologist Andrew Parrott with a "Taverner Award" as one of fourteen musicians whose "significant contributions to musical understanding have been motivated by neither commerce nor ego."

didjeridu. Also *didgeridoo.* A wooden trumpet-like instrument of the aboriginal people of Australia. Made of wood and approximately one meter in length, the instrument is an end-blown tube played by vibrating lips with simultaneous singing or vocalizations. (See figure 16.) This results in **multiphonics** and gives the didjeridu a unique, haunting quality in performance with overtones and resultant tones mixing with the drone of the fundamental. The technique of **circular breathing** is sometimes used in performance. Usually made of eucalyptus wood, the instrument has also been made out of other types of wood and materials including PVC pipe. The internal diameter (**bore**) of the didjeridu usually

measures between three and five centimeters. One of the oldest instruments in continuous use (dating back to the first century AD), it has attracted attention from contemporary musicians in more recent times.

Figure 16. Didjeridu. *Drawing by T. M. Larsen.*

disc valve. A **valve** mechanism developed by **John Shaw** in 1838 that was first called the "patent swivel valve for brass instruments." The valve operated in a manner similar to the barrel of a revolver: a disc with several holes would turn to a position that would access a hole to let the **airstream** of the instrument travel through an appended **valve slide**. J. A. **Köhler** acquired the right to manufacture instruments with disc valves for a ten-year period, and he subsequently brought out an improved version called the New **Patent Lever Valve** around 1840. Although he did not patent the invention, the Parisian maker **Halary** was the first to develop a valve using a disc mechanism in 1835 called the *plaques tournantes* or *disques mobiles.* (See appendix 2, figure A3.)

Distin, Henry John (1819–1903). English cornetist and brass instrument manufacturer. He was the second son of **John Distin** and performed with his father's pioneering brass chamber ensemble, the Distin Family Quintet, for twenty-four years. The quintet traveled widely throughout Europe and the United States, performing more than ten thousand concerts. Building on the group's association with **Adolphe Sax,** Distin and his father began distributing Sax instruments in London in 1846. Henry took control of the business three years later in 1849; his father launched his own brand of instruments in 1850. Sax ended his agreement with the Distin Company in 1853, most likely because Distin was producing a competing line of brass instruments. **Jules Levy** was secured to endorse Distin cornets in 1865, and reportedly agreed to the arrangement only because Distin instruments were modeled after those made by **Courtois**.

Henry Distin sold the business to Boosey & Company (now known as Boosey & Hawkes) in 1868; Boosey continued to operate the company under the name "Distin & Co." until 1874. Following the sale of the company, Distin worked as a music promoter in London, but was not financially successful. He moved to New York in 1877 and opened the Henry Distin Company in 1878, which specialized in importing and producing professional brass instruments, especially cornets. The company moved to Philadelphia in 1882 and later to Williamsport, Pennsylvania, in 1890, when the name was changed to the Henry Distin Manufacturing Company. During his years in Philadelphia, Distin worked as an importer for **J. W. Pepper.** Distin retired shortly after the move to Williamsport and turned over company management to Brua C. Keefer, the son of Senator Luther R. Keefer, a major stockholder. The Distin Company was sold to Keefer in 1909 and was known as the Brua C. Keefer Manufacturing Company until it went out of business in 1942. Distin's contributions to cornet design were the "light piston valve" (patented in 1864), which became the prototype for the modern cornet valve, and his "center bore cornet" (patented in 1884), whose design created a smoother **windway** by reducing abrupt bends in the tubing.

Distin, John (1798–1863). English trumpeter and pioneer of brass chamber music. A proficient soloist on both the **keyed bugle** and the **English slide trumpet,** Distin began his career playing the slide trumpet in the South Devon Militia. By 1814 he was the solo keyed bugler in the Genadier Guards, where the brilliance of his playing on the relatively new instrument attracted the attention of the Grand Duke Constantine of Russia, who subsequently purchased a keyed bugle for his own band. Distin went on to become a trumpeter with the Royal Household Band and the bandmaster for the Marquis of Breadalbane.

In 1833, Distin formed a brass chamber ensemble with his four sons known as the Distin Family Quintet. They played a variety of brass instruments: keyed bugle, cornopean, English slide trumpet, natural horns, and trombone. The Distins toured England and the European continent as well as the United States in the mid-nineteenth century performing operatic transcriptions and light repertoire. Their fame was such that jugs bearing their portrait were produced in 1845. Distin's oldest son, George (1818–1848), died in 1848, and the ensemble continued touring as a quartet thereafter with sons **Henry** (1819–1903), William Alfred (d. 1884), and Theodore (1823–1893). By the mid-1850s they were reputed to have performed over ten thousand concerts.

Distin's greatest influence came from his association with **Adolphe Sax** and the development of his family of conical brasses known as the **saxhorns.** The Distins first encountered Sax while on tour in Paris in 1844 and, in a mutually beneficial arrangement, adopted a set of five saxhorns; Distin probably was responsible for convincing Sax to call his instruments "Saxhorns" rather than *bugles à cylindres.* In 1845 he opened a music store in London with his son Henry called "Distin & Sons" to sell sheet music, which later became a "Saxhorn Dept" as British agents for Sax's instruments.

As a noted performer on the three most important high brass instruments before the advent of the valved cornet—slide trumpet, keyed bugle, and saxhorn—and as one of the first to form a successful brass chamber ensemble, John Distin played a vital role in the development of brass virtuosity in the first half of the nineteenth century. An English slide trumpet played by John Distin currently resides in the Fiske Collection at the Music Instrument Museum in Phoenix, Arizona.

Dixieland. A style of early jazz also known as **New Orleans Jazz.** Developed in New Orleans at the beginning of the twentieth century, it combined a variety of musical influences including brass band marches, ragtime, and blues with non-imitative polyphonic **improvisation.** Dixieland bands featured the **cornet** (later the trumpet) as one of the main melody instruments. Prominent Dixieland cornet and trumpet players included **Joe "King" Oliver, Louis Armstrong, Bix Beiderbecke,** and **Al Hirt.** A branch of Dixieland known as "Chicago Style" featured faster tempi and busier melodic filigree. In the 1950s it became known as a traditional form of classic jazz as distinct from more progressive styles like **Bebop** and modal jazz. Classic Dixieland standards include "When the Saints Go Marching In," "Muskrat Ramble," "Struttin' with Some Barbecue," "Tiger Rag," "Dippermouth Blues," and "Basin Street Blues."

Dodworth, Allen T. (1817–1896). American bandmaster. Born in Sheffield, England, he came to the United States at a young age and played piccolo with the family band led by his father Thomas (1790–1876), a trombonist, along with his brothers, **Harvey Dodworth,** Charles (1826–1894), and Thomas Jr. (1830–1896). Allen was the oldest of the brothers and assumed leadership of the Dodworth Band in 1836. Previously, the family had formed the first American brass band known as the National Brass Band in New York. The Dodworth family played an influential role in the development of bands and band music in the United States. Allen Dodworth also patented the first **over-the-shoulder cornet** along with a matched set of **saxhorns** with the bells pointing behind the player in 1838. He wrote his own brass band method, *Dodworth's Brass Band School,* in 1853, which spurred the formation of brass bands in towns throughout the country. Later in life he became a prominent teacher of ballroom dancing and also published eight booklets of instructions for various dances as well as *Dancing and Its Relation to Education and Social Life* (1885). The Dodworths were among the founding members of the New York Philharmonic Symphony Society (April 1842), and Allen was elected treasurer. When the orchestra gave its first concert in December 1842 the personnel included Thomas Dodworth (trombone) along with his sons Allen and Harvey (violins) and Charles (piccolo).

Dodworth, Harvey B. (1822–1891). American cornetist and bandmaster. In addition to playing the cornet in the Dodworth Band, he took over its leadership from his older brother, **Allen Dodworth**, around 1838. Also involved in music publishing, he operated Dodworth's Music Store and Publishing House in New York. During the American Civil War, the Dodworth Band served as the band for the Seventy-First National Guard Regiment of New York in the Union army. Harvey Dodworth endorsed cornets with **rotary valves** made by **Isaac Fiske**. He also played the violin.

doit. A special effect used in jazz notated with a ˇ over the note, which is usually performed with a quick descending **note bend** from the written note and back up again.

Dokshizer, Timofei Alexandrovich (1921–2005). Ukranian trumpeter. Dokshizer's ancestors originally came from Dokshizi (White Russia), settling in Nezhin (Ukraine) at the turn of the nineteenth century. His family moved to Moscow in 1932, where he attended the military band school of the Sixty-Second Cavalry Regiment and the Glazunov Music College, where he studied with Ivan Vasilevsky. He also attended the preparatory institutions for the Moscow Conservatory and the Gnesin Institute, studying with **Mikhail Tabakov**. After military service during the Second World War, he resumed studies with Tabakov at the Moscow Conservatory and the Gnesin Institute, becoming Tabakov's assistant between 1950 and 1954. Dokshizer also studied conducting with L. Ginsburg at the Moscow Conservatory between 1951 and 1957.

From 1945 to 1984, Dokshizer was the **cornet** and trumpet soloist in the Bolshoi Theater Orchestra. As a soloist, he enjoyed a prestigious status on the same level as David Oistrakh and Mstislav Rostropovich. It was during this period that he was designated the "People's Artist of Russia" by the Soviet government. In addition to his activities as a soloist, Dokshizer conducted opera performances at the Bolshoi for a number of years. As a teacher he was active at the Gnesin Institute, beginning in 1954 and ending when he moved to Vilnius (Lithuania) in 1990.

As a soloist and orchestra member, master teacher, and juror in international competitions, Dokshizer was in demand all over the world, with many visits to the United States, Western Europe, and Japan. Many composers, including **Vladimir Peskin** and Eino Tamberg, wrote new works for Dokshizer. His distinctive repertoire of more than one hundred pieces consisted in later years entirely of his own transcriptions, including significant pieces such as Gershwin's *Rhapsody in Blue* and Shostakovich's *Concerto for Piano and Trumpet, Op. 35.* In addition to performing, recording, and teaching, he wrote two pedagogical works, *From a Trumpeter's Notebook* and *The Trumpeter's Laboratory*, as well as his memoir, *Trumpeter on Horseback* (published in 1997 by the **International Trumpet Guild**). Dokshizer continued to perform and record even after quadruple bypass heart surgery in April of 1989. He had an uncanny ability to regain top form within days after a long pause of weeks or even months.

doodle tongue. A style of **articulation** popular in jazz that features a softer, nuanced attack. The movement of the tongue inside the mouth approximates the motion made when saying the words "doodle, doodle," hence the name.

doppio sordino. (It.) **Double mute.** An indication that appears in the trumpet parts for Bartok's *Violin Concerto* (1937–1938) meant to signify the use of a **Solotone mute**.

dorsal tonguing. Another term for **anchor tonguing**.

double high C. The pitch C7, an octave above **high C** (C6), often referred to as the goal of lead trumpeters in jazz bands in **altimissimo playing.** Some players are capable of reaching an octave higher (C8, the highest note on the piano keyboard), which is labeled "triple high C."

double mute. Alternate term for a **Solotone mute** or **Clear Tone mute**, which refers to the appearance of the mute with its telescoping double cone design with an open central tube. (See appendix 3.)

double piston valve. The technical name for the **Vienna valve.** (See appendix 2, figure A8.)

double tongue. A form of **multiple tonguing** that is used to play fast sixteenth notes and other rapid figures. It is produced by using the front of the tongue ("Tah") and the back of tongue ("Kah") in a rebounding fashion, as in "T K T K." At higher speeds, the movement of the tongue becomes smaller and the *T* becomes a *D* and the *K* becomes a *G*, resulting in "D G D G," which can also be used as a softer variation on the more pointed "T K T K" at slower speeds.

double water key. A feature of many **cornets** in the late nineteenth century in which a single lever at the bottom of the instrument operated **water keys** for both the first **bow** and the third **valve slide**. (See figure 11 under "**cornet**.")

Douglas, Dave (b. 1964). American jazz trumpeter and composer. He began playing piano and trombone at an early age before focusing on the trumpet. His interest in improvised music was sparked by a year-long study-abroad program in Barcelona, Spain, in high school. Douglas attended the Berklee College of Music and the New England Conservatory before moving to New York in 1984 to study at New York University. His many awards include multiple Trumpet Player of the Year awards from the Down Beat Critics Poll, Downbeat Readers Poll, Jazz Journalists Association Awards, two Grammy nominations, and a Guggenheim Foundation Fellowship in 2005. Douglas's eclectic style features influences from classical, European folk, and the avant-garde. In 2005 he launched his own record label, Green-leaf. He is also the co-founder and director of the annual Festival of New Trumpet Music in New York as well as the artistic director of the Workshop in Jazz and Creative Music at the Banff Centre in Canada, with commissions including the Trisha Brown Dance Company, the Library of Congress, and the Norddeutscher Rundfunk. Douglas's many projects bear witness to his prodigious versatility: the Tiny Bell Trio with the drummer Jim Black and the guitarist Brad Shepik; Keystone, an electric sextet (including turntables); Brass Ecstasy (a brass quartet plus drums); the mixed chamber ensemble Nomad; as well as his own quintet and big band.

dran. A simple two-note military **signal** from the Middle Ages that consisted of slurring from C3 up to G3 on an eight-foot **natural trumpet** pitched in C with a large **mouthpiece**. The name of the signal approximates its sound in performance.

draucht trumpet. A Scottish term for a trombone from the early sixteenth century. It might have also referred to a **slide trumpet** with a moveable leadpipe, but this is unlikely.

Drehventil. (Ger.) **Rotary valve.**

drip spouts. Ports on the bottom of **valve caps** on nineteenth-century **cornets** with a design more ornamental than functional. (See figure 11 under "cornet.")

Drucker, Vladimir (1897–1974). Russian-American trumpeter. He began playing the trumpet at the age of nine and was accepted into **Willy Brandt's** class at the Moscow Conservatory at the age of twelve. When Brandt left the conservatory, Drucker studied with **Mikhail Tabakov** and also pursued studies in violin and timpani. Drucker accepted his first professional position at the age of sixteen when he became Tabakov's assistant principal trumpet in Serge Koussevitzky's private orchestra. His career was interrupted by the onset of the October Revolution, when he fled Russia by way of the Trans-Siberian Railroad to China, and performed with the Shanghai Municipal Orchestra for two years. Drucker traveled to New York in 1919, where he successfully auditioned for the principal trumpet position with the newly formed Los Angeles Philharmonic.

Although Drucker stayed in Los Angeles for the rest of his career, he also performed with other orchestras including the New York Symphony Orchestra (1923–1925), the San Francisco Symphony (1925–1929), the Cleveland Orchestra (1934–1935), and the Hollywood Bowl Orchestra (1929–1947). He turned down offers from Fritz Reiner and Arturo Toscanini in 1931, as well as the principal trumpet position with the Moscow State Opera Orchestra and a professorship at the Moscow Conservatory in 1932 to stay in Los Angeles. He left the Los Angeles Philharmonic in 1945 and played in Hollywood studio orchestras at Columbia Motion Pictures until 1958. Known for his rich tone and sensitive, soft playing, Drucker played on a French **Besson** B-flat trumpet with a large mouthpiece.

drum and bugle corps. The modern drum and **bugle** corps movement began in North American after the First World War. Bugle corps were popular with the Boy Scouts in the United States as well as the American Legion and the Royal Canadian Legion. Such groups differ from contemporary marching bands in that they exclude woodwinds and trombones and feature only a matched complement of bell-front bugles with elaborate percussion and color guard. Drum corps bugles developed from the **Bersag horn** or *tromba da bersagliari* and are pitched in G and feature two or three **valves** positioned vertically, depending on the maker. Early valved bugles featured horizontal valves. Bugles with one valve were used until the 1970s when two-valve instruments came into use. The limitations of the two-valve bugles led to the adoption of three-valve instruments in 1990. Prominent makers of contemporary corps bugles are **Conn**, **Getzen** (DEG), and **Kanstul**.

Dudgeon, Ralph (b. 1948). American trumpeter, conductor, and leading figure in the **keyed bugle** revival. Dudgeon earned a bachelor's degree in music education and a master's degree in trumpet performance from San Diego State University. He received a PhD in musicology from University of California, San Diego, and pursued postgraduate studies in trumpet and conducting with John Clyman, **Gerard Schwarz**, and Frederick Fennell. Dudgeon taught high school music for eleven years in California and then became an associate professor for five years at the University of Texas at Dallas. He joined the faculty of the State University of New York (SUNY) Cortland in 1985 and taught there for 27 years until his retirement in 2013.

His published books include *The Keyed Bugle* (1993, rev. 2004) and *Das Flugelhorn* (2003), and his debut solo album, "Music for the Keyed Bugle," was the first full-length recording devoted to the keyed bugle. Dudgeon has recorded for Musical Heritage Society, Music Masters, Newport Classic, Nimbus, Hyperion, Innova, and Spring

Tree labels. He is a member of the Society for New Music in Syracuse, New York, and has directed the Miss Lucy Long Social Orchestra and Quick Step Society since 1976. He also was a member of the Syracuse Camerata, Utica Symphony, and the London Gabrieli Brass Ensemble.

Duhem, Hippolyte (1828–1911). Belgian trumpeter. He studied with C. Zeiss at the Royal Conservatory in Brussels and graduated in 1846, when he became the principal trumpet of the Royal Theater of Monnaie as well as the First Guard Regiment Band. He taught **cornet**, trumpet, and **flugelhorn** at the Brussels Conservatory between 1860 and 1888. He was a pioneer in performing Baroque trumpet literature in the nineteenth century when he com-missioned the firm of **Antoine Courtois** in 1861 to make the first **piston valve** trumpet in high D, an octave higher than a seven-foot **natural trumpet** pitched in D, and half the length of tubing. Duhem served as cornet soloist with the Kursaal Orchestra between 1870 and 1871 and later became the group's conductor from 1875 to 1877. He toured as a soloist between 1887 and 1889.

dung. dung chen. A trumpet from Tibet made of copper with a **conical bore** and built with several telescoping sections with knobs. Because it is nearly five meters long, its bell rests on the ground when it is played. It has a large, flat mouthpiece and only plays a few low notes in performance.

early music. A term generally used to refer to music from medieval times through the Renaissance or Baroque eras. With the advent of **historically informed performance** (HIP) and the rise of professional **period instrument** ensembles in the late twentieth century, the term's meaning has expanded to include any music for which **performance practice** must be reconstructed on the basis of surviving scores, treatises, instruments, and other contemporary evidence.

echo bell cornet. A type of **cornet** manufactured with a fourth **piston valve** that directed the **airstream** into a separate closed **bell** (echo bell) that was essentially a **mute**. When employed, the sound of the echo bell was very similar to that of a **Harmon mute** with the stem removed. Echo bell cornets, also known simply as "echo cornets," first appeared in the late nineteenth century and were made in the United States and Europe until 1920, with a few exceptions. Many brass instrument makers built echo bell cornets including **Besson, Conn, Courtois, Distin,** and **Holton.** The German cornet soloist **Theodore Hoch** composed the solo *"Singvögelchen aus der Thüringer Wald" Fantasie, Op. 22* in 1896 expressly to demonstrate the echo effects of his Conn echo bell cornet. Although the instrument was never expressly identified in any orchestral scores, it is possible that orchestral trumpeters at the turn of the twentieth century may have used the echo bell cornet to perform passages with quick mute changes in the symphonies of Gustav Mahler.

Egger. Swiss brass instrument manufacturer. Founded by Adolf Egger (1911–1972) in 1940, Blechblas-Instrumentenbau Egger has grown to become one of the leading makers of **period brass instruments** in the twenty-first century. Adolf's son, Rainer Egger (b. 1947), joined the company as an apprentice in 1964 and took over the business at his father's death in 1972. Rainer followed his father's lead by specializing in the crafting of modern reproduc-

tions of Baroque brass instruments with the assistance of **Edward Tarr** in 1976. In addition to trumpets with and without **vent holes**, Egger began to produce copies of sackbuts and early trombones in the 1980s. The company acquired Galileo Trumpets in 2008, a manufacturer of modern **piston** and **rotary valve** trumpets. Egger Baroque trumpet replicas are based on historic instruments by **Johann Wilhelm Haas, Johann Leonard Ehe II,** and Michael Nagel. Rainer Egger has also made reproductions of a **keyed trumpet,** a **demilune trumpet** (or *Inventionstrompete*), an early **slide trumpet,** and a coiled **natural trumpet** (or *Jägertrompete*). He has also worked with **Friedemann Immer** in 2011 to produce an improved three-hole **Baroque trumpet** with dimensions and **response** closer to that of an eighteenth-century natural trumpet. The **Historic Brass Society** honored Rainer Egger's achievements in period brass instrument craftsmanship with the **Christopher Monk** Award in 2012.

Egyptian trumpet. See **šnb.**

Ehe. German family of brass instrument makers. Active for five generations in **Nuremberg,** the Ehe family began its tradition of fine brass instruments through the work of two brothers, Isaac (1586–1632) and Georg (1595–1668). Georg's son, Johann Leonard Ehe (1638–1707), passed on the family traditions to his sons, Johann Leonard II (1664–1724)—whose **natural trumpets** are widely copied by **period instrument** makers today—and Friedrich (1669–1743). The fourth generation consisted of Friedrich's sons, Johann Leonard III (1700–1771) and Martin Friedrich (1714–1779), and Johann Leonard II's son, Wolf Magnus (1690–1722). Johann Leonard III's son, Wolf Magnus II (1726–1794), was the last important member of the trumpet-making family. The **maker's mark** for Ehe trumpets throughout the seventeenth and eighteenth centuries usually featured the head of a man wearing a turban. (See figure 35 under "maker's mark.")

Eichborn, Hermann Ludwig (1857–1918). German trumpeter. One of the first scholar-performers to produce significant research concerning the history of brass instruments, Eichborn was born in Breslau, studied law in Jena, and earned a doctorate before devoting his life to the musical profession. He was a composer and conductor as well as a proficient performer on the trumpet and French **horn**. Also a craftsman, he experimented with making his own reproductions of horns and other brass instruments, and he studied existing historic instruments. He wrote several books and articles on the history of brass instruments that were among the major sources on the topic until the middle of the twentieth century. His two works that concern the trumpet, *Die Trompete in alter und neuer Zeit* (Leipzig: Breitkopf und Härtel, 1881) and *Das alte Clarinblasen auf Trompeten* (Leipzig: Breitkopf und Härtel, 1894; English translation by Bryan Simms, Denver: Tromba Publications, 1976), display a thorough knowledge of earlier sources, a careful study of instrument collections and **organology**, and the practical knowledge of a virtuoso brass musician. He lived in the Tyrolean village of Gries bei Bozen from 1891 until his death in 1918.

Eichborn's work reflects attitudes prevalent before the twentieth-century **period instrument** movement associated with **historically informed performance** and consequently favors modern performance techniques as more expedient than the development of techniques associated with earlier periods. Although he displays a thorough knowledge of works by Sebastian Virdung, **Michael Praetorius, Girolamo Fantini**, Daniel Speer, **Marin Mersenne, Johann Ernst Altenburg**, and **Charles Burney**, Eichborn's ideas concerning early music performance practice recommended free interpretation and expressed doubts about the possibility of reviving the art of **clarino** playing on **natural trumpets**.

Eklund, Niklas (b. 1969). Swedish trumpeter. Born into a musical family, Eklund received his first musical training from his father, Bengt, a noted trumpeter and conductor. He attended the School of Music and Musicology at Göteborg University and pursued further studies in **natural trumpet** and **Baroque trumpet** with **Edward Tarr** at the **Schola Cantorum Basiliensis**. After five years as solo trumpeter with the Basel Radio Symphony Orchestra, Eklund left to pursue a solo career. In 1996, he won first prize at the first Altenburg International Baroque Trumpet Competition, held in Bad Säckingen, Germany. Since then he has appeared with many leading musicians and conductors, including Cecilia Bartoli, Zubin Mehta, John Eliot Gardiner, Heinz Holliger, Andras Schiff, Ivan Fisher, and Gustav Leonhardt. His series of recordings on the Naxos label, *The Art of the Baroque Trumpet*, received critical acclaim and wide distribution, which in turn introduced new audiences to the Baroque trumpet and **historically informed performance**.

Eldridge, (David) Roy (1911–1989). American jazz trumpeter. He began playing the drums at the age of six and later took up the trumpet. By the age of sixteen he was playing professionally with several Midwestern jazz bands and carnivals. He moved to New York a few years later and began playing with dance bands in Harlem. Eldridge went on to play with bands in Pittsburgh, Baltimore, and New York. He recorded his first solos in 1935 and joined Fletcher Henderson's orchestra as lead trumpet. The following year he moved to Chicago and started his own eight-piece band; he recorded two notable solos with the group: "After You've Gone" and "Wabash Stomp." Eldridge took his band to New York in 1939 and performed at the Arcadia Ballroom and Kelly's Stable. In 1941 he became one of the first African American musicians to perform regularly with a white jazz band when he joined Gene Krupa's band. He perfomed with Krupa in the film *Ball of Fire* (1941), and was noted for live performances of "Rockin' Chair" and "Let Me Off Uptown." After Krupa's band broke up in 1943, Eldridge joined Artie Shaw's band in 1944 and began playing with Norman Grantz's Jazz at the Philharmonic in 1948.

Considered one of the foremost jazz trumpeters after **Louis Armstrong**, Eldridge's personal style was marked by rhythmic drive, a powerful tone, remarkable virtuosity, endurance, and high-register control. His playing strongly influenced **Dizzy Gillespie** and the development of **Bebop**. Eldridge suffered a stroke in the early 1970s that caused him to reduce the physical demands of his high-energy trumpet playing and to switch to piano and drums. His legacy is captured on his best-known albums: *Little Jazz, After You've Gone, Roy Eldridge in Paris, Just You—Just Me, Happy Times, Montreaux 1977*, and *Blues in the Night*.

embouchure. *embouchure* (Fr.), *Ansatz* (Ger.) *imboccatura* (It.). The formation of the muscles around the mouth and lips to create a sound on a brass or wind instrument. In the case of the trumpet and the cornet, the facial musculature supports the vibration of the lips to optimize the control of the **aperture** for an efficient and reliable sound. The primary muscles used in embouchure formation are the **orbicularis oris**, which surrounds the mouth and compresses and protrudes the lips; the risorius (platysma strand), which depresses the lower jaw and tenses the skin of the lower face and neck; the **buccinator muscles**, which press the cheeks against the back teeth and help to expel air from the oral cavity (together with the orbicularis oris, these are the most active muscles during the actual formation of the embouchure); and the mentalis, which elevates and protrudes the lower lip. (See figure 17.) Problems with the embouchure usually originate with the teeth and jaw. A variety of **practice aids** have been developed to facilitate embouchure development and strength including the **B.E.R.P.**

(Buzz Extension Resistance Piece), **Chop-Sticks**, the **embouchure visualizer**, the **pencil exercise**, and the **P.E.T.E.** (Personal Embouchure Training Exerciser). See also **alpha angle**, **buzz**, **buzzing**, **flexibility**, **lip slurs**, **lipping**, **note bending**, **tongue-controlled embouchure**, **upstream embouchure**.

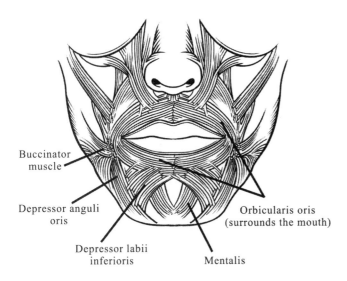

Figure 17. Facial muscles in the formation of a trumpeter's embouchure. *Drawing by T. M. Larsen.*

embouchure visualizer. A pedagogical tool consisting of a **mouthpiece rim** attached to a stick used to examine **embouchure** effectiveness. Because the tool is just a simple ring without a **cup**, it allows the teacher to view a student's **aperture** and **mouthpiece placement** without obstruction.

Endler, Johann Samuel (1694–1762). German composer. Trained in Leipzig, Endler was a violinist and singer active in Darmstadt, where he worked for many years with Christoph Graupner, eventually succeeding him as Kapellmeister. Endler wrote several solo works for trumpet including a *Sinfonia Concertante in D Major* and a *Concerto in F*.

Endsley, Gerald (b. 1945). American trumpeter, conductor, music publisher, and instrument maker. He studied with Ed Lenicheck, **Roger Voisin**, and **Robert Nagel** and earned degrees from the New England Conservatory and the University of Colorado. Endsley performed with the Colorado Symphony, the Colorado Opera, and the Colorado Ballet orchestras, and has served as the music contractor for the Denver Center Theatre Company. Developing an interest in trumpet history, Endsley amassed a private collection of historic instruments and began to make reproductions, including a **keyed trumpet**, a **natural trumpet**, and a copy of the Steinkopf-Finke trumpet played by **Walter Holy**. He formed a publishing business, Tromba Publications, and an instrument-manufacturing company, Endsley Brass, in Denver, Colorado. In 1980 he published an influential *Comparative Mouthpiece Guide for Trumpet*. He has also produced his own line of component mouthpieces, **throat** gauges for brass mouthpieces, a **leadpipe** for the **Schilke** P54 **piccolo trumpet**, and a Brandenburg Bell, which replaces the fourth valve slide of a piccolo trumpet for use in performing the high *G*s (G6) in Bach's ***Brandenburg Concerto No. 2***. Endsley is currently the director of the Denver Municipal Band (the oldest professional band in the United States) and teaches at Metropolitan State University of Denver.

endurance. The ability to play the trumpet for extended periods of time without noticeable fatigue and/or an erosion of tone quality, accuracy, or dynamic control. A vital facet of good brass playing, a player's stamina level is directly related to good physical technique involving **embouchure**, **breathing**, posture, and equipment.

English slide trumpet. An instrument unique to English trumpeters that flourished during the entire nineteenth century. The earliest English slide trumpets were converted **natural trumpets** in F that employed a slide operated by a clock-spring mechanism developed by **John Hyde**. Unlike earlier **slide trumpets** that used an elongated **leadpipe** or a double slide that moved backward (in the case of the **flat trumpet**), the English slide trumpet had a more compact design with a slide placed in the center of the instrument. The player held the instrument upside-down (with the bell section on bottom, facing the floor) and operated the slide by means of a T-shaped finger pull with the right hand. The English slide trumpet also came equipped with crooks to lower the pitch of the F trumpet to E, E-flat, D, and C; combinations of crooks could be used to reach lower keys (D-flat, B, B-flat, A, and A-flat), but with less secure intonation. Its mouthpiece was similar in dimensions to those used on natural trumpets of the time. The instrument lacked a **tuning slide**, but employed tuning **bits** that were inserted into the leadpipe.

What made the English slide trumpet so successful was its ability to correct the out-of-tune notes in the **harmonic overtone series** and play other chromatic pitches while maintaining the characteristic noble tone of the natural trumpet. It was primarily an orchestral instrument rather than a vehicle for virtuosi, but it was especially popular for performing the obbligato trumpet solos in Handel arias. Through the celebrity of **Thomas Harper** and his son, **Thomas John Harper Jr.**, the English slide trumpet enjoyed a tradition that lasted over a century. A prominent maker of the instrument was John Augustus **Köhler.** Other notable performers of the English slide trumpet were **John Distin** and **John Norton**. The instrument has been revived in the twentieth century by **Crispian Steele-Perkins**. (See figure 18.)

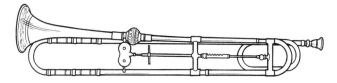

Figure 18. English slide trumpet. *Drawing by T. M. Larsen.*

Eskdale, George Salisbury (1897–1960). English trumpeter. He learned to the play the **cornet** as a boy from his father, who was a well-known brass band conductor and adjudicator. As a child prodigy, Eskdale performed solos with local bands before entering the Royal Military School of Music, Kneller Hall, where he studied the cornet with Charles Leggett as well as trumpet and violin. During the First World War he served in Palestine and Europe with the Loyal North Lancashire Regiment and was severely wounded in the leg at the Battle of Passchendaele in 1917, which left him with a slight limp for the rest of his life. After the war he played music for silent films in a small ensemble and with dance bands including the Savoy Havana Band, and later became a member of the New Queen's Hall Orchestra. Eskdale went on to become the principal trumpeter of the London Symphony Orchestra, serving in that role from 1934 until his death in 1960. Eskdale taught the trumpet at the Trinity College of Music from 1937 and at the Royal Academy of Music from 1938. The distinctive lyricism of his playing was undoubtedly influenced by his early cornet training.

Eskdale made several famous recordings including a landmark performance of **J. S. Bach**'s *Brandenburg Concerto No. 2* with the Adolph Busch Chamber Players in 1935. He played it on a small trumpet in F made especially for him by **Boosey & Hawkes**, and it was one of the first performances in the original high register. Eskdale made the first recording of **Joseph Haydn**'s *Concerto in E-flat* (the second and third movements only) in 1939 and edited a published version of the concerto the same year. His recording and published edition of the Haydn served to popularize the concerto, establish its place in the repertoire, and went a long way toward legitimizing the trumpet as a classical solo instrument in the twentieth century. Eskdale also recorded Knudåge Riisager's *Concertino for Trumpet and Strings* at the composer's request with the Danish State Radio Orchestra in 1949. He was also involved in trumpet design, and worked with a craftsman at Boosey & Hawkes to produce two trumpet models in the 1930s: a trumpet in C and another in E-flat and D. These instruments featured slightly larger bores than the previous models as well as a mouthpiece that was slightly conical.

étude. (Fr.) Study. Short instrumental pieces designed to develop or exploit a particular aspect of performing technique or musical style. Some of the most famous collections of etudes for trumpet or cornet are **Jean-Baptiste Arban**'s *Characteristic Studies* (located in the back of his *Complete Conservatory Method*), **Theo Charlier**'s *36 Transcendental Etudes*, and **Marcel Bitsch**'s *20 Etudes*.

EVI. Electronic Valve Instrument. A **MIDI** or synthesizer controller operated by blowing through a tube and pressing buttons to simulate the performing technique of a trumpet to control digital audio processing software. The EVI was marketed by Akai in 1987 in both its original trumpet design with three buttons and a saxophone-like derivative (known as the Electronic Wind Instrument, or EWI), while Yamaha's WX series (from 1987) was partly based on an earlier device called the Lyricon. Synthesizers and related electronic instruments that responded to the articulation of notes from a breath-operated controller were manufactured by Crumar, Yamaha, and Hohner.

Ewald, Viktor (1860–1935). Russian composer. A civil engineer by trade, he was an accomplished amateur cellist and tuba player. Also a student of the cornet, horn, piano, and harmony, he played cello in a string quartet at the home of music publisher Mitrofan Balyayev (or Belaieff) in St. Petersburg. This put him in contact with composers who attended the musical evenings at the Balyayev home, including Borodin, Glazunov, and Rimsky-Korsakov. When Balyayev died Ewald switched to playing tuba in an amateur brass quintet from 1890 until 1917. It was during this period that he composed his three brass quintets ("No. 1 in B-flat Minor, Op. 5"; "No. 2 in E-flat Major, Op. 6"; and "No. 3 in D-flat Major, Op. 7"); there may be a fourth quintet, but that is a point of scholarly dispute (it may be an earlier string quartet recast for brass). Ewald's quintets favor minor keys and occasionally bear resemblance to the music of Brahms with noticeable influences from Russian Romanticism and folk song.

Ewazen, Eric (b. 1954). American composer. Ewazen studied with Milton Babbitt, Samuel Adler, Warren Benson, Joseph Schwantner, and Gunther Schuller at the Eastman School of Music, Tanglewood, and the Juilliard School, where he earned a Doctor of Musical Arts degree. He has served on the faculty of the Juilliard School since 1980, and has also served on the faculties of the Hebrew Arts School and the Lincoln Center Institute as well composer-in-residence for the Orchestra of St. Luke's.

Ewazen has received numerous composition awards and prizes and his works have been commissioned, performed, and recorded by many ensembles and organizations including the **American Brass Quintet**, Detroit Chamber Winds, **International Trumpet Guild**, New York State Council on the Arts, Summit Brass, and St. Luke's Chamber Ensemble, among many others. He has written works for numerous soloists including trumpeters **Chris Gekker**, **Philip Smith**, and **Allen Vizzutti.**

A prolific composer for brass and wind instruments, some of Ewazen's works for trumpet include *Concerto for Trumpet and String Orchestra* (1990), which was later recast for trumpet and string quartet; *Trio for Trumpet Violin and Piano* (1992); *Sonata for Trumpet and Piano* (1995); *Mandala: For Flute, Clarinet (Doubling Bass Clarinet), Trumpet, Violin, and Cello*; *To Cast a Shadow Again: For Baritone or Mezzo Soprano, Trumpet, and Piano*; *Pastorale for Trumpet, Trombone, and Piano*; *Fantasia for Seven Trumpets*; *Three Lyrics for Trumpet and Piano*; *Danzante: Concerto for Trumpet and Wind Ensemble* (2004); and *Variations on a Theme by Brahms for Flugelhorn and Piano* (2011). His many works for brass quintet and brass ensembles include *Colchester Fantasy* (1987, brass quintet); *Frost Fire* (1990, brass quintet); *Shadowcatcher: Concerto for Brass Quintet and Band* (1996); *A Western Fanfare* (1997, brass quintet); *Grand Valley Fanfare* (2001, brass quintet); and *Symphony in Brass* (1991, large brass ensemble). Ewazen's brass writing is notable for its lyricism and conversational style that frequently requires trumpeters to play a subordinate, accompanying role with other instruments.

facsimile. A published copy of an original manuscript or early publication of a musical composition.

fake book. A collection of jazz and popular standards presented in **lead sheet** format with titles in alphabetical order. Fake books are used by jazz musicians for memorizing melodies and accompanying harmonic patterns and as a basis for **improvisation**.

fall. A jazz performance effect where the written note is played and then dropped off with a **glissando**. The technique of a fall varies according to its context in musical performance. Falls on shorter note durations may be performed with half-valve **smears**, fingered chromatic flourishes, or harmonic overtone slurs (using one valve combination), and will only fall by the range of a fifth or less. Falls on longer note values usually linger on the printed note initially and cover a wider range, often an octave. Usually notated with a diagonal line pointing down from the note on the right, the length and shape of that line often provides clues as to how the fall should be performed. (See figure 19.)

Figure 19. A long and a short fall. *Elisa Koehler.*

falsetto. Term used by **Praetorius** to describe the technique of **lipping**.

fanfara. (It.) 1. **Fanfare.**

    2. A bugle corps or trumpet ensemble, as in the *Fanfara per Bersaglieri*, the bugle corps of the Italian Army sharpshooters. (See also *tromba alla berseglari*.)

fanfare. A ceremonial flourish of trumpets, often with percussion. Some fanfares are long and elaborate, such as **Copland's** *Fanfare for the Common Man* (1942), while others are short, declamatory statements. Fanfare passages in orchestral music often resemble military **signals** or **bugle calls**, in order to suggest heroic or dramatic associations.

Fanfarentrompete. (Ger.) Fanfare trumpet, specifically a modern **natural trumpet** pitched in E-flat.

Fantini, Girolamo (1600–ca. 1675). Italian trumpeter. Born in Spoleto, Fantini was considered to be the greatest trumpeter of the seventeenth century. He wrote one of the earliest methods for the trumpet, *Modo per imparare a sonare di tromba* (1638), which contained the first sonatas for trumpet and keyboard ever published. Fantini most likely served as an apprentice in Spoleto before moving to Rome in 1626 to join the musical staff of Cardinal Scipione Borghese. After 1630 he moved to Florence to work for Ferdinand II, the grand duke of Tuscany. In April 1634 Fantini performed a famous concert with organist Girolamo Frescobaldi (1583–1643) in Rome, which was the first documented performance that featured the trumpet as a solo instrument with keyboard accompaniment. Two years later, in 1636, French theorist **Marin Mersenne** wrote, "Hieronymo Fantino tubicine totius Italiae excellentissimo" [Girolamo Fantini is the greatest trumpeter in all of Italy].

    Fantini left the court at Tuscany sometime after 1642 (court records from 1643–1647 are missing). Financial records from Florence show that he was still living in the city between 1640 and 1660. The last documentation of Fantini's life appears in ten letters from a prioress at a convent in 1675, who appealed to Fantini to pay the rent for his daughter, who was living there. Apparently, the great trumpeter had fallen on hard times toward the end of his life and was unable to pay the bill.

Renowned for his prowess in **lipping,** or **note bending,** to perform **nonharmonic tones** (notes outside of the **harmonic overtone series**), Fantini was praised for his rare ability to perform notes like F4 and D4, which were unobtainable by other trumpeters in the seventeenth century without the aid of **valves** or **vent holes.** These notes appear in a celebrated passage (measure 13) from Fantini's "Sonata detta dell'Adimari" in the repertoire section of his *Modo* (1638). Fantini's work was the first to treat the trumpet as a musical instrument as distinct from its role in sounding military and ceremonial signals. The complete title for the book is something like an artistic manifesto for the trumpet (translated): "Method for Learning to Play the Trumpet in a War-Like Way as Well as Musically, with the Organ, with a Mute, with the Harpsichord, and Every Other Instrument to Which Many Pieces (Sonate) Are Added, Such as Balletti, Brandi [the plural of "branle"], Capricci, Sarabande, Correnti, Passaggi, and Sonatas for Trumpet and Organ." Fantini's book also includes information on **ornamentation, articulation,** and the high **clarino** register.

Farmer, Art [Arthur Stewart] (1928–1999). American jazz trumpeter. Raised in Phoenix, Arizona, Farmer began learning the piano at the age of six. He also learned to play violin and tuba before taking up the trumpet at the age of fourteen. His twin brother, Addison, played the bass. Farmer moved to Los Angeles at the age of seventeen in 1945 and began working with jazz musicians such as Horace Henderson, Floyd Ray, Benny Carter, Johnny Otis, Jay McShann, and the Roy Porter Big Band. He was known for his mellow tone, relaxed phrasing style, and technical prowess. Farmer played with several groups in the 1950s such as Wardell Gray, Lionel Hampton, Gigi Gryce, Horace Silver, Gerry Mulligan, and **Clifford Brown**'s European tour. Between 1959 and 1962 he led the Jazztet with Benny Golson and later played in a quartet with Jim Hall.

Looking to change his sound in the 1960s, Farmer switched to the **flugelhorn** almost exclusively. He moved to Vienna in 1968 and performed with the Austrian Radio Orchestra and worked with the Kenny Clarke–Francy Boland Big Band and the Peter Herbolzheimer Orchestra. Despite regular visits to the United States, Farmer spent most of the rest of his life in Europe. In 1982 he reunited with Benny Golson in a new incarnation of the Jazztet with Curtis Fuller. In 1991 trumpet maker David **Monette** designed a unique new instrument for Farmer called the **flumpet,** which combined the characteristics of the trumpet and flugelhorn. It became his signature instrument until his death in 1999. Farmer's recorded legacy includes *Back to the City, Early Art, A Work of Art, Modern Art, Meet the Jazztet,* and *Something to Live For.*

Fasch, Johann Friedrich (1688–1758). German composer. One of most prominent contemporaries of **J. S. Bach**, he grew up as a choirboy in **Weissenfels** and later attended the St. Thomas School in Leipzig, where he studied with Johann Kuhnau (1660–1722). After studies at the university in Leipzig, he formed a *collegium musicum* in 1708. He was appointed court Kapellmeister at Zerbst in 1722, where he primarily composed sacred music, including twelve cantata cycles and a *Passio Jesu Christi* (1723). His instrumental music comprises symphonies, orchestral suites, concertos, and chamber works, and is characteristic of the transition from the late Baroque to the Classical style. Fasch wrote a concerto for trumpet and two oboes in D (Fasch Werke Verzeichnis [Fwv] number L:D 1) and featured trumpets in several of his orchestral suites, such as a suite for two trumpets in D major (Fwv K:D 3), two suites for three trumpets and winds in D major (Fwv K:D 1 and 2), and two suites for two trumpets, oboes, and bassoons in D major (Fwv K:D 3 and 4).

Feldtrompeter. (Ger.) Field trumpeter, or military trumpeter.

felt mute. A piece of felt or cloth placed over the bell to soften the sound as an alternative to the **derby mute.** A felt bag from a bottle of Crown Royal Canadian whiskey is often used as a substitute. (See appendix 3.)

Ferguson, Maynard (1928–2006). Canadian jazz trumpeter and bandleader known for exceptional high-register playing. He studied piano and violin before switching to the trumpet at the age of nine. At the age of thirteen, Ferguson performed as a soloist with the Canadian Broadcasting Corporation (CBC) Orchestra and was heard frequently on the CBC, notably featured on a *Serenade for Trumpet in Jazz* written for him by Morris Davis. Ferguson won a scholarship to the Conservatoire de musique du Québec à Montréal, where he studied from 1943 through 1948 with Bernard Baker. Following professional work in Canada, he moved to the United States, where he worked with Stan Kenton between 1950 and 1953 and in Hollywood studio orchestras until 1956, when he went to New York to form his own fourteen-piece band called Birdland Dream Band.

In the mid-1960s Ferguson primarily led a sextet. After a brief sojourn in India, he settled temporarily in England in 1968. As a Canadian citizen he was not subject to the union ban on musicians from the United States in force at the time. He established a British jazz-rock fusion band and toured widely in Europe and the United States while achieving success on the pop charts with a recording of Jim Webb's "MacArthur Park." Ferguson lived in New York in 1973 and then in Ojai, California, where he gradually replaced the British band members with younger American musicians and reduced the band's size. He attained further success in the late 1970s with Bill Conti's "Gonna Fly Now," the theme song from the film *Rocky*. The combination of Ferguson's bravura trumpet playing with disco rhythms exerted wide influence in jazz education circles in the 1970s. Ferguson led a group in the mid-1980s that in 1987 became a septet, High Voltage, which played in a fusion style. He then established his Big Bop Nouveau Band, with which he toured extensively and recorded into the late 1990s.

Ferguson was noted for his exceptional command of the trumpet's highest register, and for his ability to play a number of different brass instruments—trumpet, french horn, trombone, euphonium—competently during a single performance; he also designed and played the "firebird," a combination valve trumpet and "**slide trumpet**" (soprano trombone), and the "superbone" (a combination valve and slide tenor trombone). Although Ferguson was not known for his improvisational abilities, he has inspired many young trumpeters with his dazzling instrumental proficiency and spawned many imitators. His library of band arrangements, music, and memorabilia reside at the Ferguson Music Library Collection of the University of North Texas's College of Music.

ferrule. A metal sleeve used to join together tubing on a brass instrument, sometimes elaborately decorated with **garnishing**. (See figure 30 under "**natural trumpet**.")

Fiala, Josef (1754–1816). Bohemian composer, oboist, and cellist. A friend of **Wolfgang Amadeus Mozart**, he worked as a kappellmeister and cellist in Donaueschingen toward the end of his career. Fiala composed a *Divertimento* for the **keyed trumpet** (or *klappentromba concertante*) and small orchestra at the turn of the nineteenth century. It is not known for whom the work was written. The manuscript resides in the National Museum of Prague.

field trumpet. A **bugle** pitched in E-flat, F, or G that is used as a military signal instrument similar to the **cavalry trumpet** in the nineteenth and early twentieth centuries. **John Philip Sousa** added parts for field trumpets in F in the trio of his *Semper Fidelis* march and also used them in *The Thunderer* and *Anchor and Star*.

finger holes. 1. The holes on a **cornett** or *cornetto*, which are used to finger the notes on the instrument.
2. An alternate term for **vent holes**.

finger hook. A curved piece of metal placed on the **leadpipe** of a trumpet or cornet after the third valve that is used to stabilize the playing position with the fourth finger (pinky) of the player's right hand. It can be used to assist in maintaining the position of the fingers over the valves, to keep the third finger from sliding off the

valve button, and to allow one-handed playing when the left hand is used for turning pages, inserting **mutes**, using a **plunger mute**, or executing the **wah-wah** effect on a **Harmon mute**.

finger ring. An alternate term for a **throw ring**.

Finger, Gottfried (Godfrey) (ca. 1660–1730). Moravian composer and viol player. Growing up in Olomouc (now in the Czech Republic), he was influenced by **Pavel Josef Vejvanovský** and later emigrated to England, where he entered the service of James II in 1687, working in the Catholic chapel. When James II went into exile in 1688, Finger remained in London and embarked on a freelance career. He left London in 1701 and by 1702 was working in the service of Queen of Prussia, Sophie Charlotte in Berlin. He later worked in Breslau, Innsbruck, Heidelberg, and Mannheim. A contemporary of **Henry Purcell**, Finger wrote for the **flat trumpet** in music for the 1691 St. Cecilia Day celebrations in London, and wrote several solo trumpet works including a series of sonatas in C for one or two trumpets.

fingering. The numerical notation used to indicate **valve combinations** for specific pitches. The numbers refer to the position of the **valve** in relation to the mouthpiece, with the valve closest to the mouthpiece as "1" and the second as "2." If two or more valves are pressed simultaneously, a plus sign (+) or a comma is often written between the numbers (1+2). The system can also be applied to instruments with keys and **finger holes**.

fingering chart. A chart showing the **fingering** for every note in the complete range of an instrument as well as **alternate fingerings**. (See figure 20.)

Figure 20. Fingering chart for a B-flat trumpet. *Elisa Koehler.*

Finke, Helmut (1923–2009). German trumpeter and brass instrument manufacturer. He served in the German army during the Second World War and was badly wounded in Russia in 1943. After the war he studied engineering and joined the Herford Symphony Orchestra, playing second trumpet to **Walter Holy**. In 1950 he bought a second-hand turning lathe and began to make mouthpieces and perform brass repair work, and eventually built his first trumpet from used parts. His workshop expanded in 1954 and, encouraged by Wilhem Ehmann, he started to make copies of sackbuts and **natural trumpets**. In 1959 he worked with **Otto Steinkopf** to add **vent holes** to a coiled **natural trumpet** that resembled the *jägertrompete* held by **Gottfried Reiche** in the famous portrait by Hausmann. The instrument was known as the **Steinkopf-Finke trumpet** and was used by Walter Holy in early **period instrument** performances in 1960 with the Capella Colonienis (the chamber orchestra of the radio station in Cologne), a group with which Finke played as well. His brass instrument workshop continued to expand to include production of modern **horns** and low brass instruments.

Fiske, Isaac (1820–1894). American cornetist, bandmaster, and brass instrument manufacturer. Working in Worcester, Massachusetts, from 1842 until 1887, he obtained five American patents for improvements in valved brass instruments between 1866 and 1873. Most of his instruments were made with **rotary valves**, but he also made instruments with **Vienna valves**, keys, and **Périnet piston valves**. The most distinctive of his designs was a triangular arrangement of three string-linkage rotary valves operated by rods passing through cylinders containing coil return springs. This type of arrangement was also patented by Joseph Higham in England in 1857. Almost all Fiske's instruments were made of nickel silver. Fiske was acclaimed one of the finest makers of **cornets** in the United States by **Harvey B. Dodworth**, and **Matthew Arbuckle**, who was the cornet soloist with Fiske's own band. His business continued in spite of a disastrous fire in 1854, and on his retirement in 1887 the business was sold to the C. G. **Conn** Company.

fl., flz., flut. (abbr.) **Flutter tongue.**

Fladdergrob. (Ger.) The lowest part (sixth part) of a seventeenth-century **trumpet ensemble** as described by **Praetorius**, which was occasionally added to sound the **fundamental** (C2). The origin of the term is presumably onomatopoeic.

flat trumpet, flatt trumpet. A **slide trumpet** used in seventeenth-century England that was primarily associated with the music of **Henry Purcell** and sometimes called the "flatt" trumpet. The instrument gets its name from the fact that it usually played in minor keys, which were often referred to as "flatt keys." Its slide mechanism moved toward the back of the instrument (a U-shaped double slide) rather than the front, like a trombone. (See

figure 21.) Purcell's best-known composition for the flat trumpet is the *Funeral Music for Queen Mary.*

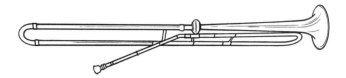

Figure 21. Flat trumpet. *Drawing by T. M. Larsen.*

Flatterzunge. (Ger.) **Flutter tongue.**

flexibility. The ability to perform **lip slurs** and **lip trills** with control and ease. A vital skill for good brass playing, flexibility results from an efficient **embouchure**, effective **breathing**, and appropriate **tongue placement**.

Flicorno. (It.) **Flugelhorn.**

flugelhorn. A high brass instrument pitched in B-flat with the same length of tubing as a trumpet, but with a wide conical **bore** and a larger **bell**. While most flugelhorns have three **valves**, some instruments are made with four to take advantage of the flugelhorn's dark, low register. Mouthpieces for flugelhorns commonly feature a deep cup or funnel design. Contemporary jazz trumpeters routinely double on the flugelhorn, most notably **Clark Terry**, **Art Farmer**, and **Freddie Hubbard**. **Chuck Mangione** popularized the flugelhorn with his 1977 crossover hit, "Feels So Good." Flugelhorn parts appear in Igor Stravinsky's *Threni*, Vaughan Williams's *Symphony No. 9*, and *Three Movements* by Heitor Villa-Lobos. Trumpeters sometimes use a flugelhorn to perform the **posthorn** solo from Mahler's *Symphony No. 3* and some high horn parts in cantatas by **J. S. Bach**. (See figure 22.)

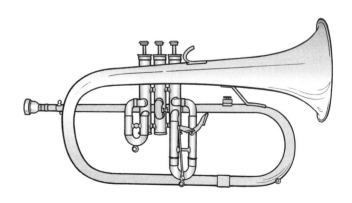

Figure 22. Flugelhorn. *Drawing by T. M. Larsen.*

flumpet. A hybrid instrument between a trumpet and flugelhorn developed by David **Monette** in 1989 for **Art Farmer**, who used it for performances of **Joseph Haydn**'s *Trumpet Concerto*. The instrument has also been used by **Charles Schlueter** to perform the **posthorn** solo from Mahler's Third Symphony.

flutter tonguing. A unique **articulation** where a trumpeter rolls the tip of the tongue while blowing as if pronouncing a rolled *R*. This technique appears frequently in twentieth-century **avant-garde** music as well as jazz, where it is descriptively called a **growl** and is produced by a player's vocal cords rather than the tongue. The growl is often performed with a **plunger mute** to create a distinctive sound. Musicians who are physically unable to roll their *R*s can substitute growling for flutter tonguing. Classical repertoire that calls for flutter tonguing includes Gershwin's *Rhapsody in Blue*, **Jolivet**'s *Concertino* and *Heptade*, Milhaud's *Creation of the World*, Ravel's *Piano Concerto in G*, and Shostakovich's Symphony No. 7 (Leningrad). Indications for flutter tonguing in musical notation appear as either symbols (three diagonal lines beneath a note, like a string tremolo) or as abbreviations (**fl., flz., flut.**).

Forestier, Joseph (1815–1882). French cornetist, trumpeter, and French horn player. He started out on the horn and studied **hand-stopping** technique with Jean-François Dauprat at the Paris Conservatory between 1832 and 1834. He later switched to the early version of the **cornet**, which was pitched in F (an octave about the horn) and used a funnel-shaped **mouthpiece** that was similar to that of the horn. He was the solo cornetist at the Théâtre Italien and the Paris Opera between 1844 and 1868. Forestier switched to the valved trumpet later in his career. He taught at the Gymnase Musical Militaire in 1856 and taught cornet to the military musicians at the Paris Conservatory between 1857 and 1870. He wrote one of the first methods for the cornet in 1844 and published *Méthode Complète pur les Saxhorns ou Bugles ou Saxotromba ou Trombone alto à trios cylindres* in 1846. Forestier published one of the first solos for cornet and piano, *Fantasie Brilliante*, in 1840 (it was jointly composed with "Mademoiselle J. Luce"). His other solo compositions for the cornet include *Variations concertantes sur un theme original* (published in his 1844 cornet method), twenty more solos and duets with piano accompaniment, and twelve duets for cornet and ophicleide.

Foveau, Eugène (1886–1957). French cornetist and trumpeter. He studied with **Merri Franquin** at the Paris Conservatory, and won first prize in the school's trumpet competition upon graduation in 1907. Foveau began his playing career in 1899 as a **cornet** soloist with the Union Musicale in Dijon. He later served as cornet soloist in the First Régiment du Génie in Versailles (1907–1910), as **flugelhorn** soloist with the Sirène de Paris, and as soloist with the Garde Républicaine (1919–1937). Foveau recorded several cornet solos for the Odeon label in the early twentieth century. He played trumpet with the Concerts Colonne between 1911 and 1914 and again after the First World War from 1919 to 1929. Foveau was the solo cornetist at the Paris Opera between 1919 and 1957. In the early 1930s he recorded several of the major works of Igor Stravinsky for the Columbia label with the composer conducting, notably the cornet part in *The Soldier's Tale*. As a teacher, Foveau served as the cornet professor at the Paris Conservatory between 1925 and 1957; he also taught trumpet beginning in 1943. Many of his students became leading French soloists, orchestral trumpeters, and teachers; these include Roger Delmotte, Ludovic Valliant (to whom **Tomasi** dedicated his trumpet concerto), Raymond Sarabich (who later taught **Maurice Andre**), and **Pierre Thibaud**. He endorsed **Couesnon** cornets during his career and also performed on cornets by Lefèvre and trumpets by Millereau.

Franquin, Merri (1848–1934). French trumpeter and pedagogue. Beginning at the age of fifteen he taught himself to play the **cornet** during a four-year period (1863–1867). He earned a position as a cornetist with the Marseille Casino Musical in 1867 and as solo cornetist with the Palais Lyrique and the Theatre Chave. In 1870 he joined the Marseille Garde Nationale as solo flugelhornist. In 1872, at the age of twenty-three, Franquin entered the Paris Conservatory, where he studied with **Arban** until 1875 and then with Jacques Hippolyte Maury (1834–1881) until 1877. After graduation in 1877, Franquin embarked on a stellar career as an orchestral trumpeter and advocated for the use of the modern trumpet in C in place of the six-foot valve trumpet in F (the **long F trumpet**) in the orchestra. He performed as first trumpet with virtually every major orchestra in Paris, including the Concerts Populaires Pasdeloup (1876–1892), the National Opera in Paris (1880–1901), Concerts Colonne (1884–1892), and the Opéra Comique.

As a teacher, Franquin served as professor of trumpet at the Paris Conservatory from 1894 until 1925. He published his *Méthode Complète de Trompette Moderne, Cornet à Pistons et de Bugle* [flugelhorn], *théorique et practique* in 1908 and reinvigorated the conservatory's trumpet class, which had languished in the shadow of the cornet class during the tenure of his predecessor, **Jules Cerclier**. Franquin also inspired composers to write an unprecedented number of solo works for the trumpet as competition pieces (*morceau de concours*), notably Georges Enescu (1881–1955), who composed *Legende* (1906) for him. Franquin's *Méthode* was the first work of its kind for the modern trumpet. His pedagogy anticipates the modern warm-up and maintenance routines of

James Stamp and **Carmine Caruso** by prescribing extensive work with long tones and soft attacks, and by emphasizing the physicality of brass playing. The subtitle of his "Principles of Study" summarizes Franquin's philosophy: "Work much; tire little; in other words, always rest before the lips are tired." Some of Franquin's most famous students were **Georges Mager, Eugene Foveau,** and Julien Porret; fifty-nine of his students won first prize in the conservatory's trumpet competitions during his thirty-one-year tenure (compared to nine during Cerclier's twenty-four-year tenure).

Franquin was also involved in the adoption of **high-pitched trumpets** and with innovations in modern trumpet design. He worked with the French instrument maker **Thibouville-Lamy** to develop a four-valve trumpet in C and D in 1912 and a five-valve trumpet that could play in four different keys (C, D, D-flat, and B-natural) in 1916. Both of these instruments employed **ascending valves**. Franquin required all of his students to play on these instruments as well as the larger long F trumpet. He also wrote the entries on the trumpet and the cornet in Albert Lavignac's *Encyclopédie de la musique et Dictionnaire du Conservatoire* (1920–1931). Franquin was largely responsible (along with **Théo Charlier**) for the rehabilitation of the trumpet as a solo instrument at the turn of the twentieth century; he exerted a seminal influence on modern brass pedagogy.

French theatre pitch, French pitch. A **pitch standard** used in eighteenth-century France where A4 ranged between 388 and 392 Hz.

frequency. The number of times per second that a cycle of sound vibrations is repeated to produce a specific pitch. The unit of measurement for frequency is the **Hertz** (Hz).

Friedrich, Reinhold (b. 1958). German trumpeter. A versatile artist comfortable with both **period instruments** and **avant-garde** modernism, he began playing the trumpet at the age of seven, and his first teachers were Lutz Köhler, Heinz Burum, and Adolf Weresch. Friedrich studied with **Edward Tarr** in Karlsruhe between 1979 and 1986, including work on the **natural trumpet** and the **keyed trumpet**. He also studied with **Pierre Thibaud** in Paris (1982–1983). Between 1983 and 2002 Friedrich served as principal trumpet of the Frankfurt Radio Symphony Orchestra. In addition to his orchestral career, Friedrich launched his solo career by winning the first prize in the ARD International Competition in Munich in 1986, and appeared as soloist with several orchestras including the BBC Symphony, the Concertgebouw Orchestra of Amsterdam, the Berlin Baroque Soloists, and many others. An advocate of new music, Friedrich has premiered and commissioned works by John Cage, Wolfgang Rihm, Herbert Willi, and many others. He has also produced several acclaimed recordings, including a disc of concerti by **Haydn, Hummel,** and Michele Puccini (Giacomo's father) on the keyed trumpet. In addition to performing and recording, Friedrich began teaching at the Karlsruhe Hochschule für Musik in 1989, and many of his students have garnered prizes at international competitions.

Frink, Laurie (1951–2013). American trumpeter and pedagogue. She studied at the University of Nebraska as well as with several private teachers, including **Jimmy Maxwell**, and began a freelance career in New York City in the 1970s. Her diverse career included performing for several Broadway shows, radio broadcasts, television shows, and film soundtracks as well as guest performances with artists such as the Talking Heads, David Bowie, and David Sanborn. She played lead trumpet with several noted bandleaders including Benny Goodman, Gerry Mulligan, Mel Lewis, Bob Mintzer, John Hollenbeck, Dave Liebman, Andrew Hill, Kenny Wheeler, and Maria Schneider. Known for her versatility, Frink also played with the Manhattan Brass Quintet, the Saturday Brass Quintet, the Gramercy Park Brass, and Concordia. Considered the foremost authority and teacher of the methods of **Carmine Caruso**, her private studio attracted professional brass players from around the world. Her personable style and warm humanity contributed to Frink's success as a clinician, lecturer, and conductor, and she was well known for her expertise in diagnosing and correcting physical difficulties associated with brass playing. She taught at several institutions including the New England Conservatory, the Manhattan School of Music, New York University, the New School University, and the State University of New York at Purchase. Together with John McNeil, Frink coauthored *Flexus: Trumpet Calisthenics for the Modern Improviser* (Gazong Press, 2009).

frullato. (It.) **Flutter tongue.**

fundamental. The lowest note and foundational pitch of the **harmonic overtone series**.

fusus. A type of shell used as a trumpet that is longer and thinner than the common **strombus** shell and shaped more like a spindle than a spiral.

Gabbard, Krin (b. 1948). American cultural analyist, jazz historian, and amateur trumpeter. He played the cornet in his school band as a child, but gave it up in college to pursue a career in comparative literature and media studies. He began teaching in the Comparative Literature Department at the State University of New York in Stony Brook in 1981. Taking up the trumpet as an adult **comeback player** after establishing an academic career, Gabbard published *Hotter Than That: The Trumpet, Jazz, and American Culture* in 2008. His theory that the high-energy style of jazz trumpeters symbolizes an assertion of male sexuality—a concept he labeled "phallic playing"—has been disputed by female trumpeters.

Gabriel. An archangel who appears in the Bible as a messenger from God and is commonly associated with the trumpet in western culture. Biblical references to Gabriel never mention the trumpet (Daniel 8:15–26 and 9:21–27; Luke 1:11–38). Gabriel's connection to the trumpet perhaps grew from the instrument's signaling function and association with royalty in medieval times. The first depiction of Gabriel with a trumpet in visual art appeared in an Armenian illuminated manuscript dated 1455 that currently resides in the Walters Art Museum in Baltimore. The first literary reference to Gabriel playing the trumpet on the day of judgment appears in John Milton's *Paradise Lost* (1667). Similar references appear in several African American spirituals, including "In Dat Great Gittin' Up Mornin'." Marc Connelly's play based on spirituals, *The Green Pastures* (1930), depicts Gabriel with his trumpet constantly at his side, and the Lord has to warn him not to blow it too soon. Other references include the song "Blow, Gabriel, Blow," from Cole Porter's musical *Anything Goes* (1934), which features a trumpet solo in the orchestration, and **Wynton Marsalis**'s 1996 album of Baroque trumpet music titled "In Gabriel's Garden."

In the Catholic Church, Gabriel is considered a saint and his feast day is September 29th (the Feast of the Archangels: Michael, Gabriel, and Raphael), which is known in the Church of England as Michaelmas. He is the patron saint of messengers and postal workers as well as those who work in the fields of broadcasting and telecommunications. In Islamic tradition, Gabriel (Jibra'il) is also considered an archangel and is credited with delivering the Quran to the prophet Muhammad as well as serving as a messenger. In the realm of science, a mathematical figure invented by Evangelista Torricelli (1608-1647) was given the modern name "Gabriel's Horn"; it is a paradoxical solid of revolution that has infinite surface area, but finite volume.

Galpin Society. An organization dedicated to **organology** founded in 1946 to carry on the work of Francis William Galpin (1858–1945), a pioneering English scholar and collector of musical instruments and canon of Chelmsford Cathedral. Dedicated to the publication of original research into the history, development, construction, and use of musical instruments, the Galpin Society publishes an annual journal and hosts visits to museums and private instrument collections.

Gambati, Alessandro (1800–1867). Italian trumpeter. An early proponent of the **keyed trumpet**, he performed throughout Italy with his brother Antonio (dates unknown) in the 1820s, as well as in Paris and London. Together they were known as the Gambati Brothers. In Paris they performed at the Opéra Italien (1826–1828), the Paris Opéra, and Académie Royale (1827–1828). They also performed on early valved trumpets and played in the orchestra for the premiere of Meyerbeer's opera, *Robert le diable*, on the new instruments. By 1829 they were performing at King's Theater in London. Alessandro Gambati came to the United States in 1833 to perform with the Italian Opera Company in New York City and remained in the country for the rest of his life. No longer playing the keyed trumpet by this time, Gambati specialized in the 1830s in playing operatic airs with variations on a trumpet with two **Stölzel valves**.

Gambati is best known for a well-documented "trumpet battle" with English trumpeter **John Norton** that took place at Niblo's Garden in New York City on August 22, 1834. Because Norton specialized in the **English slide trumpet** and Gambati did not, the instrument chosen for both to play in the contest was a "simple trumpet" (**natural trumpet** without a slide or valves). Although the contest was a publicity stunt and widely considered a draw, Norton was declared the winner and was perhaps more comfortable playing a natural trumpet, an instrument with a playing technique more similar to an English slide trumpet than that of Gambati's valved trumpet. A rematch was discussed, but never materialized. Norton and Gambati performed together in New Orleans in 1835 and eventually became friends. Gambati performed as a soloist in New Orleans in the 1830s and returned to perform at Niblo's Garden in later years; he performed in a benefit concert for Norton in 1838. Gambati eventually settled in Charleston, South Carolina, and switched from the valved trumpet to the cornet. A poster from March 1862 advertised that "Sig. Gambati" performed at "A Patriotic Music Festival" in Hibernian Hall.

Gansch, Hans (b. 1953). Austrian trumpeter. He began playing the trumpet at the age of eleven and studied with Franz Veigl at the Bruckner Conservatory in Linz, graduating with distinction in 1976. Gansch served as principal trumpet of the Austrian Radio Orchestra from 1976 until 1982, when he became principal trumpet of the Vienna State Opera Orchestra and the Vienna Philharmonic. He left Vienna in 1996 to become professor of trumpet at the Mozarteum in Salzburg, where his students have included Guiliano Sommerhalder and David Guerrier. Gansch has also performed with the German Brass, Pro Brass, Austrian Brass Connection, and the Ober Österreich Brass Band. His younger brother is **Thomas Gansch** of **Mnozil Brass**.

Gansch, Thomas (b. 1975). Austrian trumpeter. The younger brother of **Hans Gansch**, he studied with Joseph Pomberger between 1991 and 1994 and with Adolf Holler at the University for Music and Performing Arts in Vienna between 1994 and 1997. During his student years he performed on a substitute basis with the Vienna Symphony, the Vienna State Opera Orchestra, and the Austrian Radio Symphony Orchestra in addition to performing other musical styles like jazz, **avant-garde**, and folk music. In 1992 he was one of the co-founders of **Mnozil Brass** and continues to perform as first trumpet with the group. He has also performed and recorded with Pro Brass, the

Vienna Art Orchestra (1998–2006), and his own combo, Gansch & Roses. He performs on a unique trumpet, the **Ganschhorn**, which he developed in collaboration with Karl **Schagerl**. Known for his stylistic versatility, comedic timing, and dynamic stage presence, Gansch received the Hans Koller Jazz Award for "Newcomer of the Year" in 2002.

Ganschhorn. A unique trumpet in B-flat built with **rotary valves** in a vertical position and a bell section that curves down near the valve section and terminates with an upward slant. Designed by **Thomas Gansch** in collaboration with Karl **Schagerl**, it combines the smooth sound of a rotary valve trumpet with the direct and fast response of a **piston valve** instrument.

Ganter. German brass instrument manufacturer. Ganter made **rotary valve trumpets** in the twentieth century and went out of business in the early 1990s. Some prominent Ganter trumpet models were the G3, G3a (with third valve **trigger**), G5 (with a brass **bell**), G6 (gold brass bell, without a **garland**), and the G7.

garland. A metal strip on the outside of the **bell** flare used for reinforcement and decoration. On a **natural trumpet**, it also bears the **maker's mark** and signature.

garnishing. Elaborate decoration or engraving on a **ferrule** or **garland** of a brass instrument.

Gekker, Christopher (b. 1954). American trumpeter. Born in Washington, DC, he grew up in Alexandria, Virginia, and studied with Emerson Head, Sidney Mear, Adel Sanchez, and Gerard Schwarz. He earned degrees from the Eastman School of Music and the University of Maryland and went on to perform with the **American Brass Quintet** for eighteen years. Gekker was principal trumpet with the Orchestra of St Luke's and frequently performed and recorded as principal with the Orpheus Chamber Orchestra, and often as a guest with the Chamber Music Society of Lincoln Center. He has been featured as soloist throughout the United States, Europe, and Asia, and appears as soloist on more than twenty recordings and as an ensemble performer on more than one hundred chamber music, orchestra, and jazz recordings. He has served on the faculties of the Juilliard School, the Manhattan School of Music, Columbia University, and has been a professor of trumpet at the University of Maryland School of Music since 1999. A strong advocate of new trumpet repertoire, Gekker has premiered several works by **Eric Ewazen**. He has published several pedagogical works including *Articulation Studies, 44 Duos, Endurance Drills for Performance Skills*, and *Fifteen Studies for Piccolo Trumpet*, all available from **Charles Colin** Music.

gerader zink. (Ger.) Straight **cornett**.

gestopft, gest. (Ger.) Stopped. This indication appears in orchestral trumpet and horn parts by Gustav Mahler, Richard Strauss, and Richard Wagner to mean a particular kind of **hand-stopping**. It does not indicate the use of a **mute**. There are two different methods used to perform the technique. The first one involves placing the rim of the **bell** in the middle of the player's left hand (palm) and folding the fingers inside the bell (the bell is partially open). The second method requires the player to place the rim of the bell on the base of the left hand (palm) and cover the bell with the fingers (cupping the hand inside the bell). Both methods flatten the pitch of the trumpet. To make the printed note sound properly, it is necessary to **transpose** up one half step (or whole step) to compensate when using either hand-stopping technique. The second method (cupped fingers covering the bell) reduces the volume and stability of the pitch more than the first method (fingers inside the partially-open bell). Some representative passages marked *gestopft* include Mahler's Second Symphony (Mvt. I , Mvt. V), Strauss's *Til Eulenspiegel's lustige Streiche*, and Wagner's *Götterdämmerung* (Act I). (See appendix 3.)

Getzen. American brass instrument manufacturer. The firm was established in 1939 by Anthony James (T. J.) Getzen (1894–1968) in Elkhorn, Wisconsin, as an instrument repair shop. Getzen began producing student brass instruments in 1946 and expanded in 1960 by absorbing the holdings of the Hoosier Band Instrument Company of Elkhart, Indiana. The company gained prominence with the "Eterna" line of trumpets in the 1960s, and **Doc Severinsen** served as vice president for Research and Development between 1969 and 1980. Getzen's son, Donald Earl (b. 1928), branched off from the family business in 1965 to create DEG Music Products. Getzen's other son, Robert, founded Allied Music Corporation (AMC) in 1959 and Allied Music Supply Company (AMSC) in 1967. Robert's sons, Edward and Thomas Getzen, founded the Edwards Band Instrument Company in 1988 and focused on producing high-quality trumpets and trombones. These firms rescued the Getzen Company from bankruptcy in 1991.

Geyer, Charles (b. 1944). American trumpeter and pedagogue. He studied with Herbert Stoskopf, **Adolph Herseth**, and Vincent Cichowicz, and graduated from Northwestern University. He has appeared as a soloist with major orchestras and festivals as well as Music of the Baroque, Chicago Chamber Musicians, and Grand Teton Music Festival. A frequent recitalist as well, he was formerly a member of the Eastman Brass, Eastman Virtuosi, Chicago Brass Quintet, and the Chicago Symphony, Grant Park Symphony, Houston Symphony, and Lyric Opera of Chicago orchestras. Geyer has recorded and played on international broadcasts with the Chicago and Houston Symphony orchestras, as well as with the Eastman Brass, Music of the Baroque, and Chicago Chamber Musicians. He and his wife, **Barbara Butler**, have forged an extremely effective teaching partnership for more than thirty years, and many of their students have gone on to successful positions with major orchestras and other professional appointments. Geyer and Butler taught at the Eastman School of Music for eighteen years and at the Bienen School of Music at Northwestern University for fifteen years. They began teaching at the Shepherd School of Music at Rice University in July 2013.

Ghitalla, Armando (1925–2001). American trumpeter. Known for his beautifully lyrical playing, he was one of the first classical trumpet soloists in the United States. Ghitalla began playing the trumpet at the age of eight and studied with Joseph Gustat and Pattee Evenson. After graduating from high school in 1942, he enlisted in the navy and performed in a dance band during the war. He later used the G. I. Bill of Rights to attend Juilliard between 1946 and 1949 to study with **William Vacchiano**. His orchestral playing career began in 1948 with the New York Opera and the New York City Ballet Orchestras. He also performed with the Band of America directed by Paul LaValle. Ghitalla became principal trumpet of the Houston Symphony in 1949 and left in 1951 to become second trumpet of the Boston Symphony Orchestra (**Roger Voisin** was principal) and principal trumpet of the Boston Pops Orchestra. He left his position with the Pops in 1964 and became principal trumpet of the Boston Symphony in 1965, staying in that position until his retirement in 1979. During his career, Ghitalla performed mostly on a **Vincent Bach** C trumpet converted by William Tottle (ca. 1900–1976) to a four-valve C/D system patterned after the **Thibouville-Lamy** instrument played by Roger Voisin.

As a soloist, Ghitalla was one of the first to present professional trumpet recitals, most notably at New York's Town Hall in 1958 when he gave the North American premiere of the **Hummel** concerto. He played a recital in Carnegie Hall in 1960 and made the first solo recordings of trumpet concerti by Hummel, **Oskar Böhme**, and **Ponchielli**. He also recorded **Molter**'s *Concerto No. 2 in D*, cantatas by **Bach** and **Scarlatti**, and an album of contest solos for the Music Minus One series. Harold Farberman (b. 1929) wrote *Double Concerto for a Single Trumpet* for Ghitalla and the Boston Pops in 1957; it was an early **crossover** piece that alternated between jazz and classical styles. Ghitalla performed on Roger Voisin's recording series, *Music for Trumpet and Orchestra*, in the early 1960s, as well as recordings by the New England Brass Ensemble led by Voisin. He also recorded with the Boston Symphony Chamber Players, notably a 1975 disc featuring Stravinsky's *A Soldier's Tale*.

Ghitalla's legacy as a teacher includes serving on the faculties of Boston University, the New England Conservatory of Music, the Hartt School of Music, and the Tanglewood Institute. He replaced Clifford Lillya (1910–1998) as professor of trumpet at the University of Michigan (UM) in 1979 when he retired from the BSO. He retired from UM in 1993 and taught at Rice University's Shepherd School of Music until his death in 2001. Some of Ghitalla's notable students were **Timothy Morrison, Rolf Smedvig**, **David Hickman**, and Robert Sullivan (b. 1961). His many honors include the Alumni Teaching Award and Haugh Teaching Award from the University of Michigan, and an honorary doctorate from Illinois Wesleyan University.

gig bag. A soft case made of leather or nylon with internal padding designed for lightweight transport and storage of musical instruments.

Gillespie, John Birks "Dizzy" (1917–1993). American jazz trumpeter. Considered one of the leading musicians in **Bebop** and Afro-Cuban jazz, Gillespie taught himself to play the trombone and the trumpet at the age of twelve and was inspired to play jazz after hearing **Roy Eldridge** on the radio. His distinctive style of playing with puffed cheeks developed from his attempts to imitate Eldridge's playing. He earned a scholarship to study with Shorty Hall at the Lauringburg Technical Institute in North Carolina (a historic African American preparatory school) in 1933 and left school in 1935 at the age of eighteen to embark on a professional career. In 1936 he was hired to work in Frankie Fairfax's band in Philadelphia, where he played alongside Charlie Shavers and earned the nickname "Dizzy" for his fun-loving personality on and off the bandstand. He moved to New York in 1937, where he played with Teddy Hill's Orchestra for two years. Gillespie joined Cab Calloway's Band in 1939 and formed a close friendship with saxophonist Charlie Parker in 1940. His unconventional solos and penchant for practical jokes increasingly created friction with Calloway, which culminated in a famous fight that resulted in Gillespie leaving the band.

Gillespie played with several artists in the early 1940s including Ella Fitzgerald, Benny Carter, Fletcher Henderson, Lucky Millinder, and Earl Hines. His style began to evolve into what would become known as **Bebop**, featuring adventurous harmonies, complex rhythms, extended virtuosity, and impressive accuracy at blistering speed. Gillespie made one of his earliest Bebop recordings, "Woody 'n' You," in February 1944 with Coleman Hawkins. Later that year he played in Billy Eckstine's orchestra along with Charlie Parker, Dexter Gordon, and Art Blakey. Although Parker and Gillespie's artistry exerted a profound impact on jazz, they did not perform together very often because of differing artistic

agendas. Some of Gillespie's most acclaimed Bebop recordings include "Groovin' High," "Salt Peanuts," and "A Night in Tunisia." Gillespie's music began to show Afro-Cuban influences in the late 1940s when he began working with the Cuban percussionist Chano Pozo, which resulted in recordings such as "Cubana Be/Cubana Bop" and "Manteca" in 1947.

The 1950s witnessed Gillespie's return to small combo work. According to his autobiography, it was in 1953 that a dancer accidentally tripped over his trumpet and bent the bell. Gillespie liked the way the trumpet sounded with the bell bent upward by a forty-five degree angle and subsequently had trumpets built for him by **King** and **Schilke** in that design, which became his trademark.

As his celebrity grew, Gillespie was invited by the U.S. State Department to tour internationally as a cultural ambassador with a band organized by Quincy Jones in 1956. He performed with a sextet in the 1960s and 1970s and helped launch the careers of several jazz musicians, including James Moody, Lalo Shifrin, Jimmy Heath, and **Lee Morgan**. His two protégés were John Faddis and **Arturo Sandoval**. Gillespie achieved the status of a living legend in the 1980s and made guest appearances on television shows such as *The Muppet Show*, *Sesame Street*, and *The Cosby Show*. He published his autobiography, *To Be or Not to Bop*, in 1979 and formed the United Nations Orchestra to showcase talented young jazz musicians in 1989. After missing a Carnegie Hall tribute for his seventy-fifth birthday due to poor health in November 1992, Gillespie lost a battle with pancreatic cancer in January 1993.

With his puffed cheeks, stylish beret, goatee, horn-rimmed glasses, infectious enthusiasm, and distinctive trumpet with the upturned bell, Gillespie was an iconic figure of jazz recognized internationally even by those who were not fans of the idiom. He was one of the most innovative musicians in jazz history and exerted a broad cultural influence. Gillespie earned numerous awards and honors during his career. He was inducted into the Big Band Hall of Fame (1982), received a star on Hollywood's Walk of Fame, and was crowned as a traditional chief in Nigeria, and the French government made him *Commandeur de l'Ordre des Arts et des Lettres*. President George H. W. Bush presented him with the National Medal of Arts in 1989 and recognized his achievements in the Kennedy Center Honors in 1990. He also received a Grammy Lifetime Achievement Award (1989), ASCAP's Duke Ellington Award (1989), Sweden's Polar Music Prize (1993), and an honorary doctorate from the Berklee College of Music, and was named regent's professor at the University of California.

Gilmore, Patrick Sarsfield (1829–1892). Irish-American bandmaster, impresario, and composer. Regarded as the father of the modern concert band, Gilmore began his career as a **cornet** player in Ireland and immigrated to the United States in 1849 at the age of nineteen. He soon settled in the Boston area and became one of the prominent E-flat cornet soloists of the time. He later embarked on a successful career as a band conductor with the Suffolk Brass Band, the Boston Brigade Band, the Salem Brass Band, and the Charleston Band. As a pioneer in North American band music, Gilmore instituted the tradition of the outdoor Fourth of July concerts on the Boston Commons as well as a series of indoor concerts at the Boston Music Hall, both with the Salem Band. In 1858 he organized his own band, Gilmore's Band, which became part of the Twenty-Fourth Massachusetts Volunteer Regiment of the Union Army during the American Civil War.

As an impresario, Gilmore is best known for organizing two gigantic music festivals in Boston that were the largest musical events in the world at that time: the National Peace Jubilee of 1869 (organized to benefit the widows and orphans of the American Civil War and to celebrate the peace following the war) and the World Peace Jubilee of 1872 (celebrating the end of the Franco-Prussian War). A special coliseum was constructed for the National Peace Jubilee of 1869 that housed thirty thousand audience members, ten thousand chorus members, and a one-thousand-piece orchestra. Such forces performed a variety of popular and serious repertoire including Verdi's *Il Trovatore*, complete with one hundred Boston firemen striking anvils, a battery of cannon, chimes, church bells, a huge bass drum eight feet in diameter, and a colossal organ expressly built for the occasion. For the World Peace Jubilee in 1872, Gilmore presented an international lineup of twenty thousand performers including bands from England, France, Germany, and Ireland as well as the U.S. Marine Band, Johann Strauss Jr. and his orchestra from Vienna, and the German song composer Franz Abt.

Gilmore became the leader for the Twenty-Second Regiment Band of New York in 1873 and stayed with the band for nineteen years. It became the finest professional band in the United States and solidified the instrumentation of the modern concert band to include a complete array of woodwinds in addition to brass and percussion. The band presented over six hundred concerts at New York's Madison Square Garden, which became known as Gilmore's Garden. The band made several successful tours of the United States and Europe including fourteen summer seasons at Manhattan Beach and annual appearances at the St. Louis Exposition. When Gilmore died in 1892, many of Gilmore's band members joined the newly formed professional band under the direction of John Philip Sousa. As a composer, Gilmore's best-known work is the Civil War song "When Johnny Comes Marching Home," which originally appeared as part of *The Soldier's Return March* and was later

published separately under the pen name, Louis Lambert. He composed other Civil War songs including "The Voice of the Departed (Death's at the Door)" and "Good News from Home." He also wrote several marches and short instrumental pieces including the *22nd Regiment March* and *Salute to New York*.

Glantz, Harry (1896–1982). Ukrainian-American trumpeter. He was best known as principal trumpeter of the New York Philharmonic between 1924 and 1942, and with the NBC Symphony under Toscanini. His family immigrated to the United States when he was five years old. Although he was encouraged to play the violin, Glantz fell in love with the **cornet** at the age of eleven. He later took lessons with **Max Schlossberg,** Christian Rodenkirchen, and Gustav Heim. In 1915 he was invited to play first trumpet in the San Francisco Exposition Orchestra under the direction of Camille Saint-Saëns. This opportunity led to brief stints as principal trumpet with the Boston Symphony Orchestra and the Philadelphia Orchestra (between 1915 and 1917). During the First World War, he joined the U.S. Marine Band to avoid being drafted. Afterward, he was the principal trumpet of the New York Symphony Orchestra under Walter Damrosch between 1919 and 1922. Following a year as principal trumpet of the San Francisco Symphony, Glantz became principal trumpet of the New York Philharmonic in 1924 and remained with the orchestra until 1942, when he left to play principal trumpet for the NBC Symphony under Arturo Toscanini (1867–1957) until 1954. Glantz took up teaching after leaving NBC. Some of his notable students were **Bernard Adelstein,** Frank Kaderabek, Charlie Spivak, and **Charles Colin.**

glissando. A special effect used in jazz and commercial music that involves sliding up to or down from a given pitch. More idiomatic to keyboard and string instruments, where it is usually performed as a fast chromatic or diatonic scale, the glissando on brass instruments more commonly takes the form of a **rip** up to a note or a **fall** off of it or as a slow **smear.** The most famous glissando written for a wind instrument is found in the clarinet solo that opens Gershwin's *Rhapsody in Blue.*

Gordon, Claude (1916–1996). American trumpeter and pedagogue. Growing up in a musical family in Montana, his father was a clarinetist, composer, and conductor; his mother was a concert pianist. Gordon began playing the **cornet** at the age of five and progressed so rapidly that, three years later, he was a featured soloist at the age of eight with the Helena High School Band. His older brothers and sisters were also musical, and together the Gordon family performed as the staff orchestra for a local radio station under the direction of their father. With this early experience and support, Gordon began playing professionally in his teens and also began teaching cornet and accordion to private students. In 1936, at the age of twenty, Gordon became the protégé of **Herbert L. Clarke** and worked with him for the next nine years until Clarke's death in 1945. Gordon went on to enjoy a successful career in Los Angeles as a studio trumpeter and gained a reputation as "the trumpet player who never misses." He performed in studio orchestras for many popular live broadcast shows, including *Amos and Andy* and *I Love Lucy*, as well as for films and radio. He later appeared as a jazz soloist in the 1950s and formed his own big band in 1959.

As a teacher, Gordon emphasized physical conditioning, systematic practice, and wind power with the credo that "trumpet playing is a form of athletics." He published several method books that outlined his ideas including *Physical Approach to Elementary Brass Playing*, *Systematic Approach to Daily Practice*, *Daily Trumpet Routines*, *Tongue Level Exercises*, *Thirty Velocity Studies*, and *Brass Playing Is No Harder Than Deep Breathing*. Gordon also edited new publications of Herbert L. Clarke's method books and the **Saint-Jacome** method. Also involved in instrument and mouthpiece design, he worked with the **Benge** company and later developed a large bore (.470) trumpet with the **Selmer** company known as the Claude Gordon Trumpet. Legions of trumpeters traveled to Los Angeles to study with him during his lifetime as well as trombonists and horn players.

Gozzo, Conrad (1922–1964). American trumpeter. Growing up in Connecticut, his father was his first trumpet teacher. He began playing professionally in Isham Jones's band in 1938 and went on to perform with several other bands, including those led by Tommy Reynolds, Red Norvo, Claude Thornhill, and Benny Goodman. He joined the U.S. Navy in 1942, where he played in Artie Shaw's band during the Second World War. In 1945 he joined Woody Herman's First Herd and was featured as a soloist on *Stars Fell on Alabama*. As a noted lead player and studio musician, Gozzo moved to Los Angeles in 1947 and began working in television, radio, and film studios. He was the lead trumpeter on Bob Crosby's radio show (1947–1951) and recorded with numerous artists, including Frank Sinatra, Stan Kenton, Henry Mancini, Nelson Riddle, Rosemary Clooney, Peggy Lee, and Andy Williams. Gozzo also played on film soundtracks, such as *Ben Hur*, *Cleopatra*, *Bye Bye Birdie*, and *The Benny Goodman Story*. He recorded one solo album, *Goz the Great* (1955), and played the solo "A Trumpeter's Prayer" on the album *Tutti's Trumpets* (1957).

grob. (Ger.) Dirty, rough, coarse. Alternate term for the lowest part (usually a drone on C3) of the **natural trumpet** ensemble in the sixteenth century, as described by **Bendinelli** and **Fantini**. Occasionally an even lower part, labeled "*fladdergrob*" would be added to sound the **fundamental** (C2).

Gross, Joseph Arnold (1701–1784). German trumpeter and composer. He became a court trumpeter for the Elector of Bavaria in Munich in 1739 and was promoted in 1747 to *Spielgraf* for the Kurfürstentum Bavaria (Electorate of Bavaria) and the Oberpfalz (Upper Palatinate), a position similar to that of a modern union official who collected dues from musicians who weren't members of the local association for the right to perform at public functions such as weddings. Gross composed a trumpet concerto that was found in a collection from the court of Fulda (inventoried in 1788) that was acquired by the Library of Congress in 1910. The work is one of four trumpet concerti in the Fulda collection; the others are by **Joseph Riepel**, **Franz Xaver Richter**, and an anonymous composer (attributed to **Johann Stamitz**, but more likely by Johann Georg Holzbogen). American trumpeter Kevin Eisensmith (b. 1956) has suggested that Gross was the soloist for whom the four concerti were composed.

growl. A technique similar to **flutter tonguing** used in jazz during the swing era, often performed with a **plunger mute** in the lower range. It is produced by a player's vocal cords making a grinding sound rather than by the tongue, and is difficult to produce. Players who are physically unable to roll their *R*s to flutter tongue often use growling as a substitute. Masters of growl technique include James "Bubber" Miley (1903–1932), Charles "Cootie" Williams (1911–1985), and trombonist Joe "Tricky Sam" Nanton (1904–1946), who all played in Duke Ellington's band.

Guitbert trumpet. A **natural trumpet** discovered in the silt at the bottom of a well in a castle in the Dordonge region of France in the late twentieth century. The bell of the trumpet is dated 1442 and the inscription on the **garland** reads: MARCIAN GUITBERT [**maker's mark**] ME FIT A LIMOGES L'AN MIL CCCCXLII [Marcian Guibert made me at Limoges in the year 1442]. Made of seven detachable pieces, the trumpet can be configured as an S-shaped trumpet, like a Renaissance **slide trumpet** (see figure 18 under "slide trumpet"), or as a single-folded trumpet of more familiar shape with the first **bow** and the bell section crossing diagonally. It is the second-oldest surviving European trumpet next to the **Billingsgate trumpet**.

gusset. A triangular-shaped piece of metal used for reinforcement on the bell or slide of a brass instrument.

Güttler, Ludwig (b. 1943). German trumpeter and conductor. He learned to play the piano, organ, cello, accordion, and French horn before taking up the trumpet at the age of fourteen. He studied with Armin Männel at the Felix Mendelssohn-Bartholdy Hochschule in Leipzig between 1961 and 1965. Güttler became the principal trumpet of the Handel Festival Orchestra in Halle in 1965 and served as the principal trumpet of the Dresden Philharmonic and the Bach Orchestra of the Leipzig Gewandhaus from 1969 until 1980. He taught at the Carl Maria von Weber Musikhochschule in Dresden between 1969 and 1990. During most of his career, Güttler worked in what was then known as East Germany. He made numerous solo recordings in the 1970s and 1980s that were marketed in Europe and the United States after the reunification of Germany in the 1990s. The release of these recordings prompted the German Phono Academy of Hamburg to name Güttler "Discovery of the Year" in 1993. Güttler also championed the modern **corno da caccia** and made several recordings on that instrument as well. A conductor as well as a trumpeter, he founded the Ludwig Güttler Brass Ensemble in 1985 and later started both the Virtuosi Saxoniae Chamber Orchestra and the Leipzig Bach Collegium. In addition to his distinguished musical career, Güttler was awarded the Deutscher Stifterpreis in 1996 for his leadership of the efforts to rebuild Dresden's Frauenkirche, which was destroyed in the Second World War (restorations were completed in 2005).

H. In German *H* alone stands for B-natural. The German *B* is reserved for B-flat. Hence "Trompete in H" = "Trumpet in B (natural)." This practice descends from Renaissance hexachord theory in old notation where the "soft B" would be lowered (a flat) and a "hard B" would be raised (a natural). This system translates into the musical symbols for flats and naturals in use today; a flat looks like a lower-case "b" while a natural looks like a "hard" or square version of the "b," somewhat resembling a lowercase "h." This German convention also explains the "spelling" of Bach's name in musical notes, where "B–A–C–H" becomes "B-flat–A–C–B-natural."

Haas, Johann Wilhelm (1649–1723). German brass instrument maker. Descended from the most distinguished family of trumpet makers in **Nuremberg**, Haas was the clan's most illustrious member. It is likely that he apprenticed with **Hanns Hainlein**; he became a master in 1676. **Johann Ernst Altenburg** wrote in his 1795 treatise that trumpets by Haas were the best available at the time. Haas's trumpets were made in three different models with a variety of **garlands**, which most likely represented different purchase categories. The most elaborate models were made of silver with golden **ferrules** and with detailed engraving on the garlands as well as castings of angel heads with outstretched wings. Haas introduced a wider **bell flare** in his trumpets that was adopted by other trumpet makers in the late Baroque era. His youngest son, Wolf Wilhelm Haas (1681–1760), and his grandson, Ernst Johann Conrad Haas (1723–1792), carried on the business and used the same **maker's mark** on their instruments: the initials JWH [Latinized to "IWH"] and a leaping rabbit or hare (*hase*, which is German for "hare" resembles the family name). (See figure 35 under "maker's mark.") Variations in the turn of the rabbit's head (left or right) signify the identity of the maker, although some inconsistencies exist. Trumpets made by Wolf Wilhelm Haas generally depict the rabbit looking over its shoulder, to the right, while those made by his father show the rabbit looking forward, to the left. More than sixty instruments by the Haas family survive today.

hai lo. A **conch shell trumpet** used by boatmen and Buddist lamas in Tibet.

Hainlein, Hanns (1598–1671). German brass instrument maker. A member of a distinguished family of brass instrument craftsmen from **Nuremberg,** he was most likely the teacher of **Johann Wilhelm Haas.** Hainlein's trumpets featured a narrower **bell flare** than trumpets from the eighteenth century. The **maker's mark** on the **garland** of Hainlein's trumpets features the head of a hen (*hennelein*, which means "little hen" in old German, resembles the family name). (See figure 35 under "maker's mark.")

Halary (also known as Halari). French brass and woodwind instrument-manufacturing firm that flourished in Paris between 1804 and 1873. The workshop was established in 1804 by Jean Hilaire Asté (1775–1840), who adopted the name "Halary-Asté," or simply "Halary." Asté made **keyed bugles** (copied from **Haliday**'s design) and later patented the **ophecleide** in 1821. He also may have invented the **cornet**, although no patent was issued. In their **method books**, both **Joseph Forestier** and **François Dauverné** credit Halary (Asté) with applying **Stölzel valves** to the **posthorn** to create the cornet around 1831. Jean Louis Antoine (1788–1861) succeeded Asté in 1840 and used the name "Halari." His son Jules Léon Antoine (1827– after 1872) took control of the business after his father's death and sold the company to Coste & Cie in 1873. In addition to many other woodwind and brass instrument improvements, Jean Louis Antoine manufactured a kind of **disc valve** (*plaques tournantes*) for brass instruments that was similar to the design by **John Shaw**, but the mechanism was not as effective as **piston valves**.

Halbmond. (Ger.) Half moon. A crescent-shaped bugle or hunting horn commonly pitched in C at a length of approximately four feet. It was also known as the Hanoverian Bugle when used for military purposes in the late eighteenth century. (See figure 23.)

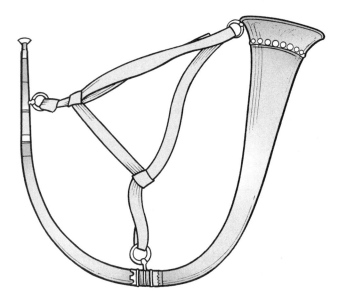

Figure 23. A semicircular bugle known as the *Halbmond. Drawing by T. M. Larsen.*

half-valve. A technique of jazz trumpet playing where one or more valves are pressed only halfway down to create a unique strangled sound. It is often used as part of a **fall** or a **horse whinny**, and sometimes appears in **avant-garde** music.

Haliday (Halliday), Joseph (1774–after 1857). Irish **keyed bugle** player and brass instrument inventor. While working as a bandmaster of the Cavan Militia in Dublin, Haliday took out a patent for the prototype of the keyed bugle. Many early keyed bugles are marked "Halliday Inventor" because the rights to the instrument, also known as the **Royal Kent Bugle**, were disputed between the Dublin dealer, Logier, and the Dublin maker, Matthew Pace.

Hall, Ernest (1890–1984). English trumpeter. He began playing the **cornet** at the age of fourteen at the Royal Court Theatre, Liverpool, and in 1910 he went on to study at the Royal College of Music with **Walter Morrow**. He played in the London Symphony Orchestra from 1912 to 1929, becoming principal trumpet in 1924, and in 1930 joined the BBC Symphony Orchestra, in which he played first trumpet until 1950. His broadcast of **Haydn**'s trumpet concerto in March 1932 was probably the first performance of the work in England. He taught the trumpet at the Royal College of Music from 1924 to 1960, and directed orchestral wind repertory classes there until 1970. Hall used a small-bore Brussels **Mahillon**

trumpet in B-flat and A (which had once belonged to his father) for most of his career, only changing to a Besson B-flat around 1945. His direct playing style featured a straight tone (without vibrato) and strict **articulation**, which contrasted markedly with the lyrical manner of his contemporary, **George Eskdale**. During his long teaching career, Hall exerted a strong influence on the modern English trumpet school; many professional players, both in the provinces and in London, were his students.

Hampel, Joseph Anton (1710–1771). German horn player who developed the technique of **hand-stopping.**

hand mute. An improvised muting effect using a cupped left hand over the bell in a manner similar to a **plunger mute**. (See appendix 3.)

hand vibrato. A technique commonly used in jazz trumpet playing where hands gently move the trumpet to simulate a wide vibrato with subtle variations of pressure on the lips.

Handel, George Frideric (1685–1759). German composer. The major differences between Handel's trumpet writing and that of **Johann Sebastian Bach** concern **range** and **endurance**. Handel's trumpet parts are generally lower and less virtuosic than Bach's, but they place more strenuous demands on a trumpeter's endurance with long passages of continuous playing. Handel's famous trumpet soloist, **Valentine Snow**, must have been an incredibly strong player. Some of Handel's most physically demanding trumpet parts appear in the overture to *Atalanta*, the *Dettingen Te Deum*, and *Music for the Royal Fireworks*. The *Suite in D* (HWV 341) for solo trumpet attributed to Handel is of doubtful authenticity. It was published in 1733 by Daniel Wright in London as "A Choice Sett [*sic*] of Aires, call'd HANDEL'S WATER PIECE" and includes movements from Handel's opera, *Partenope*, in addition to selections from the Water Music and some dances.

Handel's oratorio *Messiah* is perhaps the work most performed by trumpeters from the Late Baroque Era. It is also the work that appears in a confusing variety of editions that reflect the changing profile and abilities of the trumpet since Handel's time including editions by **Wolfgang Amadeus Mozart** from 1789 and Ebenezer Prout from 1902.

Unlike the variety of different trumpets that Bach calls for in his music, Handel overwhelmingly favors the **natural trumpet** in D; the parts are written at concert pitch rather than transposed. Although *Messiah* is undoubtedly Handel's most famous work, prominent trumpet parts appear in seventeen other Handel oratorios. Major solo arias beside "The Trumpet Shall Sound" include "Let the Bright Seraphim" from *Samson*, "Revenge, Revenge" from *Alexander's Feast*, "With Honor Let Desert Be Crowned" from *Judas Maccabaeus* (notable for being Handel's only trumpet solo in a minor key), "Vedo il ciel" from *La Ressurezione*, "To God Our Strength" from *The Occasional Oratorio*, and "Raise Your Voice" from *Susanna*. Handel's orchestra for most of his oratorios includes two trumpets pitched in D; exceptions are *Esther*, *Deborah*, *The Occasional Oratorio*, *Joshua*, *Judas Maccabaeus*, and the *Dettingen Te Deum*, where three trumpets are called for.

Other important trumpet parts appear in Handel's ceremonial music for the British court, especially the *Coronation Anthems*. One of his most beautiful trumpet solos appears in the obbligato aria "Eternal Source of Light Divine" in the *Birthday Ode for Queen Anne*. Among Handel's operas, notable trumpet parts include the demanding obbligato aria "Desterò dall'empia dite" from *Amadigi* and "Stragi, morti" from *Radamisto*. Handel wrote for his largest trumpet section—four trumpets—in the first version of his opera *Rinaldo*.

hand-stopping. A method first employed by **Anton Joseph Hampel** for the horn in the 1730s that was later applied to the trumpet by **Michael Wöggel** in the early 1770s. The technique of hand-stopping lowered any partial of the harmonic overtone series by a half step or (rarely) a whole step, depending on how much the left hand covered the inside of the bell. (See figure 24.) It worked best at softer volumes, where the contrast in sound between open and stopped notes was not as pronounced. Because of this, hand-stopping was more successfully employed in solo and chamber works rather than in large ensembles. It was used in orchestral works at times, most notably in Schubert's Fourth Symphony, where he wrote octave F-sharps for the trumpets in the first movement (produced by playing a G with a hand in the bell).

Several composers wrote for the trumpet using the hand-stopping technique. The Karlsruhe composer Joseph Aloys Schmittbaur wrote seven concerti for Wöggel in 1773 and 1774 that unfortunately have not survived. Luigi Cherubini composed six "pas redoublés et marches" for an ensemble with a hand-stopped trumpet, three hand-stopped horns, and a **serpent** (or trombone) in 1814. A trumpet designed in a crescent shape to facilitate hand-stopping was the **demilune trumpet**. Shorter, double-folded, **natural trumpets**, and **posthorns** also enabled the use of the technique, as did the *Inventionstrompete*. (See appendix 3.)

Figure 24. Hand-stopping chart for trumpet in F showing whether notes are played open, half-stopped, or fully stopped. *Elisa Koehler.*

Hanoverian Bugle. Another term for the *Halbmond*.

Hardenberger, Håkan (b. 1961). Swedish trumpeter. He began studying the trumpet at the age of eight with Bo Nilsson in Malmö, Sweden, and continued his studies at the Paris Conservatory with **Pierre Thibaud** and in Los Angeles with **Thomas Stevens**. In 1981 he won the Toulon Competition and was joint first prizewinner in the Geneva Competition. He was the first trumpeter in the twentieth century to pursue a career exclusively as a classical soloist. In addition to performing the entire solo repertoire for the trumpet, Hardenberger has been an energetic champion of new music in order to expand the repertoire. The works written for and championed by him include those by Sir **Harrison Birtwistle**, **Hans Werner Henze**, Rolf Martinsson, Olga Neuwirth, **Arvo Pärt**, Mark Anthony Turnage, Rolf Wallin, and **H. K. Gruber**'s concerto *Aerial*, which he has performed more than sixty times. In recital Hardenberger performs with Swedish pianist Roland Pöntinen as well as with percussionist Colin Currie. Hardenberger regularly appears with major orchestras worldwide and has made over twenty-five recordings. In addition to his extensive performing and recording career, Hardenberger is a professor at the Malmö Conservatoire and the Royal Northern College of Music, Manchester. In recent years he has increasingly appeared as a conductor.

Harjanne, Jouko (b. 1962). Finnish trumpeter. He studied with Raimo Sarmas at the Tampere Conservatory from 1976 to 1983 and subsequently with Henri Adelbrecht and Timofei Dokshizer. After serving as co-principal trumpeter with the Tampere Philharmonic Orchestra from 1978 to 1984, he became principal in the Finnish Radio Symphony Orchestra in Helsinki. In 1987 he won second place in the Prague Spring Trumpet Series and in 1990 he won first place in the Ellsworth Smith Trumpet Competition sponsored by the **International Trumpet Guild**. At the age of twenty-six, Harjanne began teaching at the Sibelius Academy in Helsinki as well as a number of master classes in Finland and abroad. He has played chamber music in many brass and chamber ensembles, including the Finnish Brass Ensemble, the Brasstime Quartet, and the Protoventus Ensemble. Very active as a soloist, Harjanne has given the first performances of concertos by Segerstam (1984), Gruner (1987, 1992), Linkola (1988, 1993), Wessman (1991), and Bashmakov (1992). He also gave the European première of Shchedrin's Concerto (Moscow, October 1995). In January 2012 Harjanne was appointed a guest professor of the Senzoku Gakuen College of Music.

Harmon mute, wah-wah mute. A hollow metal mute with a removable cup stem and a cork or foam collar that completely closes off the bell of the trumpet. Trumpeters create the wah-wah effect with the mute by covering and uncovering the small cup at the end of the mute's stem, which can also be extended or removed to alter the sound. Harmon mutes are made out of aluminum or copper, which creates a darker sound. Early Harmon mutes were made with a flat-bottom barrel shape, and later models adopted a rounder design, like the **Jo-Ral bubble mute**, to enhance intonation and response. (See figure 25.)

The Harmon mute was patented by George Schlüsselburg in 1924 and named for Chicago businessman P. T. "Paddy" Harmon, who owned half of the interest in the patent. Harmon, a millionaire who invested $2.5 million in the Chicago Stadium in 1929, owned the Arcadia and Dreamland ballrooms in Chicago, and was one of the first to hire African American jazz bands in the 1920s. According to trumpeter Joseph "Wingy" Manone's 1948 autobiography, *Trumpet on the Wing*, Manone's band auditioned for Harmon for a weekend gig at the Arcadia in 1928 and the businessman scolded Manone for playing unmuted by saying, "You can't play good jazz without a wah-wah mute." The Harmon Mute Company has been making mutes in Skokie, Illinois, since the 1920s.

Joseph "King" Oliver was a pioneer of wah-wah technique with a **plunger mute** as well as with the use of the left hand over the bell, which led to the development of the Harmon mute. The wah-wah effect on the Harmon mute was especially pronounced because it was easier to manipulate the smaller cup at the end of the stem and the sound came across well on early recordings. A variation of the Harmon mute was the **Solotone** or **Clear Tone mute**, which was made of hardened fiberboard with a longer shape and a softer sound. **Miles Davis** created his own distinctive sound in the 1950s by playing a Harmon mute with the stem removed. (See appendix 3.)

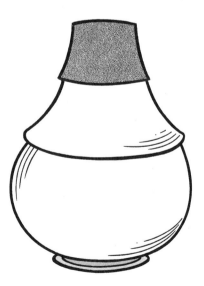

Figure 25. Harmon mute. *Drawing by T. M. Larsen.*

harmonic. A note or partial in the **harmonic overtone series** that is a whole-number multiple of the frequency of the **fundamental** pitch of the series.

harmonic overtone series. A series of pitches that is produced by a single length of tubing. With the exception of the **fundamental**, most of the notes can be sounded on a **natural trumpet** or **bugle**, depending on the length of tubing and the player's ability. (See figure 26.)

Figure 26. The harmonic overtone series based on C. *Elisa Koehler.*

harmonic trumpet. The first example of **vent holes** applied to the trumpet. An eighteenth-century silver trumpet designed by **William Shaw** in 1787 with four vent holes, three of which are covered by an adjustable metal sleeve, it was discovered in a locked leather case in the vaults of St. James's Palace in London in 1959 and studied by organologist Eric Halfpenny (1906–1979), who published an article about the instrument in the *Galpin Society Journal* in 1960 (July 1960, vol. 13) and gave the trumpet its colorful nickname. Built in E-flat, the trumpet includes **crooks** to D, C, and B-flat. The fact that it was untouched for 170 years and was built for the private royal orchestra shows that the experimental trumpet did not receive wide use. Dated just three years after **Charles Burney**'s public criticism of **John Sarjant**'s inability to correct out-of-tune notes in Handel obbligato arias on the **natural trumpet,** it was perhaps built for the Handel Commemoration in 1787.

Harper, Thomas (1786–1853). English trumpeter. Hailed as the premier trumpeter in England during his prime, Harper began his musical studies with R. T. Eley and was a member of Eley's Royal East India Volunteers Band for seventeen years. He also played horn and trumpet with the Adelphi and Drury Lane theater orchestras. Harper was elected to the Royal Society of Musicians in 1815, and was noted for his performances of obbligato arias from **Handel** oratorios, especially "The Trumpet Shall Sound" from *Messiah* and "Let the Bright Seraphim" from *Samson*. In 1821 he succeeded **John Hyde** as principal trumpet in the King's Theater in Haymarket, the Italian Opera, the Philharmonic Concerts, the Concert of Ancient Music, and all of the major festivals in and around London. Harper specialized in performing on the **English slide trumpet**, but also played the **keyed bugle** and the **cornet**.

Harper was professor of trumpet at the Royal Academy of Music from about 1829 until 1845. Around 1830 he published a collection of solos, duets, and trios for the keyed bugle. Harper revised the **bugle calls** in Hyde's *Preceptor* for the British military, and served as the inspector of trumpets and bugles for the East India Company. He published the method book *Instructions for the Trumpet* in 1835 and an expanded edition in 1837. The bulk of the book concerns the English slide trumpet, but it also covers the cornet, the keyed bugle, and the so-called Russian valve trumpet, or stop trumpet (a unique name for a trumpet with two **Stölzel valves**). Harper endorsed a slide trumpet of his own design made by **John Köhler**, which was known as "Harper's Improved Model." He had a daughter and three sons who were all professional musicians: **Thomas John Harper Jr.** (a trumpeter), Charles Abraham Harper (1819–1893, a horn player), and Edmund Bryan Harper (1826–1869, an organist).

Harper Jr., Thomas John (1816–1898). English trumpeter. The eldest son of **Thomas Harper**, he succeeded his father as principal trumpet in all of the major orchestras and festivals in London in the middle of the 1850s. He studied at the Royal Academy of Music between 1830 and 1836 and performed with Sir Michael Costa's orchestra. Harper was also a pianist and violinist; he played violin with the opera orchestra of Her Majesty's Theater. He served as professor of trumpet at the Royal Academy of Music and the Royal College of Music between 1884 and 1893. Harper served as Sergeant Trumpeter to Queen Victoria from 1884 until his death in 1898. Like his father, he specialized in performing on the **English slide trumpet,** and it was largely due to his prominence that the instrument endured into the 1890s in England when valved trumpets and cornets were favored in other countries. Harper also played the cornet, but stressed that it should not be used as a substitute for the **natural trumpet** or slide trumpet in the performance of trumpet music. He published two method books, *Harper's School for the Cornet à Pistons* (ca. 1865) and *Harper's School of the* [Slide] *Trumpet* (ca. 1875).

Hartmann, John (1830–1897). Prussian cornetist. He played both the cornet and the violin and attended a music school in Sonderhausen for four years. He was later drafted into the Prussian army and served as solo cornetist for the Cuirassiers in Cologne for three years. Hartmann's brother, Ernest, also a musician, was recruited by the British brass band at the Crystal Palace, and encouraged John to join him in England when his Prussian military service ended. John complied, joined the Crystal Palace Band as solo cornetist in 1855, and spent the rest of his career in England as a cornet soloist and band director. He composed many cornet solos, including the *Arbucklenian Polka, Facilita, The Champion, The Favorite,* and *Fantasia Brilliante on the Air "Rule Britannia."*

hassrah. Alternate name for the **chatzotzrah**, the trumpet of Ancient Israel. The transliterated Hebrew name is hasoserah.

Haydn, Joseph (1732–1809). Austrian composer. Celebrated as the father of the symphony and the string quartet and one of the leading composers of the Classical era, he wrote a trumpet concerto for **Anton Weidinger** to perform on a **keyed trumpet** in 1796. The *Concerto in E-flat Major* (Hob.: VIIe/1) is one of the most famous trumpet concertos ever written. It was premiered in Vienna on March 28, 1800, at the Burgtheater. Haydn wrote a notable solo for the second trumpet part that appears in the second movement of his *Symphony No. 100 in G Major, "Military,"* (1793–1794) that is a direct quote of an eighteenth-century military signal known as the *Generalmarsch.* With the exception of Haydn's famous concerto for the keyed trumpet, all of his other trumpet parts are written for **natural trumpets**.

Haydn, Johann Michael (1737–1806). Austrian composer. He was the younger brother of **Joseph Haydn** and served for more than forty years as an organist and composer in Salzburg beginning in 1762. He wrote the *Concerto No. 2 in C Major* (MH 60, or Perger 34) in 1763, which contains some of the highest notes ever written for the **natural trumpet**. The concerto has passages that frequently ascend up to E6 and one that goes up to F6. It may have been written for the Salzburg court trumpeter **J. B. Resenberger**, who was praised by **Leopold Mozart** for his proficiency in the high register. Michael Haydn composed a *Concerto No. 1 in D* (no MH number, Perger 52*bis*) that is not as taxing. Both of the concertos have only two movements, like Leopold Mozart's trumpet concerto, so it is possible that they may have originally been part of a serenade or inserted into a festival mass setting.

Heald, John (1843–1934). American brass instrument manufacturer. His father, Paul, played the **keyed bugle**, and John also played the instrument as well as the **cornet** in his youth. In 1863 he moved to Worcester, Massachusetts, where he later worked for **Isaac Fiske**. Heald earned his first patent in 1882 for a **water key** design while working for C. J. Hutchins in Springfield. After spending a brief time in Philadelphia, perhaps working with **Henry Distin** or **J. W. Pepper**, Heald opened his own shop in 1887, the John Heald Cornet Company. He made cornets, trumpets, and trombones before he sold the shop in 1927, whereupon it became the Springfield Band Instrument Company. Heald's surviving cornets are highly prized by modern players for their superior **response** and warm tone.

Heinisch [Hainisch, Hanisch], Johann Baptist (1706–1751). Austrian trumpeter. Considered the greatest trumpeter of the high Baroque era, Heinisch began studies with chief imperial court trumpeter (oberhoftrompeter) Franz Anton Küffel (ca. 1695–1754) in 1725 and was appointed imperial court trumpeter (kaiserlicher hoftrompeter) in Vienna in 1727. He was promoted to the rank of musical imperial court trumpeter (musikalischer kaiserlicher hoftrompeter) in 1730, and remained in that position until his death in 1751. Heinisch was celebrated for his **clarino** playing in the highest register (up to G6, the twenty-fourth partial) as well as for his accuracy, stamina, delicacy, and breath control (especially on long **trills**). Johann Joseph Fux (1660–1741), hofkappellmeister at the imperial Viennese court between 1715 and 1741, described Heinisch in 1732 as "an entirely special virtuoso in a manner that no one can surpass him. Heinisch has also happily discovered certain tones on the trumpet which the kappellmeisters indeed hitherto wanted, but no trumpeter except him could produce." Fux also recommended that Heinisch's salary be doubled on account of his "uncommon merit."

The music written for Heinisch testifies to his technical prowess and artistry. Leading Viennese court composers, including Fux, **Georg von Reutter II**, Antonio Caldara (1671–1736), and Luca Antonio Predieri (1688–1767), included numerous sinfonias and obbligato arias in operas, oratorios, and sacred music with demanding trumpet parts for Heinisch. Notable examples include the arias "Pace una volta" from Predieri's opera *Zenobia* (1740), "Chi ncl camin d'onore" from Fux's opera *Enea negli Elisi* (1731), and "Lo stuol che Apollo onora" from Reutter's opera *Il Parnaso accusato, e difeso* (1738), which was one of the most demanding pieces ever written for the **natural trumpet**. The obbligato part for the Reutter aria (written for the alto castrato Gaetano Orsini) requires the trumpeter to play G6 ten times (more than **Bach**'s *Brandenburg Concerto No. 2*), along with F6 and F-sharp6 a combined twenty-two times, and high E6 an astounding thirty-eight times, all amid virtuoso passagework, often in thirty-second notes including wide intervals. Reutter also wrote two solo concerti for him.

Heinisch was plagued by illness during the last four years of his life and was frequently replaced in the court orchestra. In addition to performing, he trained other court trumpeters, including **Johann Capsar Köstler**, a Salzburg court trumpeter who later taught **Johann Andreas Schachtner**, a friend of **Leopold Mozart**.

Hejnal Mariacki. (Pol.) "St. Mary's Dawn." A trumpet signal that is performed every hour from the highest tower of the Church of St. Mary in the main square of Krakow, Poland. It dates from the thirteenth century and continues to be sounded regularly to this day. According to tradition, the last note is abruptly cut short to commemorate a tower trumpeter who was interrupted by an enemy arrow through the neck from invading Tartar armies while sounding an alarm in 1241.

Helseth, Tine Thing (b. 1987). Norwegian trumpeter. She began playing the trumpet at the age of seven and achieved success in her teens by winning numerous competitions including first prize in the National Soloists Championship in Norway (2004), second prize in the **Theo Charlier** International Trumpet Competition (2005), second prize in the Eurovision Young Musicians Competition (2006), "Newcomer of the Year" at the 2007 Norwegian Grammy Awards, and a 2009 Borletti-Bultoni Trust Fellowship. As an international soloist and recitalist, Helseth has performed with numerous European orchestras as well as with her own all-female brass ensemble, tenThing. She records on the Simax and EMI labels.

herald trumpet. Designed with a long, straight **bell**, a twentieth-century herald trumpet pitched in B-flat is approximately four-and-one-half feet in length with three piston valves. The long bell is traditionally fitted with hooks or loops for hanging a ceremonial banner or **tabard**. Such instruments have been built by several makers including **Kanstul** and **Smith-Watkins**. Precursors include trumpets employed for use onstage during performances of operas by Richard Wagner (*Lohengrin* and *Die Meistersinger*), where they were called *Königstrompeten*, and in operas by Giuseppe Verdi (*Aida*). Herald trumpets designed for Verdi's opera earned the name **Aida trumpets**, which were subsequently and inconsistently applied to similar types of instruments. Contemporary military trumpet ensembles regularly employ matched sets of herald trumpets. For example, the U.S. Army Herald Trumpets include the following: E-flat soprano, B-flat mezzo-soprano or melody, B-flat tenor, and B-flat or G bass trumpets. Trumpet players play the E-flat soprano and B-flat melody trumpets while the tenor and bass trumpets are played by trombone and euphonium players.

Hering, Sigmund (1899–1986). American trumpeter, composer, and pedagogue. Shortly after his birth in Warsaw, Poland, Hering's family moved to the Greek island of Crete, where he began his trumpet studies at the age of seven. He received a scholarship to the Royal Academy of Music in Vienna at the age of twelve, where he studied trumpet with **Franz Rossbach** and composition with Franz Schreker, graduating in 1918. In 1923 Hering became principal trumpet of the Cleveland Orchestra and auditioned for the Philadelphia Orchestra two years later upon recommendation of Leopold Stokowski. Hering won the audition and played with the Philadelphia Orchestra between 1925 and 1964. As a teacher, Hering served on the faculties of the Granoff School of Music (1934–1939) and the Settlement School of Music (1945–1981), both in Philadelphia. In addition to his own private studio, which he maintained throughout his life, he also taught part-time at the Hartt School of Music in Hartford, Connecticut, between 1948 and 1954.

Hering was one of the most prolific trumpet pedagogues of the twentieth century. He published over twenty etude books and method books containing over four hundred etudes. His four-volume *Sigmund Hering Trumpet Course* remains a staple in the curriculum of many young trumpeters. His etude books cover all aspects of trumpet study including two posthumously published collections edited by Thomas Erdmann concerning ornamentation and multiple tonguing. Erdmann also published *An Annotated Bibliography and Guide to the Published Trumpet Music of Sigmund Hering* (Edwin Mellen Press, 1997). Some of Hering's most popular etude books include *Thirty-Two Etudes, Twenty-Eight Melodious and Technical Etudes*, and *The Orchestral Trumpeter* (a transposition method). His two solo compositions for the trumpet are *Concertino* and a polka, *Moon Shadows*.

Herodorus from Megara. Ancient Greek trumpeter who played the **salpinx** with astonishing strength and power. According to Athenaeus from Naucratis, Herodorus was over seven feet tall ("three and a half peheis" or approximately 2.24 meters), and was reputed to have an enormous appetite for food and wine as well as a habit of sleeping on a bear skin. He could play two trumpets simultaneously and was praised for his ability to inspire weary troops onward to military victories.

Herseth, Adolph Sylvester (1921–2013). American trumpeter. The longest-serving orchestral principal trumpeter in the United States, he influenced generations of musicians and defined modern orchestral trumpet playing. Born in northern Minnesota, Herseth's father was a school teacher and administrator as well as the conductor of a local youth orchestra; his mother was a pianist. His first trumpet teacher was Jimmy Greco. Herseth graduated from Luther College in Decorah, Iowa, with a degree in music and mathematics with the ambition of becoming a music teacher, but decided on a career in performance after playing in military bands while serving in the U.S. Navy during the Second World War. He studied with **Georges Mager** and Marcel LaFosse (the first and second trumpeters, respectively, of the Boston Symphony Orchestra) at the New England Conservatory between 1946 and 1948 in pursuit of a master's degree, but his studies were cut short in 1948 when conductor Artur Rodzinski invited Herseth to audition for the principal trumpet position with the Chicago Symphony Orchestra. Rodzinski offered him the job on the spot, and Herseth, at the age of twenty-six, embarked on a legendary career

with the orchestra spanning 53 years (1948–2001). His career was almost cut short in 1952 when he suffered broken teeth, a cut lower lip, and permanent nerve damage in a bad car accident. But after several months of recuperation, he relearned how to play.

Known for his rich sound, flawless articulation, and consummate musicianship, Herseth inspired generations of orchestral trumpeters. He was one of the first to require all trumpeters in the section to play the same type of instrument for a unified sound (large bore **Vincent Bach** C trumpets with the No. 229 **bell**), which in turn helped to create the distinctive sound of the orchestra's brass section. After 1965 he was also one of the first to direct his section to employ German **rotary valve trumpets** for repertoire from the Classical era, for a lighter sound. His many recordings with the Chicago Symphony under the batons of Fritz Reiner and Sir Georg Solti cemented his fame, especially his performance of Mahler's Fifth Symphony. Known to trumpeters everywhere as "Bud," Herseth preferred ensemble playing to a solo career, but frequently appeared as a soloist with the orchestra. In 1988 he premiered a *Concerto for Trumpet and Orchestra* written for him by Karel Husa that was commissioned by the Chicago Symphony. His genial personality was on display ten years later when the orchestra celebrated his fiftieth anniversary as principal trumpet in 1998. Instead of reserving the spotlight for himself, Herseth invited a large number of colleagues, former students, and old friends to join him on stage. After stepping down as principal trumpet of the Chicago Symphony in 2001, he retained the title, first trumpet emeritus, until he officially retired in 2004.

Hertel, Johann Wilhelm (1727–1789). German composer, violinist, and harpsichordist. Born into a family of court musicians, Hertel became the court composer at Schwerin in 1754. Musically, his compositions follow the conventions of the pre-classical style, and he was in contact with composers of the Berlin School such as C. P. E. Bach, Franz Benda, and Carl Heinrich Graun. Hertel composed several solo trumpet works for the Schwerin court trumpeter **Johann Georg Hoese** including three solo concerti (Nos. 1 and 2 in E-flat and No. 3 in D) and a Double Concerto for trumpet in E-flat and oboe. All of these works exploit the high **clarino** range and were written for the **natural trumpet**. Hertel was apparently contented to work at Schwerin and did not seek to have many of his compositions published during his lifetime. Consequently, a lot of his music remains in manuscript awaiting future discovery and publication.

Hertz (Hz). A unit of **frequency** equal to one cycle per second, named after the German physicist Heinrich R. Hertz (1857–1894). The unit is used to express various **pitch standards**, as in A4 = 440 Hz.

Hickman, David (b. 1950). American trumpeter, pedagogue, and music publisher. He studied with Harry McNees, Frank Baird, Walter Myers, **Roger Voisin**, **Armando Ghitalla**, and **Adolph Herseth**, and earned degrees from the University of Colorado and Wichita State University, where he served as a graduate trumpet teaching assistant. He went on to teach at the University of Illinois from 1974 until 1982, when he joined the faculty of Arizona State University; he was named a regents' professor of music at ASU in 1989. Hickman has performed as a soloist and recitalist internationally as well as throughout the United States, and has recorded seventeen solo albums. He has performed as a chamber musician with the Wichita Brass Quintet, Illinois Brass Quintet, Saint Louis Brass Quintet, Baroque Consort, and the Illinois Contemporary Chamber Players.

An active promoter of trumpet pedagogy and research, Hickman served on the original steering committee and first board of directors of the **International Trumpet Guild** (ITG) and served as the organization's president between 1977 and 1979. He founded the professional brass ensemble, Summit Brass, in 1985 and the Rafael Mendez Brass Institute in 1993. He formed his own publishing house, Hickman Music Editions, and has authored several pedagogical works including *The Piccolo Trumpet* (1973), *The Piccolo Trumpet Big Book* (1991), *Trumpet Lessons with David Hickman* (in five volumes), and *Trumpet Pedagogy: A Compendium of Modern Teaching Techniques* (2006). The ITG bestowed its Award of Merit on Hickman in 2005 to honor his lifetime achievements.

high C. The pitch C6, two octaves above middle C (C4), which is the highest note in the range of most amateur trumpeters.

high pitch. 1. A colloquial term for the **pitch standard** of A4 = 465 Hz often employed by modern **period instrument** ensembles for performances of repertoire from the seventeenth century that employ *cornetti* and **sackbuts**, which aims to approximate historic pitch standards such as **Cornet-Ton** and **Chorton.**

2. A pitch standard of A4 = 452.5 Hz known as **sharp pitch** or old philharmonic pitch, which was used by military band instruments from the late nineteenth century until the middle of the twentieth. When the international pitch standard of A4 = 440 Hz was established in 1939, band instruments using that pitch level were referred to as being "low pitch" to differentiate them from those using the higher standard.

high/low pitch slide. A component of cornets made at the turn of the twentieth century designed to accommodate changing **pitch standards**. Many bands played at high pitch or **sharp pitch** (A4 = 452.5 Hz) while others were switching to "low pitch" (A4 = 440 Hz). When the slide was pushed in, the **cornet** was in high pitch; the slide could then be extended to lower the pitch.

high-pitched trumpets. Trumpets pitched in higher keys than the common B-flat trumpet such as C, D, E-flat, F, and G. These trumpets are not the same as **natural trumpets** from the eighteenth and nineteenth centuries that changed keys by manner of **crooks**, but are instead valved trumpets used for a variety of purposes including enhanced accuracy and security in performing high-register parts that may or may not have been written for larger trumpets in B-flat and C, to facilitate more comfortable fingering patterns in alternate keys, and to provide a broader palette of tonal color. (See figure 27.)

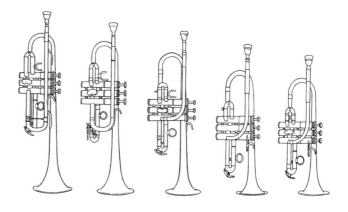

Figure 27. Trumpets pitched in high keys. From left: C, D, E-flat, F, and G. *Drawing by T. M. Larsen.*

Hindemith, Paul (1895–1963). German composer and leading figure in the **period instrument** revival. He studied composition with Arnold Mendelssohn and Bernhard Sekles at the Hoch Conservatory in Frankfurt. Hindemith was concerned that his music should serve a functional purpose and wrote his *Kammermusik* series to serve that goal. The word *Gebrauchsmusik* ("functional" or "utility" music), a term Hindemith disliked, is commonly applied to the educational works he wrote between 1927 and 1938 for students and adult amateurs, including choral songs, cantatas, orchestral pieces, and chamber music. He wrote two works featuring large brass ensembles in 1930: *Konzertmusik* (Concert music), Op. 49 for brass, harp, and piano, and *Konzertmusik*, Op. 50 for brass and strings. Hindemith composed several operas, including *Neues vom Tage* (1929) and *Mathis der Maler* (1935). He also composed the important orchestral work *Symphonic Metamorphosis on Themes of Carl Maria von Weber* (1943).

Hindemith's best-known composition for trumpet is the *Sonata for Trumpet and Piano* (1939); he also wrote a *Concerto for Trumpet and Bassoon* (1949–1952) and works for brass ensemble including *Konzertmusik, Op. 49* (1930) for brass, harp, and piano, and *Konzertmusik, Op. 50* (1930) for brass and strings. In addition to work as a composer and virtuoso violist, Hindemith also played the **cornett** (among other period wind instruments) and is considered the father of the collegiate early music movement in North America. Following an appointment at the Hochschule für Musik in Berlin in the 1930s, Hindemith joined the faculty at Yale University in 1940, where he founded the Yale Collegium Musicum. His primary goal was to broaden the horizons of his students by providing them with hands-on experience with music they were studying. Hindemith often conducted performances on period instruments borrowed from the Metropolitan Museum of Art as well as from private collections. Such performances included Dufay's Mass *Se la face ay pale* at Yale in 1946 and Monteverdi's *Orfeo* in Vienna in 1954.

hinter der Bühne, hinter der Szene. (Ger.) Behind the stage, behind the scene, off stage.

Hirt, Alois Maxwell "Al" (1922–1999). American jazz trumpeter and bandleader. He made his musical debut with the Junior Police Band in 1929 and studied with Mike Cupero at Jesuit High School in his hometown of New Orleans. He attended the Cincinnati Conservatory of Music in 1940. After 1946 he worked in the big bands of Benny Goodman, Tommy Dorsey, Ray McKinley, and Horace Heidt. While touring with Heidt's "Stars on Parade" revue in 1950 he recorded for the Magnolia label, initiating a successful recording career. Best known for his recording of "Java" (which won a Grammy for Best Non-Jazz Instrumental in 1964) and for playing the theme for the television show *The Green Hornet*, Hirt earned twenty-one Grammy nominations as well as four gold albums and one platinum album for RCA Victor. In addition to his work in jazz and popular music, Hirt recorded the **Haydn** Trumpet Concerto (on B-flat trumpet) in 1964 with the Boston Pops on the album *"Pops" Goes the Trumpet* (RCA LM–2729).

Historic Brass Society (HBS). Founded by American trumpeter Jeffrey Nussbaum in 1988, the HBS is an international music organization of amateur and professional brass musicians and scholars concerned with the entire range of brass music, from Antiquity to the present. The HBS publishes an annual journal, presents conferences and festivals, and sponsors the *Bucina* book series published by Pendragon Press.

historically informed performance. A movement that mushroomed in the 1970s following earlier efforts by Arnold Dolmetsch (1858–1940) and Wanda Landowska (1879–1959), which sought to perform music from ear-lier eras with **period instruments** informed by the latest scholarship concerning performance practice in order to explore new possibilities of musical expression. Commonly abbreviated as HIP, the movement has helped revive instruments like the **cornett** and the **natural trumpet** as well as nineteenth-century brasses such as the **keyed bugle**, the **English slide trumpet**, **cornopeans**, and vintage **cornets**. Musical issues involved include **articulation**, **pitch standards**, and **temperament**.

Hoch, Theodore (1842–1906). German cornetist. He began playing the cornet at an early age and moved to Berlin at the age of ten, when he began playing with the Kaiser Franz Guard Grenadier Second Regiment Band. In 1867 the band won first prize at the Paris Exposition and Hoch received the gold medal for his solo cornet performances. Hoch traveled with the band to the United States in 1872 to perform at the World Peace Jubilee; the band returned in 1876 to perform at the Centennial Exposition in Philadelphia. In addition to band performances, Hoch played with the Johann Strauss Orchestra in Vienna. He was also the featured soloist with the orchestra of Benjamin Bilse in Berlin. Hoch immigrated to the United States in 1881 and worked as a cornet soloist, teacher, and composer. He toured with the Mozart Symphony Club of New York in 1896. As a teacher, he advocated placing a greater degree of **mouthpiece pressure** on the lower lip, which allowed the upper lip to vibrate freely and increased high range. He outlined this theory in his *Tutor for the Cornet* (1880); his most famous student was **Ernst Albert Couturier.** Hoch composed several cornet solos such as *Alpine Flowers, American Fantasia, Echoes of the Valley, Fantasie Brilliante, Souvenir de Bellini,* and *Perle de l'Océan.* Hoch often performed on an **echo bell cornet** built for him by the **Conn** Company in his composition *Singvögelchen aus dem Thüringer Wald*, which exploited the instrument's built-in **mute** effect. He often ended concerts in the United States by performing *The Star-Spangled Banner* on a Conn **herald trumpet** with an American flag unfurled from the bell like a **tabard** at the end.

Hoese, Johann Georg (1727–1801). German trumpeter for whom **Johann Wilhelm Hertel** wrote his solo trumpet concerti. Born in Leipzig, Hoese trained in Saxony and joined the court of Schwerin in 1747 as a "court and field trumpeter." His virtuosic prowess in the high register earned him a pay raise in 1763 for his solo playing. He appears in a painting by G. D. Matthieu of Schwerin court musicians from 1770 holding a natural trumpet and a sheet of music marked "Clarino I."

Höfs, Matthias (b. 1965). German trumpeter. He began playing the trumpet at the age of six and later studied with Peter Kallensee at the University of Music and Theater in Hamburg. Höfs studied with Konradin Groth at the Karajan Academy of the Berlin Philharmonic in 1984, graduating with distinction. He was principal trumpet of the Philharmonic State Orchestra in Hamburg between 1984 and 2000, and became a member of the noted brass ensemble German Brass in 1985. Höfs has performed on many recordings, broadcasts, and videos with the German Brass; he has also written several arrangements for the ensemble. As a soloist, Höfs has recorded six CDs: *Gansch Meets Höfs*, *Trumpet Acrobatics*, *Un Concerto Italiano*, *An English Concert*, *Solo de Concours*, and *The Trumpet Shall Sound*. As a teacher, he has served as a guest lecturer at the Tchaikovsky Conservatory in Moscow, the Royal Conservatory in Copenhagen, and the Guildhall School of Music and Drama in London. He has been a professor at the University of Music and Theater in Hamburg since 2000. In addition to playing the trumpet, Höfs also performs on the modern **corno da caccia** and consults with the **Thein** brass instrument manufacturing firm on instrument design. He has won several awards such as the Eduard-Soehring Prize (1988) and first place in the International Music Competition in Markneukirchen (1990).

Hoftrompeter. (Ger.) Court trumpeter.

Holton. American brass instrument manufacturer and distributor. The firm was started by trombone soloist Frank Holton (1858–1942) and instrument maker James Warren York (1839–1927) as York & Holton, Grand Rapids, Michigan (1884–1886). Holton began marketing his trombone slide **lubricant** ("Holton's Electric Oil") in 1896 in Chicago. The first instruments produced were trombones ("Holton Special") in 1899, and the firm incorporated as Frank Holton & Co. in 1904. **Ernst Albert Couturier** was associated with the company between 1908 and 1912; Holton produced a large **bore** Couturier model **cornet** in 1910. **Herbert L. Clarke** was associated with Holton between 1917 and 1918, when the company produced the medium bore Holton-Clarke cornet. The company moved to a large new factory in Elkhorn, Wisconsin, in 1918. The "Holton Collegiate" line of student instruments began production in 1929. Company ownership changed hands in later years; in 1964 it was purchased by the G. Leblanc Corporation, and later by Steinway Musical Instruments. Holton became a division of Conn-Selmer in 2004, closed its Elkhorn factory in 2008, and relocated to Eastlake, Ohio. Notable trumpets produced by Holton include Don Ellis's quarter-tone trumpet (1965), and **Maynard Ferguson**'s Superbone (1974) and Firebird trumpet (1974), both designed by Larry Ramirez, Holton's chief design technician. The Holton archive and representative instruments now reside at the National Music Museum at the University of South Dakota in Vermillion.

Holy, Walter (1921–2006). German trumpeter and pioneer of the **period instrument** movement. At the age of twelve he saw a small **natural trumpet** pitched in G in the window of a music shop and was so fascinated by it that he saved up his pocket money, purchased it, and learned to play it. So began the musical education of the twentieth-century pioneer of the **Baroque trumpet**. After studies at the Städtischen Konservatorium Osnabrück with Karl Burmeister, he played first trumpet in orchestras in Herford, Bielefeld, Frankfurt am Main, and Hanover until 1956, when he became the assistant principal trumpet of the Cologne Radio Symphony Orchestra, a position he retained until his retirement in 1983. In addition to performing, he taught at the Folkwang Hochschule in Essen between 1968 and 1974. Holy is best known for his groundbreaking work as the first trumpeter of the Cappella Coloniensis (the chamber orchestra of the radio station in Cologne) from 1960 to 1983, where he was the first trumpeter in the twentieth century to play successfully on the valveless Baroque trumpet.

The instrument that Holy played was developed in 1959 by **Otto Steinkopf** and **Helmut Finke**, and formed in a coiled shape that resembled a *Jägertrompete*, the instrument held by **Gottfried Reiche** in the famous portrait from 1726 by Elias Gottlob Haussmann (1695–1774), but with three **vent holes**. In the 1960s, Holy performed extensively on the Steinkopf-Finke trumpet and made many pioneering recordings, including Bach's ***Brandenburg Concerto No. 2*** and various cantatas, as well as Leopold Mozart's concerto. He also taught younger players including Pieter Dolk, **Michael Laird**, and **Edward Tarr**. As the first to master this difficult instrument, Holy learned the advantage of playing modern trumpets with minimal mouthpiece pressure and ushered in the revival of **clarino** playing in the twentieth century. In 1996 he was awarded the **Johann Ernst Altenburg** Award by the **International Trumpet Guild** in recognition of his achievements.

Holztrompete. (Ger.) Wooden trumpet. **Richard Wagner** scored for a trumpet of this type in the "Shepherd's Song" in the third act of *Tristan und Isolde*. It was a long wooden instrument pitched in C with one **piston valve** and an upturned bell shaped like a bulb that was played with a trumpet mouthpiece.

horagi. A **conch shell trumpet** from Japan.

horn. 1. The modern French horn. An orchestral brass instrument with **rotary valves**.

2. Colloquial term for a **trumpet** used by professional musicians.

3. An animal horn, like that from a cow.

Horne, Florence Louise (1880–1956). American cornetist. By the age of ten, she was already performing cornet solos in public and between 1892 and 1896 she studied with Robert Brown Hall and later with Henry C. Brown. She played a solo with Hall's Military Band at the age of thirteen. In 1897, she played with the Fadettes (based in Boston) and a year later toured with the Cecilia Musical Club. Solo engagements at numerous other venues followed, often with all-female groups like the U.S. Ladies Military Band of Providence and the Tuxedo Ladies Band in Chester Park, Cincinnati. Between 1901 and 1903, she performed solos between acts of the George C. Wilson Repertory Company and between acts of the Ward & Vokes comedy team with the Talma Ladies Band. In 1903, she performed at the Iroquois Theater in Chicago on the evening of the great fire. While she played solos with the Navassar Band, she took jobs playing musicals at the Waldorf Astoria Hotel in New York City. Horne took a few lessons from **William Paris Chambers** when he returned from a solo European tour. He wanted to publicize her as his star pupil on a tour to Europe, but she declined the offer, believing it would not be fair to her first teachers, Hall and Brown. In 1910, she married Edmund Stilwell, retired from active playing, and continued to teach.

horse whinny. A special effect performed on a valved trumpet that is an extended **fall** or descending **glissando** played with **half-valve** technique to simulate the sound of a horse neighing. It famously appears at the end of Leroy Anderson's *Sleigh Ride*. The effect was described in Louis Panico's book *The Novelty Cornetist* in 1927 as the "horse neigh."

Howarth, Elgar (b. 1935). English trumpeter, composer, and conductor. His father was a brass band conductor who gave him his first lessons on the **cornet**. Howarth began playing in his father's band at the age of ten and was promoted to principal cornet at the age of eighteen. He went on to study at Manchester University and later majored in music composition at the Royal Manchester College of Music, where he formed the Manchester New Music Group with his classmates Peter Maxwell Davies (b. 1934), Harrison Birtwistle (b. 1934), Alexander Goehr (b. 1932), and John Ogdon (b. 1937). Maxwell Davies wrote his *Sonata for Trumpet and Piano* (1955) for Howarth and Ogdon. Following graduation Howarth played trumpet in the Royal Opera House Orchestra at Covent Garden between 1958 and 1963 and became principal trumpet of the Royal Philharmonic Orchestra in 1963 and again between 1965 and 1970. He was also a central member of the **Philip Jones** Brass Ensemble (PJBE) from 1965 until 1976, serving as a trumpeter, arranger, composer, and conductor. His most important work with the PJBE was his brass ensemble transcription of Mussorgsky's *Pictures at an Exhibition,* which was widely performed by other brass ensembles. Also

an active freelance trumpeter, Howarth played on the Beatles' album *Magical Mystery Tour* (1967).

Howarth conducted the London Sinfonietta during a successful tour to Italy in the late 1960s, which led to many other conducting engagements. He conducted the Grimethorpe Colliery Band (1972–1976) and the English Northern Philharmonic (1985–1989), and served as the principal guest conductor of Opera North (1985–1988). He has conducted several operatic premieres such as György Ligeti's *Le Grand Macabre* at the Grand Opera Stockholm in 1978 and Harrison Birtwistle's *Gawain* at the Royal Opera House in London in 1991. Howarth's compositions favor works for brass, such as *Concerto for Trumpet and Orchestra, Concerto for Trombone and Orchestra, Concerto for Trumpet and Brass Band, Capriccio for Solo Trumpet,* and *Concerto for Cornet and Brass Band* (written for and recorded by **Håkan Hardenberger**). Some of his compositions for brass band are *Fireworks, Mortimer's Dream, Mosaic, The Bandsman's Tale,* and *The American Dream.* Howarth's compositions were occasionally published under the pseudonym, W. Hogarth Lear.

Hubbard, Freddie (1938–2008). American jazz trumpeter. He learned to play the **mellophone** and other brass instruments before taking up the trumpet in junior high school. By the age of eighteen, he was already performing in clubs with his own group in his native Indianapolis. Hubbard performed in jam sessions with Wes Montgomery, and recorded with him in 1957. He moved to New York in 1958 and performed with several prominent jazz artists, including Sonny Rollins, Slide Hampton, J. J. Johnson, Quincy Jones, and John Coltrane. In 1961 he replaced **Lee Morgan** in Art Blakey's Jazz Messengers for three years. Hubbard formed his own quintet in 1964 and made several recordings (for the Blue Note label), which increased his popularity as a master of hard bop. By the late 1960s, critics regarded Hubbard as the next great jazz innovator after **Dizzy Gillespie** and **Miles Davis**. His fame led to a lucrative deal with Columbia Records in 1974 that resulted in several **crossover** albums featuring funk, rock, and disco influences aimed at a commercial audience. Hubbard returned to his authentic jazz roots in 1977 when he joined Herbie Hancock's band. He continued to tour and record throughout the 1980s. Hubbard ruptured his lip during a performance in 1992, and his playing declined afterward. Some of his most notable recordings are *Open Season, Ready for Freddie, Breaking Point, Backlash, Life Flight,* and *Blues at the Abstract Truth.*

huffing. A type of pulsing articulation called for in some early Baroque trumpet music that features repeated breath attacks. Similar in concept to the **trillo** performed at a slow tempo, huffing is usually notated in a manner similar to string *portato*: dots under the notes along with a slur (or tie) underneath. The technique frequently appears in the trumpet parts of **J. S. Bach** and is described by **Johann Ernst Alterburg** in his treatise (1795).

Humes & Berg. American **mute** manufacturing company. Founded by Willie Berg (1916–1996) in 1935, the company name also refers to inventor Guy B. Humes (active 1918–1941), who earned several patents for brass instrument mute designs in the early twentieth century. As a struggling clarinet and saxophone player in Chicago in the 1930s, Berg started the business by selling musical instrument accessories to musicians at local clubs. Through this work he forged relationships with many leading musicians of the day including Duke Ellington, **Harry James**, Count Basie, Woody Herman, Glenn Miller, and Tommy Dorsey. Berg developed his line of **Stonelined mutes** and they became popular with dance bands during the swing era for their colorful sound options and ability to blend brass sections with saxophones. Glenn Miller was so fond of the mutes that he helped Berg earn a contract to make mutes for all of the bands of the U.S. armed forces, which allowed him to stay home when he was drafted in 1941.

Humes & Berg manufactures mutes for all brass instruments in a variety of materials and designs. In addition to standard **straight mutes** and **cup mutes**, the company makes a full array of unique trumpet mutes including a **plunger mute, derby mute, bucket mute, Clear Tone mute** (a type of **open tube** mute), **Mica mute,** BuzzWow mute, **wah wah mute,** Mel-o-Wah mute, and a **practice mute** known as the "*Sh! Sh! Quiet Mannie Klein*" mute. The majority of Humes & Berg mutes are made of fiberboard coated with a resin mixture and paint in a characteristic white finish with red trim. (See appendix 3.)

Hummel, Johann Nepomuk (1778–1837). Austrian composer and pianist. One of the greatest piano virtuosi of his time and a sometimes-rival of **Beethoven**, Hummel was a child prodigy who studied with **Mozart** in Vienna between 1786 and 1788, and went on to study with **Joseph Haydn**, Albrechtsberger, and Salieri. He succeeded Haydn at the court of Esterházy at Eisenstadt in 1803, and became acquainted with **Anton Weidinger** and his **keyed trumpet** through this association. He left Eisenstadt to become hofkapellmeister in Stuttgart in 1816 and left in 1818 to become grand-ducal kapellmeister at Weimar, a position he held until his death in 1837.

Hummel completed his *Concerto in E* for Anton Weidinger and his keyed trumpet on December 8, 1803; it was premiered in Vienna on New Year's Day in 1804. Hummel did not assign an opus number to the concerto, and evidence suggests that Weidinger was probably the only trumpeter who performed the piece prior to the twentieth century. The concerto was revived in the twentieth century when the first published edition appeared in 1957 edited by Fritz Stein in Leipzig and transposed down one half step to the key of E-flat major in order to facilitate performance on the B-flat trumpet. The following year, Merrill Debsky, then a student at Yale University, sought to obtain a copy of the concerto's manuscript from the British Museum in order to perform it on a recital. When the copy arrived too late for Debsky's recital, he sent it to **Armando Ghitalla**, who produced an edition of the concerto for B-flat trumpet (transposed down to E-flat from the original key) that was published by **Robert King** in 1959. Ghitalla subsequently performed the Hummel concerto at a Town Hall recital and released the first recording of the piece in 1964. **Edward Tarr** produced a scholarly edition of the concerto in the original key of E in 1972 (pub. Universal Edition) and contributed historical commentary that accompanied a facsimile of the manuscript published by Editions BIM in 2011.

Hummel's other composition with a prominent trumpet part was his *Military Septet, Op. 114* (1829). Scored for a **natural trumpet** in C, flute, clarinet, violin, cello, bass, and piano, the four-movement work features typical fanfare figures restricted to notes of the **harmonic overtone series** ranging between G3 and G5. Trumpeter **Thomas Harper Sr.** (probably using an **English slide trumpet**) performed for the septet's premiere on the first concert of the Philharmonic Society's 1831 season at London's Kings Theatre. A trio by Hummel for trumpet, violin, and piano, originally thought to have been lost, has been proven to be a chamber version of the *Concerto in E*.

Hyde, John (fl. 1780–1821). English trumpeter credited with the invention of the **English slide trumpet** at the turn of the nineteenth century. One of the leading trumpeters of his day, Hyde performed as first trumpet with prominent orchestras and published a **method book** in 1799 titled *New and Compleat Preceptor for the Trumpet and Bugle Horn*.

iconography. The study of visual representations, usually paintings and other works of art, to determine the historical details and significance of the subjects depicted. Iconography is particularly helpful in determining playing positions and features of early trumpets when surviving examples of the instruments themselves do not exist. A useful example of an iconographical study for trumpeters is Tom L. Naylor's book, *The Trumpet & Trombone in Graphic Arts 1500–1800* (Brass Press, 1979).

Imboccatura. (It.) **Embouchure.**

Immer, Friedemann (b. 1948). German trumpeter. Pioneer in the early music revival and recording artist on the **vented Baroque trumpet.** His musical training began on the **Kuhlohorn** in a **Posaunenchor** with his father, a Lutheran pastor, and later continued with Freiherr Heinrich von Senden. Following studies in medicine, mathematics, and physics, he studied the trumpet between 1978 and 1984 with **Walter Holy** at the Cologne Hochschule für Musik. In 1976 he began to specialize in the **Baroque trumpet,** an instrument on which he has given numerous performances worldwide and made more than eighty recordings. He has performed Bach's ***Brandenburg Concerto No. 2*** more than two hundred times, and recorded it eight times on **period instruments**. He was the first to record Haydn's Trumpet Concerto on a modern reproduction of a **keyed trumpet** in 1987. Immer has performed and recorded with many leading period instrument ensembles including the Freiburger Barockorchester, Concentus Musicus Wien, Akademie für Alte Musik Berlin, la Stagione Frankfurt, the Academy of Ancient Music, Boston Baroque, and Aston Magna Boston. He has also worked with many notable conductors including Nikolaus Harnoncourt, Frans Brüggen, Ton Koopman, Philippe Herreweghe, Martin Pearlman, and Helmuth Rilling. In 1984 Immer joined the faculty of his alma mater, the Hochschule für Musik in Cologne, and in 1993 he began teaching at the Sweelinck Conservatory in Amsterdam. He founded the Trompeten Consort Friedemann Immer in 1988, and has also formed his own publishing house, Edition Immer, to create new editions of trumpet repertoire old and new, including music for natural trumpet ensembles.

immer mit Dämpf. (Ger.) Always with **mute**; keep the mute on.

improvisation. The art of spontaneously composing a melody, accompaniment, or countermelody based on a harmonic outline or by elaborating on an existing melody.

in der Ferne. (Ger.) In the distance. An indication for **off-stage playing**.

in stand. An indication found in music that requires the player to position the **bell** of the trumpet close to the **music stand** by a short distance (approximately one foot or less) to reduce the projection of the sound and create a subtle muting effect. Intonation and tone quality are negatively impacted if the bell is too close to the stand. (See appendix 3.)

intercostal muscles. Groups of muscles that run between the ribs that are involved in the mechanical aspect of **breathing**. They aid the expansion of the chest cavity during inhalation and its retraction during exhalation. (See figure 8 under "**breathing**.")

International Trumpet Guild (ITG). A nonprofit organization founded in 1975 to promote communications among trumpet players around the world and to improve the artistic level of performance, teaching, and literature associated with the trumpet. The ITG publishes a quarterly journal, presents annual conferences, sponsors competitions, and produces recordings as well as reprints of books and sheet music. The organization was developed in response to the urging of tubist Harvey Phillips, who advocated for the formation of an "International Brass Society" in the December 1974 issue of *The Instrumentalist*. At the time there was no organization for the trumpet to match the International Horn Society (founded in 1970), the International Trombone Association (founded in 1972), and the International Tuba Euphonium Association (founded in 1973 as TUBA, the Tubists Universal Brotherhood Association; the name changed in 2000 to be more inclusive).

Charles Gorham and **Robert Nagel** met with Phillips in the fall of 1974 to draft plans for the new organization and the first conference was held in May 1975 at Indiana University. Before the first board of directors was elected in August 1975, the steering committee of the ITG included Gorham and Nagel along with **David Hickman**, Robert Levy, **Thomas Stevens**, and Ward Cole. The first ITG officers were Lloyd Geisler, president; Clifford Lillya, vice president; David Baldwin, secretary; and Gordon Mathie, treasurer. In addition to the members of the steering committee, Bud Brisbois, **Carole Dawn Reinhart**, **Charles Colin**, **Susan Slaughter**, **Don Smithers**, and **Roger Voisin** were elected to the Board of Directors. The ITG currently has more than five thousand members from fifty-six countries including professional and amateur performers, teachers, students, manufacturers, publishers, and affiliates.

International Women's Brass Conference. Founded by **Susan Slaughter** in 1990 in response to a survey of more than fourteen hundred female brass players, the IWBC provides opportunities to educate, support, develop, and inspire female brass players who desire to pursue professional careers in music. Membership is open to both women and men. The IWBC hosts conferences and publishes a newsletter as well as a Directory of Women Brass Performers and Teachers. It also celebrates the legacy of women who were pioneers in the profession.

intervalve tubing. Short connecting tubing between valves that guides the airstream through a brass instrument when a valve is not engaged. This tubing is also called *coquille* or a **knuckle**.

intonation. The level of pitch accuracy of individual notes in musical performance. When notes or intervals are not in tune, pitch can be either too high (sharp) or too low (flat). Intonation is especially important in ensemble playing, where issues regarding **pitch standards** and **temperament** must be considered.

intrada. 1. A short instrumental work of a festive or march-like character that introduces a longer instrumental work.

2. A short piece that introduced a sonata or **toccata** written for a **trumpet ensemble** in the sixteenth and seventeenth centuries. It was also played at the end of the sonata. Prevalent in Italian music and courtly trumpet ensemble repertoire in the Holy Roman Empire, it was also popular in Scandinavia. While the intrada served to introduce sonatas for a variety of instrumental ensembles, the *Aufzug* grew to become the intrada used exclusively for trumpet ensemble repertoire. Musically, the intrada featured a processional march with triadic **fanfare** figures and repeated notes followed by a contrasting slower section and a dance-like interlude in triple meter, and concluding with a simple homophonic song. The Italian trumpeter **Alessandro Orologio** published a collection of five- and six-part intradas in Helmstaedt in 1597.

Inventionstrompete. (Ger.) Invention trumpet. Although the term is presently associated with a **natural trumpet** used for **hand-stopping** from the turn of the nineteenth century, such as a **demilune trumpet**, it was used interchangeably for a variety of different kinds of trumpets before the invention of the valve, including the **keyed trumpet** and the **keyed bugle**. The term was adapted from *Inventionshorn*, which was invented by **Anton Joseph Hampel** in the 1750s.

J

Jägertrompete. (Ger.) Hunter's trumpet, or *tromba da caccia*. A coiled **natural trumpet** from the eighteenth century that resembles a horn. This instrument is best known for its appearance in the famous portrait of Bach's trumpeter, **Gottfried Reiche,** painted in 1726 by Elias Gottlob Haussmann (1695–1774). Because of this association, it is sometimes called a Reiche trumpet. Its small size may have been advantageous for performing in cramped church choir lofts and its backward-pointing **bell** may have alleviated balance problems somewhat in small ensembles. It was the model for the **Steinkopf-Finke trumpet** with three **vent holes** that was played by **Walter Holy**. (See figure 28.)

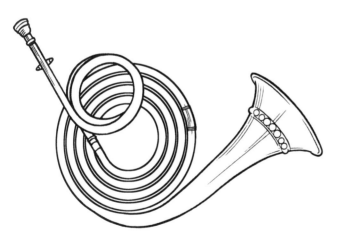

Figure 28. A coiled natural trumpet known as the *Jägertrompete.* Drawing by T. M. Larsen.

jam, jam session. To play an impromptu jazz performance; to improvise.

James, Harry (Henry Haag) (1916–1983). American jazz trumpeter, bandleader, and film star. Best known as a virtuosic trumpet soloist during the Swing Era,

James began his trumpet studies at the age of ten with his father, who was a circus bandleader in Albany, Georgia. He soon began to play professionally with the Haag Circus band and later worked with dance bands, including Ben Pollack's band. In 1937 he became a leading member of the Benny Goodman band, capturing attention with his bravura virtuosity and colossal sound throughout the entire range of the instrument. He even earned the nickname "the Hawk" for his expert sight-reading ability. James formed his own band in 1939 and enjoyed enormous popularity in the early 1940s. Two of his greatest hits were "Ciribiribin" (1939) and "You Made Me Love You" (1941), which featured James's sentimental lyricism, warm sound, and wide vibrato. He was also known for his blistering performance of Rimsky-Korsakov's "Flight of the Bumble Bee" and his own composition "Concerto for Trumpet" (1942).

James married film star Betty Grable in 1943 (his second marriage), and appeared in sixteen films including *Hollywood Hotel* (1937, in Benny Goodman's band), *Springtime in the Rockies* (1942), *Private Buckaroo* (1942), *Swing Fever* (1943), *Carnegie Hall* (1947), and *The Benny Goodman Story* (1955). He performed the trumpet solos for the soundtrack of the 1950 movie *Young Man with a Horn*, which were played by Kirk Douglas's character (a fictionalized **Bix Beiderbecke**) on screen. He also pursued an interest in racehorses and owned several prizewinning thoroughbreds. James toured extensively during the 1950s, became more involved with jazz **improvisation**, and performed frequently in Nevada and New York until his death from lymphatic cancer in 1983. A collection of his musical scores and personal papers resides in the American Heritage Center of the University of Wyoming in Laramie.

jazz trumpet. Term used in Germany and Russia in the early twentieth century to indicate the **piston valve** trumpet as opposed to the **rotary valve** instrument.

Jensen, Ingrid (b. 1966). Canadian jazz trumpeter. She studied at Malaspina College in Nanaimo, British Columbia, and graduated from Berklee College of Music in 1989. A versatile artist known for her command of hard bop styles as well as soulful lyricism, Jensen has performed with many groups including the Maria Schneider Orchestra, DIVA, her sister's Juno Award–winning group the Christine Jensen Orchestra, and the Mosaic Project. She has also performed and recorded with Clark Terry, Marc Copeland, Bob Berg, Jeff "Tain" Watts, Global Noize, Virginia Mayhew, and the Bill Cosby All-Stars. Jensen has collaborated on a wide range of projects, including performances with the soul singer Corrine Bailey Rae and *Tribute to Billie Holiday* featuring the vocalist Madeleine Peyroux, the bass player Ron Carter, and the pianist Mulgrew Miller. As a teacher, Jensen has served on the faculty of the Bruckner Conservatory of Music in Austria and the Peabody Institute of the Johns Hopkins University, and as an artist-in-residence at the University of Michigan, Ann Arbor. She has recorded numerous albums as a leader and also with the small group Nordic Connect. Jensen won a Canadian Juno Award for her album *Vernal Fields* in 1995, and has twice been a Jazz Journalist Award nominee for Best Trumpet Player.

Jericho. City in Palestine reputed to be one of the oldest inhabited cities in the world. According to a biblical account in the book of Joshua (Joshua 6: 1–27), the walls of the city fell in a battle during the year 1400 BC when members of Joshua's Israelite army marched around the city repeatedly blowing their trumpets.

jiao, tongjiao. A trumpet from Tibet made out of an animal horn (*jiao*) or made out of metal in imitation of an animal horn (*tongjiao*).

Johnson, Frank [Francis B.] (1792–1844). American **keyed bugle** soloist, violinist, bandmaster, and composer. Johnson was the earliest prominent African American musician in the United States and one of the country's most important early bandmasters. His first instruments were the violin and the horn, and he began playing the keyed bugle around 1819. Johnson performed in a black military band during the War of 1812 and was influenced by Richard Willis (ca. 1790–1830), a keyed bugle player and band director at West Point. During the 1820s Johnson led his own band in Philadelphia, which performed for a variety of municipal functions, such as parades, dances, weddings, religious services, militia drills, and concerts. As a testament to Johnson's status, he was invited to provide music for the annual celebrations of George Washington's birthday, an 1824 reception for General Lafayette, and an 1825 reception for Haitian leader Jean Pierre Boyer. He expanded his fame by performing at the spas of Brandywine, Chalybeate Springs, White Sulphur Springs (West Virginia), Congress Springs, Cape May, and Bedford Springs. Despite the growing racial prejudice in nineteenth-century America, Johnson was the first African American musician to perform in racially mixed ensembles and was popular with white audiences.

Johnson traveled with four members of his band to London and Paris between 1837 and 1838 to obtain new music and explore European trends. Following the coronation of Queen Victoria in June 1838, Johnson gave a command performance for the monarch, who presented him with a silver keyed bugle after the concert. Upon returning to Philadelphia, Johnson began performing a series of Promenade Concerts in the French style that included some of the new music he had acquired during his European travels. Between 1839 and 1844 Johnson and his band played several tours in the United States and Canada, stopping in cities such as Toronto, Detroit, Ann Arbor, Cleveland, Louisville, and St. Louis. In 1842 his band provided music for a ball honoring Charles Dickens's visit to Philadelphia. Johnson composed over three hundred pieces of band music and published widely. Although most of his musical output consists of light dance music, some of his works betray Johnson's support of the fight against slavery and the Haitian Revolution: the abolition song "The Grave of the Slave," and the *Recognition March on the Independence of Hayti* [*sic*]. Johnson's success as a published composer helped other African American musicians find publishers as well. Some of Johnson's works were recorded on period instruments by the Chestnut Brass Company in 1990 on the album *The Music of Francis Johnson & His Contemporaries* (Music Masters 7029-2-C).

Jolivet, Andre (1905–1975). French composer. He studied literature at the Sorbonne and took composition lessons with Paul Le Flem and Edgard Varèse. Jolivet's early compositional style shows a fascination with exoticism and irregular, flowing rhythmic patterns. In 1936 he formed the *Jeune France* group with Olivier Messiaen, Yves Baudrier, and Jean Yves Daniel-Lesur to promote music of substance and originality in opposition to Neoclassicism and the irreverent anti-Romanticism of *Les Six*. Jolivet was the conductor and later music director of the Comédie Française (1943–1959), adviser to the French Ministry of Cultural Affairs (1959–1962), and professor of composition at the Paris Conservatoire (1965–1970). His compositional output includes many concertos and orchestral works marked by long, modal lines. Jolivet's works that feature the trumpet in a solo capacity are the *Concertino* (1948) for piano, trumpet, and strings, *Air de Bravoure* (1952) for trumpet and piano, *Trumpet Concerto No. 2* (1954), *Arioso barocco* (1968) for trumpet and organ, and *Heptade* (1971) for trumpet and percussion.

Jones, Philip (1928–2000). English trumpeter and brass chamber music pioneer. Born into a family of trumpeters, Jones's first teachers were his father and his uncle, Roy Copestake. He earned a scholarship to the Royal College of Music, where he studied with **Ernest Hall** between 1944 and 1948. Following graduation he was appointed principal trumpet of the Royal Opera House Orchestra at Covent Garden (1948–1951). During his time at Covent Garden, he was perhaps the only trumpeter ever to perform Wagner's *Ring* in consecutive seasons on two different instruments; one season on **bass trumpet** and the next as principal trumpet, alternating roles. He subsequently served as principal trumpet with most of the major orchestras in London, such as the Royal Philharmonic Orchestra (1956–1960), the Philharmonia Orchestra (1960–1964), the English Chamber Orchestra (1960–1985), the London Philharmonic Orchestra (1964–1965), the New Philharmonia Orchestra (1965–1967), and the BBC Symphony Orchestra (1968–1972).

Jones is best known as the founder and leader of the Philip Jones Brass Ensemble (PJBE), and as a champion in furthering the art of professional brass chamber music. He was inspired to start the group when he heard the Amsterdam Koper Quartet (two trumpets and two trombones) perform on a BBC broadcast in 1947. Led by trumpeter **Marinus Komst**, the Amsterdam group was comprised of brass players from the Concertgebouw Orchestra. Jones took some lessons with Komst and started the PJBE as a quartet in 1951. The original members were all brass musicians from the Covent Garden Orchestra: Jones and his uncle, Roy Copestake, on trumpet, Charles Gregory on horn, and Evan Watkin on trombone. The group later expanded into a **brass quintet** and a ten-piece brass ensemble. The PJBE toured internationally, recorded frequently, performed on numerous broadcasts, and was widely imitated before disbanding in 1986. In addition to performing and organizing the activities of the PJBE, Jones was an energetic advocate for publishing new compositions and arrangements for brass ensembles to expand the repertoire.

As an educator, Jones served on the faculties of the Royal Northern College of Music (1975–1977) and the Guildhall School of Music and Drama (1983–1988). He was director of the Trinity College of Music between 1988 and 1994 and also served as the Governor of Chetham's School of Music in Manchester during the same period. As one of England's most esteemed musicians, Jones was awarded an Order of the British Empire (OBE) in 1977 and made a commander of the Order of the British Empire (CBE) in 1996. Other awards include the Composers' Guild Award (1979) and the **Cesare Bendinelli** Award (1993).

Jo-Ral. American mute manufacturing company. Founded by trombonist Joe Alessi (principal trombone of the New York Philharmonic) in the late twentieth century, Jo-Ral produces a full line of brass instrument mutes. In addition to a variety of **straight mutes, cup mutes** and **practice mutes,** Jo-Ral makes a unique type of **Harmon mute** known as a **bubble mute**, and a type of **bucket mute** that fits inside the bell of a trumpet, rather than being clipped onto the outside rim.

Jupiter Band Instruments. Taiwanese musical instrument manufacturer. Established by its parent company, KHS Musical Instruments, in 1980, Jupiter produces a variety of trumpets, **flugelhorns**, and **cornets**. They also make **pocket trumpets**, a "Mini-Trombone" in B-flat that they call a **slide trumpet**, and a full array of marching brass instruments. Jupiter's line of professional brass instruments, XO Brass, features trumpets in B-flat and C, a **piccolo trumpet**, and a **flugelhorn.**

just intonation. The tuning of harmonic intervals without alteration or tempering to produce pure concords with no distortion or "beating." See also, **temperament**.

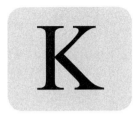

K

Kail, Joseph (1795–1871). Czech French **horn** player and brass instrument manufacturer. Although he later became an advocate of the early valved trumpet, Kail studied horn at the Prague Conservatory between 1811 and 1817, and played horn in the orchestras of the Pest Theater (1819–1822) and the Vienna Court Opera at the Kärntnertortheater (1822–1824), as well as principal horn with the Estates Theater in Prague (1824–1826). Kail also played the keyed horn, an experimental instrument unrelated to the **keyed bugle,** and performed a set of variations for the instrument by the director of the Prague Conservatory, **Bedřich Diviš Weber,** in 1819. In 1823 he worked with Joseph Riedl (d. 1840) to improve **Christian Friedrich Sattler's double piston valve** to develop the **Vienna valve.** He later worked with Riedl to develop a type of **rotary valve,** known as the "wheel valve," in 1835.

Kail became the first professor of both valved trumpet and valve trombone at the Prague Conservatory in 1826. With that appointment, he became the first professor of trumpet at a European conservatory (predating **Dauverné** at the Paris Conservatory by seven years). The following year he began to write and commission solo repertoire for the new valved trumpet and piano. His own *Variationen für Trompete in F* became the first solo work composed for the valved trumpet when it was premiered by his student, Karl Chlum, on March 23, 1827. Kail adapted the central slow movement of **Mozart's** *Horn Concerto No. 4, K. 495* for valved trumpet in F (transposed from the original key of E-flat) with embellishments, renaming it *Romanze für die Trompete v[on] Mozart.* Kail encouraged other composers to write works for the valved trumpet, including Bedřich Diviš Weber, Conradin Kreutzer (1780–1849), and Johann Wenzel Kalliwoda (1801–1866). He also composed brass duets, trios, and quartets based on popular operatic themes; wrote a **method book** for trumpet and **flugelhorn**; and adapted solo trumpet works for flugelhorn and valve trombone. Kail added the responsibility for teaching flugelhorn to his duties at the Prague Conservatory beginning in 1852; he retired in 1867.

kakaki. A long metal trumpet from Islamic areas of West Africa that dates back to the sixteenth century. Some of the instruments have been known to measure between six and thirteen feet in length.

Kammerton. (Ger.) Chamber pitch. A **pitch standard** used in Germany during the eighteenth century that was lower than **Chorton** (approximately A4 = 466 Hz), although pitch levels varied widely by region, performance medium, and time period under consideration. It developed into the contemporary standard of **concert pitch** in use today at A4=440 Hz, but in the eighteenth century, it may have been closer to A4 = 415 Hz, which is the convention known as **Baroque pitch** adopted by modern **period instrument** ensembles in **historically informed performance.**

kang t'ou, ta wang. Similar to the Tibetan **dung**, a long, straight trumpet measuring up to ten feet in length. It was played during funeral processions with its bell carried by an attendant in a sling.

kang tung. A trumpet from Mongolia made of copper in a curved shape with a brass rim approximately sixteen inches long. The instrument was made in the shape of a dragon with an open mouth for the bell.

kangling. A Tibetan trumpet made from a human thigh bone. It was played during ritual ceremonies to ward off evil spirits and to communicate with the spirits of the afterlife.

Kanstul. American brass instrument manufacturer. Founded by Zigmant (Zig) Kanstul (b. 1929) in 1981, Kanstul

Musical Instruments is based in Anaheim, California, and produces a wide variety of brass instruments. Zig Kanstul had an illustrious career in brass manufacturing before starting his own company; he worked for eighteen years for F. E. **Olds** & Son, and served as vice president for **King** Musical Instruments as well as the C. G. **Conn** Company in the 1970s. During his time with Olds, he was the first to design bell-front marching brass instruments. In addition to a complete line of trumpets and cornets, Kanstul Musical Instruments produces a highly prized flugelhorn, a full complement of brass instruments for **drum and bugle corps**, and **herald trumpets** for the U.S. Army Herald Trumpets.

karnā. A long, brass Persian trumpet that flourished during the Sassanid era (AD 224–651) that had a conical bore and was over six feet long. It was sometimes shaped like an *S*, and its Arabic name is derived from the same Greek root as the Celtic **carnyx**.

Kastenventil. (Ger.) **Box valve.**

Kendall, Edward "Ned" (1808–1861). American **keyed bugle** soloist and bandmaster. After studying the fife, drum, and clarinet, Kendall became a celebrated performer on the keyed bugle in the early nineteenth century. He made his professional debut in Boston around 1825 and appeared as a soloist with the Tremont Theatre Orchestra and the Boston Brigade Band, both conducted by his brother James Kendall (1803–ca.1874), who was also a clarinetist and trombonist. In 1835 he formed the Boston Brass Band, one of the earliest brass bands in the United States. He assumed the leadership of his brother's Boston Brigade Band in 1849, and was also a well-known circus bandsman and soloist with touring companies such as Spalding & Rogers and Nixon's Great American Circus. Like other American keyed bugle soloists, Kendall played a high E-flat instrument, equipped with extra left-hand keys for fine tuning that also extended the instrument's range. He was a dazzling soloist, greatly admired for elaborate versions of showpieces such as Joseph Holloway's *Wood Up Quick Step*. The virtuosity of Kendall and other keyed bugle soloists foreshadowed the golden era of the great **cornet** soloists.

Kent Bugle. Royal Kent Bugle. Another name for the **keyed bugle**.

Kent, Earle (1910–1994). American inventor and acoustician. Best known as the director of research, development, and design for the **Conn** Company for more than thirty years, Kent played the saxophone and studied at Kansas State University. He joined the Conn Company as a research engineer in 1940 and was charged with revitalizing Conn's Experimental Laboratory shortly thereafter.

One of his main interests was the development of electronic organs, including the Connsonata Organ. Another area of Kent's expertise was instrument tone analysis including the development of new scientific equipment and techniques for measuring acoustical qualities. One such device was an artificial **embouchure** machine designed for playing and testing brass instruments affectionately known in the Conn circles as "Hot Lips Harry." He also helped design an **acoustic** test chamber at the Conn plant with elliptical walls and a convex ceiling known as the "Bulgy Room," which neutralized directional sound properties to allow musicians to better hear the natural tone of instruments during playing tests. Kent helped develop the Connstellation line of brass instruments, which featured nickel-plated Coprion **bells**, scientifically determined adjustments of the taper and **bore**, and new electroformed **mouthpipes** and **mouthpiece receivers** patented by Kent in 1956. The holder of twenty-eight patents, Kent also developed the fiberglass bell sousaphone and the Strobotuner.

keyed bugle. A bugle with **vent holes** cut into the body of the instrument covered by keys. The keyed bugle was one of the first and most successful **chromatic brass instruments**. It was patented by Irish bandmaster **Joseph Haliday** in 1810 and subsequently appeared under a variety of names including royal Kent bugle, Kent horn, bugle horn, and patent keyed bugle. The keyed bugle was commonly built in two different sizes: B-flat (or in C with an optional crook down to B-flat) and E-flat with anywhere from five to twelve keys. (See figure 29.) Its **mouthpiece** featured a deep funnel cup similar to that of the **flugelhorn**. The keyed bugle in E-flat enjoyed wide popularity in the United States as a solo band instrument. Some of the most important soloists on the keyed bugle were Richard Willis, **Edward "Ned" Kendall**, **Francis Johnson**, and **John Distin**. The instrument flourished in bands on both sides of the Atlantic until it was replaced by the **cornet** in the 1860s. Keyed bugles and cornets both appeared together in bands between 1840 and 1860. As the precursor to the modern flugelhorn, the keyed bugle's wide bore and venting system gave it a darker and mellower sound than the cornet.

Repertoire for the keyed bugle included obbligato parts in stage works such as Bishop's *The Miller and His Men* (1813) and *Guy Mannering* (1816), Phillips's *The Opera of the Russian Imposter* (1822), Rossini's *Semiramide* (1823), and Rudolphe Kreutzer's *Ipsiboé* (1824), which were most likely written for John Distin. Two substantial solo works for the keyed bugle are A. P. Heinrich's *Concerto for Kent Bugle or klappenflügel* (1834) and Joseph Küffner's *Polonaise pour le cor de signal-à-clef obligée* (1823). North American trumpeter **Ralph Dudgeon** pioneered the revival of the keyed bugle in the twentieth century and inspired the English composer Simon Proctor to write a concerto (1991) for keyed bugle and orchestra, which Dudgeon premiered with the Richmond (VA) Philharmonic in 1994. Modern reproductions of keyed bugles have been made by Robb Stewart in the United States and Jürgen Voight in Markneukirchen, Germany.

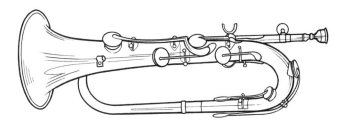

Figure 29. Keyed bugle. *Drawing by T. M. Larsen.*

keyed trumpet. A trumpet with **vent holes** cut into the tubing and operated by keys. Best known as the instrument for which the trumpet concerti by **Joseph Haydn** and **Johann Nepomuk Hummel** were both composed (in 1796 and 1803, respectively), it should not be confused with the **keyed bugle**, which had a wider **bore** and was primarily a band instrument. The keyed trumpet flourished as a solo instrument for only a brief time in the early nineteenth century until it was quickly replaced by high brass instruments with **valves** around 1840. Its tone was compared to that of the oboe or clarinet during its day, but performances on modern reproductions have shown that the tone quality of the vented (open) notes can approximate the sound of a normal trumpet at soft dynamic levels. Keyed trumpets were built with between four and six keys, but five was the most common number. They were pitched in D and E-flat at first, but after 1820 keyed trumpets commonly appeared in G, A, and A-flat, with **crooks** inserted into the **leadpipe** to play in lower keys. Keys on Austrian instruments were placed on the left side, while keyed trumpets made in Italy had keys on the right side, where they appear on most modern reproductions today. (See figure 30.)

According to Schubart's *Ideen zu einer Ästhetik der Tonkunst* (1806), the first keyed trumpet appeared in Dresden around 1770. Christoph Friedrich Nessmann, a silversmith and amateur trumpeter in Hamburg, built a keyed trumpet in 1793. The instrument's most famous exponent was the Austrian court trumpeter **Anton Weidinger**, who has often been credited with inventing the keyed trumpet, but instead he simply improved on existing designs and promoted the instrument through several solo performances. Haydn and Hummel both wrote their concerti for Weidinger, who promoted the instrument, calling it an *organisirte trompete*. Others who wrote solo and chamber works for the keyed

trumpet included Michele Puccini (Giacomo's father), Leopold Kozeluch, Joseph Weigl, **Josef Fiala**, and Sigismund Neukomm. The Italian brothers **Alessandro Gambati** and Antonio Gambati were notable keyed trumpet players in the early nineteenth century in Vienna, Paris, and London.

An influential **tutor** for the keyed trumpet and keyed bugle by C. Eugène Roy, *Méthode de Trompette sans clef et avec clefs*, first published in 1823 in Paris, enjoyed wide circulation and included a section on the **natural trumpet** along with some virtuoso repertoire in the final pages. The keyed trumpet flourished in Austria and northern Italy until 1840, especially in military music, and it was occasionally used in the orchestra. For example, Vincenzo Bellini included a *tromba colle chiavi* in the orchestra for his opera *Norma* in 1831. The keyed trumpet enjoyed a revival in the late twentieth century, and several artists have recently recorded the Haydn and Hummel concerti on modern reproductions of keyed trumpets: **Friedemann Immer**, **Reinhold Friederich**, **Crispian Steele-Perkins**, and **Gabriele Cassone**. Reproduction keyed trumpets are made by Rainer **Egger**, **Gerald Endsley**, Richard Seraphinoff, and others. The first trumpeter to perform on a keyed trumpet in the twentieth century was Åke Öst (1973) and the first to record the Haydn concerto on a keyed trumpet was Friedemann Immer (1987).

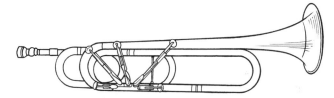

Figure 30. Keyed trumpet. *Drawing by T. M. Larsen.*

King Musical Instruments. American instrument manufacturer. The company was founded in 1893 by instrument engraver and repairman Henderson N. White (1873–1940) and was known as the H. N. White Company until 1965, when it was sold to Nate Dolan and officially became the King Company. The business was run by Henderson White's widow, **Edna (Richert) White**, between 1941 and 1962, during which time she used the name Mrs. H. N. White for business purposes. The Ohio-based company manufactured a student line of instruments called Cleveland and a professional line known as King, a name that became better known than that of the H. N. White Company. They also manufactured a limited edition of 100 **Mini Liberty Trumpets** in the late 1920s and early 1930s. Musicians who played King instruments included **Harry James**, Charlie Parker, and Tommy Dorsey. The company was sold in 1985 and became a division of United Musical Instruments (UMI).

King, Robert Davis (1914–1999). American euphonium player, music publisher, and pioneer of brass chamber music. He began his career by forming the Boston Brass Quartet in 1936, while studying composition at Harvard University. King played the euphonium and had the lofty goal of raising the artistic profile of the brass quartet to that of the string quartet. He published his first edition in 1940 (Pezel's *Sonata No. 1*) and went on to establish his own publishing house, Robert King Music Sales, in North Easton, Massachusetts. In addition to editing and publishing an extraordinary amount of repertoire for brass ensembles of various sizes, King also served as a vendor for brass music of all kinds from other publishers in addition to his own works. The annual publication of his extensive catalog, *The Brass Player's Guide*, was an essential source through which brass players obtained sheet music in the late twentieth century before the development of the Internet.

Klappe. (Ger.) Key. A venting key on a **rotary valve trumpet** that decreases resistance and improves security in the upper register. Sometimes the **water key** serves a similar purpose.

Klappenflügelhorn (also Klappenhorn). (Ger.) **Keyed bugle.**

Klappentrompete. (Ger.) **Keyed trumpet.**

Klein, Emmanuel "Manny" (1908–1994). American trumpeter. One of four brothers who became musicians, he began playing professionally as a teenager. Klein served as the assistant for **Bix Beiderbecke** in Paul Whiteman's band, taking a brief solo on its recording of *Makin' Whoopee* (1928). From 1928 to 1937 he was one of the busiest trumpeters in New York, playing on radio and on hundreds of recordings by Benny Goodman, the Dorsey Brothers, the Boswell Sisters, Red Nichols, and others. Klein was highly skilled with a **plunger mute** and was noted for his brash, bravura style. He appeared with Goodman in the film *The Big Broadcast of 1937* (1936), and moved to California the following year to help organize and lead a band in partnership with Frankie Trumbauer. In 1939 he joined Matty Malneck's orchestra. By 1940 he was one of the busiest and most respected Hollywood studio musicians, heard on the soundtracks to numerous films, including *From Here to Eternity* (1953) and *The Benny Goodman Story* (1955). He won equal critical praise for appearances at Gene Norman's Dixieland Jubilees and for performing such classical works as the Dmitri Shostakovich's *Concerto for Piano, Trumpet, and Strings*. A stroke destroyed his ability to read music in 1973, but Klein continued to appear at festivals and brass conferences late into his life.

kleiner zink. (Ger.) Small **cornett**; **cornettino.**

klephoorn. (Dutch) **Keyed bugle.**

knob, knop. Alternative terms for the **ball** on a **natural trumpet**, which is also known as the **boss** or **pommel.**

knuckle. A slang term for **intervalve tubing** that refers to the way the short, rounded tubes protrude between the valves.

Koenicke, Emile (1866–1930). German American cornetist. Also known as "Keneke" or "Kenecke," he studied at the Leipzig Conservatory of Music and emigrated to the United States in the 1890s, where he found work playing in bands and orchestras in Boston and New York. Equally proficient on the trumpet as well as the cornet, Koenicke was hired by the Victor Recording Company at the turn of twentieth century, where he played duets with **Herbert L. Clarke**, **Walter Rogers,** and trombonist Arthur Pryor. He became Herbert L. Clarke's assistant with the Sousa Band in 1909 and played first chair during Clarke's leaves of absence in 1912 and 1913. He later performed with the Innes Band, Stewart's Band in Boston, and Pryor's Band. After 1913 he worked steadily with the Victor Recording Company recording **Handel**'s famous aria, "The Trumpet Shall Sound," from *Messiah* and many other solos. In addition to his work with Victor and several professional bands, Koenicke also performed with the Philadelphia Orchestra as well as theater orchestras and freelance ensembles.

Koenig, Herman (fl. 1840–1870). German cornetist. He performed in London with the Drury Lane Theater in the 1840s and ran a business that sold brass instruments known as Pask & Koenig. His student was the Scottish cornet virtuoso **Matthew Arbuckle**. Koenig came to the United States in 1853 with the Louis Jullien Orchestra and performed in New York and Boston. He later returned to Europe with Jullien in 1854. Between 1856 and 1858 the manufacturer **Courtois** produced two "Koenig Model" cornets as well as a "Koenig-Horn" in F that was an alto brass instrument of Koenig's own design. As a composer, Koenig published a cornet **method** and several solos including *Post Horn Galop, Eclipse Polka, Bird of Paradise Waltz,* and *March in B-flat.*

Köhler. English family of brass instrument makers. John (Johannes) Nicholas Köhler (ca. 1754–1801) was originally from Volkenroda, Germany; he came to England as a Hessian mercenary around 1775 and later became a bandmaster for the Royal Lancashire Volunteers. He set up a workshop in London in 1780 and made **natural trumpets** and **horns**. His nephew, also named John Köhler (d. 1805) and identified by scholars as John (II), took over the business between the death of John (I) in 1801 and his own death in 1805. Elizabeth Köhler, the widow of John Köhler (II), managed the business between 1806 and 1809. Thomas Percival, probably a former employee of the firm, ran the business between 1810 and 1830 under the name "Köhler & Percival" or "Percival & Köhler." It is unclear whether Percival was in partnership with Elizabeth Köhler or simply maintained the Köhler name for marketing purposes.

John Augustus Köhler (1805–1878), the son of John Köhler (II) and Elizabeth, was the most important and innovative member of the family business. He was responsible for all of the innovations associated with the firm, which he managed between 1830 and 1878. He held the manufacturing rights to **Thomas Harper**'s "Improved Chromatic Trumpet" (1833, an **English slide trumpet**) and **John Shaw**'s "Patent Swivel Valves" (1838, also known as **disc valves** or **patent lever valves**), and he supplied several regimental bands with a variety of brass instruments. He also produced a **walking stick trumpet** in 1833, which was a novelty item, and two notable innovations: "Köhler's Patent Harmonic **Cornopean**," which was a prototype of the **echo bell cornet**, and "Bayley's Improved Acoustic Cornet," which had a fixed **leadpipe**, **Berlin valves**, and long **tuning slides** to facilitate pitch changes. A variation on the second instrument, a "Handelian Trumpet," was an attempt to build a cornet in F as a substitute for the six-foot English slide trumpet (it predated the **long F trumpet**). His son, Augustus Charles Köhler (1841–1890), joined the firm in 1862, and the business changed its name to "Köhler & Son." He ran the firm for eight years until his death in 1890, when his son, John Buxton Köhler (1869–1907), assumed management of the business.

While manufacturers like **Besson** and **Henry Distin** built large factories for the mass production of band instruments in nineteenth-century London, members of the Köhler family operated a small business with less than ten employees. They focused on the niche market of the English slide trumpet for sixty years and made intricately hand-crafted instruments such as the disc valve cornets and trumpets. Although they enjoyed relationships with **George Macfarlane** and Thomas Harper, no member of the Köhler family took out a patent on a design or innovation. As the market for their instruments declined near the end of the nineteenth century, the business switched to making simpler instruments like coach horns and hunting horns. After a series of financial setbacks, John Buxton Köhler sold the firm to the whip manufacturers Swaine and Adeney in February 1907 and committed suicide ten months later.

Komst, Marinus (1908–1997). Dutch trumpeter. Komst studied with Emil Kresse and served as the solo trumpeter of the Concertgebouw Orchestra from 1935 until 1972. In 1947 BBC radio broadcast **brass quartet** music with the Amsterdam Koper Quartet while on tour with the Concertgebouw, which inspired brass chamber music pioneer **Philip Jones**, who briefly studied with Komst.

Königstrompeten. (Ger.) King's trumpets, **herald trumpets**.

Kornett. (Ger.) **Cornet**.

Kosleck, Julius (1825–1905). German cornetist and trumpeter. An influential soloist and chamber musician with an international reputation in the late nineteenth century, Kosleck came from a poor family and began his education at a military boys' school in Annaburg, Saxony, at the age of eight. Ten years later he became first trumpeter in the second infantry guard regiment band in Berlin in 1843. From 1853 to 1893 he was first trumpeter in the Königliche Kapelle in Berlin, and he taught the trumpet and trombone at the Berlin Hochschule für Musik between 1872 and 1903. One of his students in Berlin was **Max Schlossberg**. Kosleck performed at Pavlovsk and St. Petersburg in the summer of 1868 and also toured Germany, England, Russia, and the United States as a cornet soloist in 1870. That same year he founded a cornet quartet with members of the Berlin Court Opera Orchestra that later came to be known as the *Kaiser-Cornet-Quartett*.

The quartet performed in the United States in 1872 as part of the World Peace Jubliee organized by **Patrick Gilmore** under the name "Emperor William's Cornet Quartette." Kosleck formed an association with the Bohemian instrument-maker Václav Červený (1819–1896), who built a unique quartet of brass instruments in circular shape (two cornets in B-flat, an alto cornet in E-flat, and a tenor in B-flat) in 1876 that were dedicated to the Crown Prince Alexander (the future Czar Alexander III). These instruments and Kosleck's ensemble both embraced the name of *Kaiser-Kornett-Quartett* (Crown Prince Cornet Quartet). As a testament to Kosleck's professional reputation, **Wilhelm Ramsøe** dedicated his sixth brass quartet to him.

In addition to Kosleck's work as a cornet soloist and chamber musician, he was also an early specialist in the high trumpet parts of **J. S. Bach**. He gained notoriety in London for a performance of Bach's B Minor Mass on March 21, 1885, the bicentenary of Bach's birth, during which he played the first trumpet part on a long, straight trumpet in A with two **piston valves** that was mistakenly called a **Bach trumpet**. Its mouthpiece was similar to that of the cornet with a deep cup; the instrument had been specially built for Kosleck and had to be played while standing because it was over four feet in length. Although the instrument bore no resemblance to a genuine **natural trumpet** from the eighteenth century, the myth of the so-called "Bach trumpet" persisted until the **period instrument** revival in the late twentieth century.

One of the most versatile trumpeters of the late nineteenth century, Kosleck published a *Grosse Schule für Cornet à piston und Trompete* in Leipzig in 1872; it was translated into English around 1907 by **Walter Morrow**, the English trumpeter who played second to Kosleck in the 1885 Bach performance. Kosleck also published a collection of fifty-four brass quartets in Boston around 1883. In 1890 he founded the Kosleck'sche Bläserbund, a large brass ensemble that won great popularity performing for public dedication ceremonies in Berlin. In many ways, Julius Kosleck anticipated the trends that would distinguish classical trumpet playing in the twentieth century: solo performance, chamber music, and the revival of Baroque repertoire.

Köstler, Johann Caspar (d. 1795). Austrian trumpeter. He studied in Vienna with **Johann Heinisch** and was known for his prowess as a soloist in the high **clarino** register. He began his career as a field trumpeter in the cuirassiers' regiment of Johann Graf Pállfy [Palfy] (1740–1744), served as trumpeter for Prince Esterházy in Bratislava (1744–1747), and was promoted to first trumpeter for the bishop of Olomouc (1747–1750) before moving to Salzburg as a court trumpeter for the prince-archbishop (1750–1769). He later served as a trumpeter for the Hungarian Noble Lifeguard until he retired in 1790. Köstler also played the violin, was a member of the Austrian Trumpeter's Society, and taught pupils including **Johann Andreas Schachtner**, who was a friend of the Mozart family. **Leopold Mozart** praised Köstler's "singing tone" and remarked that "one hears his concertos and solos with great delight."

Kresser, Joseph-Gebhardt (d. 1849). French trumpeter. Most likely of German origin, Kresser was professor of trumpet at the Gymnase de Musique Militaire in Paris until he died during a cholera epidemic in 1849. He performed with the Orchestra of the Academie Royale de Musique, the Paris Opera Orchestra, and the Société des Concerts du Conservatoire. He published a trumpet method, *Méthode complete pour la trompette d'harmonie* (ca. 1836), for use at the Gymnase de Music Militaire, an institution founded in 1836 and absorbed into the Paris Conservatory in 1859. Kresser's method was written for the *trompette d'harmonie*, a type of **natural trumpet** used in French orchestras in the early nineteenth century, and includes some challenging etudes requiring **hand-stopping** technique.

krummer zink. (Ger.) Curved **cornett**.

Kryl, Bohumir (1875–1961). Bohemian-American cornetist. He learned to play the violin at the age of ten and ran away from home the following year to join the circus as a tumbler and trapeze artist. While with the circus, he learned to play the cornet and joined the circus band, but he left in 1886 after breaking his nose in an accident during a routine. At the age of fourteen, he traveled to New York City and paid for his passage by playing violin and cornet with the ship's orchestra. He moved to Indianapolis, where he worked as a sculptor before building his musical career. Kryl became the cornet soloist of the When Clothing Store Band in Indianapolis in 1890. When the Sousa Band came to Indianapolis, Kryl sought lessons from the band's featured cornet soloist at the time, Albert Bode, who was impressed with his playing and arranged an audition for Kryl with Sousa. The audition went well, and Sousa immediately offered Kryl a contract with the band as a solo cornetist. Kryl played with the Sousa band until 1898; he may have left because he did not have the appropriate union membership to participate in international tours. He joined T. P. Brook's Chicago Marine Band in 1899 and was the cornet soloist with Frederick Innes's band between 1902 and 1906. He performed more than six hundred solos during his first year with Innes and became the band's assistant conductor in 1903.

Kryl formed his own band in 1906, the Bohemian Band, and toured for the following twenty-five years, performing at fairs, expositions, and festivals. He later formed a Women's Symphony Orchestra (later known as the Kryl Symphony Orchestra), with which he appeared as conductor and soloist. His daughters, Josephine (violin) and Marie (piano), both played with the orchestra. Kryl's cornet virtuosity was noted for his brilliant **triple tonguing**, rich tone, impressive high **register**, and phenomenal **pedal tones**. He made several recordings between 1901 and 1918 that were reissued in 2012 on the CD *Bohumir Kryl: World-Famous Wizard of the Cornet* (Archeophone 5022). As a composer, he wrote several cornet solos, including *Columbia Fantasie, Du Du with Variations, Theresa Polka, King Carnival,* and *Josephine Waltz.* Kryl performed as a cornet soloist until he was well into his sixties and once remarked that he had played over twelve thousand solos and traveled more than 1 million miles during his career. Also an astute businessman and an avid art collector, his estate was valued at more than 1 million dollars when he died at the age of eighty-six in 1961.

Kuhlo, Karl Friedrich Johannes (1856–1941). German Lutheran pastor and founder of the **Posaunenchor** movement. Together with his father, Eduard Kuhlo (1822–1891), a Lutheran pastor, he resurrected the Moravian trombone choir tradition in the late nineteenth century as a tool of evangelization. He taught himself how to play the alto trombone in 1865 and switched to **flugelhorn** five years later in 1870. In 1871 he established a Posaunenchor at his high school, the Evangelical

Stiftischen Gymnasium in Gütersloh. After graduation he studied theology in Leipzig and was ordained at the age of twenty-six in Hüllhorst bei Lübbecke. Brass choirs were always a part of his ministry. Together with the Bielefeld instrument maker Ernst David, he constructed a special type of circular flugelhorn that came to be known as the **Kuhlohorn** because he preferred the warm sound of conical brass to the trumpet in order to more closely imitate a choir of voices. In the 1930s he performed in a chamber ensemble known as the "Kuhlohorn Sextett." Kuhlo published the brass choir hymns of the Posaunenchor in piano score (treble and bass staves at concert pitch) to facilitate community participation through singing, keyboard accompaniment, and brass (trumpet and horn players had to transpose).

Kuhlohorn. A unique type of **flugelhorn** built in an oval shape with **rotary valves**, designed by **Johannes Kuhlo** and Ernst David in the 1880s in Bielefeld, Germany. Kuhlohorns were used in **Posaunenchor** ensembles (amateur church brass choirs) in Germany and have been manufactured by Miraphone, Dotzauer, and Voight. (See figure 31.)

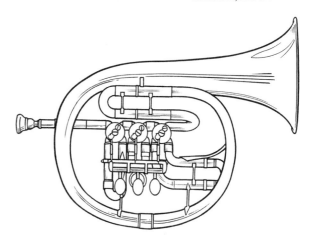

Figure 31. Kuhlohorn. *Drawing by T. M. Larsen.*

Kühnert, Albert (1825–1889). German trumpeter. He served as the principal trumpeter of the Sächsische Staatskapelle Dresden and was one of the first to introduce the use of the smaller valved B-flat trumpet into the orchestra between 1850 and 1860, in alternation with the larger valved trumpet in F.

L

laba. A Tibetan trumpet approximately five feet long made of telescoping brass sections with a flared bell and a mouthpiece with a flattened rim. It was used as a signal instrument for fire brigades and the military as well as for temple rites.

Laird, Michael (b. 1942). English trumpeter. He studied trumpet at the Vienna Musik Akademie and at the Royal College of Music with Richard Walton. Laird became interested in the **period instrument** movement when he studied with **Walter Holy** in Cologne in 1963. Through the encouragement of David Munrow, he learned to play the **cornett** and performed in Munrow's Early Music Consort for several years. An influential player and teacher of the **Baroque trumpet**, Laird standardized the system of four **vent holes** applied to a single-folded **natural trumpet** and has performed and recorded with many leading period instrument groups including those led by Nikolaus Harnoncourt, Roger Norrington, Trevor Pinnock, Sir John Eliot Gardiner, Christopher Hogwood, and Gustav Leonhardt. He has performed on the modern trumpet with the **Philip Jones** Brass Ensemble and the Academy of St. Martin in the Fields as well as studio work including films, television, and backup groups for Elton John and the Beatles. He is a Fellow of the Royal College of Music and was a professor there for fifteen years. He has also taught at the Trossingen Hochschule in Germany as well as the Birmingham Conservatoire.

LaPage. American mute manufacturer. Named for Victor J. LaPage (dates unknown), the company made aluminum **straight mutes** in the early twentieth century as well as cymbals.

lead sheet. A page of music showing only the melody of a song or instrumental composition with shorthand symbols for chords above. This form of harmonic shorthand usually appears in **fake books** and in music intended for jazz improvisation.

lead trumpet. The first trumpeter in a jazz band, who specializes in high-register **altissimo playing** rather than improvisation or soloing.

leadpipe. The initial tubing of a trumpet that includes the **mouthpiece receiver**. The **bore** on **natural trumpet** leadpipes from the seventeenth and eighteenth centuries was largely straight and untapered. Nineteenth-century **cornet shanks** introduced more taper into the bore and were eventually replaced by fixed leadpipes on cornets and trumpets in the early twentieth century that featured even more taper. In the late twentieth century, the properties of leadpipe tapers were refined through scientific research by instrument designers and acousticians, especially **Earle Kent** and **William Cardwell**; the latter is considered the father of the modern leadpipe. **Clifford Blackburn** developed a line of "Louisville Leadpipes" in the 1980s that featured enhanced **response**; he later incorporated the Louisville Leadpipes into his own line of custom-made trumpets. Orchestral trumpets in C made by the **Vincent Bach** Company in the late twentieth century featured a variety of leadpipes with different bore sizes that were named for prominent trumpeters such as the 25H (for **Adolph Herseth**), 25A (for **Bernard Adelstein**), and 25S (for **Charles Schlueter**, before he switched to **Monette** trumpets). Reverse leadpipes, where the main **tuning slide** inserts into an extended sleeve at the end, aim to reduce resistance and improve response. Other makers of custom leadpipes include Bob Malone (b. 1954) and Dennis Najoom (b. 1947).

Lechner. Austrian brass instrument manufacturer. Based in Bischofshofen, Austria, Lechner makes **rotary valve trumpets**, **piccolo trumpets**, **cornets**, **flugelhorns**, and the modern **corno da caccia**.

Leick, Mabel Keith (1883–1961). American cornetist and band director. Her first musical training consisted of piano lessons with her mother, but she later switched to the cornet. She studied with **Jules Levy** at the **C. G. Conn** Conservatory in Elkhart, Indiana, for three months in the summer of 1889 and later learned how to conduct from John Philip Sousa, who called her "the Sousa Girl." She formed her own Military Octet and served as both director and cornet soloist; she also toured as a virtuoso cornet soloist through the Rolfe and Laskey agency. She married John Leick, also a cornetist and band director, and made seven European tours with him including a performance for the coronation of King George V in 1911. In later years she and her husband both directed bands in Nebraska and ended their careers in Denver, where Mabel taught at Denver University.

Leonore Call. The offstage **signal** from Beethoven's *Leonore Overture No. 3* that originally appears in the second act of Beethoven's opera *Fidelio* (Leonore's alter ego). Scored for a trumpet in B-flat, the **fanfare** signals the arrival of the state official (Don Fernando) who will eventually secure the release of Leonore's husband, Florestan, a political prisoner about to be executed. It is one of the top audition excerpts for trumpet positions in North American orchestras.

lepatata Mambu. Term for the **vuvuzela** in Tswana (or Setswana), a language spoken in South Africa.

Levy, Jules (1838–1903). English-American cornetist and composer. One of the preeminent **cornet** soloists of the late nineteenth century, Levy began practicing on a mouthpiece at the age of twelve, and was seventeen when he eventually purchased a cornet from a pawnshop and formally began to play. The following year he was already performing with the Band of the Grenadier Guards in London, and by 1860 he was a featured soloist in the Promenade Concerts at the Royal Opera House at Covent Garden and between acts at the Princess Theater as well as with the Crystal Palace orchestra. His signature solo at the time—and for the rest of career—was his composition *Whirlwind Polka.*

Levy left England for several concert tours throughout Europe and North America between 1864 and 1876. During the summer of 1869 he was featured with the Theodore Thomas Orchestra in New York City. He joined Fiske's Cornet Band in 1871, earning $10,000 a year, an astronomical salary at the time. The Russian Grand Duke Alexis invited Levy to Russia after hearing a performance of the Fiske Band, and Levy obliged, staying in Russia for twenty months between 1872 and 1874. Although the Czarevich offered him the position of Imperial Cornetist and Chief Bandmaster of the Russian Army, Levy declined and returned to London to perform for the Promenade Concerts and later to New York to perform at the Hippodrome, commanding extremely lucrative fees in the process. He toured Australia and New Zealand between 1877 and 1878.

Levy's international celebrity and top earning power went to his head and made him famously vain, which frequently caused friction with colleagues. When he joined Gilmore's Band in 1876, he was billed as the "World's Greatest Cornet Player," and Gilmore, ever the showman, pitted Levy against another cornet soloist with the band, **Matthew Arbuckle**, in performance duels for publicity purposes. In addition to his many concert tours, Levy made several recordings and worked with instrument manufacturers as well. He was perhaps the first cornetist to make test recordings for Edison as early as 1878. He made fifteen recordings for Columbia and twenty-three for Victor, but Levy was past his prime in the 1890s when many of the recordings were made, and they do not accurately reflect the quality of his virtuosity. His association with the **C. G. Conn** Company began in 1883 when they presented him with a diamond-studded cornet when he started to endorse their instruments. Levy moved to Elkhart, Indiana, and worked as a cornet-tester for **Conn** and taught at the Conn Conservatory of Music, but later left after a disagreement and spent the last years of his life working for the **Lyon & Healy** Band Instrument Company in Chicago.

As a composer, Levy wrote several virtuosic cornet showpieces for himself, including "Carnival of Venice," "Grand Russian Fantasia," "Levyathan Polka," "Variations on Du," "Du Liegst Mir im Herzen," "Young America Polka," and "Adelina Waltz." He published his cornet method in 1895, *Levy's Cornet Instructor,* and one of his most famous students was Edwin Franko Goldman. During the height of his fame, Levy was renowned for his brilliant technique, effortless **triple tonguing**, and powerful **endurance** as well as his ability to switch registers with equally rich tone quality. Before he switched to Conn cornets in 1883, he performed on cornets by **Fiske**, **Distin**, and a special **Courtois** Artist Model named for him with a small bore and a hybrid cup-funnel **mouthpiece.**

Liberati, Alessandro (1847–1927). Italian-American cornetist, bandmaster, and composer. Liberati began studying the cornet at the age of twelve with his father, Carlo, who was a fine bugler and keyed trumpet player. His mother, Felicetta, was also musically talented. He made his public debut at the age of fourteen performing a transcription of an aria from Verdi's *Il trovatore.* Liberati enlisted in the Papal Army in 1864 and played with the First Cacciatori Band of Rome for two years before becoming a bugler for Garibaldi's army in 1866. Between 1866 and 1872 Liberati performed throughout Italy as a cornet soloist and conducted bands and taught students as well.

He joined the French Foreign Legion in 1871 and was captured as a prisoner of war in the Franco-Prussian War. **Patrick Gilmore** invited Liberati to perform as a featured soloist in his World Peace Jubilee of 1872, which was organized to celebrate the end of the Franco-Prussian War. Liberati remained in North American thereafter and became of the director and cornet soloist of the Canadian Artillery Band in 1873. In 1875 he became director of the Michigan National Guard Band in Detroit.

Liberati became an American citizen in 1876 and was invited to perform at the Centennial Exposition in Philadelphia that same year, where he heard Gilmore's Band for the first time as well as Jacques Offenbach's orchestra. He joined Gilmore's band in 1878 and alternated as cornet soloist with **Jules Levy, Matthew Arbuckle, Benjamin Bent,** and **Walter Emerson.** Liberati also played first trumpet (on cornet) with the Philharmonic Society of New York during the winter seasons of 1879 and 1880. Following a string of featured solo engagements and tours, Liberati's career increasingly gravitated toward conducting bands. He organized his own band, "The World Renowned Liberati Band," in 1889 and remained with the group for twenty years while continuing to appear as a cornet soloist and conductor with other groups. His band programs often featured transcriptions of lengthy excerpts from Italian operas, and in 1907 he formed the Liberati Grand Opera Company. At the age of seventy-two in 1919, Liberati became the bandmaster of the Dodge Brothers Concert Band Detroit and continued to appear as a cornet soloist. Liberati made several recordings in the 1890s for Edison that showcase his creamy tone, facile articulation, soft staccato playing, and secure technique in wide leaps. He was also known as an excellent sight-reader. Like **Benjamin Bent,** Liberati also played while wearing false teeth for many years with no impact on his performance.

lied horn. An amateur brass instrument similar to a **cornet** in C built in circular form with three piston valves and a bell pointing up. It was essentially designed to be a **ballad horn** pitched an octave higher. The instrument was built by Boosey & Co. beginning in 1868.

Lindemann, Jens (b. 1966). Canadian trumpeter. Raised in Edmonton, Alberta, his first teachers were Alvin Lowrey and William Dimmer. He attended McGill University between 1985 and 1988, where he studied with **James Thompson,** and went on to study with Mark Gould at the Juilliard School between 1990 and 1992. Lindemann won first prize in the Prague International Trumpet Competition and Ellsworth Smith International Trumpet Guild Solo Competition in 1992, and was also a prizewinner in the prestigious ARD Competition in Munich the same year. When **Fred Mills** retired from the **Canadian Brass** in 1996, Lindemann was hired as his replacement, tour-

ing and recording with the quintet for five years. He embarked on a solo career in 2001 and was hired as a professor of high distinction at the University of California in Los Angeles (UCLA) the same year. As a soloist he has performed in major concert halls throughout the world, at a command performance for Queen Elizabeth, at the Last Night of the Proms in Royal Albert Hall, and as a featured soloist at the Opening Ceremonies of the 2010 Winter Olympics in Vancouver. His recordings include *Flying Solo, Rising Sun,* and *The Classic Trumpet.*

lip slurs. Musical passages that involve changing pitches without the use of **valves** that include notes of the **harmonic overtone series.** Lip slurs primarily involve variations in air velocity and the shape of the **oral cavity** to change pitch while the strength of the **embouchure** remains more or less constant. The **tongue placement** inside the mouth is similar to that used while whistling rather than any rapid changes in **mouthpiece pressure** or embouchure formation. Extended lip slur studies, or **flexibility** studies, have been published for pedagogical purposes to develop embouchure strength and efficiency as well as **range.** Such studies regularly employ **alternate fingerings.** (See figure 32.)

Figure 32. A typical lip slur passage meant to be performed with one valve combination (1+3) the entire time. *Elisa Koehler.*

lip trills. Similar to a **lip slur,** but restricted to a rapid alternation of two notes adjacent to each other in the **harmonic overtone series,** usually in the high register (above G5) and known as a **shake** in jazz.

lipping. Bending a pitch up or down with the strength of the **embouchure** alone. This technique is essential for performance on the **natural trumpet** where several of the pitches are not in tune (especially F5 and A5) and need to be corrected. It is very similar to **note bending.**

lituus. Ancient Roman brass instrument. Made of a long tube that terminates in an upturned **bell,** the lituus had a detachable **mouthpiece** and primarily performed military music. Its distinctive shape resembled the letter *J* and was similar to the Celtic **carnyx,** but the lituus was Estrucan in origin and was known to the Romans before they encountered the Celts. The curved lituus is unique among ancient brass instruments because it does not have counterparts in Ancient Greece, Egypt, or Mesopotamia, unlike the **tuba,** the long straight Roman trumpet. A surviving lituus in the Museo Gregoriano Etrusco at the Vatican measures approximately 1.5 meters in length and produces six pitches of the **overtone** series in G. Following ancient times, the term *lituus* was used during the eighteenth century (mostly in Bohemia) to indicate a natural brass instrument, especially a **horn**. **J. S. Bach** called for a pair of two "litui in B-flat" in his funeral motet, *O Jesu Christ, meins Lebens Licht* (BWV 118), but the instruments intended were not those from Ancient Rome. While some have suggested that Bach intended horns to perform his lituus parts, another option might have been the **trombita**, the long wooden trumpet (similar to an **alphorn**) from the Silesian region of Poland, which had a long tradition of being played at funerals.

long-bell cornet. A design feature of cornets made after 1900 that straightened out the **shepherd's crook** to make them look more like trumpets. Long-bell cornets featured a more cylindrical bore and began to resemble trumpets in sound as well as in appearance and eventually evolved into the modern B-flat trumpet.

long F trumpet. A valved trumpet six feet in length (folded twice) pitched in F that flourished during the late nineteenth century. The trumpet was able to play in lower keys such as E, E-flat, and D through the use of **crooks** inserted into the leadpipe. (See figure 33.) The "long F" (as it was called in England) was a prominent orchestral trumpet in the late Romantic era and was particularly prized by the English trumpeter **Walter Morrow**.

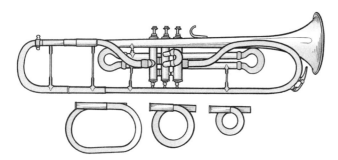

Figure 33. A valved trumpet in F with crooks from the late nineteenth century, also known as "the long F." *Drawing by T. M. Larsen.*

lontano. (It.) Distant. An indication to play off stage, as in the solo in Respighi's *Pines of Rome*.

lubricant. A substance such as **valve oil** or **slide grease** that is applied to the moving parts of a trumpet's valves, slides, or other tubing to facilitate smooth operation. In the early nineteenth century, a pure strain of olive oil known as Provence Oil was used on trombones and was most likely used on other brass instruments like the

English slide trumpet. Before the mass marketing of valve oil in the twentieth century, saliva was often used as a valve lubricant.

lur. One of the oldest surviving brass instruments, the lur dates from the Nordic Bronze Age (ca. 1000–600 BC). The instrument consists of a conical tube, approximately six feet long, made of several sections joined by bands and shaped like a graceful letter "S" (see figure 34). The bell section features a bronze disc ornamented with geometric figures. Some examples of the instrument have small metal plates hanging from rings near the mouthpiece which swing to create a rattle effect. A large number of lurs have been excavated from peat bogs in the vicinity of the Baltic Sea, particularly in Denmark and southern Sweden, where they have been remarkably well preserved. Many of the lurs that have been excavated appear to have been deposited in pairs with each instrument curved in the opposite directions, like a pair of animal horns.

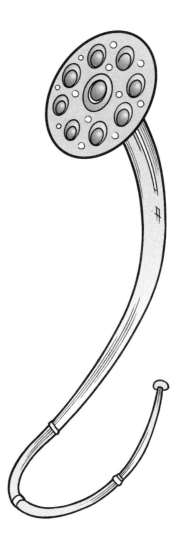

Figure 34. Lur. *Drawing by T. M. Larsen.*

Lyamin, Pyotr Yakovlevich (1884–1968). Russian trumpeter. He graduated from the music school of the Moscow Philharmonic Society in 1906 and studied with **Willy Brandt** at the Moscow Conservatory between 1906 and 1911. While still a student, he performed with the orchestra for Sergei Diaghilev's Ballets Russes in Paris. Lyamin played for the premieres of Igor Stravinsky's *Petrouchka* on June 13, 1911 (the famous **cornet** solo "The **Ballerina's Dance**" was written for him) and *The Rite of Spring* on May 29, 1913. Lyamin served as principal trumpet at the Bolshoi Theater (1912–1924 and 1931–1948) as well as with several prominent Russian orchestras. He also taught at the conservatory in Saratov (1923–1926) and the Moscow Music College (1933–1945).

lyre. A small metal clip shaped like a small harp (hence the name) attached to a cornet or trumpet or other wind instrument to hold small sheets of music for marching band performances. Lyres for cornet and trumpet usually have a long metal rod that fits into a slot that also holds a removable **throw ring** for the third valve slide.

M. M. Abbreviation for "Maelzel's Metronome" (or in German, "Metronom Maelzel"), which often precedes a metronome marking indicating the tempo for musical composition quantified in beats per minute based on a determined rhythmic value.

Macfarlane, George (fl. 1830–1860). English keyed bugle player, cornetist, and brass instrument maker. He began his career as a **keyed bugle** player, eventually switched to the **cornet**, and was also active as a conductor and a composer. He performed in the Duke of Devonshire's Band and was also active as a soloist. Macfarlane introduced the **cornopean** to England in 1833 and wrote several pieces for it as well as a method book, *The Cornopean Instructor*, which went through many editions and was still in print as late as 1863. In 1845, he is credited with the invention of the Macfarlane clapper-key, also known as the **clapper shake key**, a device that produced trills on certain notes on the three-valve cornopean. Also in 1845, Macfarlane produced a "New Cornopean" and in 1860 he patented an eleven-keyed ophicleide with W. E. Newton and R. Carte.

Madeuf, Jean-Francois (b. 1966). French trumpeter and **period instrument** specialist. One of the first to perform on the **natural trumpet** in the twentieth century without **vent holes** or other compromises such as tapered leadpipes and modern mouthpieces, Madeuf studied with Pierre Dutot (**modern trumpet**) and Jean-Pierre Canihac (natural trumpet). He performs with many of the leading period instrument ensembles in Europe including Les Arts Florissants, Orchestre des Champs Elysée, and Le Petite Bande. In 2001 he succeeded **Edward Tarr** as professor of trumpet at the **Schola Cantorum Basiliensis**, and in 2009 he became the first to record Bach's *Brandenburg Concerto No. 2* on a natural trumpet without vent holes (Accent ACC 24224). The **Historic Brass Society** bestowed its prestigious **Christopher Monk** Award on Madeuf in 2009.

Mager, Georges (1885–1950). French-American trumpeter. He served as the principal trumpet with the Boston Symphony Orchestra from 1919 until his death in 1950, and was a renowned trumpeter in Paris before the First World War, playing at the Paris Opera and the Concerts Lamoureux. He first musical training was on the horn, violin, and cornet, and he later studied with Jean-Joseph Mellet (a student of **Jean-Baptiste Arban**) at the Paris Conservatory. In 1905 and 1906 he won the first prize for cornet at the conservatory. After serving in the French army during the war he came to America as flugelhorn soloist with the Garde Republicaine Band and was engaged to play in the Boston Symphony, first as a violinist, since there was no vacancy for trumpet, sharing a stand with Arthur Fiedler. He assumed the first trumpet position in 1920. Mager advocated for the use of the C trumpet as an orchestral instrument and had great influence on its development and acceptance in America, working most notably with **Vincent Bach**. He also was the first trumpeter in North America to play Bach's *Brandenburg Concerto No. 2* in its original high range. Mager served on the faculty of the New England Conservatory, and taught some of the most influential trumpeters of the twentieth century, including **Adolph Herseth**, **Roger Voisin**, **Bernard Adelstein**, and **Renold Schilke**.

Magosy-Buscher. North American instrument-making firm located in New York City that flourished in the first half of the twentieth century. They patented a series of Non-Pareil trumpet straight mutes made of aluminum in 1929 that was popular with orchestral trumpeters as well as jazz musicians up until the 1960s.

Mahillon, Victor-Charles (1841–1924). Belgian wind instrument maker, acoustician, and organoloist. One of the first to make a **piccolo trumpet** and other **high-pitched trumpets**, his father, Charles Borromée Mahillon (1813–1887), manufactured woodwind and brass instruments for the Belgian military. Victor-Charles attended the Brussels Conservatory and worked in his father's establishment until 1865. Mahillon founded the musical journal *L'Echo* in 1869, which was published until 1886. He became the curator of the Musée Instrumental du Conservatoire Royal de Musique in Brussels in 1877 and added more than three thousand instruments to its collection over the following fifty years. Mahillon compiled a detailed five-volume catalog of the collection that set new standards for scholarship regarding musical instruments. The first volume (1880) included an *"Essai de classification méthodique de tous les instruments anciens et moderns* [Essay on the Methodical Classification of All Instruments, Ancient and Modern]," which marked the first attempt to create a systematic classification of musical instruments. Mahillon's system was revised by Hornbostel and Sachs in 1914, and forms the framework still in use today. He made numerous replicas of historic instruments that were too fragile to be restored, including an ancient **lituus** and a Roman **buccina**. He also made a straight *cornetto* with keys, which was used in a performance of Gluck's *Orphée*.

As a maker, Mahillon began manufacturing high-pitched trumpets in D in 1870. He patented the **compensating valve** system in 1886, and by 1892 his D trumpet had replaced the so-called **Bach trumpet** previously used by **Julius Kosleck** and **Walter Morrow** for performances of Baroque orchestral repertoire. In 1905 he produced a piccolo trumpet pitched in B-flat that was championed by **Théo Charlier**, who had previously performed **J. S. Bach**'s *Brandenburg Concerto No. 2* on a Mahillon G trumpet in Liége (1898) and Paris (1902). Mahillon also collaborated with Charlier in 1909 to produce a unique trumpet in B-flat known as the "Charlier-model." Mahillon's instrument designs and publications exerted a broad influence on the industry, including scholars as well as makers like **Besson** and **Schilke**. He contributed several articles to the ninth edition of the *Encyclopedia Brittanica* and received the Cross of the Legion of Honour from the French government in 1889. Following Mahillon's death in 1924, C. Mahillon and Company continued to produce instruments until 1935.

maker's mark. A distinctive symbol inscribed on an instrument that identifies the maker, workshop, factory, dealer, or region of manufacture. Similar to a trademark or hallmark, the symbol is important to the field of **organology** because it is sometimes the only clue to determining the origin of an instrument. Of particular interest to trumpeters are the marks employed by the master trumpet makers in **Nuremberg**, Germany, during the Baroque era, especially those of **Ehe**, **Haas**, and **Hainlein**. As different members of a family took up the trade, the individual marks often featured subtle differences to reflect unique identities. For example, Johann Leonard Ehe II and Johann Leonard Ehe III had the same initials (ILE;

I was the Latinized *J*), so their marks included a man's head wearing turbans of different designs. In the Haas family, marks for individual makers featured a rabbit (or hare; *hase* in German) leaping with the head turned left or right, depending on the craftsman represented. (See figure 35.)

Figure 35. Marks from three Baroque trumpet makers. From left, Haas, Hainlein, Ehe. *Drawing by T. M. Larsen.*

mandrel. A cone-shaped piece of wood or metal used for shaping the bell of a brass instrument.

Mangione, Charles Frank "Chuck" (b. 1940). American jazz trumpeter, flugelhorn artist, composer, and bandleader. Best known for his jazz-rock fusion compositions and for popularizing the flugelhorn in mainstream pop culture, Mangione studied music at the Eastman School between 1958 and 1963, and later moved to New York, where he led a hard-bop group, the Jazz Brothers, with his brother, Gap, a pianist. He first gained notice as a trumpeter in the bands of Woody Herman, **Maynard Ferguson**, and Art Blakey, playing in the style of **Miles Davis** and **Clifford Brown**. Mangione served as director of the Eastman jazz ensemble from 1968 to 1972, and eventually switched to playing the flugelhorn exclusively. He achieved success with several hits in the 1970s including "Bellavia" (for which he won a Grammy for Best Instrumental Composition in 1977); "Chase the Clouds Away," which was performed at the 1976 Summer Olympics in Montreal, Quebec; and his biggest hit of all, "Feels So Good" (1977).

Mangione won his second Grammy Award (Best Instrumental Pop Performance) in 1979 for "Children of Sanchez." His instrumental composition "Give It All You Got" was used as the theme to the 1980 Winter Olympic Games, held in Lake Placid, New York, and Mangione performed it live at the closing ceremonies, which were televised globally. After achieving celebrity status in Adult Contemporary Jazz, Mangione took on occasional acting work in television shows and a voice-over role (playing himself) in the animated series *King of the Hill.*

mariachi. A form of Mexican folk music that prominently features the trumpet. From its origins in Jalisco, western Mexico, in the mid-nineteenth century, mariachi ensembles did not include the trumpet, but primarily featured string instruments such as the violin, guitar, vihuela (a guitar-like instrument), guitarron (a large acoustic bass guitar), and a diatonic harp. The term itself refers to a festive style of dancing on a wooden platform, similar in concept to the Spanish *flamenco* tradition. Mariachi ensembles grew in prominence along with the rise in nationalism following the Mexican Revolution in the early twentieth century. A **cornet** was first added to the ensemble in 1908, and **clarinets** were added in the 1920s. The trumpet replaced the cornet in the 1930s and pairs of trumpets became a regular fixture of the group. Mariachi ensembles grew in popularity through appearances on radio broadcasts, recordings, and in films in the 1930s. One of the first documented international performances of a mariachi ensemble occurred in 1933, when the Mariachi Coculense of Cirilo Marmolejo performed at the World Exposition in Chicago. Beginning in the 1950s, some professional mariachi ensembles began including three or four trumpets in the instrumentation.

Valentin Cobarrubias (ca. 1908) was one of the first trumpeters to perform in a mariachi ensemble. Other prominent mariachi trumpeters include Ignacio Rodriguez, Jesús Salazar, José Marmolejo, Miguel Martinez Dominguez, Isidro Martinez, and José Hernandez. Mariachi styles influenced the playing of twentieth-century trumpet soloiosts **Rafael Mendez** and **Herb Alpert**. North American trumpeter Jeff Nevin (b. 1968) has devoted his career to mariachi music including performances and publications, such as the book *Virtuoso Mariachi* (University Press of America, 2002) and a method for learning mariachi style, *Mariachi Mastery* (Kjos Music, 2006).

Marsalis, Wynton (b. 1961). American trumpeter, composer, educator, and bandleader. Born into a musical family in New Orleans, his father, Ellis (b. 1934), is a jazz pianist, and three of his brothers are also musicians: Branford (b. 1960, saxophonist), Delfeayo (b. 1965, trombonist and record producer), and Jason (b. 1977, drummer). Named after the pianist Wynton Kelly, he was given his first trumpet at the age of six by **Al Hirt**, who was performing with Ellis Marsalis at the time. Wynton progressed quickly and by the age of eight was already playing in Danny Barker's Fairview Baptist Church Band. He studied both jazz and classical styles and performed **Haydn's** Trumpet Concerto with the New Orleans Philharmonic at the age of fourteen. He attended the Tanglewood Institute at the age of seventeen and studied with **Roger Voisin**. Marsalis received a full scholarship to Juilliard in 1979 and studied with **William Vacchiano**. While a student in New York, he joined Art Blakey's Jazz Messengers in 1980 and made his first recordings with the band. In 1981 he toured in a quartet with Herbie Hancock, Ron Carter, and Tony Williams and recorded his first album as a leader. Early in 1982

he left the Jazz Messengers to form a quintet with his brother, Branford.

Marsalis achieved international fame in 1983 at the age of twenty-two by becoming the first musician to win Grammy Awards for both jazz and classical recordings: *Think of One* (his first jazz solo album) and *Classical Trumpet Concertos* (Haydn, **Hummel**, and **Leopold Mozart**). He achieved the same feat the following year and went on to win additional Grammy Awards in jazz for the next three years. Marsalis signed with Columbia Artists Management and performed as soloist with numerous symphony orchestras in both jazz and classical styles, but within a few years, he opted to discontinue classical performances and concentrate solely on jazz. His jazz playing resembled that of **Clifford Brown**, **Freddie Hubbard**, and **Miles Davis**, with brilliant technical facility and a marked affinity for early New Orleans jazz. He formed his own septet in 1988 that included trombonist Wycliffe Gordon and pianist Marcus Roberts.

In addition to his impressive trumpet performances, Marsalis attracted attention as an articulate speaker, a gifted teacher, and a passionate advocate for jazz education and appreciation. He became the driving force behind efforts to establish a home for jazz at Lincoln Center that would be on an equal footing with the Metropolitan Opera and the New York Philharmonic. What started as the "Classical Jazz" concert series in 1987 eventually became known as Jazz at Lincoln Center, with Marsalis as artistic director. By 1995 it had become an autonomous division of Lincoln Center with its own facilities. That same year he also produced and starred in a four-part educational series on Public Broadcasting titled *Marsalis on Music*, which won the George Foster Peabody Award as well as comparisons with Leonard Bernstein's televised *Young People's Concerts*. While Marsalis achieved enormous success with his educational and promotion efforts, he also received criticism for his lack of sympathy for progressive jazz styles, which were not adequately represented in his educational programs and concert series.

As a composer, Marsalis won a Pulitzer Prize in 1997 for his oratorio *Blood on the Fields* (1994). His large-scale jazz works include elements of swing, **Bebop**, blues, gospel, New Orleans jazz, **avant-garde**, and the symphonic style of Duke Ellington. Some of his other notable compositions include *In This House on This Morning* (1992), *All Rise*, *Congo Square*, *Abyssinian 200: A Celebration* (for the bicentennial of Harlem's Abyssinian Baptist Church), *Blues Symphony* (2009), and *Swing Symphony* (2010). He has also authored several books, including *Sweet Swing Blues on the Road* (1994), *To a Young Musician: Letters from the Road* (2005), *Jazz ABZ* (2007), and *Moving to Higher Ground: How Jazz Can Change Your Life* (2008). More than thirty institutions have awarded him honorary degrees, including Columbia, Harvard, Princeton, and Yale universities. He received the U.S. Medal of Arts in 2005. The French government bestowed its highest honor on him, the insignia chevalier of the legion of honor, in 2009.

Martin Committee trumpet. A B-flat trumpet developed in the 1930s by a committee, literally, of the Martin Company, to be uniquely different from the French **Besson** trumpet popular at the time. Known for its ability to produce a wide range of timbres, it was a popular instrument with many jazz trumpeters including **Miles Davis** and **Chris Botti**.

Mase, Raymond (b. 1951). American trumpeter and member of the American Brass Quintet. From 1969 to 1973 he studied with **Armando Ghitalla** and Roger Murtha at the New England Conservatory. Following graduation he joined the American Brass Quintet (ABQ), which has been the mainstay of his career. He has also performed with New York City Ballet Orchestra (principal), Summit Brass (co-founder), the Orpheus Chamber Orchestra, the New York Philharmonic, and other ensembles in the New York area. With these groups and as a soloist, he has performed on over 100 recordings. In addition to performing and recording, Mase published editions of repertoire from the sixteenth, seventeenth, and nineteenth centuries for ABQ. He also learned the *cornetto* and performed with the New York Cornet & Sacbut Ensemble in the 1980s. Mase joined the faculty of the Juilliard School in 1987 and became chair of the brass department in 1991. He retired from the American Brass Quintet in December 2013.

Mason, David (1926–2011). English trumpeter. Mason was born in London and educated at Christ's Hospital and the Royal College of Music, where he studied with **Ernest Hall**. After leaving the Royal College of Music, Mason became a member of the orchestra of the Royal Opera House, moving on later to the Royal Philharmonic Orchestra, where he eventually became principal trumpet. After seven years in that role he moved to the Philharmonia, where he remained for the majority of his orchestral career. He was a professor of trumpet at the Royal College of Music for thirty years. Mason performed the flugelhorn solo in Ralph Vaughan Williams's *Symphony No. 9* for the work's premiere on April 2, 1958. He is best known for having recorded the **piccolo trumpet** solo on the Beatles song "Penny Lane" in 1967. Mason also performed on other Beatles songs, including "A Day in the Life," "Magical Mystery Tour," "All You Need Is Love," and "It's All Too Much."

Mathez, Jean-Pierre (b. 1938). Swiss trumpeter, author, and publisher. He studied trumpet with **Ernest Hall** in London and with Paolo Longinotti at the Geneva Conservatory, graduating in 1961. He performed with several musical groups including the Bern Symphony Orchestra, the Niedersächsisches Sinfonie-Orchester in Hanover (as principal), and the Lausanne Chamber Orchestra, as well as several jazz groups and theater orchestras. Mathez was a founding member of the **Edward Tarr** Brass Ensemble in 1967 and also performed with the Edward Tarr Trumpet Ensemble in the 1970s. He served on the faculties of the Lausanne Conservatory (1962) and the Fribourg Conservatory (1971) in Switzerland. In 1969 Mathez established a publishing company called *Bureau d'Imformation Musicale* (BIM), which included Editions BIM, a leading publisher of brass music, and produced the influential periodical *Brass Bulletin* between 1971 and 2003. In addition to hundreds of articles for the *Brass Bulletin*, Mathez wrote a biography of **Jean-Baptiste Arban** (1974) and published his own *Trumpet Method* (1976).

Maxwell, Jimmy (1917–2002). American jazz and commercial trumpeter. Maxwell's first instrument was the **cornet** and he studied with **Herbert L. Clarke** in the early 1930s. He went on to play with several bandleaders including Gil Evans (1933–1934), Jimmy Dorsey (1936), and Benny Goodman (1939–1943). He worked as a studio musician at NBC after 1943 and played first trumpet on hundreds of recordings, commercials, and broadcasts until 1980. In addition to working as a sideman for artists like Count Basie, Duke Ellington, Quincy Jones, and Maynard Ferguson, Maxwell recorded the iconic trumpet solo on the soundtrack for *The Godfather* in 1972.

Mega mute. A trade name for a type of **Solotone mute** or **open tube mute** made by **Shastok**. (See appendix 3.)

Meinl. German brass instrument manufacturer. The firm was founded by Franz Meinl (1910–1992) and his son Ewald (b. 1937) in 1956. Father and son were later joined by Johann Lauber (1919–1988) and the company changed its name to Meinl & Lauber. Although they specialized in making **bells** at first, the firm earned an international reputation in the late 1960s for building reproductions of historic brass instruments. Of particular note is the modern **Baroque trumpet** with three **vent holes** that Ewald Meinl developed in consultation with **Edward Tarr** in 1972. Commonly known as the "short model" Baroque trumpet, the instrument is widely used by **period instrument** specialists such as **Friedemann Immer**. Ewald Meinl took over the firm in 1981 and the company became known under his name.

mellophone. *Cor alto* (Fr.), *altkorno* or *alt-corno* (Ger.), *genis corno* (It.). A brass instrument with valves pitched in E-flat or F commonly played in marching bands in the United States. Lower in pitch than the trumpet or the **cornet** and with a wider **bore** profile, the mellophone performs in the alto or tenor range and often doubles or replaces parts for the French horn in band music. One of the first instruments of this type was made by **Antoine Courtois** in the 1850s. It was similar in design to a French horn, but with a smaller bell and with valves operated by the right hand. **Besson** and **Distin** made similar instruments in the mid-nineteenth century known as *tenor cors*. The **mouthpiece** for the mellophone was similar to that for the cornet and some instruments were made with smaller receivers or adapters for use with horn mouthpieces. A bell-forward model known as the mellophonium was developed in the 1950s by **Conn** in collaboration with Stan Kenton for use in his band.

Méndez, Rafael (1906–1981). Mexican-American trumpeter. Born in Jiquilpan, Mexico, his musical training began when he was five, when his father needed a **cornet** player for the family orchestra. Méndez took to the cornet quickly and practiced enthusiastically. In 1916, the Méndez orchestra performed for guerrilla leader Pancho Villa, who was so taken with the family orchestra, that he "drafted" them into his army. Rafael quickly became Villa's favorite player, but was sent before a mock firing squad at the age of ten when he wanted to desert. He was eventually released and moved to the United States at the age of twenty to work in steel mills in Gary, Indiana. Méndez later moved to Flint, Michigan, where he began working at the Buick Company plant, and playing in the company band. After winning a last-minute audition for the Capitol Theatre orchestra, Méndez moved to Detroit, where he began working with other orchestras in the area, including the Ford orchestra and the Fox Theatre orchestra.

In 1932, Méndez suffered the first of two horrific embouchure accidents. While warming up at the Capitol Theatre, a door was carelessly thrown open, and his trumpet smashed into his face. After studying with several famous trumpet teachers to recover without success, he returned to Mexico to study with his father. A year later, Méndez returned to the United States, moved to New York and joined the band of Rudy Vallee. After touring Southern California with Vallee's band, Méndez and his wife fell in love with California and moved there in 1937. Méndez's twin sons, Rafael Jr. (known as Ralph) and Robert, were born shortly before the move to California.

Méndez joined the MGM orchestra in 1939 and he became an American citizen in 1940. He played on several movie soundtracks at MGM and performed regular live concerts; he also performed on screen in some films including *Holiday in Mexico* (1946) and *Cowboy* (1958). After hearing an MGM concert featuring Méndez, a Decca records representative offered him a twelve-record contract. He was also contracted to arrange, compose, and author trumpet method books by the Carl Fischer Company. Méndez began to appear more frequently as a soloist with orchestras away from the movie studio. He appeared on television shows such as the *Bing Crosby Show*, the *Red Skelton Show*, the *Art Linkletter Show*, and Milton Berle's the *Texaco Star Theater*, and Xavier Cugat and his orchestra featured Méndez as a regular soloist at the Hollywood Bowl. Méndez's popularity as a trumpet soloist led to conflicts with his MGM schedule, and in 1949, he left the orchestra. In 1956 he was featured by the Mills Picture Corporation in an educational film in the series *Concerts on Film*, which highlighted famous musicians including violinist Jascha Heifetz and cellist Pablo Casals.

As the premier Hollywood trumpeter of his era, Méndez performed on the B-flat trumpet exclusively and specialized in arrangements of popular and classical favorites as well as virtuoso showpieces. Some of his trademark selections included *La Virgen de la Macarena*, the finale of Mendelssohn's Violin Concerto, his own *Scherzo in D Minor*, and *Perpetual Motion* (featuring four minutes of continuous double tonguing). Méndez's technical brilliance and work ethic were legendary, as were his colossal sound and dynamic stage presence. In addition to his solo performances, he was also a devoted advocate for music education who performed extensively at high schools in the United States in addition to his work as a talented composer and arranger. He often performed trios with his twin sons, endorsed trumpets made by F. E. **Olds**, and wrote a method book, *Prelude to Brass Playing* (1961).

Late in his career Méndez began experiencing health problems related to asthma that negatively impacted his trumpet playing. In 1967, he was hit in the face with an errant bat while attending a baseball game in Mexico. He eventually healed, but the accident, combined with his failing health, led him to drastically reduce his performance schedule. He finally retired from performing in 1975, but continued to compose and arrange until his death in 1981. He was awarded a posthumous star on the Hollywood Walk of Fame in 1983. In 1993, his musical scores, personal papers, and other materials were deposited at the Méndez Library at Arizona State University through the influence of **David Hickman,** and the Rafael Méndez Brass Institute was established by Summit Brass.

Mersenne, Marin (1588–1648). French music theorist, mathematician, philosopher, and polymath. He was the first to explain the relationship of **partials** and **harmonics** to the fundamental of the **harmonic overtone series**. His *Harmonie Universelle* (1636) expanded on the work of **Michael Praetorius** and included a wealth of information about early instruments (Eastern as well as Western) and is one of the first important studies of **organology**. He was also one of the first to suggest the application of **vent holes** to the trumpet, "as do serpent players," in order to improve intonation.

metatrumpet. An instrument developed in 2001 by English trumpeter and composer Jonathan Impett that is comprised of a trumpet covered with electronic sensors connected to a computer. The connected computer reacts to the player's sound and movements transmitted by the sensors in order to produce an improvised electronic duet with the musician playing the trumpet.

method book. A pedagogical work designed to provide instruction in techniques for playing an instrument through musical exercises and explanatory text. Method books often contain etudes, duets, and solo material as well. One of the most famous and widely imitated method books is the *Complete Conservatory Method for Cornet* (1864) by **Jean-Baptiste Arban**.

Mica mute. A type of **cup mute** made by **Humes & Berg** with a rubber rim around the edge of the cup and felt lining inside, which is positioned closer to the **bell** and creates a softer sound. Its name comes from the fact that it is often used for playing up close to a microphone. (See appendix 3.)

microphone technique. When a microphone is used for acoustic sound enhancement during live performance, the type of microphone used and the position of the **bell** of a trumpet or **flugelhorn** in relation to the microphone influence the quality of the sound. Dynamic cardioid microphones are favored for use with brass instruments in both live performance and studio recording. Wireless microphones mounted to the bell with a framework extension enable the distance from the bell to be stabilized, but usually do not allow for adjustment during performance.

When working with a microphone on a fixed stand, a trumpeter has more flexibility in bell placement and sound options. Ideally, the microphone should be approximately six inches from the bell, positioned where the end of a **Harmon mute** would extend beyond the bell. In this position, the player should not be able to see the microphone; if the mike can be seen, the bell is too far away and may not receive adequate coverage, depending on the strength of the recording input levels (whether a mike is "hot"). The sound of a trumpet close to a microphone is darker and lower frequencies are well represented; higher frequencies are accented from a further distance and lower frequencies are reduced.

Sound engineers also play a role in determining the sound of a trumpet played into a microphone for live performance or recording, especially how the sound factors into the mix of an amplified ensemble. If a trumpeter is performing live as a jazz soloist, it is best to request that the engineer use recording settings suitable for a vocalist to obtain the best quality and to avoid getting lost in the mix. When a trumpet is miked as part of an ensemble, it may be difficult for the player to hear his or her individual sound, and an additional amplifier pointing toward the musicians, known as a monitor, should be used.

microtuner. A mechanism attached to some **cornets** in the early twentieth century to improve fine tuning. It comprised a vertical hump **tuning slide** that was adjusted by a micrometer dial placed in front of the valve section before the **bell bow** of the cornet under the **leadpipe**. Cornets with microtuners included the Conn *New Wonder* model and the *Victor New Wonder*.

MIDI. Musical Instrument Digital Interface.

Mills, William Frederick (1935–2009). Canadian trumpeter and member of the **Canadian Brass**. Mills began his musical studies on the cornet purchased from a traveling salesman. He went on to study at the Juilliard School of Music and later performed with the American Symphony Orchestra, the New York City Ballet Orchestra, the Houston Symphony Orchestra, the Casals Festival Orchestra, and the New York City Opera Orchestra. He joined the Canadian Brass in 1972 and exerted a major influence on the group's sound with his brilliant **piccolo trumpet** playing and arrangements of Baroque repertoire, notably **J. S. Bach**'s *Toccata and Fugue in D Minor*. Mills left the group in 1996 and joined the faculty of the University of Georgia, where he taught until he was killed in a car accident in 2009 on the way home from the airport after an international solo appearance.

Mini Liberty Trumpet. A small trumpet pitched in high B-flat or A manufactured by the H. N. White Company (later known as **King Musical Instruments**) in the late 1920s and early 1930s. Designed to be half the size of the King "Liberty" Trumpet, the instruments were novelty items not intended for performance. Only 100 Mini Liberty Trumpets were made. They were produced with special mouthpieces and custom-made hard cases, and frequently presented as gifts to prominent industry executives and musicians including **Harry James** and **Rafael Méndez**. Although the instruments were manufactured with similar dimensions to the modern **piccolo trumpet**, they were designed as presentation trophies rather than vehicles for the performance of Baroque repertoire.

mmẹn. Plural of **abẹn**; Asante side-blown trumpets made from elephant tusks.

mmẹntia. Plural of **abẹntia**; short Asante side-blown ivory trumpets.

Mnozil Brass. Austrian brass septet. Formed in 1992 by students at the University for Music and Performing Arts in Vienna and named after a local tavern owned by Joseph Mnozil, the group performs a variety of musical styles along with comedic skits, choreography, and technical virtuosity. Their elaborate stage shows—all performed from memory—are usually built around a unifying theme that includes jazz and popular music along with classical music and Austrian drinking songs. Known as the "Monty Python of Brass," the current members of Mnozil Brass are **Thomas Gansch** (trumpet), Robert Rother (trumpet), Roman Rindberger (trumpet), Leonhard Paul (trombone and **bass trumpet**), Gerhard Füssel (trombone), Zoltan Kiss (alto and tenor trombone), and Wilfried Brandstötter (tuba).

mock trumpet. A term applied to the chalumeau, a single-reed woodwind that was an early form of the **clarinet**, around 1700. Similar in size to the treble **cornett**, it was pitched in G with seven **finger holes** and reputedly had a strident, loud sound, which may have inspired the instrument's name.

modèle anglais. (Fr.) English model. Term used by French **cornet** makers in the middle of the nineteenth century to describe instruments with **bells** positioned to the left of the valve section, as they appear on most trumpets and cornets today.

modèle français. (Fr.) French model. Term used by French **cornet** makers in the middle of the nineteenth century to describe instruments with **bells** positioned to the right of the valve section, as they appear on most **flugelhorns** today.

modern trumpet. A trumpet that is currently in use by most professional players, as distinct from a **period instrument**.

Molter, Johann Melchior (1696–1765). German composer and violinist. He studied in the Gymnasium in Eisenach and began working as a violinist in Karlsruhe in 1717. Molter studied composition in Italy between 1719 and 1721. He served as court Kapellmeister at Karlsruhe between 1722 and 1733, and became Kapellmeister at the court of Duke Wilhelm Heinrich of Saxe-Eisenach in 1734. Following his wife's death in 1737, Molter returned to Italy to observe new trends in Italian music and heard music by Giovanni Battista Pergolesi (1710–1736) and Giambattista Sammartini (1700–1775) while there. He returned to Karlsruhe in 1742 and worked there for the rest of his life. Molter composed in all of the contemporary genres of his time. His works bear witness to his affinity for creative instrumental combinations and the Galant style.

Molter wrote four trumpet concertos in D (MWV 4/12–14, 35); five concertos for two trumpets all in the key of D (MWV 4/7–11); three "concertinos" for trumpet, two oboes, and bassoon (MWV 8/5–7); two sinfonia concertantes for trumpet, two horns, two oboes, and bassoon (MWV 8/1–2), and a "sonata grossa" (an instrumental genre unique to Molter) for three trumpets, two oboes, and timpani (no MWV number). Molter wrote his solo trumpet works for **Carl Pfeiffer** in Karlsruhe during the 1750s. In addition to his trumpet works, he also wrote several concerti for the clarinet, which was a new instrument at the time. The final movement of Molter's Second Trumpet Concerto can be heard as the theme music for the television news program *Washington Journal* on C-SPAN in the United States. Molter's complete repertoire for trumpet, including several chamber pieces, was recorded by German **piccolo trumpet** soloist Otto Sauter (b. 1961) in 2007 for Brilliant Classics.

Monette. Custom trumpet manufacturing company founded by David G. Monette (b. 1956) in 1983 and based in Portland, Oregon. Monette's instruments are custom made to suit the needs of individual trumpeters using scientific methods and often feature elaborate decorations and heavy weighted construction. The first Monette trumpet was produced in May 1983 and the company started making mouthpieces in 1985, inspired by the work of acoustician Arthur Benade as well as by the practice of yoga and the Alexander Technique. Models range from the one and a half pound 2000LT to the luxuriously ornate seven-pound Raja Samadhi. Trumpeters who have embraced Monette's trumpets include **Wynton Marsalis**, **Charles Schlueter**, Adam Rapa, Andrea Giuffredi, and Patrick Hession.

Monk, Christopher (1921–1991). English *cornetto* maker and major figure in the **period instrument** revival. Following studies in history at Oxford University's Lincoln College and trumpet studies with **George Eskdale** in the 1940s, Monk embarked on a career as a period instrument maker and performer. He produced his first *cornetto* in 1955 and his first *cornettino* the following year. On April 25, 1958, Monk played the *cornetto* on a radio broadcast for the first time. Ten years later in 1968 he conceived of a way to make *cornetti* out of resin along with his colleague Len Ward at a fraction of the cost of wooden instruments. These affordable resin *cornetti* played a vital role in the revival of the *cornetto* by making the instruments more accessible to those desiring to learn the instrument. While the manufacture of inexpensive resin *cornetti* spread the instrument to thousands of early music enthusiasts around the globe, Monk's connections with David Munrow and his Early Music Consort of London introduced the *cornetto* to professionals and audiences.

Monk was also a devoted player and maker of the **serpent**, a bass instrument made of wood shaped like an *S* with finger holes, covered with leather, and played with a brass embouchure into a cup-shaped mouthpiece. The serpent is not a "bass cornett"—such an instrument does exist—because its bore profile is more conical and it lacks a thumb hole. Not only did Monk play the serpent with the London Serpent Trio (beginning in 1976), but he also began making the instruments as well as *cornetti* of different sizes. His serpents (made of sycamore and sometimes walnut covered in leather) played a significant role in the revival of the instrument. What started as a small enterprise eventually became Christopher Monk Instruments. Cornett virtuoso **Jeremy West** took over the business at Monk's request after his death in 1991 and formed a partnership with Keith Rogers (1943–2008). Nicholas Perry joined the team during Rogers's lifetime and took over his duties following his death in 2008. As a tribute to Monk's achievements, the **Historic Brass Society** established its highest honor—the Christopher Monk Award—in 1995 to recognize scholars, performers, instrument makers, or teachers who have made significant and life-long contributions to study and/or performance in the field of brass history.

Monke. German brass instrument manufacturer. Founded by Josef Monke (1882–1965), the firm began producing **rotary valve trumpets** in 1922. He developed the "Cologne Model" trumpet with a wider **bore** and a larger **bell** diameter. A third **valve slide trigger** was added to Monke trumpets in 1950. Monke invented the screw-rim **mouthpiece** in 1908. After his death in 1965, the business was run by his daughter Liselotte, who sold the firm to Stephen Krahforst in 1997. Hermann Helmich served as foreman between 1941 and 1997. Josef Monke's son, Wilhelm Monke (1913–1986), opened his own independent shop in 1945, which sold a variety of instruments until it closed in 1994.

morceau de concours. (Fr.) Competition piece. A solo for student performance examinations on woodwind and brass instruments. The tradition of commissioning such works began in the early nineteenth century at the Paris Conservatory and was later adopted by other national conservatories throughout Europe. Many of these pieces have become standard recital repertoire including Jolivet's *Concertino* (1948) and Francaix's *Sonatine* (1950).

Morgan, Lee (1938–1972). American jazz trumpeter. Growing up in Philadelphia, he began playing the trumpet at the age of thirteen and started performing professionally at the age of fifteen. He joined **Dizzy Gillespie**'s Orchestra in 1956 and produced his solo album, *Introducing Lee Morgan*. Other notable recordings included *The Cooker* (1957), *Candy* (1957), and *City Lights* (1958). His perfor-

mances and recordings drew attention as reviewers called him "the new **Clifford Brown**." When Gillespie's group disbanded in 1958, Morgan played with Art Blakey's Jazz Messengers until 1961. His biggest commercial hit came from his album *The Sidewinder* in 1963. His influence as an innovative jazz stylist continued throughout the 1960s with more than twenty recordings. Morgan leveraged his celebrity to advocate for wider coverage of jazz artists on television between 1970 and 1971. He died in 1972 at the age of thirty-three, when his longtime girlfriend shot him at Slug's jazz club in New York's East Village after discovering he had been unfaithful.

Morrison, Timothy (b. 1955). American trumpeter. Growing up in Oregon, his first trumpet teacher was Fred Sautter, principal trumpeter of the Oregon Symphony. He later attended the New England Conservatory, where he studied with **Roger Voisin** and **Armando Ghitalla**. Morrison joined the Boston Symphony in 1980 and ended his first tenure in 1984 to tour and record with the Empire Brass, performing over 100 concerts a year with the quintet. He returned to the Boston Symphony in 1987 as associate principal, a post he held for the next ten years, also serving as the principal trumpet of the Boston Pops Orchestra and appearing frequently with the orchestra as a soloist for concerts, television broadcasts, and recordings. Morrison's singing lyricism and purity of tone attracted the attention of Boston Pops conductor laureate John Williams, who subsequently composed several prominent trumpet solos for Morrison in his film scores including *Born on the 4th of July, JFK, Apollo 13, Nixon, Amistad, Saving Private Ryan, Bobby,* and *Lions to Lambs*. Williams also composed "Summon the Heroes," the theme music for the 1996 Summer Olympic Games in Atlanta for Morrison. In addition to performing, Morrison has served on the faculties of Boston University, Boston Conservatory, and the New England Conservatory of Music, where he was the recipient of an Outstanding Alumnus award, and is currently on the faculty of California State University, Long Beach.

Morrow, Walter (1850–1937). English trumpeter. He studied with **Thomas John Harper Jr.** at the Royal Academy of Music and began to play the **cornet** and the **English slide trumpet** in London concerts around 1873. He was a professor at the Royal College of Music from 1894 to 1920, and also at the Guildhall School of Music. When Harper retired in 1885, Morrow assumed the status of the most prominent trumpeter in England. Also an accomplished pianist, Morrow began to reduce his trumpet-performing commitments around 1910. Morrow represented a conservative voice in the debate over the changing instrumentation of the orchestral trumpet section at the turn of the twentieth century. With the decline of the English slide trumpet and the rise of the valved cornet, Morrow energetically championed the valve trumpet in F, also known as "**the long F trumpet**," a relatively unfamiliar instrument at the time, on the grounds that it alone had the proper length of tubing to reproduce the classical trumpet tone. By 1905, however, the modern B-flat trumpet supplanted the cornet in the orchestra and gained wider acceptance. Morrow objected to the use of the B-flat trumpet in the orchestra—he derisively called it a **trumpetina**—because its tubing was the same length as that of the cornet, but bowing to pressure from his colleague **John Solomon** and his student **Ernest Hall** (the leading British player of the following years), he began to teach and use the B-flat trumpet, at least occasionally, from about 1912. Inspired by **Julius Kosleck**'s performance of Bach's B Minor Mass in 1885 on a so-called **Bach trumpet**, Morrow had a similar instrument made by the firm of Silvani & Smith, which he introduced at the Leeds Festival of 1886. He also translated Kosleck's *Grosse Schule für Cornet à piston und Trompete* into English around 1907.

mouthpiece. The part of a brass instrument into which a player buzzes his or her lips to generate sound. Each mouthpiece has several parts of varying dimensions that can impact the sound: the **rim**, the **cup** or funnel, the **throat**, and the **backbore**. (See figure 36.)

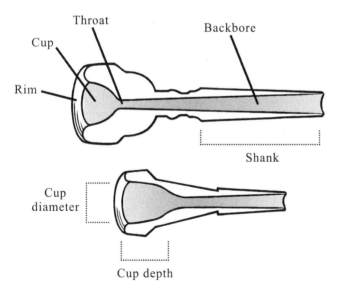

Figure 36. Cross section of mouthpieces for a trumpet (top) and a cornet (bottom) with parts identified. *Drawing by T. M. Larsen.*

mouthpiece brush. A cone-shaped brush designed for cleaning the inside of the mouthpiece, usually inserted into the **shank** of the **backbore**.

mouthpiece gap. The distance between the end of the mouthpiece shank inside receiver and the beginning the

tapered dimensions of the **leadpipe**. If the gap is too large, it can cause the player to experience problems with **response** and comfort in playing. Gaps can be caused by flaws in the taper in the receiver, the size of mouthpiece shank, and poor tolerances by manufacturer as well as the age of the instrument.

mouthpiece placement. The specific location of the **mouthpiece rim** on a brass player's **embouchure**. Depending on an individual's physiognomy, the percentage of the rim on the top lip typically ranges from one half to one third or two thirds. The shape of a player's teeth (overbite or underbite) also plays a role.

mouthpiece pressure. The amount of pressure applied to a musician's lips from a brass instrument while playing. Because the **rim** of a mouthpiece naturally compresses the **aperture** and excessive reliance on this technique can lead to injury, many trumpeters strive to minimize the use of pressure as much as possible. There have even been players who lean toward playing with no pressure whatsoever.

mouthpiece puller. A device that operates like a vise with jaws and long screws to slowly extract a mouthpiece stuck in the **leadpipe** of a brass instrument so as to prevent damage to the instrument's **tubing** or **brace** structure.

mouthpiece receiver. The opening of the first tube of a trumpet into which the mouthpiece is inserted; the first part of the **leadpipe**.

mouthpipe. Another term for **leadpipe**.

Mozart, Leopold (1719–1787). Austrian composer and violinist. The son of an Augsburg bookbinder, Johann Georg Mozart (1679–1736), and his second wife, Anna Maria Sulzer (1696–1766), he began studies in jurisprudence and philosophy at the university in Salzburg in 1737, but was expelled in 1739 for poor attendance. Subsequently turning to a musical career, he began composing trio sonatas and church music in 1740. He joined the court orchestra in Salzburg as a violinist in 1743 and played with the orchestra for forty-four years. In 1756, the year **Wolfgang Amadeus Mozart** was born, Leopold published his influential violin treatise, *Versuch einer gründlichen Violinschule*. One year later he was named a court and chamber composer. Although Leopold was named a vice kappellmeister in Salzburg in 1763, he failed to receive future promotions because of his frequent absences from court during European tours with young Wolfgang. He is best known to history for his training and promotion of Wolfgang's talents as a child prodigy.

As a composer, Leopold Mozart exemplified the preclassical style. He wrote a great deal of church music (masses, cantatas, litanies) as well as keyboard sonatas, symphonies, serenades, divertimenti, dance music, and chamber music. He did not write any operas or theatrical music, and gave up composition altogether after 1771. His best-known work for trumpet is the *Concerto in D*, which originally appeared as two movements of his nine-movement *Serenade in D Major* composed in 1762. Three other movements of the serenade contain a concerto for trombone (*posaune*). Leopold Mozart's trumpet concerto was most likely premiered by Leopold's close friend, **Johann Andreas Schachtner**, or Schachtner's teacher, **Johann Caspar Köstler**.

Mozart, Wolfgang Amadeus (1756–1791). Austrian composer and pianist. Universally acknowledged as one the greatest of all classical composers, Mozart began his career as one of the most famous child prodigies in the history of music. Under the guidance of his father, **Leopold Mozart**, Wolfgang toured the European continent and England as a boy and astonished audiences and dignitaries alike with his performances on the piano and violin, especially in his own compositions. Mozart composed his first piano sonata at the age of six, his first symphony at the age of eight, and his first opera at the age of twelve. He developed a keen awareness of international styles through his youthful tours of Germany, Italy, France, and England, and met leading musicians of the day, especially **J. S. Bach**'s youngest son, Johann Christian Bach (1735–1782). Equally adept at all musical genres, Mozart composed some of the world's most beloved symphonies, string quartets, operas, sacred music, piano sonatas, chamber music, and concerti during his short life.

Mozart's favorite brass instrument was the horn, not the trumpet. He favored the horn with four major concerti, and several fine chamber compositions. One of Mozart's best friends was a horn player, Joseph Leutgeb (1732–1811), for whom he wrote most of his major horn works. Although Mozart inserted a **posthorn** solo in the trio of the second minuet of his *Serenade in D, K. 320* (1779), he did not write any significant melodic parts for the trumpet in his operas, symphonies, or other genres. Mozart's trumpet parts primarily feature harmonic reinforcement and rhythmic punctuation. When Mozart rescored Handel's *Messiah* for a German-language performance in 1789 (K. 572), he gave most of Handel's trumpet solo in "The Trumpet Shall Sound" to the horn and shortened the aria considerably. And in his *Requiem, K. 626*, he scored a similar text, "Tuba mirum spargens sonum [The Trumpet Will Send Its Wondrous Sound]," with a famous obbligato solo for tenor trombone.

While it is true that Mozart wrote a trumpet concerto at the age of twelve (K. 47c), the manuscript is lost and the only evidence of its existence is a reference in one of his father's letters from November 1768. The work was originally performed at the dedication of the Waisenhaus (Orphanage) Church in Rennweg, Vienna on December 7, 1768, along with Mozart's *Missa Solemnis in C Minor (Waisenhausmesse), K. 139 (47a)*. Two divertimenti for five trumpets, two flutes, and timpani (K. 187 and K. 188) originally attributed to Mozart have now been shown to be spurious. These two outdoor works were most likely arranged by Mozart's father, Leopold, from dance movements by Starzer and Gluck.

Documentary evidence—especially an incident involving the trumpeter **Johann Andreas Schachtner**—shows that Mozart was extremely sensitive to loud sounds as a child and indeed had a morbid fear of the trumpet. Some have speculated that such sensitivity suggests that Mozart suffered from a condition on the autism spectrum, but that diagnosis was unknown in the eighteenth century. His sensitivity to poor intonation also diminished his view of the trumpet after experiencing some bad performances. Later in life, Mozart's affinity for warm sounds and dark instrumental colors—especially the viola, horn, and clarinet—further confirm his disregard for the trumpet, especially when it was played stridently and out of tune. Although Mozart did not favor the trumpet with solo repertoire, his musical influence is noticeable in the concerto written by his student **Johann Nepomuk Hummel** for the **keyed trumpet** in 1803.

multiphonics. An extended technique used in twentieth-century music and some progressive jazz that involves playing and singing through the trumpet simultaneously.

multiple tonguing. A form of rapid **articulation** in which both the front and the back of the tongue alternate in a rebounding fashion. The front of the tongue produces the syllable "Tah," while the back produces "Kah," as in "Tah Kah Tah Kah" (or TKTK) for **double tonguing** and TTK or TKT for **triple tonguing**. (See figure 37.) Uneven groupings can be performed with a variety of patterns that best suit the passage under consideration and the player's preference. For example, the running sixteenth note quintuplets in the "Royal March" from Stravinsky's *L'histoire du soldat* can be performed with a combination of double and triple tonguing or with continuous double tonguing with irregular accents where alternate groups start with *K* rather than *T*, as in TKTKT—KTKTK. At higher speeds the movement of the tongue becomes smaller to change the *T* to a *D* and the *K* to a *G*, resulting in "DGDG," which can also be used as a gentler variation of the more pointed "TKTK" at slower speeds. The vowel sounds that follow the consonants can be altered to suit the **tongue placement** most appropriate for the **range** of the passage. For example, a high passage (around F5 or higher) might be performed "Tee Kee Tee Kee," while a phrase requiring multiple tonguing below the staff (C4 and below) could be played "Taw Kaw" or "Toh Koh." In jazz, **doodle tonguing** engages the front of the tongue in a vertical fashion—up and down—rather than the front and back of the tongue to produce a softer, more nuanced articulation.

Figure 37. Examples of different tonguing syllables used for single, double, and triple tonguing. *Elisa Koehler.*

Murphy, Maurice (1935–2010). English trumpeter. He grew up in Yorkshire and started playing the cornet at the age of six with his father as his first teacher. He became the British All-Junior Champion Cornet Soloist at the age of twelve, and went on to play with several British brass bands, including the Crook Hall Colliery Band and the Yorkshire Engineering and Welding Band. He served as principal cornet of the Black Dyke Mills Band from 1956 until 1961, when he was appointed principal trumpet of the BBC Northern Symphony Orchestra. In addition to performing, he taught at the Royal Northern College of Music between 1974 and 1977. Murphy became principal trumpet of the London Symphony Orchestra in 1977 and stayed with the orchestra for thirty years. He is best known for his performances on many film soundtracks recorded by the LSO, including *Star Wars, Superman, Raiders of the Lost Ark, Batman, Alien,* and *Gladiator.* The **International Trumpet Guild** honored him with its Honorary Award in 2008 and he became a member of the Order of the British Empire (MBE) in 2010.

music stand. A small piece of furniture designed to display sheet music at comfortable height and distance for a musician while playing. Comprised of a large rectangular panel, or desk, with a small shelf at the bottom to hold the pages or book of music, the stand is connected to a pole attached to a tripod for stability. The height of music stands can be adjusted as well as the angle of the desk. A music stand can also serve as a kind of **mute** for trumpeters when composers require that passages be played "**in stand.**" It can also be a portable table on which to place mutes for convenient access when performing solo literature that requires them. When used as a mute stand, it is advisable to fold the desk flat, like a table, and cover the surface with a soft cloth or hand towel to dampen unnecessary metallic sounds made when setting mutes on the stand during performance. Music stands are made of metal, wood, or plastic, and come in a variety of designs from ornate wooden furniture to collapsible folding stands.

muta. (It.) Change. A direction found in some orchestral parts from the nineteenth century that indicates when **crooks** should be changed to put a trumpet into a different key. A typical direction would be "muta in D" or "change to D" from the previous trumpet pitch (B-flat or D, for example).

mute. An object that fits inside of or over the bell of a trumpet to alter the tone color, pitch, or volume of the instrument. The variety of mute designs has changed over the years as well as the materials from which they were made and the musical situations in which they were used. From the beginning of recorded history, trumpet mutes were associated with death and funeral processions. They were also used to prevent military trumpet calls from being heard by the enemy during clandestine maneuvers and to lower the volume of trumpets played indoors.

Because early wooden mutes fit completely inside the **bell**, they shortened the length of the vibrating air column at the point of contact and raised the pitch of the trumpet; the airstream exited the trumpet through an **open tube** in the center of the mute. (See figure 4 under "**Baroque mute.**") Later mute designs, such as the common **straight mute**, employed three strips of cork to suspend the mute inside the bell in order to be nontransposing: the vertical cork strips allowed air to escape around the sides of the mute so that they would not alter the pitch of the trumpet. Twentieth-century mutes that used bands of cork to seal the bell, such as the **Harmon mute, Solotone mute (Clear Tone** mute) and **practice mute**, feature larger internal chambers designed to mimic the shape of the bell to prevent them from excessively raising the pitch.

Although wooden stoppers were found with the trumpets (**šnb**) in the tomb of Ancient Egyptian King Tutankhamun (ca. 1323 BC), they were most likely intended to protect the instrument during transport or to absorb moisture rather than to serve as mutes. The first mention of trumpet mutes appears in a 1511 account of a carnival in Florence where a pageant involving a *Carro della Morte* (Chariot of Death) designed by Piero di Cosimo featured singers dressed as skeletons who reminded spectators of their mortality to the accompaniment of muted trumpets. The opening "Toccata" of Monteverdi's opera, *L'Orfeo* (1607) features a muted trumpet ensemble, and a note in the score, "to be played one tone higher as it is desired that the trumpets play muted," indicates that the mutes were expected to change the pitch (transpose the key). Musicologist Wolfgang Osthof has suggested that Monteverdi muted the trumpets because *L'Orfeo* was first performed in an intimate chamber in Mantua for a small audience.

Marin Mersenne notes the use of muted trumpets during stealth military maneuvers and presents a drawing of a Baroque mute in his *Harmonie Universelle* (1636), and **Girolamo Fantini** mentions mutes in his 1638

Metodo, including several solo works for muted trumpet and keyboard. Dietrich Buxtehude scores for transposing muted trumpets in his 1672 cantata *Auf Stimmet die Saiten* with the trumpets in C, but with the strings playing in D. Daniel Speer discusses mutes in his *Vierfaches Musicalisches Kleeblatt* (1697), writing that they make the trumpet's tone "more delicate" and would cause "the pitch to rise and make the sound seem to come from afar," also noting that "it is more difficult to play muted."

Mozart scored for nontransposing muted trumpets in his opera *Idomeneo* (1780), and as **Tom Crown** has pointed out, letters from Mozart asking his father to send "the mutes made in Vienna" from Salzburg to Munich for the opera's premiere, shows that nontransposing mutes were a relatively new invention at the time. **Johann Ernst Altenburg** discusses the traditional uses of mutes in his 1795 treatise (hushed military signals, funeral processions, and transposing pitch) as well quiet practice for embouchure development (perhaps due to increased **back pressure** and to minimize disturbance to others while practicing on a regular basis).

The first patent for a trumpet mute in the United States appeared in 1865, when John F. Stratton (1832–1912) patented a prototype of an early **Harmon mute** in New York that was not commercially produced. Wagner scored for muted trumpets in several of his works (*Siegfried* was the first in 1871) and so did Gustav Mahler and Richard Strauss, whose tone poem *Don Quixote* (1889) requires the entire brass section to play muted while **flutter tonguing** to simulate the sound of a flock of sheep. The metal **straight mute** was commonly assumed by composers who requested muted passages in their orchestral trumpet parts. The **echo bell cornet** (with a built-in mute accessed by a fourth valve) was a novelty at the turn of the twentieth century.

Jazz trumpeters created an array of colorful mutes in the twentieth century including the **cup mute**, the **Harmon mute**, the **Solotone mute**, the **bucket mute**, the **derby mute**, and **the plunger mute**. As mute makers strove for continuous innovation and new colors in the Swing Era, fanciful trade names for unique mutes proliferated, such as the **Mica mute**, the **Velvet tone mute**, and the **Buzz-Wow mute**. Some mutes were improvised such as putting the hand in the bell or covering the bell using found materials such as a handkerchief or a beer glass. **Joseph "King" Oliver** was a noted innovator in jazz mute techniques. Although he never used a Harmon mute, he was known for creating wah-wah effects (without a plunger) and other unique sound options, such as putting a handful of kazoos in the bell.

These mutes and several variations on their designs appear in **avant-garde** contemporary works and continue to develop as musicians innovate to create new sounds and improve the acoustical properties of existing mutes. Yamaha developed an electronic **practice mute** that operated in conjunction with a sound processor known as the Silent Brass system that enabled the player to simulate reverberant acoustic environments through headphones while playing. Prominent makers of trumpet mutes include **Shastock**, **Humes & Berg**, **Tom Crown**, **Jo-Ral**, **Denis Wick**, and **TrumCor**. (See appendix 3.)

mute cornett. A type of **straight cornett** bored out of a single piece of wood that features a mouthpiece carved into the body of the instrument. Because of the unique design of the mouthpiece, the bottom of its **cup** merges gently into the **bore** of the instrument without a **backbore** and with a gentle **shoulder** that influences the warm, dark sound of the mute cornett. Boxwood and fruitwoods are often used to make the instrument.

Nagel, Robert (b. 1924). North American trumpeter and pioneer of brass chamber music. Nagel earned degrees in composition and a diploma in trumpet performance from the Juilliard School of Music and performed in concerts and recordings in New York City for twenty years, including a recording of Stravinksy's *L'histoire du soldat*, with the composer conducting. In 1954 he founded the **New York Brass Quintet**, the first professional ensemble of its kind, and led the quintet for thirty-one years until the group disbanded in 1984. He was a co-founder of the **International Trumpet Guild** in 1975 and taught at several institutions including the Yale University School of Music (for thirty-one years), the New England Conservatory, the North Carolina School of the Arts, the Manhattan School of Music, and Juilliard. In 1999 he received the **Cesare Bendinelli** Award. Also involved in composition and publishing, he is a member of the American Composers Alliance and the president of Mentor Music.

Nakariakov, Serge (b. 1977). Russian trumpeter. He began his musical studies on the piano at the age of six with his father, Mikhail, but moved on to the trumpet at the age of nine (also studying with his father) after a spinal injury ended his piano studies. He made astonishingly rapid progress and began to perform with orchestras in major concert halls of the Soviet Union at the age of ten. His family moved to Israel in 1991 to circumvent Soviet travel restrictions. The next year he won the Prix Davidoff at the Schleswig-Holstein Festival in 1992 and released his debut album later that year at the age of fifteen. Since then he has appeared in many of the world's leading music centers, including the Hollywood Bowl, Lincoln Center, the Royal Festival Hall, and the Royal Albert Hall in London. In 2006 Nakariakov premiered "Ad absurdum" with the Munich Chamber Orchestra, a concerto written for him by Jörg Widmann, featuring his unique **circular breathing** ability. In recent years he has performed transcriptions of cello and bassoon repertoire on a **Courtois** four-valve **flugelhorn** to critical acclaim.

natural trumpet. A trumpet comprised of a single length of tubing without **valves**, **vent holes**, a **slide**, or any other devices to modify the pitch. The classic trumpet of the seventeenth and eighteenth centuries, the natural trumpet was limited to the notes of the **harmonic overtone series** of a key determined by the length of the tubing (eight feet of tubing produced a harmonic series on C while seven feet of tubing produced a series on D). A diatonic scale could be played in the upper octave starting on the eighth partial and composers in the Baroque era exploited this high register, known as the **clarino** range, by writing some of the trumpet's greatest repertoire. The technique of clarino playing was marked by the necessity to adjust pitches by **lipping** because several notes of the harmonic series (especially the seventh, eleventh, and thirteenth partials) are naturally out-of-tune with equal **temperament**.

The **mouthpiece** for the natural trumpet differs from that of the modern trumpet in several ways. The rim is flatter and wider, and there is a sharp edge between the **cup** and the **throat**, which is also larger. The **shank** is longer and thicker, and the sharp edge or **shoulder** between the cup and the throat enhances the precision of the trumpet's response. These mouthpiece dimensions, along with the trumpet's wider **bore**, facilitate the practice of lipping out-of-tune partials into tune and also make it possible to produce usable notes between the partials (like B-natural and C-sharp). The parts of the natural trumpet are freely adjustable and are not soldered together including the first **yard** (including the **leadpipe**), the second yard (on the bottom), the bell section, and the connecting U-shaped **bows**. (See figure 38.)

The **period-instrument** revival in the twentieth century inspired several instrument makers to craft natural trumpets using historic methods, especially Robert Barclay, who wrote the essential guide *The Art of the Trumpet-Maker* (Oxford University Press, 1992), and organized annual summer trumpet-making workshops beginning in 1993. Other makers of natural trumpets include Michael Münkwicz, Graham Nicholson, and Markus Raquet. It is important not to confuse the natural trumpet with the **Baroque trumpet**, which is a twentieth-century compromise instrument with **vent holes**.

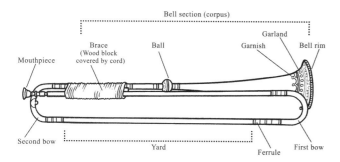

Figure 38. An eighteenth-century natural trumpet with parts identified. *Drawing by T. M. Larsen.*

naubat. A Persian trumpet ensemble featuring the long, straight trumpet known as the **karnā**.

Neruda, Jan Křtitel Jiři (ca. 1711–1776). Czech composer active in Germany. His name is rendered in German as Johann Baptist Georg Neruda. Trained as a violinist and cellist, Neruda began working at the court of Count Rutowski in Dresden in 1742 as a violinist and remained there for the rest of this life. Of his ninety-seven compositions, one that is familiar to trumpeters is the concerto written in 1750 for a "corno" in high E-flat that is often performed on a modern E-flat trumpet today. The concerto was written for the horn virtuoso Johann Georg Knechtel (ca. 1715–after 1766), who played in the Dresden court orchestra between 1734 and 1756 and specialized in the high register. In the twentieth century, **Edward Tarr** was the first to perform the concerto on a modern **corno da caccia**. Other trumpeters who also recorded the concerto on small piccolo horns in trumpet range were **Ludwig Güttler** and **Franz Streitwieser**.

New Orleans Jazz. See Dixieland.

New York Brass Quintet. One of the pioneer ensembles in the history of brass chamber music. Formed in 1954 by trumpeter **Robert Nagle** and tubist Harvey Phillips, the quintet was the first professional group of its kind. The original members of the NYBQ were Robert Nagel (trumpet), John Glasel (trumpet), Frederick Schmidt (horn), Erwin Price (trombone), and Harvey Philips (tuba). By 1966 the personnel stabilized to include Nagel and Allan Dean on trumpet, Paul Ingraham on horn, John Swallow on trombone, and Toby Hanks on tuba. The repertoire of the NYBQ started out with works like **Eugène Bozza**'s *Sonatine* (1951) and Ingolf Dahl's *Music for Brass Instruments* (1944) as well as numerous transcriptions of Renaissance and Baroque works. They began touring in 1960 and spread the popularity of the **brass quintet** medium around the world and prompted more composers to write brass chamber music. The NYBQ officially disbanded in 1984 after thirty-one years of pioneering work to establish the brass quintet as a vehicle for artistic brass playing though extensive tours, recordings, and the development of repertoire from composers like Gunther Schuller, Jacob Druckman, Alvin Etler, Karel Husa, and Alec Wilder.

nodal point. A location where sound waves rebound off the inner walls of the tube of a wind instrument when it is played. The sound waves pulse at a rate of speed determined by the velocity of the **airstream** along with the intensity of the lip vibration in the **embouchure**. Low notes generate slow pulses which in turn create long sound waves with fewer nodal points while faster pulses for higher notes produce shorter sound waves with more nodal points. **Vent holes** are cut at selected nodal points on some brass instruments including some nineteenth-century **posthorns** and modern **Baroque trumpets** to enable **nodal venting**, which is a twentieth-century compromise technique employed in **historically informed performance**.

nodal venting. When a **vent hole** is opened (uncovered) to access the **harmonic overtone series** of the shortened tube rather than the complete length of the trumpet in order to make additional notes accessible; however, this negatively affects the tone quality because it reduces the overtones in the sound by half. It causes the sound wave pulsation to stop at the point of the hole, cutting the vibrating air column in half. The use of vent holes on a brass instrument was first suggested by **Marin Mersenne** in the early seventeenth century. The first surviving trumpet with vent holes is an eighteenth-century silver trumpet designed by **William Shaw** in 1787 known as a **Harmonic trumpet** with four vent holes, three of which are covered by an adjustable metal sleeve. Nodal venting played an important role in the invention of the **keyed trumpet** and the **keyed bugle** at the turn of the nineteenth century, instruments later eclipsed by the invention of the **valve** and its application to trumpets and cornets. The first trumpet in the twentieth century to employ nodal venting was made by **Otto Steinkopf** and **Helmut Finke** in 1959 and played by **Walter Holy**.

It was a coiled trumpet with three vent holes designed after the *Jägertrompete* held by **Gottfried Reiche** in the famous portrait by E. G. Haussman from 1727.

nominal pitch. The pitch by which a brass instrument is named, such as a C trumpet or an E-flat cornet. This pitch is the **fundamental** of the **harmonic overtone series** produced by the primary length of tubing of which the instrument is made, such as eight-foot C or seven-foot D.

nonharmonic tones. Pitches that are not included in the **harmonic overtone series**. Such pitches played an important role in early trumpet music of the seventeenth and eighteenth centuries before the invention of the valve. Some, like B-natural4 and C-sharp5, were available through the process of **lipping**, or **note bends**, but some notes were not, such as A4, although **Girolamo Fantini** was reputed to be able to perform it and included it in some of his compositions.

note bending. A practice technique designed to strengthen the **embouchure** and improve pitch centering by bending a given note down one half step with only the lip muscles, not the valves. Similar to the technique of **lipping** used to correct notes on the **natural trumpet**, note bending was an important component of the pedagogy of **James Stamp**.

ntahera. 1. The ivory **side-blown trumpet** ensemble of the Asante nation in Ghana, closely attached to the Asantehene (King of the Asante).

2. A powerful spirit released through the playing the Asante ivory trumpets or, **mmen**.

Nuremberg. A city in the German state of Bavaria with a long tradition of brass instrument manufacturing. Nuremberg was of particular importance during the seventeenth and eighteenth centuries when it benefitted from a rich supply of copper and zinc ore (calamine) accessible through the trade agreements of the Hanseatic League as well as a tradition of fine craftsmanship. Many of the great trumpet makers of the Baroque era came from Nuremberg including **Ehe, Haas, Hannlein,** and **Schnitzer**.

off-stage playing. Trumpet or cornet solos in orchestral works or operas that require the trumpeter to perform off-stage. Off-stage solos appear in several works, notably **Beethoven**'s *Leonore Overture Nos. 2 and 3*, Mahler's *Symphony No. 1* (the entire trumpet section), *Symphony No. 3* (the **posthorn** solo in the third movement), and **Respighi**'s *Pines of Rome*. When playing off-stage, the acoustics of the performance space should be taken into account. Distance tends to make pitches sound flat, so tuning sharp is usually necessary to compensate.

offen. (Ger.) Open, not muted. The term can also be an instruction to remove a **mute**.

ohne Dämpfer. (Ger.) Without a **mute**.

Olds. American brass instrument manufacturer. Founded by trombonist Frank Ellsworth (F. E.) Olds (1861–1928) in 1908, the company initially specialized in making trombones and went on to produce a famous line of trumpets and cornets. The company changed its name to F. E. Olds and Son when Frank's son, Reginald B. Olds (1899–1970), joined the business. The company moved into a new factory in Los Angeles in 1922. Following his father's death in 1928, Reginald took over the company and began producing a prestigious line of trumpets. Following the Second World War, Chicago Musical Instruments (CMI) purchased the company and Foster A. Reynolds (1884–1960) joined the staff as plant supervisor. Reynolds was responsible for signing **Rafael Mendez** as a clinician and endorser of Olds trumpets in the 1940s. Zigmant **Kanstul** joined the team in 1953 and Dale Olson (b. 1935) served as director of research between 1961 and 1968 before the company went out of business in 1979. Some of the respected Olds trumpet models included the large-**bore** "Opera," the "Super," the "Recording," and the "Ambassador."

olifant (also oliphant). Medieval hunting horn made of ivory. Its name was derived from the Old French word for *elephant*, the source of the tusk from which the end-blown horn was made. Olifants were made in the tenth and eleventh centuries primarily in Italy. A surviving instrument is the "Horn of Ulf" in York Minster, UK. The use of the olifant as a **signal** instrument is immortalized in the *Chanson de Roland*.

Oliver, Joseph Nathan "King" (1885–1938). American cornetist, bandleader, and jazz pioneer. Widely known as Louis Armstrong's mentor, Oliver's innovations, in the use of **mutes** and novelty cornet playing style, transformed the sound world of early jazz. Born in Abend, Louisiana, Oliver's family moved to New Orleans in his youth. His first instrument was the trombone and he also played alto and baritone **saxhorns** before switching to the **cornet**. His first teacher was Walter Kinchin and he also studied with George McCullum Sr., Willie "Bunk" Johnson, and Frank Guarante. Oliver played cornet in a number of New Orleans brass bands and dance bands between 1908 and 1917. He led a successful band during that time with trombonist Kid Ory that enjoyed wide popularity as the best group of its kind in New Orleans with audiences across all economic and racial lines. Oliver earned the nickname "King" when he defeated Freddie Keppard and Manuel Perez in a cornet-playing contest.

After moving to Chicago in 1918, Oliver started his own band and toured the Chicago area as well as California by 1921. King Oliver's Creole Jazz Band made a series of recordings in 1923 that included a young **Louis Armstrong** on second cornet. Oliver's band toured in the Midwest and Pennsylvania in 1924, but Armstrong left the group to play with Fletcher Henderson in New York. Between 1925 and 1927 Oliver reorganized and enlarged the band as the Dixie Syncopaters. When the group disbanded, Oliver performed with a variety of jazz groups until 1931 and recorded on several labels including Gennett, Okeh, Columbia, Paramount, and Victor. Suffering from financial problems caused by the Great Depression as well as dental ailments caused by tooth decay and gum disease, Oliver retired from performing and moved to Savannah, Georgia, in 1937. He spent the last year of his life working as a pool hall attendant until his death in 1938 at the age of fifty-two.

Oliver pioneered many of the mute techniques and expressive styles that came to be associated with jazz trumpet playing. Some of Oliver's best-known recordings include *Dippermouth Blues*, *Sugar Foot Stomp*, *Sweet Like This*, *Snag It*, *Doctor Jazz*, *Canal Street Blues*, *Wa Wa Wa*, and *West End Blues*. Although he never used a **Harmon mute**, Oliver experimented with placing various objects inside of and in front of the **bell** to create **wah-wah** effects like a plumber's rubber **plunger**, a **derby** hat, a drinking glass or cup, and a bottle. He also favored the use of a small metal mute by C. G. **Conn**, and was known to place a handful of kazoos inside the bell and to shape his right hand over the bell to create unique sounds. These innovations inspired many of the mutes later created by **Humes & Berg** and **Shastok**, such as the **Buzz-Wow mute**, the Harmon (or wah-wah) mute, and the **Solotone mute** (or **Clear Tone mute**). One of Oliver's students, Louis Panico (1898–1986), published the book *The Novelty Cornetist* (Forster Music, 1927), which includes photos demonstrating some of the techniques he learned from Oliver. The subtitle of Panico's book catalogs the unique sounds created: *A Complete, Thorough Exposition of How to Execute Every Known Trick on the Cornet Such as Baby Talk, Baby Cry, Blues, Chinese Effect, Flutter Tongue, Horse Neigh, Laugh, Sneeze, Improvisation, and Other Effects.*

open. To play without a **mute**. The term most often appears as a performance indication to direct a player to remove a mute after a specific passage.

open tube mute. A type of **mute** that fits completely into the **bell** of a trumpet and includes a hollow tube through the center. While this description is not a common name for a mute, it is a suitable classification for several different types of mutes, such as the wooden **Baroque mute**, the **Harmon mute**, the **Solotone mute**, the **Clear Tone mute**, the **Mega mute**, and the **double mute**. (See appendix 3.)

ophicleide. *Ophicléide, basse d'harmonie, contrebasse d'harmonie* (Fr.), *ophikleide* (Ger.), *oficleide* (It.). An ancestor of the tuba that is a bass version of the **keyed bugle**. Invented by **Halary** in Paris in 1817, the ophicleide has a wide, conical bore, and eleven **finger holes** covered by keys. Its sound and intonation are more stable than that of the **serpent**, but it lacked the strength and presence of the tuba, which eventually supplanted it. It was the main brass bass for bands and orchestras for most of the nineteenth century and has been revived for those parts that Berlioz, Mendelssohn, and others wrote for it. The instrument's unusual name betrays its development from the serpent before the invention of the modern tuba. The bass wind instrument in bands before the ophicleide was an upright serpent built in the shape of a bassoon, known as the bass horn. Therefore, the ophicleide is essentially an upright serpent with keys, from the Greek word for *serpent* (*ophis*) plus *kleis* (cover or key). Both the serpent and the ophicleide have enjoyed a revival in the twentieth-century **period-instrument** movement.

oral cavity. The interior of the mouth.

orbicularis oris. The O-shaped sphincter muscle that surrounds the mouth and controls the ability of the lips to pucker like a drawstring. This muscle is crucial to the function of a trumpeter's **embouchure**, and has been known to rupture in cases of extreme overuse. (See figure 17 under "**embouchure**.")

organisirte Trompete. (Ger.) Organized trumpet. Term used by **Anton Weidinger** to describe the **keyed trumpet** on concert programs at the turn on the nineteenth century.

organology. The study of musical instruments including their history, design, evolution, and performance considerations as well as their social and cultural uses. Organology plays a vital role in the study of trumpet history because the instruments of the trumpet family have changed so radically and so frequently over the centuries. One of the first studies of organology was **Praetorius**'s *Syntagma musicum ii* (1618), which included illustrations of contemporary musical instruments in its *Theatrum instrumentorum*. Erich Moritz von Hornbostel and Curt Sachs devised a classification system in 1914 that enabled ethnomusicologists to discuss instruments from nonwestern cultures in terms of their sound production methods. For example, brass instruments are classified in this system as lip-vibrated **aerophones**. Organologists who have accomplished important work studying instruments of the trumpet family include Eric Halfpenny, Sabine Klaus, and Arnold Myers. The leading society for organology is the **Galpin Society**.

ornamentation. The decoration of a melodic line in order to enhance expression or to provide a vehicle for virtuosic display. Other terms for the practice include *pasaggi*, divisions, and embellishment. Rules for ornamentation from earlier style periods appear in **treatises** and **method books** and are considered an important facet of **performance practice**.

Orologio, Alessandro (ca. 1550–ca. 1633). Italian composer and trumpeter. Orologio spent most of his career in German-speaking lands and was one of the first ensemble instrumentalists to achieve a successful career as both a performer and a composer in the sixteenth century. He published a set of **intradas** in 1597 dedicated to King Christian IV of Denmark.

Osiris. The god of the afterlife in Ancient Egypt who was worshipped with the sound of the trumpet (**šnb**).

Öst, Åke (b. 1941). Swedish trumpeter. The first trumpeter to perform **Haydn**'s Trumpet Concerto on a modern reproduction of a **keyed trumpet** in the twentieth century. The performance took place on March 24, 1973, in Gotland with the Motala Orkesterförening on a trumpet made by Adolph **Egger**, while Öst was a student of **Edward Tarr**. He eventually gave up the trumpet to pursue a medical career as the head of pathology and cytology at a prominent Stockholm hospital.

ottoni. (It.) Brass instruments.

over-the-shoulder cornet. A unique type of brass instrument that flourished in the United States between approximately 1850 and 1890. Patented by **Allen Dodworth** in 1838, over-the-shoulder (OTS) brass instruments developed from upright saxhorns and were designed for marching, with the bell pointing behind so that troops marching behind the band could hear the music. Cornets in this shape were made in both B-flat and E-flat and figured prominently in brass bands, especially during the American Civil War (1860–1865) when over-the-shoulder (OTS) brass bands led troops in parades. Instruments of this design featured top-action, string-operated **rotary valves** and **Allen valves**, known for their swift and efficient operation. (See figure 39.)

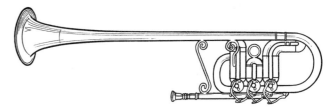

Figure 39. An over-the-shoulder cornet (ca. 1865) with top-action rotary valves. *Drawing by T. M. Larsen.*

Pakhmutova, Alexandra Nikolayevna (b. 1929). Russian composer. She began playing the piano and composing music at an early age, and eventually went on to study at the Moscow Conservatory, graduating in 1953. In 1956 she pursued advanced composition studies with Vissarion Shebalin. As an award-winning song composer in the Soviet Union known for her lyric romanticism and popular style, she composed a single-movement *Concerto for Trumpet and Orchestra* in 1955.

Park, Anna (ca. 1867–after 1903). American cornetist. She was the oldest of four sisters from the Boston area who together formed a versatile quartet known as the Park Sisters. The **cornet** was her main instrument and contemporary reviews consistently praise her skills. For example, a letter to the editor from 1889 claims that "Miss Annie A. Park truly handles the cornet like a man." A review from London's *Court Circular* reports that Park's performance of **Jules Levy**'s *Polka de Concert* "fairly brought down the house," and several encores were required. Anna and her three sisters—Georgia, Katibel, and Ada—played cornet quartets as well as other instruments including piano, trombone, zither, and mandolin (perhaps to allow rest for the embouchure and musical variety on concert programs). The Park Sisters toured throughout the United States as well as two European tours, managing all of their business affairs themselves. Also active as a teacher, one of Park's students toward the end of her career was **Edna White**.

patent lever valve. A variation on the **John Shaw**'s **disc valve** developed by John Augustus **Köhler** around 1840. The levers were long rods attached to a **valve button**. When the button was pressed, the rod would turn a disc that positioned a hole to allow the **airstream** of the instrument to flow through an appended **valve slide**. Köhler improved Shaw's design by replacing the watch spring mechanism with helical compression springs in the push-rod guide cases, which made the instruments easier to lubricate and maintain. (See appendix 2, figure A3.)

pavillon. (Fr.) **Bell**.

peashooter. Slang term for a small or narrow bore **cornet**.

pedal tones. The notes from F3 down to C3 (or E-flat 3 down to B-flat 3 in **concert** pitch on a B-flat trumpet) that are not part of the normal playing **range** on the **modern trumpet**. Their name is derived from the lowest notes of the organ, which are played with the foot pedal keyboard. The **fundamental** pitch produced by any length of **cylindrical** tubing is usually a pedal tone; **fingerings** are the same as those for the standard notes in the lower octave of the trumpet's playable range. The fundamental on a **natural trumpet** is a playable note on a seventeenth-century instrument with a narrow **bell** flare (such as those made by **Hanns Hainlein**), but it is a pedal tone on later bell designs with a more pronounced flare (such as those by **Ehe** and **Haas**; see figure 6 under "bell"). Although they are not commonly found in performance repertoire, pedal tones are frequently prescribed as a method to build **embouchure** strength and extend a player's high range by developing the muscles below the lower lip and corners that help support the jaw. (See figure 17 under "embouchure.") The **cornet** soloist **Bohumir Kryl** was famous for his unusual ability to produce deep, rich pedal tones and frequently showcased them in performance, especially in his version of Karl Ludwig Fischer's song "Deep Down in the Cellar."

Although trumpeters call them pedal tones, the term is colloquial because the notes are not genuine acoustic pitches, as they are on the trombone; trumpeters approximate the notes and have to work to play them in tune with an acceptable sound. Two methods for producing them include a "fixed jaw" approach, where the corners are firm and the **aperture** is relaxed, and the "floating jaw" approach, where the lower jaw is deliberately moved forward to align the teeth vertically. The "fixed jaw" approach works best for players without an overbite; excessive pucker of the aperture leads to faulty embouchure formation. Teachers who have advocated pedal tone exercises in their pedagogy include **Jerome Callet, Claude Gordon,** and **James Stamp. Rafael Méndez** used them to help him recover from a severe lip injury in 1932.

pencil exercise. An isometric exercise intended to build **embouchure** strength, in which the eraser end of a common pencil is held between the lips at the focal point of the **aperture,** without the aid of the teeth. Resistance is added by extending the length of time that the pencil is held between the lips as well as by using longer and heavier pencils (or similar objects). Some **practice aids** that simulate the pencil exercise with customized rods include **Chop-Sticks** and **Warburton's P.E.T.E.** (Personal Embouchure Training Exerciser).

Pepper, J. W. American musical instrument manufacturer and distributor. Best known today as the largest seller of sheet music in the United States, the company was started in 1876 by James Walsh Pepper (1858–1919) in Philadelphia as a music-publishing business. Pepper began selling brass instruments in 1880 and engaged **Henry Distin** to supervise the building of a new factory in 1882. Distin **cornets** and Pepper cornets were both produced by the factory, including models such as the "American Favorite," "Excelsior," and "Imperial." The firm also produced **echo bell cornets** and was a leading publisher of band music. The business moved to Philadelphia in 1890 and the company name changed to "J. W. Pepper & Son" in 1910. The firm stopped manufacturing brass instruments in 1910 and continued to import instruments and publish sheet music thereafter.

perce droit. (Fr.) Straight **bore**, direct bore. A term used by French **cornet** makers in the mid-nineteenth century to describe the design of **intervalve tubing** with straight tubing as opposed to *perce pleine*.

perce pleine. (Fr.) Full **bore**. A term used by French **cornet** makers in the mid-nineteenth century to describe the design of **intervalve tubing** that was "knuckled out" as it is on most modern trumpets and cornets, also known as *coquilles* or **knuckles**.

perfect pitch. A colloquial term for **absolute pitch**.

performance practice. The manner in which music from previous style periods is performed with special attention paid to methods, techniques, and practices of earlier times. Usually associated with **early music, historically informed performance,** and **period instruments,** performance practice encompasses issues regarding notation, ornamentation, instruments, vocal production, **pitch standards, temperament,** and the size of instrumental and vocal performing forces.

Périnet, Etienne François (fl. 1829–1860). French inventor and brass instrument manufacturer. Although he is the inventor of the modern **piston valve** that is universally adopted today, biographical information about Périnet is scarce. He learned to make brass instruments at the Raoux shop and opened his own establishment in Paris in 1829. That same year he added a third valve to the **cornet** (the early **cornopean** originally had only two **Stölzel valves**). The improvements that Périnet made to Stölzel's valve and Wieprecht's **Berlin valve** involved making the diameter of the piston larger than the **bore** of the instrument, which in turn made the holes inside the valves larger to provide a better fit for the valve tubing. His patent for the *système Périnet* became effective on October 27, 1838. In 1841 he created a tuba prototype called the *piston basse* with four valves. In later years he was unable to compete with the manufacturing achievements of **Adolphe Sax** and focused on making hunting horns. Périnet left Paris in 1859 and moved to Passy, where he established his company under the name Francios Périnet, Pettex-Muffat & Cie.

Périnet valve. A **piston valve** developed by **Francois Périnet** in 1838. It was superior to previous types of piston valves such as the **Stölzel valve** and the **Berlin valve** because it eliminated the sharp angles in the tubing inside the valves and had smoother operation. Trumpets and cornets with Périnet valves became standard in France and England as well as the United States. (See appendix 2, figure A4.)

period instrument. An instrument from an earlier time, whether an original or a reproduction, that differs from those in current use. At the beginning of the early music revival in the twentieth century, such instruments were often called "historic" or "authentic," but the term *period instrument* has become the accepted alternative because it covers a wider category of instruments and allows for a variety of interpretations. High brass instruments that fit into this category include the **Baroque trumpet, cornett, cornopean, keyed bugle, keyed trumpet,** and **natural trumpet** as well as nineteenth-century valved cornets and trumpets.

Peskin, Vladimir (1906–1988). Russian composer and amateur trumpeter. As a boy he began composing songs for his mother, Vera, who was a singer. From 1914 to

1916 Peskin lived in Geneva and studied piano at the Académie de Musique de Genève while his father was an exiled revolutionary in Switzerland. Returning to Russia in 1917 after the revolution, he studied at the Moscow Conservatory beginning in 1922 with the pianist and composer Samuel Feinberg. An overuse injury forced him to discontinue his piano studies and his attention turned increasingly to composition. Peskin worked as a pianist in the Balalaika Orchestra at Red Army headquarters in the 1930s when his father was persecuted by Stalin's regime and his mother was deported to Kazakhstan. It was at the Red Army headquarters that he met **Timofei Dokshizer**, who was a young trumpet student at the time, and began writing works for him in a style similar to that of Rachmaninoff.

The first work that Peskin wrote for Dokshizer was *Scherzo for Trumpet and Piano* in 1937. Other works included *Concerto No. 1 in C Minor* for trumpet and orchestra (1948), *Concert Allegro (Concerto No. 2) in B Minor* for trumpet and orchestra (1954), and *Concerto No. 3 in F Minor* for trumpet and orchestra (1971). Shorter works included "Melody" for trumpet and piano, "Poeme" for trumpet and piano, and "Nocturne and Scherzo" for trumpet and piano. Peskin also composed concerti for clarinet and horn as well as a "Poème" for violin and piano.

P.E.T.E. Personal Embouchure Training Exerciser. A **practice aid** developed by **Warburton** Music Products that is used for isometric exercises to develop **embouchure** strength. Similar in concept to the **pencil exercise**, the P.E.T.E. is a short metal device with a small disc on one end that is inserted in the mouth through the **aperture** of the lips in front of the teeth. When the lips grip the stem of the device to hold the rod in place, the facial muscles that support the embouchure, such as the **bucinnator muscles** and the **obicularis oris**, are strengthened.

petite trompette. (Fr.) Small trumpet. Term used by **Ravel** to indicate a **high-pitched trumpet** in D in *Bolero* (1928).

Pfeiffer, Carl (fl. 1730–1770). German trumpeter. He worked as a court trumpeter in Karlsruhe and was known for his proficiency in the high **clarino** register. **Johann Melchior Molter** wrote three significant concertos for Pfeiffer around 1750. He may have also premiered the concerto by **Franz Xaver Richter**.

phorbeia. Ancient Greek version of the **capistrum,** a strap used to support the cheeks while playing at loud volumes on the **salpinx** or the aulos.

piccolo horn. An alternate term for the modern **corno da caccia** or **Clarinhorn,** not to be confused with the descant horn, which is a different instrument.

piccolo trumpet. A small trumpet usually pitched an octave higher than the modern B-flat trumpet and approximately half its length with a smaller **bore**. In addition to the key of B-flat, such instruments are commonly built in the keys of A and G. Often confused with the **pocket trumpet**, which features the same length of tubing as the B-flat trumpet twice coiled, the first piccolo trumpet was built by **Besson** in 1885 and pitched in G for a performance of Bach's *Magnificat.* **Theo Charlier** was the first to perform Bach's ***Brandenburg Concerto No. 2*** on a similar instrument made by **Mahillon** in 1898. These early instruments and other high-pitched trumpets in D were often referred to as "**Bach trumpet**" because they were employed for Baroque repertoire. Modern piccolo trumpets appear in a variety of shapes and configurations including both **piston** and **rotary valves**. Important specialists on the modern piccolo trumpet include **Maurice André, Håkan Hardenberger**, and **Adolf Scherbaum**. Prominent makers include **Getzen, Kanstul, Scherzer, and Schilke**. (See figure 40.)

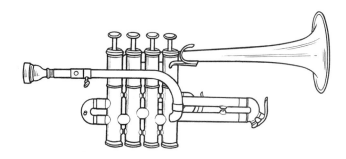

Figure 40. Piccolo trumpet. *Drawing by T. M. Larsen.*

pinky ring. An alternate term for a **finger hook** on a trumpet or cornet.

piston valve. A mechanism the redirects the **airstream** of a brass instrument from its primary length of tubing into an attached slide through holes inside a piston that moves up and down vertically when pressed. Piston valves were made by Heinrich Stölzel (**Stölzel valve**), **François Périnet** (**Périnet valve**), and Wilhelm Wieprecht (the **Berlin valve**). (See appendix 2.)

piston, pistone. (It.) Colloquial term for a **cornet** with **piston valves**.

pitch standard. A reference pitch level devised to coordinate satisfactory **intonation** for performances with instruments and voices. Usually expressed in terms of **Hertz** (Hz), or cycles per second, pitch standards have been labeled by names associated with the circumstances of their use since the sixteenth century. Early pitch standards included **Chorton** (for sacred music) and **Kammerton** (for secular music) as well as regional variations such as **French theatre pitch**. The term *concert pitch* is a vestige of this system. Strict measurement of pitch levels was an elusive proposition before the Industrial Revolution in the early nineteenth century, and the terms meant different things in different regions. For example, Chorton in the seventeenth century was lower in Italy and higher in Germany. The universal pitch standard of A4 = 440 Hz was established in 1939 and confirmed in 1953, but is still subject to slight variations (usually higher).

The measurement of pitch levels on organ pipes and wind instruments, especially wooden *cornetti*, provided evidence of standards used at the time of their construction. Because *cornetti* were usually made to produce A4 at an average of 465 Hz, the standard became known as **Cornet-ton.** Trumpeter **John Shore** invented the first tuning fork in 1711; it rendered A4 at 423.5 Hz. With the advent of **historically informed performance** of earlier repertoire in the twentieth century, the establishment of historic pitch standards for performances using **period instruments** resulted in the conventions of **Baroque pitch** (A4 = 415 Hz) and **Classical pitch** (A4 = 430). Seventeenth-century repertoire performed on *cornetti* and **sackbuts** was often performed at **high pitch** (A4 = 465 Hz) to approximate Cornet-ton or Chorton as a standard. Various historic **temperaments** were also used in period instrument performances.

Another high pitch standard known as **sharp pitch** or old philharmonic pitch (A4 = 452.5 Hz) was employed for band instruments as late as 1965 when Boosey and Hawkes and the Salvation Army agreed to abandon the manufacture of high-pitch instruments and switch to a "low pitch" standard (A4 = 440 Hz). An even higher standard, military band sharp pitch, was set at A4 = 462.5 Hz. Some **cornets** were made with a **high/low pitch slide** in the early twentieth century to cope with pitch standard discrepancies. The proliferation of different pitch levels also required musicians to transpose when instruments built for differing standards were combined in the same ensemble. For example, 415 Hz (Baroque pitch or eighteenth-century Kammerton) is one half step below 440 Hz and one whole step below 465 Hz (Cornet-ton or eighteenth-century Chorton).

pixie mute. A short **straight mute** that fits completely inside the **bell** and does not protrude much beyond the **rim**. Approximately the size of a **piccolo trumpet** mute, but wider, the pixie mute is most often used in conjunction with a **plunger mute** for special effects in jazz. The mute's name is a trademark of the **Humes & Berg** Company, but has widely been adopted to refer to a mute of similar size from other manufacturers. (See appendix 3.)

plating. Metal coating applied to the raw brass of a trumpet or cornet for purposes of protection, sound enhancement, and decoration. Silver is used most often, and some instruments are gold-plated as well. Student brass instruments often substitute lacquer for more expensive plating.

Plog, Anthony (b. 1947). American trumpeter, composer, and conductor. Plog's first trumpet teacher was his father, Clifton Plog, and by the time he was nineteen, he was playing extra trumpet with the Los Angeles Philharmonic. He earned a degree from the University of California at Los Angeles (UCLA) and studied with Irving Bush, **Thomas Stevens,** and **James Stamp.** Plog performed with several orchestras including the San Antonio Symphony (principal), the Utah Symphony, and the Los Angeles Chamber Orchestra (principal) as well as studio orchestras for several film scores (*Star Trek, Rocky 2,* and *Altered States* among others). He also played with several chamber groups such as the Fine Arts Brass Quintet, Summit Brass, and the St. Louis Brass Quintet, and performed and recorded as a soloist.

Plog moved to Europe in 1990 to become the solo trumpeter of the Malmo Symphony in Sweden and has been a professor at the Staatliche Hochschule für Musik in Freiburg, Germany, since 1993. Already active as a composer since 1976, Plog retired from performing in 2001 to devote all of his energies to composing. He has written numerous solo and chamber works for brass including a popular series of *Animal Ditties* scored for various instrumental combinations, a *Sonata for Trumpet and Piano* (2009), and two trumpet concerti (1988, 1994). In recent years he has directed his attention to works for orchestra and other ensembles including the children's opera *How the Trumpet Got Its Toot* (2004).

plunger mute. A rubber plumber's plunger held by the left hand and cupped over the bell of the trumpet while playing. The sink plunger (approximately four inches wide) is the appropriate size for use with the trumpet; the toilet plunger is too large and is used for the trombone. Popular in early jazz, the technique developed from a similar use of the left hand as a **hand mute** and other found items like a beer glass. **Joe "King" Oliver** was a master of plunger mute technique, although he used his hand and other objects rather than a plunger. James "Bubber" Miley (1903–1932) was another master of plunger mute technique, especially on the recording of his composition *Black and Tan Fantasy* (1927) with Duke Ellington's Orchestra. When open and closed effects with a plunger are notated in printed music, the symbols *o* and + are used to indicated an open (o) or closed (+) bell. Commercially produced plunger mutes have been made of metal cups with rubber or felt rims often with grip handles or loops. (See appendix 3.)

pocket cornet, pocket trumpet. A small, tightly-wrapped **cornet** or trumpet made of the same length of tubing as a normal instrument, but in a more compact size (often as short as seven inches long). The earliest models began appearing in the 1850s and were made in the keys of B-flat, C, and E-flat. Advertised as pocket, parlor, miniature, or tourist models, these cornets were marketed as appropriate for children, travel convenience, and novelty performances, and for playing in confined spaces. Pocket cornets were sold up until the early 1940s and made up less than 1 percent of all cornets manufactured during that period.

A pocket trumpet is nearly indistinguishable from a pocket cornet except for its larger **mouthpiece receiver**, which accommodates the larger **shank** of a trumpet mouthpiece. **Calicchio** began making pocket trumpets in the 1940s, and other manufacturers of the instruments include Amati, **Benge**, **Getzen**, **Jupiter**, **Kanstul**, and Marcinkiewicz. After 1960, pocket trumpets began to replace pocket cornets on the market. **Holton** stopped manufacturing the C-150 model in 2002, which was the last professional-grade pocket cornet ever made. Only pocket trumpets are made today. Musicians known to have played them included **Herbert L. Clarke** (who owned a one-of-a-kind "Baby" model made by **Henry Distin**), jazz artist Don Cherry (who played the **Besson** "MEHA" model), and Ringling Brothers Circus band leader Merle Evans (who played the Holton "Mighty Midget" model). Musicians in the Salvation Army also played the instrument (hence the occasional term, *preacher's cornet*). Like the **bicycle bugle**, some models were made with oval-shaped bells.

pommel. An alternate term for the **ball** on a **natural trumpet**.

Ponchielli, Amilcare (1834–1886). Italian composer. A prominent Italian opera composer from the nineteenth century, his father was a church organist and shopkeeper. Ponchielli entered the Milan Conservatory while still a child, and studied piano with Arturo Angeleri, theory with Pietro Ray, and composition with Felice Frasi and Alberto Mazzuccato. Following graduation in 1854, he became a church organist and music teacher in Cremona. In 1860 he directed several operas at the Teatro Carcano in Milan as well as in Alessandria. Ponchielli's masterpiece is the opera *La Gioconda* (1876), which contains the popular ballet "Dance of the Hours" often performed in orchestral concerts. Some of his other operas include *I lituani* (1874), *Il figliuol prodigo* (1880), and *Marion Delorme* (1885); he also composed sacred music, cantatas, and ballet music along with assorted piano pieces and songs. Ponchielli was appointed a professor of composition at the Milan Conservatory in 1880 and among his students were Puccini, Mascagni, and Leoncavallo.

Throughout the 1860s Ponchielli made his living as a municipal bandmaster, first in Piacenza and later in Cremona. While in these positions he composed several band pieces including solo works for trumpet (and **cornet**) and band including *Concerto per tromba in Fa, Op. 123* (1866), *Concerto per cornetto* [cornet], *Op. 198* (1867), *Fantasia per tromba sopra motivi dell'opera* La Traviata, *Op. 146* (1868), and *Aria e cavatina from* Maria Rohan *by Donizetti [Son leggera, è ver.], Op. 208* for solo cornet. The trumpet concerto was written for Giuseppe Cesare, the *primo* **tromba** of the band in Cremona, and was played on a **rotary valve trumpet** in F. The solo cornet works were written for Achille Bissocoli (d. 1915), the *vicemaestro* and *primo* **flicorno** in the band as well as its highest-paid member (the first trumpeter, Cesare, earned the next-highest salary). Ponchielli also composed solo works for other members of the band including a *Concerto per flicornobasso* [euphonium], *Op. 155* (ca. 1872) and several solo works for B-flat clarinet and E-flat clarinet, many based on popular operatic themes.

Posaune. (Ger.) Trombone. The instrument's name descends from *busaun*, an alteration of the term for the medieval herald trumpet, the **buisine**.

Posaunenchor. (Ger.) Trombone choir. German amateur brass band movement started by Lutheran pastor Eduard Kuhlo and his son, **Johannes Kuhlo**, in the late nineteenth century. Inspired by earlier Moravian trombone choirs, the groups played chorales and hymns in church services and were comprised of conical brass: **flugelhorns**, alto horns, euphoniums, and tubas. Music was published in piano score format at concert pitch and musicians learned to transpose their parts. In the second half of the twentieth century, Posaunchor ensembles adopted more prevalent trumpets and trombones into the instrumentation. Such groups continue to flourish in Germany today.

posthorn. Coiled in a circle like a miniature **horn** and commonly pitched in A or B-flat, the instrument literally gets its name from its association with the postal service, which dates back to the fifteenth century. The internal dimensions of the posthorn differed from the **bugle** in that its **bore** profile is narrower and more **cylindrical**. Best known today for its participation in Mozart's "Posthorn Serenade" (K. 320) and Mahler's *Symphony No. 3*, the posthorn was an integral part of everyday life in most of the Western world during the eighteenth and nineteenth centuries. Many European postal services still maintain the image of the posthorn as a trademark symbol today. (See figure 41.)

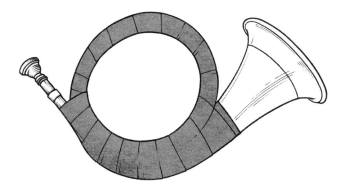

Figure 41. Posthorn. *Drawing by T. M. Larsen.*

practice aid. A device intended to strengthen a trumpet player's **embouchure**, finger dexterity, or breath control away from the instrument or an addition to the instruments. Such devices include the **B.E.R.P.**, the **Breath Builder**, a **spirometer**, and the **Volydne**.

practice journal. A notebook similar to an athlete's training log where a trumpeter keeps track of progress and records benchmarks for improvement as well as perceptions of physical symptoms, especially when developing new skills.

practice mute. A mute designed like a **straight mute** or a closed-off **Harmon mute** without a stem to allow trumpeters to practice quietly to minimize disturbance to others. Designed with a cork collar sealing the bell, small holes are placed near the bottom of the mute chamber. Practice mutes are made by **Denis Wick**, **Jo-Ral**, and **TrumCor**. A miniature practice mute that is smaller than a **Pixie mute** is made by Best Brass. **Yamaha** developed an electronic practice mute in 1995 that operated in conjunction with a sound processor know as the Silent Brass system that enabled the player to simulate reverberant acoustic environments though headphones while playing. Best Brass developed a similar system in 2013 called eBrass III.

Praetorius, Michael (1571–1621). German musical theorist, composer, and organist. His *Syntagma musicum* (3 volumes, 1614–1618) includes an extensive discussion of early Baroque instruments in the *Theatrum instrumentorum* (also published separately), which features a series of woodcuts showing a variety of early brass instruments. In addition to its abundant theoretical content, it is considered the first published document of **organology**, because it displays the wide variety of instruments available to composers in the early seventeenth century.

preacher's cornet. Term sometimes used to describe the **pocket cornet** when it was used by members of the Salvation Army.

principal trumpet. The first or solo trumpeter of an orchestra.

principale. (Ger.) Principal. The low register of the **natural trumpet** from G3 to C5. The term also designated the part to be played by a member of a trumpet corps (ensemble section) in that register. Trumpeters who played higher parts were *clarino* players, and their musical roles were often designated as "*clarino,*" while *principale* parts were labeled, "*tromba.*" *Principale* players in a trumpet corps were expected to be proficient in **double** and **triple tonguing**, which featured prominently in military signals from the sixteenth to the eighteenth centuries.

Prokofiev, Sergey (1891–1953). Russian composer. He studied privately with Reinhold Glière before entering the St. Petersburg Conservatory in 1904, where he studied harmony and counterpoint with Anatol Liadov, orchestration with Nikolai Rimsky-Korsakov, and piano with Alexander Winkler and Anna Yesipova. Prokofiev's compositional style combined **avant-garde** modernism with melodic lyricism; he included prominent parts for trumpet and cornet in his symphonies, ballets, operas, and film music. Although he did not write any solo works for the trumpet, Prokofiev's orchestral writing for the trumpet is notable for its **angularity**, expressive soaring melodies, and sardonic muted passages. Prokofiev included parts for cornets in several of his works, including the *Lt. Kije Suite* and the ballet *Romeo and Juliet*. When scoring for both cornet and trumpet in the same piece, Prokofiev tended to give more lyrical, delicate material to the cornet, and more forceful passages to the trumpet. In his *Scythian Suite* (1914), he scored for a *tromba piccola* in E-flat and four trumpets in C, and in his *Symphony No. 5 in B-flat Major, Op. 100* (1944) he scored for three trumpets in B-flat with several soaring melodic solos for the first trumpeter. Prokofiev's orchestral scores are usually printed in concert pitch, though the orchestra parts are transposed for the appropriate instruments.

pTrumpet. A plastic trumpet in B-flat made in England by trombonist Jiggs Whigham, who produced the world's first plastic trombone, the pBone, in 2010. First produced in 2014, the pTrumpet features a fully plastic **piston valve** system, a patented polymer **leadpipe**, and a **bore** size of 0.460 inches. Like the plastic **Tiger Trumpet**, the valves are interchangeable by virtue of identical positioning of the slide ports, unlike traditional trumpets where the ports differ for each valve.

Pumpenventil. (Ger.) **Piston valve**.

Purcell, Henry (1659–1695). English composer. Henry Purcell wrote melodic and idiomatic music for the trumpets of his day. He introduced the trumpet into English art music in 1687 by featuring a solo part for Matthias **Shore** in the ode *Sound the Trumpet, Beat the Drum.* Most of Purcell's scores feature parts for two trumpets, but only one trumpet usually appears in scores during the last year of his life (1694–1695). One of the unique characteristics of Purcell's trumpet writing is the equality of scoring between two independent trumpets, which often features imitative passagework. In fact, the second trumpet occasionally plays higher notes than the first part at cadences (especially in act IV of *The Fairy Queen*). Another distinctive feature is the inclusion of parts for the predecessor of the **English slide trumpet** known as the **flat trumpet**. Parts for these instruments appear in Purcell's incidental music for the play *The Libertine* (1692) and the *Funeral Music for Queen Mary* (1695), which is scored for a quartet of flat trumpets. Several trumpet solos appear in Purcell's works in addition to his well-known sonata including the birthday songs for Queen Mary, "Celebrate This Festival!" (1693) and "Come Ye Sons of Art" (1694), as well as the "Trumpet Overture" in *The Indian Queen* (1695). An obbligato aria with solo trumpet, "To Arms, Heroic Prince," appears in *The Libertine*. Purcell included trumpet parts in only twenty of his compositions, most of which were written for royal celebrations or for the stage. He included trumpet parts in only two of his sacred works, the *Te Deum Laudamus* and *Jubilate Deo* in 1694, and the anthem *Thou Knowest Lord* in 1695. Purcell wrote two trumpet sonatas for **John Shore**.

pututu. A **conch shell trumpet** used by the Incas. It was played as a signal instrument as well as for solemn religious ceremonies of the winter solstice.

quarter-tone trumpet. A unique trumpet built by the **Holton** Company for the jazz trumpeter Don Ellis (1934–1978), who was fond of using micro-tonal effects in his solos. The trumpet featured a fourth valve that lowered any **valve combination** by a quarter-tone. Holton made the trumpets during the 1960s and 1970s. More recently, Joseph Marcinkiewicz, a former member of the Don Ellis Orchestra, built a quarter-tone trumpet with a more cornet-like design.

quick-change valve. A **rotary valve** attached to some **cornets and trumpets** at the turn of the twentieth century to switch between high pitch (A4 = 452.5 Hz) and low pitch (A4 = 440 Hz) because bands, orchestras, and church organs performed at various pitch standards before the Second World War. Such valves were also used to switch between B-flat and A, like the *barillet*.

quinta. (It.) Fifth. The second-highest part (C4 to C5) of the **natural trumpet** ensemble in the sixteenth century, as described by **Bendinelli** and **Fantini**.

Ramsøe, Emilio Wilhelm (1837–1895). Danish violist and composer. Ramsøe wrote the first of his six brass quartets in 1866 for a group in Copenhagen consisting of B-flat cornet, trumpet in F, tenor horn, and trombone. One of Ramsøe's quartets was the first piece of brass chamber music performed professionally in Russia during the St. Petersburg Chamber Music Society concerts in 1873–1874. He dedicated his sixth brass quartet to **Julius Kosleck**.

range. 1. The full compass of pitches from the lowest to the highest note in a musical composition.

2. Term used informally to describe a trumpeter's ability to play in the high register.

Rasmussen, Mary Helen (1930–2008). American brass historian. Her articles in the *Brass Quarterly* and the *Brass and Woodwind Quarterly* (1957–1969) and *A Teacher's Guide to the Literature of Brass Instruments* (1964) inspired those who launched the historic brass movement. She graduated from the University of New Hampshire with a bachelor's degree in 1952 and then attended the University of Illinois, earning master's degrees in both low brass performance (1953) and library science (1956). Her primary instrument was the horn, and she also played the cello. Rasmussen taught public school in Gorham, New Hampshire, for two years and was appointed to the faculty of the University of New Hampshire in 1968, where she taught until her retirement in 1997. The recipient of a Fulbright award and grants from the Ford and Guggenheim foundations, she lectured at many different institutions, including Harvard University, Boston University, and the University of Wisconsin. She founded the periodical *Brass Quarterly* in 1957, merging it soon with *Woodwind Quarterly*, and the combined journal continued until 1969. She also contributed program notes to many editions of music

published by **Robert King.** From the 1970s she became increasingly active in the field of musical **iconography** and collected photographs from all over the world. In 1998 the **Historic Brass Society** presented her with the **Christopher Monk** Award "in recognition of pioneering scholarly research in brass music."

Regent's Bugle. A **keyed bugle** with a **slide**. The instrument got its name from its inventor's association with the prince regent's private band. Johann Georg Schmidt was the trumpeter and he was given credit for developing the instrument in an 1815 article in the *Allgemeine musikalische Zeitung* of Leipzig. The name of the awkward, obscure instrument may also be a reference to an alternate name for the keyed bugle: the "**Royal Kent Bugle**" because the prince regent was the older brother of the duke of Kent. In other words, the name "Regent's Bugle" was a marketing attempt to pull rank on the keyed bugle. The only surviving example of the instrument (made by Curtis of Glasgow) resides in the Albert Spencer Collection in the Brighton Museum. The main tubing of this instrument is cylindrical and includes a telescopic mouthpipe and a U-shaped tuning slide capable of putting the instrument into C, D-flat, D, E-flat, E, or F. When one or more of the five keys on the bell are used, the pitch can be raised one half step, a whole step, or a minor third above the notes produced by each slide position.

register. A segment of the complete **range** of pitches in an instrument's compass, usually qualified with terms like *low*, *middle*, *high*, and *altimisso*.

Reiche, Gottfried (1667–1734). German trumpeter. Born in **Weissenfels**, he moved to Leipzig in 1688, as journeyman to the local *Stadtpfeifer*. In 1694 the Leipzig city council paid him a sum of money to prevent him from seeking employment elsewhere during a period of mourning (when trumpet music was not performed). Reiche progressed through the professional ranks from Kunstgeiger (1700) to city piper (1706), and on to senior city piper (1719). From **J. S. Bach**'s arrival in Leipzig in 1723 until his own death in 1734, Reiche played all of Bach's first trumpet parts, and perhaps those for **horn** and **cornett** as well. He played not only the trumpet but also the violin, the Waldhorn, and alto trombone as well as the **slide trumpet**. In addition to performing, Rieche composed *Vier und zwantzig neue Quatricinia* as well as many five-part sonatas. It was probably in celebration of his sixtieth birthday that the Leipzig town council engaged Elias Gottlob Haussmann (1695–1774), an artist who later painted a portrait of Bach, to paint a portrait of Reiche in 1726. The portrait is famous for its portrayal of Reiche holding a *Jägertrompete*, a coiled **natural trumpet**, which may have been his favorite instrument. Reiche collapsed at the age of sixty-seven from a stroke on the way home after an outdoor performance of BWV 215 on October 5, 1734, and died the next day.

Reinhart, Carole Dawn (b. 1941). American trumpeter. Her mother, who played trombone, began teaching her to play a **slide cornet** (soprano trombone) when she was only two and a half years old. By the time she was seven, Reinhart was playing duets in concert with her older brother, who was an accomplished trumpeter. She earned a scholarship to study with Edward Treutel at the Juilliard School at the age of ten. As well as being first chair in the New Jersey All-State Band and Orchestra during high school, Reinhart was chosen as a soloist for the Juilliard Preparatory Division graduation concert. At sixteen, she was commissioned as the youngest and only woman bandmaster in the Salvation Army. After graduating from high school, she attended the University of Miami on scholarship, where she worked under Fabian Sevitzky and graduated *cum laude* with a Bachelor of Arts degree.

She earned a Fulbright scholarship to study with **Helmut Wobisch** in Vienna, Austria, where she was the first female brass player to achieve the coveted "Reifezeugnis" with honors at the Academy of Music. She returned to the United States to complete her education at the Juilliard School of Music, where she was first trumpet in the Juilliard Orchestra under Jean Morel, and earned Bachelor of Music and Master of Science degrees. Reinhart performed professionally in New York with the orchestra at Radio City Music Hall and in Leopold Stokowski's American Symphony Orchestra, and also made several television solo appearances on *The Tonight Show*, *The Mike Douglas Show*, and Al Hirt's *Fanfare* shows in the 1960s.

Reinhart moved to Berlin in 1971, where she performed studio work, filled in as first trumpeter at the Deutsche Oper, and continued her solo performances on television and with symphony and chamber orchestras. She recorded for the Deutsche Grammophon and BASF labels with the Munich Philharmonic, the German Bach Soloists, the Amsterdam Chamber Orchestra, and the Wuerttemberg Chamber Orchestra, as well as numerous radio broadcasts. In 1983 she was offered a professorship at the University of Music in Vienna, Austria, and she later served as the head of the Department of Winds and Percussion between 1996 and 1998. Retiring from active performance in 1996, Reinhart earned a PhD from the University of Music and Performing Arts in Vienna, Austria, in 2009 with her dissertation, *Women Brass Musicians: Historical Documentation and the Influence of the International Women's Brass Conference on Their Profession.*

repertoire. A collection of musical compositions for a specific instrument or in a specific musical style. For example, trumpet solo repertoire or symphonic repertoire.

repiano cornet. An ensemble part designation in the British brass band. The term is a variant spelling of *ripieno* (It., filled or stuffed), which denoted supporting ensemble parts as distinct from the solo instruments in the Baroque concerto grosso. Performed by a single musician on a B-flat **cornet**, the part serves the function of an assistant for the soprano E-flat cornet (often doubling at pitch or an octave lower) and the solo B-flat cornet parts as well as the **flugelhorn**. The repiano cornet now serves a unique purpose in contemporary British brass compositions, which often give the part solo passages and material not doubled in other cornet parts. The importance of the repiano cornet's role has grown to the extent that it is usually assigned to the third-strongest cornetist in the band, after the solo and first B-flat cornet parts.

Resenberger, Johann Baptist (1700–1781). Austrian trumpeter. He served as a distinguished court trumpeter in Salzburg during the late Baroque era, especially noted for his command of the high **clarino** register. Following his apprenticeship he served as a field trumpeter and court trumpeter between 1725 and 1742, and as chief court trumpeter from 1742 until his death in 1781. Between 1733 and 1781 he also served as a *spielgraf*, a position similar to that of a modern union official who collected dues from musicians who weren't members of the local association for the right to perform at public functions such as weddings. Resenberger performed as a soloist, most notably in the concerti by **Michael Haydn**. He was praised by **Leopold Mozart** as "a fine trumpeter who has made himself very famous . . . particularly in the high [register], through the extraordinary purity [of his tone], through his quickness in runs, and through his good trills."

Respighi, Ottorino (1879–1963). Italian composer. A brilliant musical colorist who was the most popular Italian composer after Puccini, Respighi included many notable parts for the trumpet in his compositions. He was also one of the few Italian composers better known for writing symphonic music rather than opera. Respighi did not write any solo concerti or chamber works for the trumpet, but he did feature the trumpet in his *Concerto a cinque* (1933) for oboe, trumpet, violin, double bass, piano, and strings. He is best known for three symphonic poems known as the Roman Trilogy: *Fontane di Roma* [*Fountains of Rome*] (1916), *Pini di Roma* [*Pines of Rome*] (1924), and *Feste Romane* [*Roman Festivals*] (1928). Other works with prominent trumpet parts include the first two suites of *Antiche Danze ed Arie* [*Ancient Dances and Airs*] (1917, 1923), *Vetrate di Chiesa* [*Church Windows*] (1925–1926), *Trittico Botticelliano* [*Three Botticelli Pictures*] (1927), and *Gli Uccelli* [*The Birds*] (1928).

Respighi's trumpet writing features high range (up to D6), sustained passages above the staff at loud volumes, lyrical solo lines, vigorous **multiple tonguing**, and muted passages. He scored for the trumpet in B-flat most often, but also wrote for valved trumpets in C, D, and A. As in most Italian works, the keys of the trumpets are expressed using **solfège** syllables such as *Do* (C), *Re* (D), and *Sib* (B-flat). (See appendix 3.) It is likely that Respighi wrote for **piston valve trumpets**, but **rotary valve trumpets** may have been used in Italian orchestras in the early twentieth century.

All of Respighi's trumpet parts are written for *tromba* (trumpet) with the exception of the some parts for *buccina*. The offstage brass parts in the final movement of *The Pines of Rome* are scored for six *buccine* (two sopranos, two tenors, and two basses, all in B-flat). The two high parts are labeled *Buccina (**Flicorno** Soprano in Sib)*; the other *buccina* parts consist of pairs of *Flicorni tenori* and *Flicorni bassi*. These parts are commonly performed on trumpets and trombones today, but they were originally conceived for the unique family of *flicorni* (**flugelhorns** or conical **saxhorns**) used in Italian wind bands. The opening movement of *Roman Festivals* includes three *Buccine (Soprani) in Sib*. The score lists the parts with the added direction, "*opp. Trombe*," which were trumpets, not the band instruments (*flicorni*) of *Pines of the Appian Way* meant to portray marching ghosts of ancient Roman legions. The *buccine* parts in *Roman Festivals* may have been intended for **natural trumpets** (the pitches all fall within the **harmonic overtone series**) for their unique sound and theatrical flair.

response. The ease with which a player can make sound on a trumpet. Poor response can be caused by large **mouthpiece gaps**, **back pressure**, and a fatigued or faulty **embouchure**.

Reutter II, Georg von (1708–1772). Austrian composer. The son of Georg von Reutter I (1656–1738), he began his musical studies with his father on the organ. He later studied composition with Antonio Caldara (ca. 1670–1736). After three unsuccessful attempts to gain employment as a court organist in Vienna and further study in Italy, Reutter finally earned a position at the imperial court. He succeeded his father as kappellmeister at St. Stephen's Cathedral in 1738 and later became court kappellmeister in 1769. Reutter composed over five hundred pieces of sacred music including numerous masses, psalm settings, and motets. He composed several operas and oratorios in the grand imperial style favored at the time as well as several instrumental works, especially a series of *Servizio di tavola* or Tafelmusik for the imperial court. He composed two trumpet concerti for **Johann Heinisch** that featured extremely high **clarino** range (up to G6) as well as several arias with notable obbligato parts for trumpet, especially "Lo stuol che Apollo onora" from the opera *Il Parnaso accusato, e difeso* (1738), perhaps the most difficult virtuosic solo part ever written for the **natural trumpet**.

Reveille. (From the French *réveillez!* "Awake!") A **bugle call** sounded at the beginning of the day by the armed forces to awaken the troops. The origin of the call dates back to the Crusades.

Richter, Franz Xaver (1709–1789). German composer. Following studies in Vienna and Italy, Richter moved between several positions before joining the Hofkapelle of the Elector Palatine Carl Theodor in Mannheim as a bass singer in 1746. He became *maître de chapelle* at Strasbourg Cathedral in 1769, where his assistant was Ignace Pleyel. Writing in the pre-Classical style of the Mannheim school, Richter composed a variety of instrumental and vocal works including a *Concerto à5 Voc. per Clarino Principale*, which features extremely high passagework up to F6. The trumpeter for whom the concerto was written is not known, but it may have been **Carl Pfeiffer**, who worked in Karlsruhe (close to Richter's job in Mannheim) and for whom **Molter** wrote his concerti. **Joseph Arnold Gross** may have also performed the concerto.

Riedl, Joseph Felix (ca. 1786–1840). Austrian brass instrument manufacturer. He worked with **Joseph Kail** to develop the **Vienna valve** in 1823 and a type of **rotary valve** known as the "wheel valve" in 1835. In 1844 his widow, Anna, was appointed by the Austrian government to supply **posthorns** for the postal service.

Riepel, Joseph (1709–1782). Austrian composer, theorist, and violinist. He came to a musical career relatively late, beginning his studies instead in philosophy at the Jesuit university in Linz in 1733. He also studied Fux's *Gradus* *ad Parnassum* on his own and later attended the University of Graz (1735–1736). Following two years of service as valet to General Alexander Graf d'Ollone during the Turkish wars, he moved to Dresden in 1739, where he studied with **Jan Dismas Zelenka** until 1745. Unable to secure positions in Poland or Vienna, Riepel eventually became Kapellmeister at the court of the Prince of Thurn und Taxis in Regensburg in 1749 and remained there for thirty years. In addition to his musical works, Riepel wrote two theoretical treatises: *Anfangsgründe zur musicalischen Setzkunst* [*Rudiments of the Art of Composition*] (1752–1768) and *Harmonisches Sylbenmass* (1776). He composed a trumpet concerto, *Concerto à Clarino Principale*, during his time at Regensburg that exemplifies the height of *clarino* playing with range that frequently ascends to E6 and extreme demands placed on **endurance**. The trumpeter for whom the concerto was written is unknown, but it may have been performed by **Joseph Arnold Gross**. The work is one of four trumpet concerti in the Fulda manuscript collection at the Library of Congress; the others are by Gross, **Franz Xaver Richter,** and an anonymous composer (attributed to **Johann Stamitz**, but more likely by Johann Georg Holzbogen).

rim. The part of the **mouthpiece** that comes into contact with the trumpeter's lips. Shaped in a ring, the thickness and relative sharpness of the edge plays an important role in the way that a player's **embouchure** interacts with the mouthpiece to create the sound as well as the player's feeling of control and comfort in performance. A wider rim with smooth edges reduces the pressure on a player's lips and aids **endurance** at the expense of **flexibility**, while a flatter rim with sharper edges affords a player more control (which is why such dimensions are found on mouthpieces used for the technique of **lipping** on **natural trumpets**). The inner diameter of the rim also plays a role. Larger rim diameters are favored for lower notes while smaller rims aid playing in the high register. The rim dimensions interact with the other components of the mouthpiece such as the **cup**, **throat**, and **backbore** in performance.

rip. A special effect used in jazz where a note is approached from approximately a fourth or more below with a slide using a variety of different techniques based on the musical context such as half-valve technique, a slurred chromatic scale, or a **lip slur**. As its name implies, a rip usually happens quickly, as opposed to a **glissando**, which usually covers a wider range at a slower tempo. It is usually notated with a diagonal line on the left, pointing up to the intended pitch. (See figure 42.)

Figure 42. The jazz technique known as a rip. *Elisa Koehler.*

Robinson mute. An exceptionally soft type of **cup mute** made by trombonist Ray Robinson between the 1930s and 1950s. The mute had a distinctive black cone and a white cup with absorbant fiber material inside the cup. No longer in production, existing Robinson mutes are highly prized for their unique sound. Robinson also made straight mutes for trumpets and trombones in a cone shape similar to those made by **Humes & Berg**. **Andre Jolivet** calls for a Robinson mute in the second movement of his *Concerto No. 2* (1954). (See appendix 3.)

Rodenkirchen, Christian (1858–1915). German-American trumpeter. He was the first principal trumpeter of the Chicago Symphony Orchestra at its founding in 1891. Originally from Cologne, Germany, Rodenkirchen played cornet in the orchestra until 1898 and then trumpet until 1901.

Rogers, Walter Bowman (1865–1939). American cornetist and conductor. He studied the **cornet** and violin with his father as a boy and continued cornet studies with Captain John Lathrope, eventually performing as a soloist with Lathrope's Cornet Band. Rogers entered the Cincinnati Conservatory at the age of seventeen, where he studied theory, harmony, and composition. He went on to perform as a cornet soloist and member of the Indianapolis Municipal Band and became friends with **Herbert L. Clarke** (two years younger than Rogers), who had moved to Indianapolis in 1884. Clarke and Rogers performed together in the Schubert Brass Quartet (a church ensemble), the When Clothing Store Orchestra and Bellringers, and Biessenhertz's English Opera House Orchestra.

In 1885, the twenty-year-old Rogers became the cornet soloist for Cappa's Seventh Regiment Band in New York, as well as Cappa's personal assistant. When Cappa died in 1894, Rogers assumed leadership of the band until 1897. He substituted for Clarke in the Sousa Band in 1898 and shared soloist duties with Clarke during the band's European tour in 1900. Rogers remained with the Sousa Band until 1904, when he moved to Camden, New Jersey, to become the musical director of the Victor Phonograph Company. With Victor, he made arrangements and led instrumental accompaniments for the leading soloists of the time, including Caruso, Melba, Tetrazzini, and McCormack. He also recorded several cornet solos and duets for Victor including his own compositions, *Echoes of the Catskills, Harp of Tara, The Volunteer*, and *War Songs (Columbian Fantasy)*.

Rogers left Victor in 1916 to pursue other positions in the burgeoning recording industry, including recording manager with the Paroquette Record Company, music director of both the Paramount Record Company and the Emerson Phonograph Company, and band director for the Brunswick Phonograph Company. Following a temporary hiatus from playing while devoting time to teaching, Rogers became the cornet soloist with Clarke's Anglo-Canadian Leather Company Band in Huntsville, Ontario, in 1929. He later taught and played in New York theaters until 1932. During his career Rogers recorded twenty-two cornet solos and thirteen duets (often with trombonist Arthur Pryor), and played on numerous other recordings as an ensemble musician.

Romm, Ronald (b. 1946). American trumpeter. Best known as a member of the **Canadian Brass** for nearly thirty years, Romm grew up in Los Angeles as part of a musical family. He started his solo career at the age of ten and performed with his family's dance band, "The Romm-Antics" at the age of twelve. His trumpet teachers during his school years were Al Ruby, Eddie Ehlert, and Lester Remsen. By the age of eighteen he was already a veteran freelance trumpeter in Los Angeles, performing regularly with the Los Angeles Philharmonic Orchestra and the Los Angeles Brass Quintet. Romm studied with **James Stamp** at the University of Southern California between 1964 and 1967, and later transferred to the Juilliard School to study with **William Vacchiano**, earning a bachelor's degree in music in 1970 and a master's degree in 1971. Following his years at Juilliard, he earned a position with the Hamilton Philharmonic in Ontario and joined the Canadian Brass, who all became principal players of the orchestra. The quintet eventually broke away from the Hamilton Philharmonic and embarked on an international performing and recording career. Romm performed more than 4,500 concerts with the Canadian Brass and made sixty recordings as well as numerous television and radio broadcasts, videos, and DVDs.

After retiring from the Canadian Brass in 2000, Romm became a professor of trumpet at the University of Illinois in 2002. He also formed a chamber music group with his wife, Avis (a pianist), and his son, Aaron (a trumpeter). Romm's many awards include honorary doctorates from the New England Conservatory, McMaster University, and Hartwick College as well as the Honorary Award from the **International Trumpet Guild** (2012). In addition to serving as a Yamaha Artist/Clinician, Romm is also an instrument-rated private pilot.

Rossbach, Franz (1864–1941). German trumpeter. Following studies in trumpet and violin at the Leipzig Conservatory, he performed on both instruments with the municipal orchestra in Meißen between 1881 and 1882. Rossbach later performed as principal trumpet of the Infantry Regiment 134 (and occasionally on violin) as well as first trumpet in the Kurkapelle Bad Elster and the Frankfurt Zoological Gardens Orchestra. In 1892 he became the principal trumpet of the Vienna Court Opera Orchestra as well as the Vienna Philharmonic, where he performed under Gustav Mahler. In 1896 he began per-

forming with both the Vienna Hofmusikkappelle and the Bayreuth Festival Orchestra. Rossbach became one of the first to perform the **Haydn** Trumpet Concerto in the twentieth century when he performed the work with the Vienna Philharmonic in 1908. As a teacher, he served on the faculty of the Vienna Conservatory between 1907 and 1908 and was a professor at the Vienna Music Academy from 1909 until 1931. Rossbach also edited an orchestral excerpt book devoted to the works of Richard Strauss.

rotary trumpet. Colloquial term for a **rotary valve trumpet**.

rotary valve. A mechanism that redirects the **airstream** of a brass instrument from its primary length of tubing into an attached slide through holes inside a cylinder that rotates back and forth when activated by a lever. Rotary valves were first made by **Friedrich Blühmel** in 1814. The standard German design is known as the side-action rotary valve because the levers are positioned horizontally on the instrument. Another design prevalent on American **cornets** in the mid-nineteenth century was the top-action string-operated rotary valve, which was prized for its quick action. Top-action rotary valves appeared on instruments by such makers as **Fiske**, Louis Schreiber (1827–1910), John F. Stratton (1832–1912), and Hall & Quinby. A variation on this design with narrower rotors for faster operation was the **Allen valve**. (See appendix 2.)

rotary valve trumpet. Trumpets with rotary valves possess a narrower bore than **piston valve trumpets**, shorter valve movement, and a larger bell with a wider flare. (See figure 43.) The placement of the valve section is significantly closer to the mouthpiece (just eight inches on a B-flat trumpet) with the bulk of the rotary trumpet's tubing placed afterward. Some instruments include as many as three venting keys or *Klappen* that decrease resistance and improve security in the upper register on certain notes (usually B-flat, A, and C as well as related notes in the **harmonic overtone series**); the water key can also act as a venting key. The narrower bore requires more control when playing at loud volumes to avoid overblowing and the lower register responds differently than it does on piston valved trumpets and requires slower airflow (similar to fogging up a mirror). Rotary valve trumpets are capable of producing a wider variety of tone colors at different dynamic levels than piston valve trumpets. Following the example set by **Adolph Herseth** in 1965, many North American orchestras employ rotary valve trumpets for repertoire from the Classical era because they respond well for soft playing and blend more easily with the rest of the orchestra. Orchestras in Austria and Germany favor the use of rotary valve trumpets for most repertoire. **Piccolo trumpets** with rotary valves, especially those made by **Scherzer**, are increasingly popular for solo playing. Prominent manufacturers of rotary valve trumpets include **Ganter**, **Lechner**, **Monke**, and **Schagerl**. A popular **mouthpiece** for orchestral playing on rotary valve trumpets is the Breslmair G2 developed by Kurt Breslmair for players in the Vienna Philharmonic Orchestra. Such mouthpieces feature a deep V-shaped **cup**, a larger **throat**, and a larger **backbore** than those used on trumpets with **piston valves**.

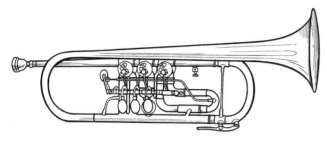

Figure 43. Rotary valve trumpet in B-flat. *Drawing by T. M. Larsen.*

rotta. A section in seventeenth-century **trumpet ensemble** sonatas where the top **clarino** part rests and the lower parts in the group perform triadic passages with vigorous rhythm and **multiple tonguing**.

Ruhe, Ulrich Heinrich Christoph (1706–1787). German trumpeter. Born into a family of musicians in Halberstadt, Ruhe succeeded **Gottfried Reiche** as **J. S. Bach**'s first trumpeter in Leipzig in 1734 and performed as a *Stadtpfeifer* for sixteen years until 1751. He premiered the first trumpet parts on several of Bach's works including the *Christmas Oratorio,* the *Ascension Oratorio*, and many of the later cantatas. Ruhe also played the violin and preferred that instrument to the trumpet toward the end of his career. In addition to playing for Bach, he was an early member of the Gewandhaus Orchestra (founded in 1743).

S

Sachs, Michael (b. 1961). American trumpeter. Originally from California, Sachs earned a degree in history from the University of California at Los Angeles (UCLA) in 1983 while studying trumpet with **Anthony Plog** and **James Stamp**. After a summer at the Aspen Music Festival, he decided to pursue an orchestral playing career and enrolled at the Juilliard School to study with Mark Gould. During his third year, in 1986, he won a position with the Houston Symphony and the Houston Grand Opera Orchestra. Two years later in 1988, he became principal trumpet of the Cleveland Orchestra, a position he has held ever since. Also an active teacher, Sachs served on the faculty of the Shepherd School of Music at Rice University while in Houston, and is currently chair of the brass department at the Cleveland Institute of Music. As a soloist Sachs premiered the *Trumpet Concerto* by **John Williams** in 1996, a work commissioned for him by the Cleveland Orchestra. In 2012 he premiered Michael Hersch's *Night Pieces for Trumpet and Orchestra* and Matthias Pintscher's *Chute d'Etoiles* (concerto for two trumpets), which were also Cleveland commissions. Sachs has written several pedagogical works including *Daily Fundamentals for Trumpet* (Interational Music Company, 2002), *Mahler: Symphonic Works for Trumpet* (International Music Company, 2004–2005), *14 Duets for Trumpet and Trombone* (with Joseph Alessi and Carl Fischer, 2007), and *The Orchestral Trumpet* (Tricordia, 2012).

Sachse, Ernst [Friedrich Ludwig Jr.] (1813–1870). German trumpeter. Considered the best German trumpeter of the mid-nineteenth century, his playing was praised by **Hector Berlioz** in 1844 for its "extraordinary force." Sachse was named after his father, who was a municipal musician in Eisenberg, Germany. Leaving home at the age of twenty-one in 1834, he moved to Leipzig and successfully auditioned for the position of court trumpeter and chamber musician in Weimar, under the direction of **Johann Nepomuk Hummel**, who described Sachse as "a first-rate musician." He played first trumpet in the orchestra at Weimar until 1869, and performed in the premieres of several operas by Richard Wagner including *Lohengrin* (1850), directed by Franz Liszt. Also an active teacher, one of his students was **Christian Ferdinand Weinschenk**. He published a set of *100 Etudes* for E-flat trumpet around 1850; the book may have been written in response to increasing demands for transposition found in Wagner's music, and is commonly used for **transposition** practice today. As a soloist and composer, Sachse wrote a *Concertino in D for Trumpet and Orchestra* (which is better known in its transposed version for trumpet and brass band in the key of E-flat), a *Concertino für Posaune und Orchester in B-Dur [B-flat Major]*, and *Variationen für Trompete & Pianoforte in Es-Dur [E-flat Major]*. A review of Sachse's 1844 solo performance in London in the *Neue Zeitschrift für Musik* reported that "the power, the charming songlike style, and the surprising agility with which he handles his instrument brought him universal recognition."

Sachse, Friedrich (1809–1893). German trumpeter. The older brother of **Ernst Sachse**, Friedrich's playing was also praised by **Hector Berlioz**, who said he was "a most excellent trumpeter." At the age of twenty he joined the music corps of the seventh infantry regiment of the Hanover army. Between 1833 and 1865 he served as first staff trumpeter of the Royal Hanovers as well as a member of the court orchestra. Also active as a soloist, Sachse performed Ferling's *Introduction and Variationen* with the Leipzig Gewandhaus Orchestra in 1842, as well as concerts in Berlin, Riga, Frankfurt am Main, Vienna, and Hanover between 1843 and 1865. Contemporary reviews praised the beauty of his tone along with his dexterity, virtuosity, and tasteful artistry. Upon leaving military service in 1866, he made several concert tours of southern Germany and Switzerland. Between 1871 and 1873 he performed in the United States in the cities of New York, Baltimore, and Philadelphia.

sackbut, sagbut. The early English term for the **trombone** used between the fifteenth and eighteenth centuries. It derived from the French term *sacqueboute*, which literally described the "push-pull" motion of the slide. Modern reproductions of sackbuts used in **period instrument** ensembles and **historically informed performance** feature smaller **bells**, thinner metal, and narrower **bore** sizes than modern trombones.

saddle. Another name for the **thumb hook** on a trumpet's first **valve slide**.

Saint-Jacome, Louis-Antonie (1830–1898). French cornet soloist. He began his musical studies at the age of seven on the violin and piano with his stepfather, Martel, the bandmaster of the Bal de la Cour. He went on to study at the Paris Conservatory, graduating in 1850 with the first prize in cornet. He played solo cornet and keyed bugle with the Chaseurs a Creval de al Garde between 1855 and 1858, and later moved to London to play with the Alharmbra Orchestra under Revierre. In 1870 he became a musical arranger for the Messers La Fleur Publishing Company and published his *Grand Method for the Cornet* the same year. In 1883 he became a cornet tester for the Besson Company in London, where he worked until his death in 1898. In addition to playing the cornet, Saint-Jacome was considered a "connoisseur" of the violin and played the flageolet, a simple woodwind instrument similar to the recorder.

salpinx. A long, straight trumpet with a narrow **bore** and a small **bell** used in Ancient Greece primarily for military **signals**. The length of the instrument was approximately five feet (or 1.5 meters). A salpinx from the fifth century BC currently resides in the Museum of Fine Arts in Boston that is of unknown origin. It measures a little more than five feet (155 cm) and is made of thirteen cylindrical bone tubes (perhaps from a cow or an ox) fastened together with bronze rings flanked by a narrow bronze bell and a small bone mouthpiece on the ends. The **mouthpiece** was a simple enlargement of the end of the tubing devoid of a distinct cup, **throat**, or **backbore**. The instrument is longer than iconographical depictions of the salpinx on Greek vases, which portray a shorter instrument with a bell that resembles a cup or bulb shape. Some of the instruments were completely made of bronze, and mouthpieces were often fashioned out of bone and included chains used to facilitate a more secure playing position. (See figure 44.)

The strident, piercing sound of the salpinx resembled "screaming," according to Aeschylus, and was described as "rough" by Aristotle as well as "sharp and penetrating." Although little is known about the music the salpinx performed, contests for trumpet playing were included in the Ancient Greek Olympic Games after 396 BC, primarily as tests of volume, tone, and **endurance** for signaling purposes. According to the Ancient historian Julius Pollux, a man named **Archias from Yvla** won the Olympic prize three times and a column was built in his honor. Other notable salpinx players were **Herodorus from Megara,** Molovros, and Aglaisi Megakleous, a woman. Those who played the instrument were called *salpingtis* (in the military), *keryx* (heralds), and *komastes* (street entertainers).

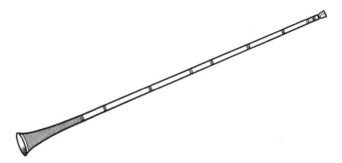

Figure 44. An ancient Greek salpinx. *Drawing by T. M. Larsen.*

salpinx thalassia. An ancient Greek trumpet that was made from a conch shell (literally "trumpet of the sea"), referred to by the poet Archilochus in the seventh century BC as the instrument played by sea god **Triton,** Poseidon's trumpeter.

Sandoval, Arturo (b. 1949). Cuban trumpeter and composer. He began studying the trumpet at the age of twelve and played in his hometown band in Artemisa outside of Havana. He attended the Escuela Nacional de Arte in Havana on scholarship for three years and studied classical trumpet technique. His early career was spent playing in circus bands, Latin bands, and orchestras in Havana. In 1971 Sandoval was drafted into the military and spent the next three years playing in the Orquesta Cubana de Música Moderna. In 1974 he formed the group Irakere with saxophonist Paquito D'Rivera and pianist Chucho Valdes, which became extremely popular in Cuba, and earned a Grammy Award for Best Latin Recording in 1980. He met **Dizzy Gillespie** in 1977 when the famous jazz trumpeter visited Cuba, and the two became fast friends, often performing together. As his fame grew, Sandoval earned accolades as "Cuba's Best Instrumentalist" from the country's hit parade between 1982 and 1990.

Despite his success in Cuba, Sandoval was eager to leave the repressive communist government, which limited his artistic freedom and commandeered a large percentage of his concert income. Gillespie, through his association with the United Nations Orchestra, helped Sandoval gain political asylum in the United States in 1990, and he subsequently moved to Miami and joined the faculty of the Florida International University. He made his first American recording in 1991, *Flight to Freedom*, followed by over twenty-five more as a leader, including one that features Sandoval playing piano (*My Passion for the Piano*, 2002). He became a naturalized American citizen in 1999, and was the subject of an HBO movie in 2000 titled *For Love or Country: The Arturo Sandoval Story.* Known for his versatility and high-energy style reminiscent of **Maynard Ferguson** and Gillespie, Sandoval earned numerous honors, including four Grammy Awards, six *Billboard* Awards, and an Emmy Award. He also published three volumes of *Playing Technique and Performance Studies* (Hal Leonard) and *Brass Concepts* (Editions BIM). In 2013 Sandoval received the Presidential Medal of Freedom from President Barack Obama.

sankh. A **conch shell trumpet** played in India. In Hinduism the conch shell is usually associated with the god Vishnu, Lord of the Waters.

Sarjant, John (d. 1798). English trumpeter. His solo performances of Handel repertoire on the natural trumpet with uncorrected intonation famously drew the criticism of **Charles Burney** in 1784. He served as first trumpeter and soloist at Vauxhall and also played at the ceremony at Oxford University when Haydn was awarded an honorary doctorate.

Satchmo. Nickname for **Louis Armstrong**; short for "satchel mouth" in reference to his wide mouth and infectious grin.

Sattler, Christian Friedrich (1778–1842). German brass instrument manufacturer who invented the **double piston valve,** later known as the **Vienna valve.** He trained with Johann Gottfried Moritz (1777–1840) between 1799 and 1805 in Leipzig and set up his own workshop in 1809. Sattler became the first brass instrument maker in Saxony to build a horn with three valves in 1819. His double piston valve first appeared in 1821 on a trumpet with two such valves; the mechanism was improved by **Josef Kail** and Joseph Riedel in 1823 in Vienna (hence the name) and later adapted by Leopold Uhlmann in 1830. Sattler also developed a trigger mechanism for the trombone in 1839.

Sax, Adolphe (1814–1894). Belgian wind instrument manufacturer. Best known as the inventor of the saxophone, he studied clarinet and flute at the Brussels Conservatory and learned the craft of instrument making in the workshop of his father, Charles-Joseph Sax (1790–1865). His talents for invention and self-regard were not matched by a head for business, and he generated controversy, attacks, and lawsuits throughout his highly influential career. His first instruments presented at the Brussels Industrial Exposition of 1830 were a flute and an ivory clarinet. He patented a bass clarinet in 1838 that was superior to contemporary models, and he most likely began to develop the saxophone around the same time. Sax moved to Paris in 1842 and forged contacts with influential composers such as **Berlioz**, Rossini, Halévy, and Meyerbeer. French patent records of the next ten years bear witness to Sax's extraordinary powers of invention, including families of **saxhorns** (1845) and **saxotrombas** (1845) as well as saxophones (1846).

He won a competition to supply musical instruments to the French military in 1845, which gave him a monopoly on the lucrative trade that angered competing instrument manufacturers. Sax also adopted innovations from other inventors such as **Wieprecht's Berlin valve.** His family of conical brass saxhorns was embraced by the **Distin** Family Quintet in the middle of the nineteenth century and later formed the foundation of the British brass band. While the quartet of saxophones became a fixture in the wind band, Sax never envisioned the enormous popularity the saxophone would come to enjoy in the realm of jazz in the twentieth century.

saxhorn. Brass instruments produced by **Adolphe Sax** in the 1840s and 1850s in Paris that were built in a family of sizes of consistent design. First made with **Berlin valves,** saxhorns were later built with **Perinet piston valves** and **rotary valves.** The instruments featured a **conical bore** with the exception of the **valve slides,** which were cylindrical, and deep cup **mouthpieces.** Although some of the smaller saxhorns were made with bells pointing forward, like **cornets,** most were built with vertical bells. Sax became embroiled in a series of lawsuits from competing instrument makers because valved brass instruments in different sizes were not new at the time; only the idea of a matching family, like that of the saxophones (which were developed later) was new. Sax spent so much on legal fees to defend his patents that he declared bankruptcy three times.

The full complement of saxhorns included a sopranino in high C or B-flat (known as the *saxhorn sur-aigu;* similar to a modern **piccolo trumpet**), a soprano in E-flat or F, an alto in B-flat or C, a tenor in E-flat or F, a baritone in B-flat or C, a bass in B-flat or C, a contrabass in E-flat or F, and a contrabass in low B-flat or C. High-pitched saxhorns were similar to cornets, but featured a slightly wider **bore** in between that of a cornet and a **flugelhorn.** Tenor and baritone saxhorns became the modern tenor horns and baritone horns of the British brass band. The bass saxhorn became the modern euphonium and the contrabasses became known as tubas ("bombardons" or "basses" in bands).

Adolphe Sax met trumpeter **John Distin** and his pioneering brass chamber ensemble, the Distin Family Quintet, in 1844, who quickly adopted a matching set of saxhorns. It might have even been John Distin who suggested that the instruments be named for their inventor rather than called *Bugles à cylinders*. **Henry Distin**, John's son, became the London agent for Sax's instruments in 1845 and began making his own line of brass instruments five years later. Largely through the agency of the Distins, saxhorns were adopted by brass bands in England as early as 1845 and later in the United States. The instrumentation of early brass bands was virtually identical to the family of saxhorns and several groups even called themselves "saxhorn bands," such as the "Hawick Saxhorn Band."

In the United States **Allen Dodworth** patented an **over-the-shoulder** (OTS) **cornet** with **rotary valves** in 1838 (predating the saxhorns) that later inspired a family of OTS brass instruments best known through their use in bands during the American Civil War (1860–1865). Although the OTS instruments may resemble saxhorns with upright bells played horizontally (bells pointing backward), they were unique instruments. Dodworth mentions saxhorns (referring to them as "Sax Horns") as distinct from cornets and **keyed bugles** in the section on instrumentation in his 1853 band method, *Dodworth's Band School.*

saxotromba, saxtromba. A family of valved brass instruments created by **Adolphe Sax** in 1845 for mounted bands of the French military. Featuring a **bore** that was moderately **conical**, the instruments were pitched in B-flat and E-flat and designed with a vertical bell. An additional saxotromba was built in F to substitute for the French horn in band instrumentation. The instrument's unique bore profile may be the reason why its name included "*tromba*" rather than "**horn**," like the contemporary **saxhorns**. Saxotrombas flourished for only a short time and disappeared from the ranks of French cavalry bands by 1867; no original instruments survive today.

Schachtner, Johann Andreas (1731–1795). Austrian trumpeter and writer. He studied at Ingolstadt University and subsequently moved to Salzburg, where he studied with court trumpeter **Johann Caspar Köstler**. He was appointed court and field trumpeter in 1754 and became a close friend of **Leopold Mozart** as well as a frequent visitor to the Mozart home. A versatile musician, Schachtner also played the violin and the cello, and regularly participated in chamber music evenings with the Mozart family. Leopold was a witness at Schachter's wedding and described his trumpet playing as "elegant"

and displaying "good taste." It is very likely that Leopold wrote his *Concerto in D* for Schachtner in 1762. In 1781 he was named a *spielgraf*, which was a position similar to that of a modern union official who collected dues from musicians who weren't members of the local association for the right to perform at public functions.

In 1792, after the death of **Wolfgang Amadeus Mozart**, Schachtner wrote down his recollections of Mozart's childhood at the request of Wolfgang's sister, Maria Anna "Nannerl" (1751–1829). One of the episodes captures Mozart's dislike of the trumpet:

> Until he was almost nine he was terribly afraid of the trumpet when it was blown alone, without other music. Merely to hold a trumpet in front of him was like aiming a pistol at his heart. . . . Papa wanted me to cure him of this childish fear and once told me to blow [the trumpet] at him despite his reluctance, but my God! I should not have been persuaded to do it; Wolfgangerl scarcely heard the blaring sound when he grew pale and began to collapse, and if I had continued he would surely have suffered a convulsion.

Also a poet and librettist, Schachtner published a collection of poetry, *Poetischer Versuch in verschiedenen Arten von Gedichten* (1765) and wrote the text for Adlgaser's oratorio, *Die wirkended Gnade Gottes, oder David in der Busse* (1756). He collaborated with Mozart on several of his operas; he revised the libretto for *Bastien und Bastienne* and wrote the German version of Varesco's libretto for *Idomeneo*. Schachtner also supplied the text for *Zaide* and wrote the German version of the libretto for Mozart's early opera, *La finta giardiniera.*

Schagerl. Austrian brass instrument manufacturer. Founded in 1961 by Karl Schagerl (b. 1929), the company specializes in **rotary valve trumpets** and also produces **piston valve** trumpets, **cornets**, **flugelhorns**, trombones, and saxophones. **Hans Gansch** has collaborated on trumpet design for Schagerl, as has his brother, **Thomas Gansch**, for whom Schagerl has built a custom B-flat trumpet with an upturned **bell** called the **Ganschhorn**. The management of the company was turned over to Karl Schagerl Jr. (b. 1962) in 1989. Several other members of the Schagerl family work in the business. Karl Jr.'s brother, Robert Schagerl (b. 1966), has been instrumental in developing the company's professional line of rotary valve trumpets. Most of the members of **Mnozil Brass** play Schagerl instruments.

Schallstück. (Ger.) The **bell** of a trumpet.

Schalltrichter auf, Schalltricher in die höhe. (Ger.) **Bells** up, bells in the air. A performance indication found in the music of Gustav Mahler to instruct the musicians to point their instruments up higher than the normal playing position for intensified sound projection. The term for bells (*schalltricher*) is sometimes abbreviated as *schalltr.*

Scheibenventil. (Ger.) **Disc valve.**

Scherbaum, Adolf (1909–2000). Czech trumpeter. He was the first international soloist on the **piccolo trumpet** when he began recording Baroque repertoire in the late 1950s on a piccolo trumpet in B-flat of his own design made by Leistner of Hamburg. He performed Bach's *Brandenburg Concerto No. 2* over four hundred times and recorded over eighty albums of Baroque trumpet music. Scherbaum began playing the trumpet at the age of eight and studied at the Military Music School in Prague between 1923 and 1928. He later played with the Czech Philharmonic in Prague from 1939 until 1941, when he became principal trumpet of the Berlin Philharmonic under Wilhelm Furtwängler. Political pressures caused him to leave Berlin in 1945 and he became solo trumpet of the Pressburg Radio Orchestra (Pressburg is now Bratislava in the Slovak Republic). He went on to serve as a professor at the Pressburg Conservatory from 1945 until 1951, when he became solo trumpet of the Hamburg Radio Orchestra until 1967. He was a professor at the Saarbrücken School of Music between 1966 and 1977.

Scherbaum's solo career flourished between the 1950s and 1970s. He was the first classical trumpet soloist to garner international fame in the twentieth century and he paved the way for those who followed, such as **Maurice Andre**. His expertise in the high register was the result of a highly compressed **airstream** rather than **mouthpiece pressure**. Although Scherbaum's specialty was Baroque repertoire, Bernd-Alois Zimmermann (1918–1970) wrote the **avant-garde** solo work *Nobody Knows de Trouble I See* for him in 1954. Scherbaum recorded more than thirty solo albums, as well as **J. S. Bach**'s large choral works and many cantatas. His recordings earned five *Grand Prix du Disque* awards and one Edison Award. Scherbaum performed as a soloist with major orchestras throughout Europe and the United States, and received numerous awards including the Albert Schweitzer Peace Medal in 1979.

Scherzer. German brass instrument manufacturer. Johannes Scherzer (b. 1922) apprenticed with his uncle in Markneukirchen and became a master in 1951. His brand is best known for the **piccolo trumpet** with rotary valves that he developed in conjunction with the trumpeter Willi Krug (1925–2000). Scherzer piccolo trumpets are highly prized for their warm tone quality and are used by many prominent soloists including **Håkan Hardenberger** and **Alison Balsom**. The company was absorbed into the B&S Group (Blechblas- und Signalinstrumente) in 1984.

Schilke, Renold (1910–1982). American trumpeter and brass instrument manufacturer. He began playing the cornet at the age of eight and was playing as a soloist with the **Holton** factory band at the age of eleven. His first teacher was Del Wright and he later studied with **Max Schlossberg, Georges Mager,** Edward Llewellyn, and **Herbert L. Clarke**. In 1921 he began playing professionally with the Orpheum Vaudeville circuit while also working part-time in the Holton factory. Schilke moved to Chicago in 1929 and played with the Chicago Civic Orchestra between 1932 and 1936. He joined the Chicago Symphony Orchestra (CSO) in 1933 and played with the orchestra in various roles until 1962; he started as a substitute, progressed to assistant first trumpet (1934), then first trumpet (1939), and spent the rest of his time with the orchestra as a section member when he devoted more time to making trumpets. Schilke also played with **Adolph Herseth** in the CSO Brass Ensemble (a **brass quintet**) between 1949 and 1962. In addition to performing, Schilke taught at Northwestern University (1939–1958), De Paul University (1953–1958), and Roosevelt University (1945–1968). Some of his notable students were Vincent Cichowicz, **Thomas Crown**, and William Scarlett.

Schilke met **Elden Benge** in 1933 when they were both playing in the CSO. The two men shared an interest in trumpet design and spent many hours working on instruments together in Schilke's home workshop. When Benge opened his own trumpet-making business in 1939, Schilke made many of the first tools and dies for Benge. Schilke began making his own high-quality trumpets in 1947 and incorporated as Schilke Music Products in 1956. His acoustical research and interest in the work of **Victor-Charles Mahillon** led to the development of the **tuning bell** trumpet design in 1968 (patented in 1970). **High-pitched trumpets** with tuning bells and **piccolo trumpets** with narrow **bore** tuning **shanks** helped establish Schilke as a leading brand among professional trumpeters in the late twentieth century. Schilke's success attracted the attention of the **Yamaha** Corporation and he was subsequently engaged as a design consultant by the Japanese firm. When he retired in 1982, his son, Renold E. Schilke, took over the company and sold it to Andrew Naumann twenty years later in 2002.

Schiltz, Jean Baptiste (fl. 1831–1854). French cornetist. He was a **cornet** player in the Paris Opéra orchestra between 1831 and 1854 who was also active in early brass chamber music. Schiltz composed several works that were published in Paris including a number of *divertissements facile et brilliant* (1837) for two cornets, horn or **ophicleide**, and trombone; *Quartours sur des motifs de Lucia di Lammermoor* (ca. 1839); and *Six Trios* (op. 101) for two cornets and bass ophicleide. Schiltz wrote some of the first solos for cornet and piano ever published, including numerous fantasias based on popular operatic airs (especially those by Rossini and Meyerbeer) and a set of six grand duets. He also published methods for trombone, ophicleide, cavalry trumpet, cornet, and the complete range of **saxhorns** from soprano E-flat to contrabass B-flat. Richard Wagner's autobiography mentions that Schiltz was "the leading cornet player in Paris" in 1840.

Schlossberg, Max (1873–1936). Russian-American trumpeter. Considered to be the father of the American school of trumpet playing, Schlossberg was born in Libau, Courland (now known as Liepaja, Latvia), in the Russian Empire. At the age of nine he went to Moscow to study with his older brother, Joseph, who was studying at the Moscow Conservatory. He later studied with August K. Marquardt (fl. 1882–1915) and Franz Puttkammer (fl. 1883–1903) in Moscow, most likely at the music school of the Russian Musical Society. Between 1889 and 1894 Schlossberg moved between St. Petersburg and Berlin, studying with **Julius Kosleck** and performing with orchestras under the direction of noted conductors Arthur Nikisch, Felix Weingartner, and Hans Richter. He returned to Riga to complete compulsory military service in 1895, where he conducted the 171st Regiment Band as well as the orchestra at the Russian Club Theater. In 1902 he married Jenny Lohak (1879–1947), deserted the Russian Army, and fled to America, never to return. He became a naturalized American citizen in 1914.

Settling in New York, Schlossberg performed with several freelance groups as well as Edwin Franko Goldman's band and taught at the Hebrew Orphan Asylum in Manhattan. In 1910 he accepted a position with the New York Philharmonic-Symphony Orchestra (as it was then known), when Gustav Mahler was chief conductor. He stayed with the orchestra for the rest of his life with the exception of the 1920–1921 season. In 1923 he began teaching at the Institute of Musical Art (later to become the Juilliard School) and later preferred to teach an ever-growing number of private students at home in the Bronx. His classic book, *Daily Drills and Technical Studies for the Trumpet*, was first published in 1937, the year after his death.

As the master trumpet teacher in early twentieth-century America, most of the professional players of the younger generation studied with him at one time or another. These trumpeters included **Charles Colin**, Louis Davidson, **Vladimir Drucker**, **Harry Glantz**, Bernie Glow, **Harry James**, **Mannie Klein**, **Renold Schilke**, **James Stamp**, and **William Vacchiano**, among others. His pedagogy emphasized strength of tone, long tones in octaves, tongue-level studies, and secure mouthpiece placement.

Schlueter, Charles (b. 1940). American trumpeter. He grew up in Illinois and studied the **cornet** with Charles

Archibald at the age of ten. Between 1953 and 1955 he studied trumpet with Don Lemasters and later with Eddie Brauer in Saint Louis. Schlueter went on to study with **William Vacchiano** at the Juilliard School, graduating in 1962. He served as principal trumpet with the Kansas City Philharmonic between 1962 and 1964 and with the Milwaukee Symphony between 1964 and 1967. He became associate principal trumpet of the Cleveland Orchestra in 1967 and left in 1972 to become principal trumpet of the Minnesota Orchestra, a position he held for ten years. Schlueter joined the Boston Symphony as principal trumpet in 1981 and remained with the orchestra for twenty-five years until his retirement in 2006. As a teacher, he served on the faculties of Wisconsin State University, the Cleveland Institute of Music, the University of Minnesota, the University of Connecticut, the New England Conservatory, and the Tanglewood Institute. He has also led master classes in Europe, Canada, Japan, and South America. Since the 1980s, Schlueter has been a regular visitor to Brazil, presenting numerous master classes, recitals, and solo appearances. Schlueter recorded several CDs for Kleos Classics including *Bravura Trumpet*, *Virtuoso Trumpet*, and *Song from the Heart*. He was named "Musician of the Year" by the Boston Musicians' Association in 2006 and received an Honorary Award from the **International Trumpet Guild** in 2007.

Schola Cantorum Basiliensis. A music academy and research institution located in Basel, Switzerland, that specializes in **historically informed performance** and the instruction of **period instruments**. Founded in 1933 by Paul Sacher and the Swiss musicologist Wilhelm Merian, the current brass faculty includes **Bruce Dickey** (**cornett**) and **Jean-Francois Madeuf** (trumpet). **Edward Tarr** taught there between 1972 and 2001.

Schreiber, Johann Ludwig (fl. 1715–1723). German trumpeter. He was the principal trumpeter at the court of Cöthen during the tenure of **J. S. Bach** (1717–1723) and may have been the soloist for whom Bach wrote *Brandenburg Concerto No. 2*. No evidence exists that Schreiber performed the work, but Bach may have had his abilities in mind when he composed the difficult concerto.

Schreiberhorn. Any of the fanciful brass instruments built by Louis Schreiber (1827–1910) in the nineteenth century whether they are cornets, alto horns, tenor horns, or baritone horns. One feature of these unique instruments is the gently curved bell section that often resembles the letter *S*, depending on size.

Schubventil. (Ger.) Push (piston) valve, **Stölzel valve**.

Schuster, Friedrich Wilhelm (1798–1873). German brass instrument maker. Working in Karlsruhe, Schuster was the first to apply **Friedrich Blümel**'s invention of a **box valve** to a brass instrument in the early nineteenth century. He stopped making such instruments after 1833.

Schwarz, Gerard (b. 1947). American conductor and trumpeter. He attended New York City's High School for Performing Arts and later studied with **William Vacchiano** at Juilliard. Schwarz joined the **American Brass Quintet** in 1965 and remained with the group until 1973, performing several international tours. During the same period he also played with the American Symphony Orchestra, the Aspen Festival Orchestra, and the Casals Festival Orchestra. Schwarz made several recordings with the American Brass Quintet and as a soloist. Known for his interest in contemporary music and adventuresome programming, Schwarz commissioned new works from several composers including Brant, Cervetti, Dlugoszewski, Hellerman, Moryl, and Whittenberg. He earned a Ford Foundation grant to commission **Gunther Schuller** to write a trumpet concerto in 1973 (it was completed in 1979). That same year Schwarz succeeded Vacchiano as co-principal trumpet of the New York Philharmonic. He left the position four years later in 1977 to pursue a full-time conducting career. As a conductor Schwarz founded the Y Chamber Symphony (later known as the New York Chamber Symphony) in 1977 and served as music director until 1986. He concurrently served as music director of the Los Angeles Chamber Orchestra from 1978–1985 and New York's Mostly Mozart Festival from 1982–2001. Schwarz served as music director of the Seattle Symphony from 1985 until 2011, winning several awards during his tenure including thirteen Grammy nominations and Musical America's Conductor of the Year in 1994 (the first American so honored). He also served as the music director of the Royal Liverpool Philharmonic Orchestra between 2001 and 2006.

schwarzer zink. (Ger.) Black **cornett**. A term used to differentiate the curved treble cornett from the **straight cornett** because it was covered with black leather while the straight cornett was made of plain wood, usually boxwood.

scoop. A special effect used in jazz and commercial music similar to a **rip** up to note, but performed by **lipping** or through a **note bending**, and usually starting approximately a half step below the printed note.

screaming. Term often used to describe the altissimo playing of jazz lead trumpet players at high volumes. It was also used by Aeschylus to characterize the strident sound of the Ancient Greek **salpinx**.

screw pins. External pins that pierce the **valve casings** on **Stölzel valves** to serve as **valve guides**.

Seefeldt, William (1829–1909). American brass instrument manufacturer. He established his shop in Philadelphia in 1858 and produced **cornets** with **rotary valves** at first; later he made cornets modeled after **Courtois** artist models with **piston valves** beginning around 1880. His nephew, Albert Hentschke (ca. 1850–ca. 1918), joined him in the business in 1875 and took over when Seefeldt retired in 1890, when the firm adopted the name "Seefeldt Musical Instrument Manufacturing Co." The firm stopped making instruments after Seefeldt died in 1909 and the business changed to making "brass metal goods" under the name "A. Hentschke & Son."

Seifert, Eduard (1870–1965). German orchestral trumpeter and soloist nicknamed by his colleagues "Mr. Never-Miss" ("Der Unfehlbare," literally, "the infallible one"). Seifert attended the Leipzig Conservatory between 1887 and 1889, and again from 1893 to 1894, where he studied with **Christian Ferdinand Weinschenk** and performed Wilhelm Herfurth's *Concertino in E Major* as a graduation piece. He served as principal trumpet of the Royal Saxon State Orchestra (Sächsische Staatskapelle Dresden) for forty years from 1898 until his retirement in 1938. Because the Dresden Opera and the Staatskapelle had a close association with Richard Strauss, Seifert played for the premieres of many of the composer's works including *Salome* (1905), *Elektra* (1909), *Der Rosenkavalier* (1911), *Eine Alpensinfonie* (1915), *Arabella* (1933), and *Daphne* (1938).

Known for his musicianship, endurance, and unfailing consistency, Seifert was also a soloist who specialized in Baroque repertoire on his small Heckel F/G **rotary valve trumpet**. He was one of the first to play the Haydn concerto in the twentieth century when he performed the work in 1914, and was also one of the first to perform Bach's ***Brandenburg Concerto No. 2*** regularly in concert. When he retired from orchestral playing in 1938, he specialized in performing the music of Bach, especially the *B Minor Mass* and several cantatas. Many of Seifert's students earned principal trumpet positions and university posts including Horst Eichler (Berlin Philharmonic), Erwin Wolff (Staatskapelle Dresden), and Hans-Joachim Krumpfer (Berlin Symphony Orchestra). Seifert's personal papers and instruments are preserved by the Trumpet Museum Bad Säckingen, including his own manuscript solo parts for over a dozen compositions.

Selmer. French musical instrument manufacturer and distributor. The firm was founded in Paris by the French clarinetist Henri Selmer (1858–1941) in 1885. His brother, Alexandre Selmer (1864–1953), also a clarinetist, traveled to the United States in 1898 to become a member of the Boston Symphony Orchestra; he later played with the Cincinnati Symphony (1902–1906). Beginning in 1903, Alexandre began acting as an agent for the distribution of Selmer clarinets in the United States. He moved to New York in 1906 and opened an import and retail business. In 1909 he joined the New York Philharmonic and hired George Bundy (1886–1951) as an assistant in the shop. After the First World War, the firm was incorporated as H. & A. Selmer Inc. with Bundy as president. The firm grew steadily and merged New York operations with **Conn**; the result was known as Selmer-Conn until 1928. The American branch of Selmer began producing clarinets and flutes under the Bundy name in 1944 and expanded into the mass production of student instruments. The Bundy Band Instrument Company was formed in 1958. Selmer acquired the **Vincent Bach** Corporation in 1961 and several other subsidiary companies before reincorporating as the Selmer Company in 1976. Selmer began working with **Maurice André** in 1958 to produce a **piccolo trumpet** that was marketed in 1960, revised in 1967, and became widely adopted by professional players. In 1983 Selmer-USA marketed a large **bore** trumpet in B-flat that was designed with **Claude Gordon**. In 2003, Selmer merged with United Musical Instruments (UMI) to form Conn-Selmer, a subsidiary of Steinway Musical Instruments Inc.

sennet. Similar to "sonata," a long flourish for trumpets, more elaborate than a **tucket** (toccata) or **fanfare**. The term appeared as a stage direction in Elizabethan plays to indicate a type of fanfare, played before actors entered or left the stage. The first movement of Leonard Bernstein's orchestral work *Divertimento* (1980) is titled "Sennets and Tuckets."

serpent. An ancestor of the bass tuba made of wood and covered with leather that featured a widely **conical** tube formed in the shape of a letter *S* (as its name implies) to enable the musician playing it to reach the six finger holes in the center of the instrument. The top of the serpent had a curved metal pipe extending from it, similar in concept to the bocal on a bassoon, to hold the trombone-like cup mouthpiece. Initially devised as a bass instrument to support voices in French churches, it became a popular military instrument throughout Europe at the turn of the nineteenth century. The serpent also served as the orchestral brass bass before the invention of the **ophicleide** and the tuba. Its wide bore gives it a rich tone, which was soft and flexible, but often required adjustments such as **lipping** and **alternate fingerings** to achieve accurate tuning. Some serpents had auxiliary keys to assist with tuning and trills. Although it appears to be part of the **cornett** family, the serpent is not a "bass cornett"—such an instrument does exist—because its bore profile is more conical, and it lacks a thumb hole on the back.

serpentine trumpet. A trumpet configured in the shape of a letter *S* or a figure eight for decorative purposes or to make the instrument appear to be shorter. Such a trumpet was built by Anton Schnitzer (ca. 1525–1608) for **Cesare Bendinelli** in the seventeenth century. Because of this association, it is sometimes called a "Bendinelli trumpet."

set. The position of the muscles surrounding the lips to form an **embouchure**.

Severinsen, Carl Hilding "Doc" (b. 1927). American trumpeter and conductor best known for his tenure as the bandleader of *The Tonight Show* Band for thirty years (1962–1992). His father (also named Carl) was a dentist and amateur violinist, so he earned the nickname "Little Doc" as a boy, eventually becoming known simply as "Doc." Severinsen started playing the trumpet at the age of seven, was soon good enough to join the local high school band, and won the Music Educator's National Contest at the age of twelve. He began playing professionally in high school with the Ted Fito Rio Orchestra, but had to leave the group to serve in the army during the Second World War. After the war, Severinsen toured with the Charlie Barnett Band as well as Tommy Dorsey and Benny Goodman.

In 1949 Severinsen moved to New York and started his career playing in studio bands at NBC. He began appearing on *The Steve Allen Show* in the 1950s and became first trumpet in *The Tonight Show* Band under director Skitch Henderson in October 1962. He eventually became the leader of the band and music director for the television show in 1967. Known for his terrific trumpeting and melodic artistry, Severinsen was also a consummate entertainer with a commanding stage presence, a dynamic wardrobe, and a gift for comedy. He often served as co-host on *The Tonight Show* in the absence of Ed McMahon and introduced several musical skits into the programming such as "Stump the Band." His recording career included albums with *The Tonight Show* Band as well as Henry Mancini and the Cincinnati Pops.

After leaving *The Tonight Show* in 1992 when host Johnny Carson retired, Severinsen embraced a second career as a conductor of symphonic pops programs, which he had begun before retiring from NBC. He served as the principal pops conductor of several American orchestras including the Phoenix Symphony, the Colorado Symphony Orchestra, the Milwaukee Symphony Orchestra, the Minnesota Orchestra, the Buffalo Philharmonic Orchestra, and the Pacific Symphony Orchestra. Following his retirement from active conducting in 2007, Severinsen continues to perform with small groups like the San Miguel 5, appear as a guest artist, present master classes, and perfect his own line of "Destino" trumpets manufactured by the S. E. Shires Company.

shake. 1. An alternate term for a trill favored in nineteenth-century British usage.

2. A technique in jazz trumpet playing that involves a **lip trill** in the high register between two notes close together in the **harmonic overtone series** (for example, G5 and B-flat5).

shank. 1. The stem of a brass instrument **mouthpiece** that fits into the **mouthpiece receiver** or **leadpipe**.

2. A short piece of tubing inserted into the leadpipe of a nineteenth-century **cornet** or a twentieth-century **piccolo trumpet** for tuning and bore taper adjustments.

sharp pitch. A pitch standard (A4 = 452.5 Hz) used in military bands in the late nineteenth-century and early twentieth century. It was also known as Old Philharmonic pitch.

Shastock. American **mute** manufacturing company based in Cleveland, Ohio. Started by Louis W. Shastock (dates unknown) in the 1920s, the company catered to jazz trumpeters and made a variety of different **straight mutes**, **cup mutes**, and **practice mutes**; they were best known for creating the **Solotone mute**. Some of Shastock's unique models were the LWS Trumpet Mute (a straight mute with six offset corks, later known as the Shastock Mute), the Vocatone mute (a type of straight mute), the Tonalcolor mute (an adjustable cup mute), and the Charlie Spivak **Wispa mute** (a practice mute). Shastock mutes were marked by a quest for new tone colors and sometimes featured experimental materials and designs. While most of the mutes were made from hardened fiberboard, some had bottoms made of maple wood, and others were variations on the solotone mute with appended filters to change the sound such as the Krooner mute (with an enlarged double bell), the Buzz mute (with a kazoo-like disc on the bottom), and the EE-MO-YE mute (featuring a large appended chamber with holes). In the 1940s Shastock mutes began to appear under the name "Micro Products." Many of Shastock's designs were adopted by other mute manufacturers such as **Humes & Berg**.

Shaw, John. (fl. 1824–1867). English brass instrument manufacturer. He referred to himself as "a farmer of Salop" and developed a form of the **disc valve** in 1838 that was patented as the "patent swivel valve" (see appendix 2). He sold the rights to John Augustus **Köhler**, who modified its design and called it the **patent lever valve** and applied the mechanism to trumpets and cornets.

Shaw, William (ca. 1754–after 1823). English brass instrument manufacturer. He built the first trumpet with **vent holes** in the eighteenth century in 1787. Known as a **Harmonic trumpet**, it was a silver trumpet with four vent holes, three of which are covered by an adjustable metal sleeve. Shaw is also credited with transforming the shape of the **bugle** from the crescent-shaped **Halbmond** into the familiar single-looped trumpet shape with the bell pointing to the front.

Shaw, Woody (1944–1989). American jazz trumpeter. He began playing the trumpet at the age of eleven and took private lessons with Jerome Zierling between 1955 and 1957. When he was fourteen, he played in a YMCA big band with Wayne Shorter. At the age of nineteen, he made his recording debut on Eric Dolphy's album *Iron Man* and later went to Europe to perform with Dolphy. He remained in Paris until 1965, playing and recording with Nathan Davis, Jef Gilson, and others. Shaw returned to the United States and performed with several noted musicians including Horace Silver, Chick Corea, McCoy Tyner, Art Blakey, and Max Roach. He also served as a pit musician on Broadway. Known for his versatility, sweet tone, and fluency with free jazz and hard bop styles, Shaw made a series of notable recordings in the 1970s and 1980s, including *The Moontrane, Time Is Right, Song of Songs, Little Red's Fantasy,* and *Last of the Line.* He began to lose his eyesight as a result of retinitis pigmentosa and curtailed performing in the 1980s. He moved to Bern, Switzerland, and later to Amsterdam to teach at several jazz schools. Shaw returned to the United States in 1988, suffered from declining health, and died in 1989 at the age of forty-four following a tragic fall in a subway station.

Shchelokov, Vjacheslav (1904–1975). Russian composer. He wrote the first Russian trumpet concerto in the twentieth century, *Trumpet Concerto No. 1 in D-flat Major,* in 1929 for **Mikhail Tabakov**. His other compositions for trumpet and piano include *Poem in C-sharp Minor, Scherzo in B-flat Major, Trumpet Concerto No. 3 in C Minor, Concert Etude,* and *Etudes No. 1 and 2.*

shed. Shortened version of the term *woodshed*; to practice intensely for long periods of time usually in seclusion.

shell trumpet. A trumpet made from a sea shell. Such instruments have ancient origins, like the Greek **salpinx thalassia,** were commonly used for **signal** purposes, and were blown from a small hole on the end (often cut or sanded down for comfort). Shell trumpets are usually identified by their distinctive shapes—**cassis, fusus, triton,** and **strombus**—than merely as **conch shell trumpets**. (See figure 10 under "conch shell trumpet.") Shell trumpets are used in Oceania and Polynesia.

shepherd's crook. The **bell crook** or **back bow** on a nineteenth-century **cornet** with a wide curved designed. Its name comes from its resemblance to a crosier, or bishop's staff, which is itself patterned after a walking stick traditionally associated with shepherds with a open semicircular loop at the top.

Shew, Bobby (b. 1941). American jazz trumpeter. His given name was Robert Joratz, but he assumed his stepfather's name, Shew, at the age of five. Almost entirely self-taught, he began playing professionally at local dances at the age of thirteen, and he decided to pursue a musical career after performing in bands during his military service. Shew joined the Tommy Dorsey Orchestra in 1964 and went on to play with Woody Herman, Benny Goodman, and Buddy Rich. He worked in Las Vegas for nine years, accompanying popular singers, playing in show bands, and working in films and television. In 1973 he moved to Los Angeles, where he continued to be active as a studio musician and resumed his career in jazz. He received critical acclaim in the late 1970s for his work in the Toshiko Akiyoshi–Lew Tabackin Big Band. In the early 1980s, he switched from big-band work to playing with many small groups, in which he performed solos on trumpet, **flugelhorn**, and his own custom-made "Shewhorn," which was similar in concept to an **echo bell cornet** with two bells—one open and one muted—that could be played in alternation.

shofar. A trumpet-like instrument made from a ram's horn. One of the oldest instruments in continuous use, it dates from biblical times and was the only Jewish liturgical instrument to survive the destruction of the Second Temple of Jerusalem by the Romans in AD 70. The shofar is still in use today and is traditionally sounded on Rosh Hashanah (New Year's) and Yom Kippur (the Day of Atonement). Although the horn of a ram is traditionally preferred, shofars have also been made out of horns from other animals including sheep and goats, but cows are not preferred. The blowing end of the shofar is often modified through the application of heat to fashion a smoother, more comfortable opening, but modern trumpet or horn mouthpieces have occasionally been added (although this is not authentic).

Capable of only playing three or four pitches because of its small size (determined by the source of the horn), the shofar performs **calls** and **signals** that use the first notes of the **harmonic overtone series**, typically intervals of a fifth and a fourth. The length and internal dimensions of the horn determine the specific pitches. Edward Elgar scored a part for a shofar in his oratorio *The Apostles*, which is sometimes played by a **flugelhorn** in modern performance.

Shore, John (ca. 1662–1752). English trumpeter. His father, Matthias Shore (ca. 1640–1700), was the sergeant trumpeter of the royal household and a close personal friend of **Henry Purcell**. His older brother, William

Shore (d. 1707), was also a trumpeter. John Shore was first trained as a lutenist and musical instrument maker before taking up the trumpet. He entered the King's Music as a trumpeter in 1688 and later succeeded his father as sergeant trumpeter of the royal household in 1708, remaining in the post until his death in 1752. He also served as a royal lutenist and is credited with inventing the tuning fork in 1711. As the leading English trumpeter of his time, Shore's playing was praised by Sir John Hawkins (1719–1789) for having "extended the power of the noble instrument . . . beyond the reach of the imagination, for he produced from it a tone as sweet as that of the hautboy [oboe]." Henry Purcell wrote two sonatas for Shore, and **Jeremiah Clarke** also wrote solo works for him. Shore retired from playing in 1695 due to lip paralysis, but remained in royal service. He played trumpets made by **William Bull**, one of which (ca. 1680) currently resides in the London Museum. Like his father and brother, John Shore occasionally performed on a type of **slide trumpet** known as the **flat trumpet**.

shoulder. The part of a **mouthpiece** where the bottom of the **cup** transitions into the **throat**. Most U-shaped cups have a fairly sharp shoulder, which results in easy **response** and a bright sound. Mouthpieces with a funnel or V-shaped cup have a rounder shoulder, which lowers resistance and produces a soft, dark tone.

side-blown trumpet. A type of organic trumpet used primarily in Africa and made from animal horns (cow or ox) or elephant tusks, or carved out of wood. A rectangular or oval hole is cut into the side, which facilitates the playing position and allows the entire length of the horn or tusk to be sounded (rather than cutting a hole at the end). Side-blown trumpets are used for **signal** purposes as well as religious ceremonies. The musical selections performed by the instrument often feature a form of surrogate speech (like a talking drum), where the rhythms of well-known texts are reproduced by the players. In some African cultures, the dissonant sound of a large group of side-blown trumpets was meant to summon powerful spirits and ward off evil spirits and military enemies as well as dangerous animals and insects. (See figure 45.)

Figure 45. A short side-blown trumpet (abentia) made from an elephant tusk from the Asante nation of Ghana. *Drawing by T. M. Larsen.*

sight reading. The ability to read (and play or sing) unfamiliar music accurately. Work with *solfège* and rhythmic training develops this skill.

signal. A short musical passage performed on a brass or wind instrument (most often a **bugle** or military trumpet) to transmit information to large groups or at a distance. Signals varied in complexity from mere blasts of sound on ancient trumpets like the **salpinx** to short musical fragments with distinctive melodic and rhythmic contours that resembled a unique kind of language. In the military, signals directed armies during battle and rallied troops to fight on or retreat. In peacetime, signals directed military maneuvers and highway traffic through the use of **posthorns** and **coach horns**. Less ceremonial than **fanfares**, signals also made their way into concert music in the eighteenth and nineteenth century, most notably in Mozart's "Posthorn Serenade" (K. 320), Haydn's "Military Symphony" (No. 100 in G Major: the second trumpet famously quotes an Austrian *Generalmarsch* signal in the second movement), and the posthorn solo in the third movement of Mahler's Third Symphony. Two of the best-known signals are "**Reveille**" and "**Taps**."

Simon, Frank (1889–1967). American cornetist, bandmaster, and composer. Born in Cincinnati, Ohio, his first instrument was the flute, but he switched to the **cornet** at the age of eleven. Beginning at the age of thirteen, he studied with **Herman Bellstadt** for three years. He made his first solo appearance with William Kopp's band in 1909. The following year he joined the trumpet section of the Cincinnati Symphony. Simon was engaged as **Herbert L. Clarke**'s assistant in the Sousa Band in 1914 and replaced him as solo cornetist when Clarke left the band in 1917. He remained with the Sousa Band until 1920, when he established the Armco Band for the Armco Steel Corporation in Middletown, Ohio. A charter member of the American Bandmasters Association, Simon served as the organization's president between 1935 and 1937. He joined the faculty of the Cincinnati Conservatory in 1949, toured as a cornet soloist, and conducted the National Band of the Air. In 1950 he joined the faculty of the University of Arizona, but returned to the Cincinnati Conservatory in 1966. Also a composer, Simon wrote the cornet solo *Willow Echoes* and several band works such as *Cincinnati Post*, *Four Square*, and *Crusaders*.

single tonguing. A technique of **articulation** that uses only the forward motion of the tongue (as in *tah tah tah*) as opposed to various forms of **multiple tonguing** that add the rebound action of the back of the tongue (as in *tah kah tah kah*).

Slaughter, Susan (b. 1945). American trumpeter. She studied with Herbert Mueller, **Bernard Adelstein**, **Arnold Jacobs**, **Robert Nagel**, **Claude Gordon**, and **Laurie Frink** and graduated from Indiana University, where she received the coveted performer's certificate in recognition of outstanding musical performance. Slaughter served as principal trumpet with the Toledo Symphony for two years before she joined the trumpet section of the St. Louis Symphony Orchestra in 1969. Three years later she was promoted to principal, becoming the first woman to be named principal trumpet of a major symphony orchestra, and held the position until her retirement in 2010. Slaughter has served on the faculty of the Grand Teton Orchestra Seminar, the National Orchestra Institute, and her own week-long workshop, Trumpet Lab. In 1990, she performed with the Bay Area Women's Philharmonic in San Francisco, and in 1991, at the invitation of baseball commissioner Fay Vincent, Slaughter performed the National Anthem for game 3 of the World Series. She founded the **International Women's Brass Conference** in 1990, an organization dedicated to providing opportunities and recognition for female brass musicians.

slide. Tubing on a brass instrument that extends telescopically to lengthen the overall tubing. On a Renaissance or Baroque **slide trumpet**, the tubing was a long **leadpipe** on which the body of the instrument slid back and forth. On the seventeenth-century **flat trumpet**, a U-shaped slide was fitted to the back of the instrument, while the nineteenth-century **English slide trumpet** featured a slide in the center. On trumpets and cornets with **valves**, auxiliary tubing added when valves were engaged did not move, but were known as **valve slides** because they could be moved in order to adjust intonation.

slide cornet. A colloquial term for the soprano trombone.

slide grease. A **lubricant** applied to the main **tuning slide** and **valve slides** of a modern trumpet usually made from petroleum substances and lanolin, a yellow wax-like substance secreted by sheep to protect their wool. Slide grease products vary in thickness depending on the circumstances of their use. Products applied to main tuning slides—or slides that require minimal adjustment rather than continuous, free movement—are thicker than the lighter substances applied to valve slides. Sometimes oils rather than grease are applied to valve slides. For the trombone, special creams or grease are used that are sprayed with water on a regular basis; the water beads act like ball bearings to allow free movement of the slide. In the early nineteenth century, a pure strain of olive oil known as Provence Oil was used on trombones and was most likely used on other brass instruments like the **English slide trumpet**. Provence Oil was advocated for use on trombone slides by Joseph Frölich (1780–1862) in his *Vollständige theoretisch—pracktische musicschule* (1813).

slide trumpet. *Trompette à coulisse* (Fr.), *Zugtrompete* (Ger.), *tromba da tirarsi* or *tromba con coulisse à resort* (It.). A trumpet with sliding tubing that can be elongated during performance in order to play notes outside of the **harmonic overtone series**. Classified as a **chromatic trumpet** rather than a **natural trumpet**, different kinds of slide trumpets appeared beginning in the fifteenth century.

The earliest form of the slide trumpet featured a long **leadpipe** on which the body of the entire trumpet was moved back and forth. It was commonly built in the shape of an "S" with the player holding the mouthpiece and leadpipe like a cigarette in the left hand (similar to the modern trombone) and gripping the body of the instrument with the right hand. (See figure 46.) The early slide trumpet usually doubled the slow-moving chant line (cantus firmus) in the small medieval wind band known as the **alta cappella** (two shawms and a slide trumpet) and played along with choral music, much like the early trombone into which it evolved. The slide trumpet was known in France as the *trompette des menestrels* (trumpet of the minstrels) as distinct from the *trompette de guerre* (trumpet of war). Sebastian Virdung labeled the instrument as a *thurner horn* (tower horn) in his *Musica getutscht* of 1511. These names underscore the point that the slide trumpet was the instrument of the civic musicians known as the "town waits" or *Stadtpfeifer*. When the trumpet guilds were formed in the seventeenth century, many of the subsequent "mandates against the unauthorized playing of trumpets" concerned municipal trumpeters taking work away from military and court trumpeters during peace time by performing ceremonial music (**fanfares**) on a slide trumpet.

In the Baroque era the slide trumpet appeared under a variety of names. The Italian term *tromba da tirarsi* only appears in the scores of **Johann Sebastian Bach**. The German equivalent is *Zugtrompete*, which literally means "gliding trumpet." The slide trumpet was capable of lowering the pitch of each harmonic of the overtone series (usually in the lower register) by as much as two whole steps through five positions. Although this system does not produce a complete chromatic scale, it covered many of the gaps in the lower range of the overtone series. The earliest surviving slide trumpet dates from 1651, an instrument made by Huns Veit of Naumberg, Saxony. In the late seventeenth century, **Henry Purcell** wrote for a unique English instrument known as the **flat (flatt) trumpet**. It gets its name from the fact that it usually played music in minor keys, which were often called "flatt keys" at the time. Its slide mechanism differed from that of the *zugtrompete* by moving the back of the instrument (a U-shaped double slide) rather than the front.

A unique instrument, **the English slide trumpet**, flourished in England during the entire nineteenth century. First developed by **John Hyde** in the late eighteenth century, it stemmed from converted natural trumpets in F that employed a slide operated by a clock-spring mechanism in a more compact design with a slide situated in the center of the instrument. Like other orchestral trumpets in the early nineteenth century, it could be equipped with **crooks** to lower the pitch to keys other than F. The instrument enjoyed a vogue in England because of its ability to correct the out-of-tune notes in the harmonic overtone series and play other chromatic pitches while maintaining the characteristic noble tone of the natural trumpet.

French trumpeter **Joseph-David Buhl** designed his own version of a slide trumpet in 1833, but it suffered from a slow, resistant slide mechanism and was not widely used. Buhl's nephew, **François Dauverné**, designed a type of slide trumpet later in the nineteenth century that featured a forward-moving slide mechanism, but it also failed to attract players. In contemporary jazz performances, trombonists have occasionally been known to use the soprano or piccolo trombone, and this instrument has sometimes been referred to as a slide trumpet.

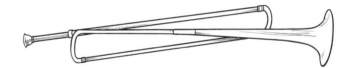

Figure 46. Renaissance slide trumpet. *Drawing by T. M. Larsen.*

slurring. A technique of **articulation** in which **tonguing** is not used. Only the valves are employed to change pitch in order to create a smooth connection between notes in a passage, which is indicated by a curved line above or below the notes to be slurred. Passages where notes of the **harmonic overtone series** are played without changing valves are known as **lip slurs**.

smear. A special effect used in jazz where a note is **lipped** down about a half step. Unlike the technique of **note bending** used in brass pedagogy to strengthen the **embouchure**, a smear is meant to sound "dirty" and not strictly rhythmic and controlled. **Louis Armstrong** popularized the technique, which imitated the slides of blues singers.

Smedvig, Rolf (b. 1952). American trumpeter. He grew up in Seattle and made his solo debut with the Seattle Symphony at the age of thirteen. He studied with **Armando Ghitalla** at Boston University and also studied briefly with **Rafael Méndez**, Don Jacoby, and **Maurice André**. At the age of nineteen, Smedvig won the position of third and assistant principal trumpet with the Boston Symphony Orchestra. Following Ghitalla's retirement from the orchestra, he served as acting principal trumpet between 1979 and 1981. Smedvig left the orchestra in 1981 to pursue a solo career and to devote more time to the Empire Brass, a quintet he formed in 1974. With the Empire Brass he toured more than thirty-five countries and recorded over a dozen CDs. He was also a composer, and the Boston Ballet premiered his work *Passage* in 1996. As a conductor, Smedvig has served as music director of the Williamsport Symphony and the Cambridge Chamber Orchestra in addition to guest conducting.

Smith, Leonard Bingley (1915–2002). American cornetist, trumpeter, and band director. He began playing the cornet at the age of eight and won a scholarship to the New York Military Academy when he was fourteen. After graduation, he studied with **Ernest Williams** and attended New York University and the Curtis Institute. His teachers included Mayhew Lake, Erik Leidzen, Pierre Henrotte, and Rosario Scalero. Smith was hired as a cornet soloist in Edwin Franko Goldman's Band at the age of nineteen and played with the band for six years. In 1937 he became principal trumpet of the Detroit Symphony Orchestra and held that position for six years. During the Second World War Smith served as cornet soloist with the U.S. Navy Band in Washington and returned to the Detroit Symphony in 1945. In 1946 he formed a professional municipal band in Detroit. Its name became the Detroit Concert Band in 1969 and Smith conducted and soloed with the band until 1991, when its funding was eliminated. He also conducted the Blossom Festival Concert Band in Cleveland from 1972 until 1997. As a teacher, he served on the faculties of Wayne State University (trumpet instructor) and the University of Detroit (band director). Smith composed more than 450 band works; his band warm-up method, *Treasury of Scales*, was widely used throughout the United States. He composed several cornet solos and trios such as *Ecstasy, Spanish Caprice, Venture,* and *The Three Bluejackets*. Throughout his solo career, Smith performed on a cornet made for him by the Reynolds Company (the Leonard Smith Model).

Smith, Philip (b. 1952). British-born American trumpeter. Best known as the principal trumpeter of the New York Philharmonic for thirty-six years (1978–2014), Smith was born in London and moved to New York with his family as a child. His father, Derek Smith, was a noted cornetist and conductor with the Salvation Army. Smith began **cornet** studies with his father at the age of eight and later attended the Juilliard School, where he earned bachelor and master of music degrees studying with Edward Treutel and **William Vacchiano**. Smith won the position of fourth trumpet with the Chicago Symphony Orchestra during his final year at Juilliard and played with the orchestra for three years, where he benefit-ted from **Adolph Herseth**'s mentoring. Smith won the audition to replace **Gerard Schwarz** in the New York Philharmonic in 1978 and served as co-principal trumpet with John Ware until 1985, when he became principal trumpet. After thirty-six years he retired from the orchestra in June 2014 to become the William F. and Pamela P. Prokasy Professor of Trumpet at the University of Georgia. Smith had previously served on the faculties of the Juilliard School and Manhattan School of Music.

Smith has appeared as soloist with dozens of leading brass bands, wind ensembles, and orchestras in the United States and Europe. Several works have been written for him, including Joseph Turrin's *Trumpet Concerto, Caprice, Intrada, Four Miniatures, Elegy, Two Portraits,* and *Escapade,* and concertos by Jacques Hêtu, Lowell Liebermann, and Siegfried Matthus. He has also appeared as recitalist and clinician at numerous festivals, including the Caramoor International Music Festival, Grand Teton Music Festival, Scotia Festival of Music, and several **International Trumpet Guild** conferences. Smith's recordings include *Fandango* (Summit), *New York Legends* (CALA), *Music of Zwilich* (New World), *Orchestral Excerpts for Trumpet* (Summit), and *Contest Solos for Young Trumpeters* (ITG). He also performs with the gospel group Resounding Praise and has recorded many albums of worship music, such as *World's Greatest Hymns, The Trumpet Shall Resound* (Heritage), and *He Restores My Soul.*

Smithers, Don (b. 1933). American trumpeter, musicologist, and leading figure in the **period instrument** revival. His first instrument was the oboe and he began playing the trumpet when he was in college, studying with Roger M. Smith. He studied music history at the University of Long Island, Columbia University, and Oxford University, where he earned a doctorate in musicology in 1967. His dissertation on Baroque trumpet repertoire was expanded into the important book *Music and History of the Baroque Trumpet Before 1721* (London: Dent, 1973; second edition, 1988). He taught at Syracuse University from 1973 until 1976, when he left to teach music history at the Royal Conservatory of Music in the Hague. As a trumpeter, he made several solo recordings between 1968 and 1975 on a piccolo trumpet made by **Victor Mahillon**. He also played the **natural trumpet,** a copy of the **Steinkopf-Finke trumpet,** and the *cornetto,* and made recordings on those instruments, including a performance of **Gottfried Rieche's** *Abblasen* on natural trumpet that was used as the theme for the *CBS Sunday Morning* television program in the United States between 1979 and 1998. Smithers retired from active performing in the late 1970s. A noted scholar and author, Smithers has published numerous articles on trumpet history as well as new editions of music by early Baroque composers such as **Biber**, Schmelzer, and **Vejvanovsky**.

Smith-Watkins. British brass instrument manufacturer. The firm was established in 1985 as a joint venture between acoustics expert Richard Smith (b. 1944) and trumpeter Derek Watkins (1945–2013). Prior to starting the company Smith had been the chief brass designer for Boosey and Hawkes between 1974 and 1985. Smith-Watkins produces trumpets in B-flat, C, and E-flat as well as cornets in B-flat and E-flat. They also make flugelhorns and a unique four-valve trumpet that can be configured to play in B-flat, C, D, and E-flat with five different leadpipes. Since 2005 the company has been a contractor for the British Ministry of Defense, providing specialist brass instruments to most of the British military bands. Smith-Watkins also builds customized fanfare or **herald trumpets** that were featured at various important ceremonial events: the Royal Wedding (2011), ceremonies marking the Queen's Jubilee (2012), and the opening of the 2012 Summer Olympic Games in London.

snake. A tool used for cleaning the internal tubing of a high brass instrument designed with a long metal coil with small brushes on each end.

šnb. A straight metal trumpet used in Ancient Egypt made of bronze, silver, or gold. It is the earliest kind of trumpet known to scholars; the English rendering of its name is determined from hieroglyphic inscriptions. These trumpets appear in artwork as early as 1348 BC and were used for military purposes and religious ceremonies. Two such instruments were found in the tomb of King Tutankhamun (ca. 1323 BC), which are the oldest surviving trumpets known to exist. One is made of silver that is nearly two feet long (58.2 cm) and the other is made of copper-alloy bronze and gold that is approximately one and a half feet long (50.5 cm). Both trumpets have elaborately decorated long wooden cores that fit inside the instrument presumably for protection during transport. **Tom Crown** has suggested that the wooden stoppers may have been intended for cleaning (to absorb moisture). The trumpets do not have separate mouthpieces; the players simply blow into the end of the instrument's tubing opposite the cone-shaped bell, which features a wire ring over which the metal is rolled to create a smooth surface for the player's lips.

According to acoustic tests performed by Hans Hickmann, the shorter bronze trumpet produced a note between C4 and C-sharp4 (264.3 Hz) and a playable higher harmonic close to E-flat5 (608.1 Hz). Tests on a copy of the longer silver trumpet determined its playable notes to be a low note between B-flat3 and A3 (220 Hz) and a higher harmonic near C5 (503 Hz). The metal of the trumpet was quite thin (between 0.2 and 0.25 mm in the main tubing and close to 0.1 mm at the end of the bell) and the bore was narrow (approximately 1.7 cm).

The Greek historian Herodotus compared the sound of ancient trumpets to the braying of a donkey in the fifth century BC.

Snow, Valaida (1904–1956). American trumpeter, singer, and dancer. Born in Chattanooga, Tennessee, she was raised on the road in a show-business family. She learned to play the trumpet along with several other instruments and was playing professionally by the age of fifteen. An accomplished entertainer, she also performed as a singer and dancer. Snow soon earned acclaim as a trumpeter and was nicknamed "Little Louis" after **Louis Armstrong**, who was impressed with her playing. She traveled extensively and played concerts throughout the United States, Europe, and Asia. From 1926 to 1929 she toured with Jack Carter's Serenaders in Shanghai, Singapore, Calcutta, and Jakarta. Her most successful period was in the 1930s when she performed in London and Paris and made films with her husband, Ananias Berry, a professional dancer. Snow performed at New York's Apollo Theater, the Cotton Club in Los Angeles, and with Earl Hines's band in Chicago, and again toured Europe in the late 1930s. During the Second World War, she was detained in Denmark in 1941 and was released on a prisoner exchange in May 1942. Returning to the United States, she settled in California in 1945 and resumed touring for the rest of her life, most often as a singer. Through her many recordings from the 1930s, she is the only female trumpet player of the vintage or swing eras to be extensively documented on record.

Snow, Valentine (1685–1770). English trumpeter. Described by **George Frideric Handel** as "the finest trumpeter of his day," Snow premiered the first trumpet parts of several Handel works in London orchestras during the 1730s. Many of Handel's obbligato trumpet solos were written for him including "The Trumpet Shall Sound" from *Messiah*, "Let the Bright Seraphim" from *Samson*, and the overture to *Atalanta,* as well as first trumpet parts in many other works, including the "Dettingen" *Te Deum*, *Judas Maccabaeus*, and *Music for the Royal Fireworks*. Snow's playing was marked by his extraordinary capacity for **endurance** rather than the extreme high register. In 1737 he was mentioned as a trumpeter in George II's First Troop of Horseguards, and in 1738 he became a charter member of the Royal Society of Musicians. Snow frequently performed in such venues as the New Theatre in the Haymarket, Hickford's Room on Brewer Street, and Vauxhall Gardens (where **Charles Burney** remarked that he "was justly a favourite"). In 1753 he succeeded **John Shore** as sergeant trumpeter to the king. He wrote several duets for trumpets that were published in a collection by Bremner in London. A painting that is reputed to be a portrait of Snow hangs in the Fenton House in northwest London.

solfège. (Fr.) *Solfeggio* (It.). A method of singing scales and intervals with solmization syllables as an aid for developing skill in musicianship and **sight reading**. Traditionally ascribed to Guido d'Arezzo (ca. 995–1033), the syllables of the major hexachord (C D E F G A) were expressed as *ut, re, mi, fa, sol,* and *la.* The seventh syllable, *si,* was added in the seventeenth century when the syllable for *ut* was also changed to *do.* French schools retained the use of *ut* for the first syllable. The term *solfège* developed from the syllables *sol* and *fa,* which were also used to describe the system in England (*sol-fa*). Different approaches to solmization gained acceptance in the nineteenth century, the most prevalent of which were the fixed *do* method (where *do* is always associated with the note *C*), and the moveable *do* method (where *do* represents the tonic pitch of the scale, regardless of the note). Variations in syllable vowel sounds for chromatic alterations (for example, *mi* for the third degree of a major scale and *me* for the minor) are an additional feature of the moveable *do* method. Solmization syllables are used to identify pitches in most European countries in place of note letter names (*re* = D, *mi* = E, etc.). Trumpeters benefit from work with *solfège,* especially in the ability to learn (and hear) music away from the instrument, and as an aid for **transposition**.

Solotone mute. The trade name for a type of **open tube mute** made by **Shastock** with two telescoping cones and a small center tube. Made from cardboard or synthetic materials with a cork collar that sealed the bell, it was more resonant than a **Harmon mute** and less stuffy to play. Other names for the mute are **Clear Tone mute,** *doppio sordino,* **double mute,** and **Mega mute.** The name "Solotone" has gained wide acceptance as a universal term for the open tube mute. (See appendix 3.)

sordino. (It.) **Mute.**

sourdine. (Fr.) **Mute.**

sourdine bol. (Fr.) **Cup mute.**

spirometer. A **practice aid** for developing lung capacity and breath control. Originally designed as a therapeutic device for patients with respiratory problems, the spirometer features an enclosed column that houses a hollow plastic ball that moves up and down to provide visual feedback regarding the speed and intensity of airflow provided by the user through a blowing tube. Airflow resistance can be increased by a dial that limits the amount of air that moves into the device. The spirometer can be used to develop smooth inhalation as well as exhalation depending on the position of the air column (up or down).

spit valve. A colloquial term for the **water key** on a trumpet or cornet.

Stadtpfeifer, Stadtpfeiffer. (Ger.) City pipers. Municipal musicians in European cities and towns who performed for civic and ceremonial occasions including weddings, public processions, funerals, and worship services, and signaling the passage of hours in the day (also known as "tower music"). Such organizations flourished between the fourteenth and eighteenth centuries and were largely comprised of brass and wind instruments. Many *Stadtpfeifer* were extremely versatile and played multiple instruments; some doubled on string instruments as well. Bands of civic musicians in Italy were known as *piffari,* and in England, they were the "town waits." Trumpeters who served as *Stadtpfeifer* included Johann Pezel (1639–1694), **Gottfried Reiche,** and Daniel Speer (1636–1707).

Stamitz, Johann (1717–1757). Bohemian composer, violinist, and teacher. Best known as one of the most important early symphonists of the Classical era, he worked at the court of the Elector Palatine at Mannheim, which he made a leading center of orchestral performance and composition in the middle of the eighteenth century. His innovations in symphonic composition include the addition of a minuet to the three-part Italian *sinfonia* and bold dynamic effects such as the orchestral crescendo known as the "Mannheim steamroller." Although he composed one of the first concertos for the clarinet, Stamitz most likely did not write the *Concerto à Clarino Principale* that is often attributed to him. The manuscript of the trumpet concerto bears no signature and resides in the Fulda manuscript collection at the Library of Congress along with three other trumpet concerti by **Joseph Arnold Gross, Franz Xaver Richter,** and **Joseph Riepel.** According to the research of Kevin Eisensmith (b. 1956), the concerto was most likely composed by Johann Georg Holzbogen (1727–1775), who was a violinist in the Mannheim court orchestra between 1751 and 1752, during Stamitz's tenure, and again in 1771.

Stamp, James (1904–1985). American trumpeter and pedagogue. Stamp's father was an amateur cornet player in a Salvation Army band who started him on the instrument as a boy. After high school he attended North Dakota Agricultural College. He married and moved to Rochester, Minnesota, where he played with the Mayo Clinic Band for five years and subsequently moved to St. Paul. He performed as principal trumpet of the Minneapolis Symphony Orchestra for seventeen years before moving to Los Angeles in 1944, where he performed as first trumpet at the Hollywood Bowl as well as a studio trumpeter for films, television, and radio. Stamp suffered a heart attack at the age of fifty in 1954 and devoted the rest of his life to teaching. The lessons learned through his recuperation impacted his teaching because he went against the medical wisdom of the time, which prescribed a sedentary lifestyle and instead embarked on a slow, methodical approach to gradually increasing exercise and physical stamina. His unique gift for curiosity and problem solving put him ahead of his time and made him an insightful master teacher.

Stamp's teaching philosophy was influenced by the work of **Max Schlossberg** and emphasized breath attacks ("poo"), pure tone, the reduction of tension, **note bending**, and efficient **embouchure** movement by opposing conventional thinking. Some of his best-known sayings included "keep thinking down" while going up (and vice versa), and "blow great gusts of air through the trumpet." He was also an advocate of dedicated mouthpiece practice (**buzzing**) and work with **pedal tones**. Stamp's book, *Warm-Ups + Studies* (Editions BIM, 1978), has been translated into five different languages and is an international best-seller. Because the written text in the book is sparse, some of his students have produced books and supplemental studies elaborating on Stamp's methods including Roy Poper, **Thomas Stevens**, and Jean-Christophe Wiener.

stay. Another term for a **brace** on a trumpet or cornet.

Steele-Perkins, Crispian (b. 1944). English trumpeter and **period instrument** specialist. He began playing the trumpet at the age of ten, and by the age of sixteen was playing with the English National Youth Orchestra. He studied with Bernard Brown at the Guildhall School of Music as well as with **Ernest Hall**. Steele-Perkins began his professional career playing with the Sadler Wells Opera (later the English National Opera) and the Royal Philharmonic Orchestra, and he also performed for radio, television, and film studio broadcasts and recordings. Inspired by David Munrow, he developed a special interest in **historically informed performance** and **period instruments**. He amassed his own collection of **natural trumpets** and antique high brass instruments of many different kinds and worked at learning to play them as well as restoring them. These instruments included **cornopeans, cornets**, trumpets with a variety of early valve mechanisms, the unique seventeenth-century **slide trumpet** known as the **flat trumpet**, and especially the **English slide trumpet**, which he revived and promoted on several fine recordings.

Steele-Perkins has performed and recorded on many of these instruments with leading period instrument ensembles such as the Academy of Ancient Music, the English Baroque Soloists, Tafelmusik, the Taverner Players, the London Gabrieli Brass Ensemble, and the King's Consort. He even recorded the theme music for the popular BBC television show *Antiques Roadshow*. Known for his entertaining stage presence and charming wit, he is much in demand as a recitalist and lecturer, and has given several concert tours and master classes to help educate audiences and students about period brass

instruments. He has also published articles in the ***Galpin Society*** Journal and the ***Historic Brass Society*** Journal as well as a book, *The Trumpet* (Kahn & Averill, 2001). In 2004 the **Historic Brass Society** presented him with the **Christopher Monk** Award to honor his achievements and contributions to the field.

Steinkopf, Otto (1904–1980). German woodwind instrument maker and important figure in the **period instrument** revival. He learned to play several different wind instruments and studied music in Berlin, and later musicology with Curt Sachs. After performing for several years as a bassoonist with the Leipzig Gewandhaus Orchestra, the Berlin Philharmonic and the Berlin Radio Symphony Orchestra, he also worked at the Berlin Instrument Collection of the Institut für Musikforschung as a restorer of woodwind instruments, and began to copy old instruments. He was the first to reproduce many Renaissance and Baroque woodwind instruments in the twentieth century, including crumhorns, rackets, dulcians, shawms, and **cornetts** as well as Baroque bassoons and oboes. In 1959 he worked with **Helmut Finke** to add **vent holes** to a coiled **natural trumpet** that resembled the *Jägertrompete* held by **Gottfried Reiche** in the famous portrait by Haussmann. The instrument was known as the **Steinkopf-Finke trumpet** and was used by **Walter Holy** in early period instrument performances with the Capella Colonienis (the chamber orchestra of the radio station in Cologne) in 1960.

Stephenson, James (b. 1969). American composer, trumpeter, and conductor. Stephenson studied trumpet at the Interlochen Arts Academy and the New England Conservatory of Music. He won a position with the Naples (FL) Philharmonic Orchestra directly after graduation and went on to spend seventeen seasons with the orchestra before turning his attention to composition full-time. A prolific composer for trumpet and brass as well as orchestra and wind band, Stephenson's accessible, tonal style has attracted a large number of commissions and performances. His growing catalog features forty-four works for trumpet including *Sonata for Trumpet and Piano* (2001), *Concerto No. 1 for Trumpet* (2003), *Vignettes for Trumpet and Percussion* (2005), and *Rextreme Concerto: Concerto No. 2 for Trumpet* (2010).

Stevens, Halsey (1908–1989). American composer, scholar, and musicologist. Stevens studied composition with William Berwald at Syracuse University in the 1930s and with Bloch at the University of California, Berkeley. Stevens went on to teach at several institutions including Dakota Wesleyan University, the University of Redlands, and the University of Southern California, Los Angeles. He received many awards and commissions including two Guggenheim Fellowships in 1964 and 1971. Stevens is a noted authority on the life and music of **Bela Bartok**, and has written the definitive book on Bartok in English. He composed a *Sonata for Trumpet and Piano* in 1956 for Theodore Gresh that has become a staple of the trumpet's recital repertoire.

Stevens, Thomas (b. 1938). American trumpeter, composer, and arranger. He studied with Lester Remsen and **James Stamp** in California as well as with **William Vacchiano** at the Juilliard School in New York. Stevens joined the trumpet section of the Los Angeles Philharmonic in 1965 and was named principal trumpet by conductor Zubin Mehta in 1972, a position he retained until 1999. He also performed with the Los Angeles Brass Quintet and as a studio player for film soundtracks in Hollywood. A noted exponent of new solo works for the trumpet, several compositions were written for Stevens, notably Luciano Berio's *Sequenza X* (1984). As a teacher, he has served as a member of the faculties of the University of Southern California, the California Institute of the Arts, and the Music Academy of the West. Also a founding board member of the **International Trumpet Guild**, Stevens was named an outstanding alumnus by the University of Southern California's Thornton School of Music in 1996. He has published several trumpet studies through Editions BIM including *Changing Meter Studies* (1978), *Contemporary Interval Studies* (1981), *48 Lyrical Studies* (1997), and *After Schlossberg: Trumpet Studies as Taught by Leading Members of the Schlossberg School* (2011).

stiller zink. (Ger.) **Mute cornett.**

Stockhausen, Markus (b. 1957). German trumpeter and composer. The son of German **avant-garde** composer Karlheinz Stockhausen (1928–2007), he attended the Cologne Hochschule für Musik, where he studied the piano as well as classical trumpet with Robert Platt and jazz trumpet with Manfred Schoof. Stockhausen made his jazz début in 1974 at the Newcomer Jazz Festival in Frankfurt, and his classical début in 1976 in his father's work, *Sirius*, at the American Bicentennial celebrations in Washington, DC. In 1981 he won the German Music Competition as a trumpet soloist. His most famous collaboration with his father was *Licht: Die sieben Tage der Woche* (1977–2003), an ambitious seven-part operatic cycle in which the main character, Michael, was written for him. To perform the demanding role of Michael in the operas, Stockhausen had to play from memory in costume on stage, often wearing a unique tool belt carrying several mutes. The trumpet was the "voice" of Michael and the part involved acting and movement as well.

In addition to performing as a trumpet soloist in contemporary repertoire, Stockhausen leads or collaborates in various jazz ensembles like Electric Treasures and Trio Lichtblick, and plays contemporary and intuitive music (free improvisation) in the group Moving Sounds with clarinetist Tara Bouman, pianist Fabrizio Ottaviucci, and many others. His new group, Eternal Voyage, features musicians from India, Greece, and Lebanon. In 2000 he instituted a concert series called *Klangvisionen* that features performances of intuitive music in the church of St. Maternus in Cologne with expressive stage lighting by the artist Rolf Zavelberg.

As a composer he has received commissions from several organizations including the London Sinfonietta, the Orchestra d'Archi Italiana, the Winterthur Chamber Orchestra, the Cheltenham Music Festival, and the 12 Cellists from the Berlin Philharmonic. In 2007 he wrote *Dancing Light* for trumpet, big band, and string orchestra for the Swiss Jazz Orchestra and the Camerata Bern, as well as *Symbiosis*, a double concerto for clarinet and trumpet with string orchestra, written for the Franz Liszt Chamber Orchestra.

Stölzel valve. A **piston valve** invented by Heinrich Stölzel (1777–1844) in the early nineteenth century that featured a **valve casing** that was the same width as the tubing of the trumpet or cornet to which it was applied, which was necessarily thinner than the design of the later piston valve designed by **François Périnet**. Stölzel valves were used on **cornopeans** and featured the distinctive appearance of gently looping tubing through which the **windway** exited the bottom of the valves. (See appendix 2, figure A7.)

Stomvi. Spanish brass instrument manufacturer. Founded by Vicente Honorato in 1984 as Horiba S.A. (*Sociedad Anónima*, a type of Spanish business corporation), the company is based in Xirivella, a suburb of Valencia. Stomvi specializes in making **piston-valve** trumpets in B-flat and C as well as **high-pitched trumpets** in E-flat/D and E/F/G inspired by the **tuning bell** design of **Schilke** trumpets. Stomvi's **piccolo trumpet** is widely used. In recent years they have added **flugelhorns, rotary valve trumpets**, and **cornets** in B-flat and E-flat to their line. Stomvi also makes trombones, **horns**, several different trumpet **mutes, mouthpieces**, and instrument cases. The firm offers a variety of different models of trumpets for students and professionals such as the Elite, Mahler, Master, and Titán. Most recently, Stomvi has added a modern **corno da caccia** to their line and has begun producing trumpets made with titanium components. Between 2008 and 2014 Spanish Brass Luur Metals (a **brass quintet**) was involved with testing and promoting Stomvi brass instruments.

Stonelined mute. A trade name used by **Humes & Berg** for their line of **mutes**. The name refers to the properties of durability and resonance provided by the substance used to treat the fiberboard inside the central cone region of the mute. The substance was most likely a mixture of resin and stone dust of some kind.

stop rod. A mechanism attached to movable valve slides designed to aid the alignment of the tubing and to limit the distance the slide can be extended. It can also prevent the slide from falling off of the instrument.

straight cornett. A form of the treble **cornett** made out of boxwood with a detachable mouthpiece. Unlike the curved cornett, it was not covered in leather, but it shared the same range and was also pitched in G. The instrument flourished in Germany, primarily, and survived into the nineteenth century as a church instrument in the Moravian community.

straight mute. A cone or pear-shaped **mute** made of aluminum, copper, brass, cardboard, wood, plastic, fiber, or synthetic materials. Three vertical strips of cork hold the mute inside the bell of the trumpet. The material of which the mute is made impacts the sound of the mute as well as its shape. Because most composers intended a straight mute to be used when they wrote the generic indication "mute" (or *Dämpfer*, *sordino*, or *sourdine*) in their trumpet parts, trumpeters employ as many as three or four different kinds of straight mutes made of various materials to produce a wide palette of expressive sounds ranging from penetrating loud passages to soft lyrical lines and distant fanfares. Most straight mutes are made for use in B-flat or C trumpets, but smaller models are made for higher-pitched trumpets in D or E-flat as well as **piccolo trumpets**. (See figure 47 and appendix 3.)

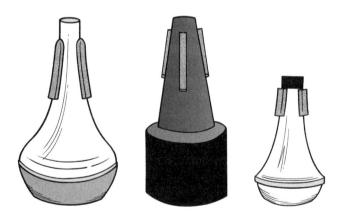

Figure 47. Three different straight mutes. From left: metal (loud), fiber (soft), small (for piccolo trumpet). *Drawing by T. M. Larsen.*

Streitwieser, Franz X. (b. 1939). German trumpeter. He studied with Fritz Krammer at the Mozarteum in Salzburg and graduated in 1961. He later studied with Josef Levora in Vienna and moved to New York, where he studied with **William Vacchiano** and **Mel Broiles**. Streitwieser developed a fascination with exotic brass instruments, started collecting old trumpets as a student, and continued adding to his collection throughout his life. With the help of his wife, Katherine Schutt, he established the Streitwieser Foundation in 1979 and converted a large historic barn in Pottstown, Pennsylvania, into the Streitwieser Trumpet Museum in 1980. The museum housed over one thousand instruments, several exhibition rooms, and a library, and occasionally presented concerts. Following the death of his wife from leukemia, Streitwieser moved his instrument collection in 1996 to the Kremsegg Castle in Kremsmünster, Austria. In addition to his work collecting instruments, Streitwieser served as principal trumpet of the Philharmonic Orchestra of Freiburg, Germany, and as assistant professor at the Freiburg Music Academy in the 1970s. He returned to the United States and became an American citizen in 1975. In addition to the trumpet, Streitwieser plays a version of the modern **corno da caccia** that he calls the **Clarinhorn**. In 1978 he recorded the **Neruda** concerto and repertoire by **Leopold Mozart** and Sperger on the album *Virtuoso Clarinhorn* (Hännsler Verlag, LC 4047). He co-authored the book *Das Flügelhorn* (Edition Bochinsky) with **Ralph Dudgeon** in 2004.

strombus. A conch shell commonly sounded as a trumpet by blowing into its narrow end. The term also refers to a specific shape of a conch shell that features the basic spiral design usually associated with the shell.

swing. 1. An attribute of jazz performance that defies precise definition. Although commonly associated with performing rhythms notated in duple beat division with a triplet feel, swing also encompasses subtleties of unequal articulation and nuance that highlight the **backbeat**. Tempo plays an important role in the style; more rhythmic alteration may occur at slower tempi, while articulation emphasizing the backbeat is more prominent in faster music, especially **Bebop**.

2. A style of big band dance music popularized in the 1930s and 1940s. Prominent swing-era bandleaders include Count Basie, Duke Ellington, Benny Goodman, and Glenn Miller.

T

Tabakov, Mikhail Innokent'yevich (1877–1956). Ukrainian trumpeter. Considered the father of the Soviet School of trumpet playing, he began playing the trumpet at the age of twelve. Following studies at the Odessa Music Academy between 1889 and 1892 and lessons with **Willy Brandt**, Tabakov embarked on a professional career playing in several orchestras, including those in Yalta, Sevastopol, Kiev, and Rostov-on-the-Don. He joined the Bolshoi Theater Orchestra in 1898 as second trumpet and became first trumpet in 1903, a position he held until 1938. Known for his powerfully expressive sound, Tabakov was praised by Scriabin for his performance of the prominent trumpet part in the composer's *Le Poème de l'Extase*. Between 1910 and 1917 he was the first trumpet and manager of Koussevitzky's virtuoso symphony orchestra, and he was a founding member and manager of the Persimfans Orchestra (an experimental orchestra that performed without a conductor) between 1922 and 1932. As a teacher, Tabakov served on the faculties of the Music College of the Moscow Philharmonic Society (1914–1917), the Moscow Conservatory (1918–1956), and the Gnesin Music Institute (1947–1956), where he was head of the department of wind instruments. Two of his best students were **Timofei Dokshizer** and **Vladimir Drucker**. Tabakov published a four-volume *Progressive Trumpet Method* (1945–1953) and *Daily Exercises for Trumpet* (1952). **Vjacheslav Shchelokov**'s *Trumpet Concerto No. 1 in D-flat Major* (1929), the first Russian trumpet concerto written in the twentieth century, was dedicated to him.

tabard. A ceremonial banner hung from the elongated bell of a **herald trumpet**.

Taps. A **bugle call** of the U.S. military performed for funerals, memorial services, wreath ceremonies, and at the end of a military day. Comprised of twenty-four notes, the call was written in July 1862 and originally attributed to General Daniel Butterfield (1831–1901), but was later found to be adapted from the last five measures of an 1835 version of the call "Tattoo," traditionally played at dusk. "Taps" was first sounded by Union Brigade bugler Oliver Willcox Norton (1839–1920) and soon replaced the performance of the call "Extinguish Lights," at the end of the day. By 1891 the performance of "Taps" at military funerals was mandated in the U.S. Army Infantry Drill Regulations. The sounding of "Taps" at ceremonies is the most sacred duty a bugler can perform.

The name of the call descends from the term *tattoo* and its surrounding traditions. It most likely originated during the Thirty Years War in the seventeenth century. The word *tattoo* is derived from the Dutch *tap* (faucet) and *toe* (cut off, stop); it signified the time for innkeepers to stop serving drinks and for troops to return to camp for roll call before turning in for the night. "Tattoo" was also called "Tap-toe," which was subsequently shortened to "Taps" in military slang. The term may have also come from the traditional drum beats—a series of three taps played at four count intervals—performed at the end of the day for the same purpose as "To Extinguish Lights." The drum beats became known to common soldiers as "the Taps," and the term was presumably transferred to the bugle call that replaced the drum beats in later years.

tarantara. Poetic imitation of the sound of a trumpet **fanfare** in literature in the English language.

Tarr, Edward Hankins (b. 1936). American trumpeter and musicologist. A pioneer in the **period instrument** revival and brass scholarship, Tarr is known worldwide as a preeminent authority on trumpet history through his work as a prolific author, editor, and teacher in addition to his many performances and recordings. Born in Norwich, Connecticut, his family moved around the country frequently during his childhood. He began to play the trumpet at the age of nine; his first teacher was

Don Pratt, a former student of **Herbert L. Clarke.** Tarr attended Phillips Exeter Academy in New Hampshire between 1951 and 1953, and studied with **Roger Voisin** the summer after graduation. He went on to Oberlin College (1953–1957), where he studied trumpet with Arthur Williams and earned a Bachelor of Arts degree in music. Tarr earned a master's degree in music history and literature from Northwestern University in 1959, and also studied trumpet with **Adolph Herseth** while in the Chicago area. He moved to Switzerland in 1959 to study musicology with Leo Schrade in Basle and later earned a doctorate at the University of Hamburg in 1987.

Tarr's career as a period instrument specialist began on the *cornetto*. He acquired an instrument from **Otto Steinkopf** in 1959 and taught himself how to play. In Basle he performed with the university's Collegium Musicum and went on to perform with early music groups throughout Europe on the instrument. In 1960 he heard **Walter Holy** perform Bach's *Mass in B Minor* on a **Steinkopf-Finke trumpet** and soon purchased one of the instruments to learn how to play the early **vented trumpet**, eventually progressing to perform with Holy and **Helmut Finke** in performances and recordings. Tarr continued his work with period instruments by forming the Edward Tarr Brass Ensemble in 1968, a group of four trumpeters and four trombonists who specialized in Baroque and Renaissance repertoire as well as new music. He also performed on **modern trumpet** with Mauricio Kagel's Cologne Ensemble for New Music in the 1960s and 1970s. During the same period Tarr made a series of recordings of Baroque and Classical concerti as well as brass ensemble music and works for trumpet and organ.

As a scholar, Tarr has published more than two hundred modern performing editions of previously unavailable early trumpet repertoire. His annotated translations of major treastises by **Bendinelli**, **Fantini**, and **Altenburg** made the works accessible in English for the first time, and his own seminal book on the trumpet's history, *Die Trompete* (Schott, 1977), was translated into English in 1988 (the third edition was published in 2008). Tarr authored a three-volume method for the **natural trumpet**, *The Art of Baroque Trumpet Playing* (Schott, 1999–2000), and co-edited with Uwe Wolf the seven-volume collection covering the complete repertoire of **J. S. Bach** for trumpet, horn, and trombone, *Bach for Brass* (Carus Verlag, since 2002; volumes 6 and 7 forthcoming). The *Bach for Brass* series is designed for study and performance with the complete trumpet repertoire published in score format with timpani parts and commentary. His book *East Meets West* (Pendragon Press, 2003) explored the history and traditions of Russian trumpet playing. Tarr also contributed numerous articles to the *New Grove Dictionary of Music*, *Historic Brass Society Journal*, *International Trumpet Guild Journal*, and other

scholarly journals. He has also consulted on instrument design with several trumpet makers including Ewald **Meinl** (formerly Meinl & Lauber), **Egger**, and **Yamaha**.

As a teacher, Tarr has served on the faculty of the Rheinische Musikschule, Cologne (1968–1970), and the **Schola Cantorum Basiliensis** (1972–2001) as well as visiting professor and artist-in-residence positions in Europe, Australia, and the United States. He served as the founder and director of the Trumpet Museum in Bad Säckingen, Germany, between 1985 and 2004. Some of his students include Wolfgang Bauer, **Bruce Dickey**, **Niklas Eklund**, **Reinhold Friedrich**, Håkan Hardenberger, Graham Nicholson, and Marc Ullrich. Tarr's pioneering work in trumpet performance, repertoire, and scholarship has garnered numerous awards and honors including the inaugural **Christopher Monk** Award (1995) from the **Historic Brass Society** and the ITG Honorary Award from the **International Trumpet Guild**.

tecciztli, tekiztli. The **conch shell trumpet** of the Aztecs. It was played for rituals connected with death and the afterlife.

Telemann, Georg Philipp (1681–1767). German composer. Telemann was the hiring committee's first choice in 1723 for Bach's job at the Thomaskirche in Leipzig, but he went to Hamburg instead and composed a staggering wealth of repertoire, much of which is yet to be published in modern editions. Telemann's musical style bridges the late Baroque and early Classical eras favoring melodic charm and rhythmic vigor over counterpoint. He composed several solo works for the trumpet including the *Concerto in D*, TWV 51: D7, *Concerto for Trumpet, Two Oboes and Strings in D*, TWV 53:D2, *Concerto for Three Trumpets, Timpani and Strings*, TWV 54:D4, *Concerto for Three Trumpets, Two Oboes, Timpani and Strings in D*, TWV 54:D3, and a *Sinfonia* for Trumpet and Strings, TWV 44:1. Prominent solo trumpet parts also appear in many of his orchestral suites including the *Tafelmusik (Musique de table)*. Organist Marie-Claire Alain (1926–2013) made a popular transcription of Telemann's *Twelve Heroic Marches* for trumpet and organ in 1971, but despite the martial associations of the title, the pieces were originally scored for violin, oboe, "or other instruments" in 1728, not the trumpet.

Telemann composed a large number of cantatas, oratorios, and sacred works, and many of them included trumpet parts. Unlike Bach and Handel, a complete edition of Telemann's works has not yet been published, like the *Neue Bach Ausgabe (New Bach Edition)*. Perhaps this is because Bach monopolized scholarly attention for the past century or more, and also because Telemann was one of the most, if not *the* most, prolific composers in music history: he composed over two thousand cantatas. Most of the cantata manuscripts are extant and reside in the city and university library of Frankfurt am Main.

One of Telemann's five sacred oratorios with trumpet parts is particularly interesting. *Die Donner-Ode* (TWV 6: 3a/3b), or "The Ode of Thunder," was composed in two parts. The first, "Wie ist dein Name so groß," was composed in 1756 to celebrate the one-year anniversary of the catastrophic Lisbon earthquake and tsunami that occurred on November 1, 1755. The second part, "Mein Herz ist voll vom Geiste Gottes," was composed six years after the first in 1762. The score calls for three trumpets in D and features several choruses with active section playing and a virtuoso trumpet solo obbligato part for the tenor aria, "Deines Namens, des herrlichen," in the second part of the oratorio. It is tantalizing to contemplate what other great music by Telemann is languishing in the archive at Frankfurt am Main awaiting discovery by curious musicians. An important recent catalog by Simon Rettlebach is *Trompeten, Hörner und Klarinetten in der in Frankfurt am Main überlieferten "Ordentlichen Kirchenmusik" Georg Philipp Telemanns* (Tutzing: Hans Schneider, 2008).

temperament. A tuning system in which enharmonic notes (such as D-sharp and E-flat) are made to sound alike by tempering—raising or lowering them—slightly. When this system is applied to all of the notes (especially on a keyboard instrument), it is known as "equal temperament." When only the keys that are used most often are selectively altered in this manner, the resultant temperament is referred to as "unequal." A variety of unequal temperaments that are used in **period instrument** ensembles and **historically informed performance** include Pythagorean (for Medieval music), mean-tone (for Renaissance music), and various "irregular" temperaments devised by seventeenth-century theorists such as Vallotti, Werckmeister, and Kirnberger. Equal temperament gained acceptance in the eighteenth century, despite its preponderance of sharp major thirds. Natural notes performed without any tempering system are described as examples of **just intonation**.

Teste, Xavier-Napoléon (1833–1905/1906). French trumpeter. He served as the principal trumpeter of the Paris Opéra in the late nineteenth century and was one of the first to introduce the use of the valved trumpet in C (and D) into the orchestra in 1874. He also was one of the first trumpeters in France to perform on a high D trumpet in Handel's *Messiah*, and on a trumpet in high G built for him by **Besson** for Bach's *Magnificat* (1885) and *B Minor Mass* (1891).

Thein. German brass instrument manufacturer. Founded in 1971 in Bremen, Germany, the firm is run by two brothers, Max and Heinrich Thein. The company produces a full complement of brass instruments, including trumpets with **rotary valves** and **piston valves, piccolo trumpets, high-pitched trumpets** in D and E-flat (with four valves), flugelhorns, **cornets**, and the modern **corno da caccia**. They also produce a trumpet in low F (similar in concept to the **long F trumpet**), an **Aida trumpet**, and a "Tristan-trumpet" to perform the part for *Holztrompete* in **Wagner**'s opera *Tristan und Isolde*. In addition to modern instruments, the Thein brothers also produce reproductions of historic brass instruments including a **natural trumpet**, a coiled natural trumpet (*Jägertrompete* or *tromba da caccia*), a Baroque **slide trumpet**, natural horns, and **sackbuts**. Thein trumpets are endorsed by **Matthias Höfs**, who also assists with instrument design.

Thibaud, Pierre (1929–2004). French trumpeter. He studied the violin at the Bordeaux Conservatoire and studied trumpet with **Eugène Foveau** at the Paris Conservatory, where he won a *premier prix* for the trumpet at the age of eighteen after only one year's study. He joined the Israel Philharmonic Orchestra as first trumpeter in 1960, played with the band of the Garde Républicaine from 1964 to 1966, and from 1966 to 1992 was first trumpeter of the Paris Opéra. A master teacher, he was professor at the Paris Conservatory from 1975 to 1994, where he taught many students, including **Håkan Hardenberger**. Toward the end of his life he published three method books, *Daily Routine and Vocalises for the Advanced Trumpeter*, *Method for the Advanced Trumpeter*, and *Chromatic and Technical Studies for the Advanced Trumpeter* (all by Balquhidder Music, 2002).

Thibouville-Lamy, Jerome (1833–1902). French brass instrument manufacturer who successfully applied a **compensating valve** mechanism and an **ascending valve** to the trumpet.

Thompson, James (b. 1949). American trumpeter and pedagogue. He began studying the trumpet at the age of ten with Richard Longfield in Phoenix, Arizona, and continued his studies with Ray Lichtenwalter at the Interlochen Arts Academy, and **Roger Voisin** at the New England Conservatory. Thompson performed with the Phoenix Symphony Orchestra between 1970 and 1973, the Mexico State Orchestra from 1973 to 1974, and the National Orchestra of Mexico between 1974 and 1976. In 1979 he competed in the first Maurice Andre International Trumpet Competition and was a prizewinner. Thompson became principal trumpet of the Montreal Symphony Orchestra in 1976 and held that position until 1990, when he became the principal trumpet of the Atlanta Symphony. He has performed as principal trumpet on over eighty recordings. In 1987 he performed the world premiere of Malcolm Forsyth's *Concerto for Trumpet*, which was written for him and the Montreal Symphony. Thompson left the Atlanta Symphony in 1998 to become a professor of trumpet at the Eastman School of Music. He is the author of *The Buzzing Book: Complete Method* (Editions BIM, 2001).

Thomsen, Magnus (fl. 1596–1609). German trumpeter. As a German trumpeter working at a Danish court, he published one of the first collections of military trumpet **signals** in the late sixteenth century (ca. 1596). It was also the first trumpet music published in Europe.

throat. The part of a **mouthpiece** at the bottom of the **cup** that directs the **airstream** through the **backbore** into the instrument's **leadpipe**. The relative size of the throat impacts the sound as well as the response of the instrument.

throw ring. An upright ring attached to the top **branch** of a **valve slide** (most often the third valve slide on a trumpet or cornet) to facilitate small intonation adjustments.

thumb hook. A U-shaped piece of metal attached to the top **branch** of a **valve slide** (most often the first valve slide on a trumpet or cornet) to facilitate small intonation adjustments.

Thurner Horn. (Ger.) Tower horn. Term used by Sebastian Virdung (ca. 1465–after 1511) to label an S-shaped **slide trumpet** in his *Musica getutscht* (1511), the first book published about musical instruments.

Tiger Trumpet. A plastic trumpet in B-flat made by **War-burton** Music Products in collaboration with Rheinsound Music of Beijing. Made of acrylonitrile butadiene styrene (ABS) plastic in a variety of colors (black, blue, pink, red, and purple), the Tiger Trumpet was first produced in 2013. The instrument weighs one pound, has a **bore** size of 0.464 inches, and features interchangeable valves that position the slide ports in the same location on each valve. The **piston valves** and **valve casings** are coated with aluminum sleeves that require a unique proprietary **lubricant** rather than regular **valve oil**.

toccata. (It.) Touch piece. A short composition designed to showcase instrumental dexterity. It was a fixture of the repertoire of courtly **trumpet ensembles** in the seventeenth century, where it usually included vigorous **double tonguing**, as in the opening toccata of Monteverdi's opera *L'Orfeo* (1607). In the twentieth century, Igor Stravinsky included a toccata movement in his ballet *Pulcinella* (1920), which included a prominent solo trumpet part.

Tomasi, Henri (1901–1971). French composer and conductor. He studied with Philippe Gaubert, Vincent d'Indy, Georges Caussade, and Paul Vidal at the Paris Conservatory, won the Prix de Rome in 1927, and was awarded the Grand Prix de la Musique Française in 1952. During the 1930s he was one of the founders of the contemporary music group "Triton" along with **Prokofiev**, Poulenc, Milhaud, and Honegger. He composed operas, ballets, chamber music, and orchestral works, including a notable series of concertos for most wind, brass, and string

instruments, of which his trumpet concerto (1948) is the most widely performed. Tomasi's other works for trumpet include *Three Etudes* (1955), *Triptych* (1957) for trumpet and piano, *Holy Week in Cuzco* (1962) for trumpet and organ, *Variations on a Gregorian Salve Regina* (1963) for trumpet and organ, and a *Suite for Three Trumpets* (1964). He also composed an important work for symphonic brass ensemble, *Fanfares Liturgiques* (1944).

Tomes, Francis James "Frank" (1936–2011). English maker of reproduction early brass instruments. He played the banjo and the sousaphone and worked making bronze sculptures for the Morris Singer foundry before pursuing studies at the Wimbledon School of Art. He first took up brass instrument restoration in 1982 to fix rare instruments in his own private collection. Following a course in brass instrument repair, he began making **sackbuts** (early trombones) for **Christopher Monk** and branched out to make **natural trumpets**, **Baroque trumpets**, and **flat trumpets**, as well as alto, tenor, and bass sackbuts. He made 387 instruments in his Wimbledon workshop before he lost a battle with cancer. His collection of thirty-six historic brass instruments now resides at Edinburgh University.

tongue placement. The degree to which the back of the tongue is raised inside the **oral cavity** of a musician playing a brass instrument. When the tongue is raised (as in saying "ee"), the airflow is compressed and the airspeed increases in velocity. When the tongue is lowered (as in saying "ah"), the slower airflow reduces the velocity. (See figure 48.)

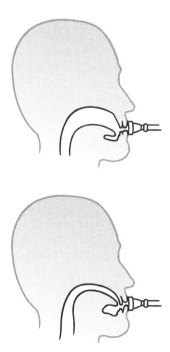

Figure 48. Two different tongue positions used to direct airflow in the oral cavity: low, as in saying "ah" (top), and high, as in saying, "ee" (bottom). *Drawing by T. M. Larsen.*

tongue-controlled embouchure. A method where a trumpeter anchors the tongue on the inside of the mouth behind the lower lip while playing to increase strength, stamina, and performance in the high register. Other characteristics of the technique include a more open jaw position with the tongue stretched between the teeth, looser muscles at the corners of the **embouchure**, and a sensation of articulating notes similar to "spitting seeds." Players using the technique sometimes exhibit puffed cheeks as well. **Jerome Callet** is the leading teacher of the technique and has written several books on the subject along with Robert "Bahb" Civiletti (b. 1946). According to Callet, some of the trumpeters who have employed the tongue-controlled embouchure (often abbreviated as TCE) have been **Roy Eldridge** (who lost all of his teeth at age seventeen), **Harry James**, Fats Navarro, **Jules Levy**, and **Alessandro Liberati**. Civiletti has also suggested that some of the great **natural trumpet** soloists of the high Baroque era may have used the technique, including **Johann Heinisch**.

tonguing. The manner in which **articulation** is applied in trumpet playing. There are several different types of tonguing including **single tonguing** and various combinations of **multiple tonguing**.

Torelli, Giuseppe (1658–1709). Italian composer. As the most prolific composers of early Baroque trumpet music, he wrote the first solo concertos for the trumpet and developed the genres of the concerto and the concerto grosso. He studied violin and composition at the Accademia Filarmonica in Bologna and was admitted to the *cappella musicale* at the Basilica of San Petronio in 1686. Economic hard times caused the orchestra to disband in 1695, and Torelli worked in Ansbach and Vienna. He returned to San Petronio in Bologna in 1701 and worked there until his death. Torelli composed more than thirty pieces for one, two, or four trumpets and strings bearing the titles "concerto," "sinfonia," or "sonata." One of the leading trumpeters at San Petronio who performed Torelli's music was **Giovanni Pellegrino Brandi**.

town waits. English term for *Stadtpfeifer*, or town musicians.

transposing mute. See **Baroque mute**.

transposition. An essential skill for trumpeters that involves reading one note on a page while playing a different one. Reasons for transposing include performing parts written for old trumpets on new trumpets (in different keys), performing orchestral parts from the late nineteenth century that include frequent key changes (of trumpet **crooks** or tunings, not just the harmony), and for choosing to perform a passage on a smaller trumpet for increased security or a different sound. The method of transposition

is not difficult, in theory, but to transpose fluently in five or more keys (intervals)—at sight—requires extensive practice. Transposing is a mental discipline that sharpens the mind and refines overall musicianship; it develops fluency in all major and minor keys in a manner similar to the **woodshedding** preparation of jazz improvisers. (See figure 49.)

Figure 49. The opening measures of the finale from Dvořák's Eighth Symphony in the original key (trumpet in D) and transposed for B-flat trumpet. *Elisa Koehler.*

treatise. A thorough and systematic treatment of a subject in writing. The idea of the treatise in the eighteenth century was to instruct the entire musician, not just an instrumental technician. This was the design of the great treatises that were published in the 1750s: Johann Joachim Quantz's treatise on the flute (1752), Carl Philip Emanuel Bach's treatise on keyboard playing (1753), and Leopold Mozart's violin treatise (1756). The only treatise written for the trumpet was *Versuch einer Anleitung zur heroisch-musikalischen Trompeter- und Pauker-Kunst* (1795) by **Johann Ernst Altenburg**. Most important volumes on the trumpet, like those by **Arban**, **Dauverné**, **Fantini**, and **Franquin**, are not treatises, but **method books**.

trémolo avec la langue. (Fr.) **Flutter tonguing.**

trigger. An alternative to the **throw ring** or **thumb hook** (**saddle**) on a trumpet or cornet **valve slide** that involves a lever mechanism that pushes the slide out when engaged.

trill. A musical ornament consisting of a rapid alternation of two neighboring pitches. The performance of trills varies depending on the historical era of the music under consideration, the method of notation, and the instrument used.

trillo. A musical ornament found in the works of Monteverdi and **Fantini** that requires the rapid repetition of a single pitch. Similar to **huffing**, the ornament is meant to simulate the sound of a singer making rapid glottal stops (similar to a nervous laugh) that begins slowly and accelerates. Because the trillo is usually indicated in musical notation by the abbreviation *tr*, which can be confused with a **trill**, it is important to understand that it primarily occurs in seventeenth-century repertoire and is not preceded by a grace note or followed by a resolution.

triple tonguing. A form of **multiple tonguing** employed for rapid passages with groups of three notes (usually triplets) that are too fast to be performed by **single tonguing**. Syllables commonly used are "ta ta ka" or "ta ka ta."

Triton. The mythological sea god of Ancient Greece who was the son of Poseidon as well as his trumpeter. Traditionally portrayed as a man with the tail of a fish, he lived in the deep sea and played a shell trumpet known as a **strombus** or **salpinx thalassia**. He is depicted in Virgil's *Aeneid* as winning a conch-shell-blowing contest with Aeneas's helmsman, Misenus, subsequently hurling the loser overboard to his death. In the seventeenth century the sculptor Gian Lorenzo Bernini created the Triton Fountain in Rome's Palazzo Barberini, which depicts the sea god as a merman blowing a large conch shell up in the air, from which the water of the fountain flows. Triton is also the name of the largest moon of the planet Neptune (the Roman name for Poseidon).

triton. The distinctive shape of a shell with a large, pronounced opening, similar to the bell of a trumpet.

Trognée, Emile Joseph (1868–1942). Belgian trumpeter and cornet player who spent most of his career in Russia. He studied at the Brussels Conservatory, won a European competition in 1902, and became the solo trumpeter of the Mariinsky Theater (home of the Kirov Opera and Ballet) in St. Petersburg (Leningrad) shortly thereafter. Trognée worked at the Mariinsky for twenty-five years and was praised for his outstanding musicianship and expressive soft playing. He taught at the Baltic Fleet Music School between 1911 and 1917 and at the Rimsky Korsakov Music School from 1928 until 1941. Trognée wrote several **etude** books and solo works for trumpet and cornet including *Valse lente* and *Fantasia-Caprice*. His career was cut short by the German siege of Leningrad during which he died of starvation.

tromba. (It.) **Trumpet.**

tromba a chiavi, tromba colle chiavi. (It.) **Keyed trumpet.**

tromba a piston. (It.) Trumpet with **piston valves**.

tromba alla berseglari. (It.) Trumpet of the Berseglieri. A valved **bugle** invented by Giuseppe Clemente Pelitti (1837–1905) for the *fanfara* (bugle band or trumpet ensemble) of the Bersaglieri, or sharpshooter corps, of the Italian army (*bersaglieri* means "marksmen" in Italian). Later known as the **Bersag horn**, the bugles were pitched in B-flat and E-flat with a single piston valve that lowered the pitch by a fourth and evolved into the instruments used in the modern **drum and bugle corps**.

tromba alta in Fa. (It.) Trumpet in low F. While orchestral parts for trumpet in F are performed on **modern trumpets** with a **transposition** of either a fourth up on a C trumpet or a fifth up on a B-flat trumpet, the indication "alta" requires transposition down (a fifth on a C trumpet, a fourth on a B-flat). Instances of *tromba alta in Fa* are rare. The most famous appearance is in the third trumpet part for Shostakovich's *Symphony No. 1* (1925). The instrument was invented at the request of Nicolai Rimsky-Korsakov (1844–1908) for his opera *Mlada* (1892) and was essentially an F trumpet with a wider **bore** that specialized in low-**register** playing.

tromba brevis. (Lat.) Short trumpet. Term used by **Vejvanovský** to indicated a trumpet pitched in D, which was shorter than a trumpet in C, in his compositions.

tromba con coulisse à resort. (It.) **Slide trumpet**.

tromba da caccia. (It.) Hunter's trumpet. A coiled **natural trumpet** like the *Jägertrompete*.

tromba da tirarsi. (It.) Trumpet that is drawn or pulled; **slide trumpet**. Specifically, the Baroque slide trumpet or *zugtrompete*. **J. S. Bach** used this Italian term to describe the instrument. (See figure 50.)

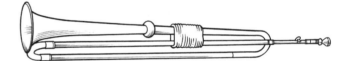

Figure 50. A Baroque slide trumpet known as the *tromba da tirarsi* or *Zugtrompete*. Drawing by T. M. Larsen.

tromba interna. (It.) Interior (offstage) trumpet. Term used by **Ottorino Respighi**.

tromba marina. (It.) **Trumpet marine**.

tromba piccolo. (It.) Small trumpet. Term used by Stravinsky in *The Rite of Spring* (1913) to indicate a **high-pitched trumpet** in D, but not a modern **piccolo trumpet**, which is usually pitched in B-flat or A and is a much smaller instrument. **Prokofiev** used the term for a high E-flat trumpet in his *Scythian Suite* (1914).

tromba squarciata. (It.) Trumpet torn apart (or opened up). A long, straight trumpet played during civic processions in Venice in the sixteenth and seventeenth centuries with a bell that was wider than normally used. The term *squarciata* ("opened up") probably referred to the unusual shape of the bell.

trombe lunghe. (It.) Long trumpet. Long, straight trumpets used in Venetian processionals and outdoor ceremonies in the seventeenth century. Usually longer than the standard eight-foot **natural trumpet** pitched in C, they were carried by boys during processionals in addition to the trumpeter playing the instrument.

trombetta. (It.) **Trumpet**. The term was used by **Cesare Bendinelli** when he published the first trumpet **method book**, *Tutta l'arte della Trombetta* in 1614.

trombetti della signoria. (It.) Trumpeters of the city (government). The civic trumpet corps in fourteenth-century Italy.

trombita. A long, straight trumpet of the Silesian Zywiec Beskid region of Poland that was up to thirteen feet in length. It was commonly played at funerals and was also used in other countries such as the Czech Republic, Romania, and Ukraine.

trombula. (It.) Jew's harp, jaw harp. Archaic term used by Johann Georg Albrechtsberger (1736–1809) for the solo instrument in his *Concerto per trombula in E, for viola (da gamba), 2 violini, viola e basso (con sordini)* in 1771. The abbreviation for the instrument in the manuscript score (*tromb.*) caused the mistaken impression that it may have been written for the trumpet during the Baroque revival in the late twentieth century.

trommet. Term used to describe a **natural trumpet** by **Michael Praetorius** in his *Syntagma Musicum* (1614–1620).

trompe. An early Latin term for the **trumpet** used by writers during the Crusades instead of the older Latin terms that referred to Roman brass instruments such as *tuba, cornu, bucina,* and *lituus*.

trompe de chasse. (Fr.) Hunting horn.

Trompe de Lorraine. A hunting horn designed with its tubing tightly wound in a spiral around a short, curved conical bell down and back up again. The concept for a more compact hunting horn was patented by Pierre Théodore Grégoire in 1867 and named for his homeland, the Lorraine region of France. The total length of the tubing was that of a typical hunting horn of the period: fourteen feet and pitched in D. Some instruments were made with a leather sheath covering the tubing to simulate the appearance of a short cow horn and others were made uncovered. (See figure 51.)

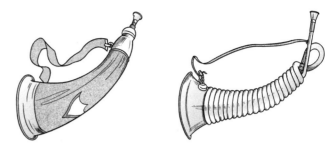

Figure 51. Trompe de Lorraine. *Drawing by T. M. Larsen.*

trompete. (Ger.) **Trumpet**.

trompetengeige. (Ger.) **Trumpet marine**.

trompette. (Fr.) **Trumpet**.

trompette à clef. (Fr.) **Keyed trumpet**. The term also referred to the **keyed bugle** in the early nineteenth century before instrumental terminology was standardized.

trompette à coulisse. (Fr.) **Slide trumpet**.

trompette à l'angle. (Fr.) A fanfare trumpet designed for military parades by **Adolphe Sax** in the middle of the nineteenth century. Perhaps inspired by the long trumpets from antiquity, the instrument features tightly compressed tubing with small loops near the mouthpiece and bell to resemble a straight trumpet from a distance. The leadpipe is angled slightly to accommodate performances on horseback so that the bell would not point directly at or collide with the horse's head.

trompette de basse. (Fr.) See *basse de trompette*.

trompette de guerre. (Fr.) Trumpet of war; military trumpet.

trompette des menestrel. (Fr.) Minstrel's trumpet; a Renaissance **slide trumpet**.

trompette dessus. (Fr.) High trumpet. This term was used by Charpentier and André Danican Philidor l'Aîné (ca. 1652–1730), the royal oboist and music librarian for King Louis XIV, to indicate high trumpet parts as opposed to lower parts (*trompette de basse*).

trompette d'harmonie. (Fr.) Harmonic trumpet. A French orchestral trumpet pitched in G that was a **natural trumpet** fitted with **crooks** down to lower keys designed for use with **hand-stopping** technique.

trompette d'ordonnance. (Fr.) **Cavalry trumpet**. A French military trumpet pitched in E-flat used for signal purposes.

trompette marine. (Fr.) **Trumpet marine**.

TrumCor. American **mute** manufacturing company. Founded by trumpeter Richard Giangiulio in 1994, the company makes a full line of mutes for all brass instruments. Their line of trumpet mutes includes a variety of different **straight mutes**, **cup mutes**, and **practice mutes** made from fiber and aluminum. Unique to the company is a fiber mute for playing at soft dynamic levels known as the Lyric Mute. Like the **Denis Wick** Company, TrumCor also makes mutes for different size trumpets (piccolo, E-flat trumpet, and B-flat trumpet). In 2013 TrumCor introduced a new type of **Harmon mute** known as "the Zinger."

trumpet. *Trompette* (Fr.), *trompete* (Ger.), *tromba* (It.). 1. A lip-vibrated instrument comprised of a tube of a given length and diameter that usually ends in a flared **bell** of some kind. Often categorized as a "brass instrument," trumpets from various cultures and historical eras have been made out of materials other than brass or other metals including wood (**didjeridu**), bone (human and animal), seashells (**conch shell**), tree bark (*borija*, **dau- dytė**), animal horns (**shofar**), ceramics, glass, plastic (**vuvuzela**), and even elephant tusks (**aḅẹn**). Most Non- western trumpets and instruments from antiquity consist of a straight tube that is blown through an opening on one end; **side-blown trumpets** from Africa feature a hole cut near the end of a closed tube, on the side. Such instruments are usually employed for signaling purposes rather than the performance of melodies.

In Western cultures the trumpet, **horn**, and **trombone** all evolved from the same principle of an end-blown tube (of varying lengths) sounded through lip vibration, and terminology can be confusing. Trumpets are sometimes called "horns" and the term *trombone* literally means "big trumpet." Horns are generally thought to have a higher proportion of **conical** tubing than trumpets, but that is not always the case in modern instruments.

2. (v.) to sound forth, to proclaim; as in "to trumpet the good news."

3. A brass instrument with predominantly **cylindrical** tubing, a **mouthpiece**, and a **bell** at the end. The oldest surviving trumpet is an ancient Egyptian **šnb** (ca. 1300 BC) found in the tomb of King Tutankhamun. The trumpet of ancient Israel was the **chatzotzrah**, and the trumpet of the ancient Greeks was the **salpinx**. The long, straight trumpet of ancient Rome was known as the **tuba**, but other Roman trumpet-like instruments were the **buccina**, the **cornu**, and the **lituus**. The ancient Celtic trumpet was the **carnyx** and an ancient trumpet-like instrument of Nordic origin was the **lur**. In the middle ages, a long, straight trumpet like a **herald trumpet** was known as a **buisine** and was most likely designed in imitation of the Arabian trumpet known as the *bûq*

al-nafîr. A trumpet (buisine) of this type (ca. 1375) was discovered in a bog in the Billingsgate area of London in 1984 and is known as the **Billingsgate trumpet**, the oldest surviving trumpet in Europe. These early trumpets and their relatives mainly produced a few notes in the low register for signaling purposes; their shorter length precluded melodic playing in the high register.

By the fifteenth century, trumpets were made with longer tubing and rendered easier to hold by looping the tubing into the familiar bugle shape of the **natural trumpet**. At first the U-shaped bends in the tubing were assembled in an *S* shape. These instruments were still primarily used for signaling purposes and gradually made their way into concert music in the late sixteenth century. Natural trumpets were limited to the notes of the **harmonic overtone series** with the key determined by the length of the tubing (eight feet of tubing produced a harmonic series on C, while seven feet of tubing produced a series on D). Trumpeters developed their technique on the longer trumpets in order to extend the range of the instrument above the eighth **partial**, where a diatonic scale was accessible and melodies could be performed. Playing in this high register, from C5 to C6 (and even higher) was known as **clarino** playing, and Baroque composers like **Bach**, **Handel**, **Telemann**, **Purcell**, and many others exploited the technique, favoring the trumpet with some of its most impressive repertoire.

The limitations imposed by the harmonic overtone series (in one key) were challenged by several different attempts to enable a trumpet to play in different keys, and even chromatically. The first was the application of a simple **slide** mechanism in the fifteenth century that operated through a sliding **mouthpipe**, rather than a U-shaped slide. These **slide trumpets** were played by tower watchmen and minstrels (*stadtpfeifer*, *piffari*, **waits**) in shawm bands, in churches, and for outdoor ceremonies, usually in the performance of slow-moving chorales and other melodies. The Renaissance slide trumpet eventually evolved into the trombone as it is known today with its U-shaped slide, but the mechanism of the sliding **leadpipe** persisted in the eighteenth century in the form of the Baroque slide trumpet referred to by Bach as the *tromba da tirarsi* and in Germany as the *zugtrompete*. In England, two different types of slide trumpets evolved: the **flat trumpet** (which appears in scores by Purcell) and the **English slide trumpet**, a unique instrument with an improved clock spring slide mechanism, which flourished in England with its own performance tradition throughout the entire nineteenth century.

Unrelated to the slide mechanisms applied to trumpets were the removable lengths of auxiliary tubing known as **crooks**. Smaller pieces of straight tubing were known as **bits**. These extra loops were commonly inserted into the leadpipe before the mouthpiece and served to lower the pitch of the trumpet. For example, a trumpet in D could add a crook to lower the pitch to C; longer crooks could be inserted to further lower the pitch to B-flat or A. To accommodate crooks down to lower keys, natural trumpets in the eighteenth century were usually pitched in seven-foot D (or E-flat), and nineteenth-century orchestral trumpets were pitched in six-foot F (or G). A trumpet with interchangeable slides positioned in the center of the instrument (rather than crooks inserted before the mouthpiece) appeared at the turn of the nineteenth century known as the *inventionstrompete*. This instrument was also double wrapped to make it appear smaller and to allow the hand to reach the bell to use **hand-stopping** technique to lower certain pitches. Some trumpets were built in circular form or in crescent shape, like the **demilune trumpet**, for this purpose. The first trumpeter to use this technique was **Michael Wöggel** in Karlsruhe, Germany.

At the end of the eighteenth century **nodal venting** was applied to the trumpet and the bugle through the application of **vent holes** covered by keys. Viennese trumpeter **Anton Weidinger** perfected the **keyed trumpet** and encouraged both **Haydn** and **Hummel** to compose concerti for it, but the instrument's vogue was brief. Its conical relative, the **keyed bugle**, was a more successful instrument, but keyed brasses were supplanted by the invention of various **valve** mechanisms in the early nineteenth century.

The first valve applied to the trumpet was a **piston valve** by **Heinrich Stölzel**. Both **Stölzel** and **Friedrich Blühmel** earned a joint patent in 1818 for the principle of a valve mechanism applied to brass instruments, generally, which made it difficult to patent specific modifications in the years that followed. The **rotary valve** was invented by Blühmel, and **François Périnet** patented an improved piston valve in 1838. Many other valve designs were applied to trumpets and **cornets**, but Blühmel's rotary valve and Périnet's piston valve enjoy the widest use today. (See appendix 2.) The first works in France to use valve trumpets were Chelard's *Macbeth* (1827), Berlioz's *Les francs-juges Overture* (1826) and *Waverley Overture* (1827–1828), Rossini's *Guillaume Tell* (1829), and Meyerbeer's *Robert le diable* (1831).

The development of the cornet in the 1830s threatened the status of the trumpet in the orchestra and led to innovations in virtuoso technique. Composers experimented with instrumental combinations—natural trumpets with cornets, valved trumpets with cornets, cornets alone—and brass instrument manufacturers experimented with making trumpets in higher keys, like cornets. Trumpeters also experimented with instrument selection, enjoying the freedom to use the latest equipment, not necessarily the instrument the composer requested. Composers and critics argued that the cornet's sound was inferior to that of the trumpet, but when the smoke cleared, smaller trumpets in B-flat and

C eventually replaced the **long F trumpet** and cornets as well. Dresden trumpeter **Albert Kühnert** starting using the B-flat trumpet in the orchestra around 1850 and French trumpeter **Merri Franquin** began using the C trumpet in the orchestra in the early twentieth century. Another Frenchman, **Georges Mager**, advocated for the use of the C trumpet in the United States.

Even smaller trumpets were making their way into the orchestra in the early twentieth century including trumpets in D, E-flat, F, and G as well as the **piccolo trumpet**. Jazz trumpeters like **Louis Armstrong** redefined the limits of range, expression, and virtuosity on the trumpet in the early twentieth century, which in turn inspired **avant-garde** composers to stretch the limits of trumpet technique even further.

trumpet ensemble. A group of two or more trumpets that can range in size from a duet to upward of twenty parts. A relatively new genre that has grown sharply over the past thirty years, especially at North American universities, the modern trumpet ensemble has inspired an increasing number of composers to write new literature highlighting creative combinations of diverse high brass instruments (from **piccolo trumpet** to **flugelhorn**) and exploiting the full arsenal of **mutes** and extended playing techniques. Ceremonial trumpet ensembles have a long history from the origins of courtly trumpet guilds in the Baroque era to the U.S. Army Herald Trumpets and the Royal Air Force Fanfare Team in the UK today. These contemporary military ensembles include **bass trumpets** as well soprano trumpets in E-flat and B-flat, and straddle a line between brass ensemble, drum and bugle corps, and trumpet ensemble in structure. They are distinguished by their matched sets of custom herald trumpets by **Kanstul** (USA) and **Smith-Watkins** (UK) as well as their stunning precision in performance. In the realm of early music, several notable period-instrument trumpet ensembles include the **Friedemann Immer** Trumpet Consort, the ensemble of the **Schola Cantorum Basiliensis** (led by **Jean-François Madeuf**), and the Historic Trumpet Ensemble of the U.S. Army Old Guard Fife and Drum Corps. Two unique trumpet ensembles in the twentieth century that deserve mention are the Trompeterchor der Stadt Wien, for which Richard Strauss composed his expansive *Festmusik der Stadt Wien* (1942), and the largest group of trumpets ever assembled (thirty-six) outside of a conference of the **International Trumpet Guild** for the performance of **Malcolm Arnold**'s *A Hoffnung Fanfare* (1960) at the memorial service in honor of British musical humorist Gerard Hoffnung.

trumpet marine. *Trompette marine* (Fr.); *trumscheit, nonnengeige, marien trompet, trompetengeige* (Ger.); *tromba marina* (It.). A unique string instrument that bears no resemblance to a trumpet or other brass instrument, but was instead designed to play notes of the **harmonic overtone series** in imitation of a **natural trumpet**. A bowed monochord (instrument with a single string) equipped with a vibrating bridge in common use from the fifteenth century until the middle of the eighteenth century. In its fully developed form the instrument is capable of sounding all of the pitches of the harmonic series up to the sixteenth partial. The trumpet marine was approximately four feet long with a three-sided body that tapered upward toward the pegbox.

trumpet stand. A device that allows musicians to set a trumpet down on its bell with a stable resting position for quick retrieval. Designed with a central cone or stick on which to place the bell with tripod legs splayed underneath, trumpet stands usually fold up for easy transport. Models with the cone-shape center fit into the bell like a mute for storage. Some models include five or more legs for enhanced stability.

trumpetillas barstardas. (Sp.) Bastard trumpet or **slide trumpet**. The term was used in describing the **alta cappella** that performed for the wedding festivities of Philip II of Spain in 1543.

trumpetina. A derisive term for the B-flat **trumpet** sometimes used in the late nineteenth century to distinguish the instrument from the **long F trumpet**, which was considered to have a superior tone. English trumpeter **Walter Morrow** used this term repeatedly in his address on "The Trumpet as an Orchestral Instrument" to the Royal Musical Society in 1895 to differentiate the B-flat trumpet from the cornet.

tuba. The long, straight trumpet of Ancient Rome. (See figure 52.)

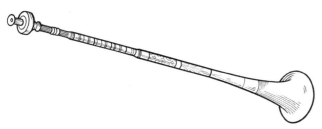

Figure 52. A Roman tuba. *Drawing by T. M. Larsen.*

tuba campestris. (Lat.) Field trumpet or military trumpet. This term was used by **Vejvanovský** in some of his works to distinguish military trumpets from a smaller trumpet for clarino playing that he called a ***tromba brevis.***

tuba pastoricia. (Lat.) **Alphorn**. The term was used by Fux in a *Pastorella* from the early eighteenth century.

tubatores. (Lat.) Trumpeters. The Latin term used in official documents for the civic trumpeters of fourteenth-century Italy instead of ***trombetti della signoria*** because Latin was still the official language of the government at the time.

tubicines. (Lat.) Trumpet players. Musicians who played the Roman **tuba**.

tubing. Any length of pipe used in the construction of a brass instrument.

tuck, tucket. A flourish or **signal** for trumpets and drums, thought to be derived from the Italian word ***toccata***. The term *tuck* appears in Old English as early as the fourteenth century to indicate the sound of a trumpet. The related term *tucket* appears frequently in stage directions for Shakespearean plays as in "Then let the trumpets sound the tucket sonance, and the note to mount" (*Henry V*, act IV, scene ii).

tuning bell. A removable bell that connects to the second **bow (bell bow)** of a **modern trumpet**. Its position is adjusted and secured by means of a screw-tightening mechanism. Trumpets made with tuning bells do not have a main **tuning slide** to adjust the general pitch of the instrument; instead, the bell assembly slides on a pipe that exits the first valve casing and a stabilizing rod on the left side of the valve section. **High-pitched trumpets** employ this design most often, but B-flat **trumpets** and C trumpets have also been made with tuning bells because the design reduces the bracing to the body of the trumpet and results in a brighter sound. **Victor-Charles Mahillon** was the first to develop this concept in 1910, and **Renold Schilke** applied it to his trumpets in 1968 and patented his design in 1970. In Schilke's design the **leadpipe** entered the third valve, rather than going straight into a main tuning slide. Schilke later sold the patent to **Yamaha** when he was working as a consultant for them.

tuning fork. A two-pronged piece of tempered steel that produces a reliable reference pitch for tuning instruments in an ensemble. Unlike strings or wooden instruments, the steel tuning fork was not vulnerable to changes in temperature and did not lose its pitch with age. It also produced a pure tone with minimal overtones. The tuning fork was invented by **John Shore**, an English trumpeter who played for Purcell and Handel, around 1711.

tuning slide. The largest slide on a **modern trumpet** that serves to adjust the overall pitch of the instrument. On a B-flat trumpet the tuning slide appears in the first **bow**, next to the **bell**. On many nineteenth-century **cornets**, it is located in the center of the instrument, pointing toward the **mouthpiece**.

tutor. A **method book** that provides instructional material for learning an instrument.

Twiselton, [?] (fl. 1710–1715). English trumpeter. He performed a benefit concert on March 20, 1713, that advertised him as "Trumpet to His Excellency the Duke of Aumont." The piece he performed at the concert was the trumpet sonata by **Arcangelo Corelli**, which was reportedly written "on purpose for Mr. Twiselton when he was at Rome."

U

upstream embouchure. A manner of playing a brass instrument in which the **mouthpiece placement** rests primarily on the lower lip and directs the **airstream** upward. This results in good response for high-register playing and produces a bright sound. It does not increase a player's range, but it can increase a player's comfort in high-register playing. Some trumpeters use this **set** because of dental considerations (an underbite).

urtext. (Ger.) Original text. The earliest surviving version of a musical or literary composition. The term is also applied to a modern published edition of a musical composition based on that primary source.

Utley, Joe (1935–2001). American trumpet collector. Growing up as a talented trumpeter in western Oklahoma, Utley pursued a medical career, but enjoyed a life-long fascination with the trumpet that led him to amass one of the largest collections of antique, historic, and unique trumpets as well as related brass instruments from around the world. In 1999 Utley and his wife, Joella, donated their collection of more than six hundred brass instruments to the National Music Museum at the University of South Dakota in Vermillion. The collection includes instruments spanning four centuries including rare **natural trumpets** by **Nuremberg** makers **Ehe** and **Haas** up through an ornate **flumpet** custom made for Utley by David **Monette**.

Vacchiano, William (1912–2005). American trumpeter. One of the most influential orchestral trumpeters and teachers in the United States, his career spanned more than six decades. Vacchiano grew up in Portland, Maine, where he began studying the **cornet** with Frank Knapp, cornet soloist with **Liberati's** band; he also studied piano and **solfege**. At the age of fourteen he joined the 240th Artillery Coast Guard Band of Portland. During high school he performed as third trumpet of the Portland Symphony Orchestra and took lessons with **Herbert L. Clarke** and Del Staigers. He also traveled to Boston to take lessons from **Georges Mager**, Lois Kloepfel, Walter M. Smith, and Gustav Heim, who encouraged him to explore the use of **high-pitched trumpets**. After high school he won a scholarship to study with **Max Schlossberg** at the Juilliard School (known then as the Institute of Musical Art). While still a student in 1935, Vacchiano auditioned on the same day for the Metropolitan Opera Orchestra (first trumpet position) and the New York Philharmonic (third/assistant principal trumpet) and won both auditions. He chose to join the Philharmonic and remained with the orchestra for thirty-eight years (thirty-one as principal), retiring in 1973. In addition to his work with the Philharmonic, he also performed with numerous studio orchestras and radio broadcasts, appearing on more than four hundred recordings.

Vacchiano's career as a teacher was legendary. He taught more than two thousand students and professionals over the course of nearly seventy years. Vacchiano served on the faculties of the Juilliard School (1935–2002), the Mannes College of Music (1937–1983), and the Manhattan School of Music (1937–1999). He also taught a legion of trumpeters who traveled to New York for private lessons and coaching. Because he began his professional career without graduating from Juilliard, Vacchiano went back to school to earn bachelor and master of music degrees from the Manhattan School of Music in 1952 and 1953, respectively. His studio produced hundreds of professional trumpeters, notably **Mel Broiles**, **Armando Ghitalla**, **Gerard Schwarz**, **Philip Smith**, **Thomas Stevens**, **Fred Mills**, **Ronald Romm**, Stephen Chenette, Edward Carroll, Maurio Guaneri, Manuel Laureano, Louis Ranger, **Charles Schlueter**, and **Wynton Marsalis**.

In addition to performing and teaching, Vacchiano published several books of trumpet studies including *Advanced Etudes*, *The Art of Bel Canto*, *The Art of Double Tonguing*, *The Art of Solo Playing*, *Trumpet Routines*, *A Study of Intervals*, *Necessary Technique for Trumpet*, and *Comprehensive Trumpet Studies*. He co-designed the Alessi-Vacchiano **straight mute** that was marketed by **Holton**, and he also had a lifelong interest in **mouthpiece** design, especially the function of different mouthpiece cups and proportions. He received many honors during his career including an award from the New York Brass Conference for Scholarships (1978), the Honorary Award from the **International Trumpet Guild** (1984), and an honorary doctorate from the Juilliard School (2003).

valve. A mechanism the redirects the **airstream** of a brass instrument from its primary length of tubing into an attached slide (and back again) to change the fundamental pitch of the instrument and enable the performance of diatonic and chromatic scales in all registers. The added tubing of the auxiliary slide serves to access overtones from the **harmonic series** of tubing longer than that of the primary pitch of the instrument, such as from B-flat down to A, A-flat, or G, and so on. Trumpets and cornets with three valves added slides (tubing) that lowered the **nominal pitch** of the instrument by a half step (second valve), a whole step (first valve), and a minor third or three half steps (third valve). The seven available valve combinations enabled a trumpet or cornet to access the harmonic series of seven different lengths of tubing. (See figure 53.)

Figure 53. Notes playable on trumpets with three valves (seven different valve combinations). Enharmonic pitches assumed; higher notes follow the pattern of the harmonic overtone series (see figure 26). *Elisa Koehler.*

While most high brass instruments positioned the shortest **valve slide** (the half step) in the middle (operated by the second valve), some instruments were designed with the half step slide operated by the first valve. This unconventional system of manufacture was known as **"Catholic" fingering**. In the twentieth century, some trumpets and **flugelhorns** were equipped with a fourth valve to expand the lower range of the instruments. Fourth valves became standard on most **piccolo trumpets** to reach the lower notes (especially D4) in Baroque repertoire; they were also added to some trumpets in E-flat by **Schilke** to maximize the utility of the facile smaller trumpets.

Valve mechanisms are operated by pressing levers, buttons, or rods, which in turn move an internal device (the valve itself) to access holes that redirect the **windway** of the instrument into the appended slide(s). The earliest type of valve used on a brass instrument was a **box valve** developed by **Charles Clagget** in 1788 for his **Cromatic [sic] Trumpet**, which simply toggled between two conjoined natural trumpets in D and E-flat. Other mechanisms developed in the early nineteenth century included a **rotary valve** by **Friedrich Blühmel; piston valves** by **Heinrich Stölzel, François Périnet**, and Wilhelm Wieprecht; a swivel **disc valve (patent lever valve)** by **John Shaw**, and the **double piston valve** or **Vienna valve** by **Christian Friedrich Sattler**. The invention of the valve revolutionized brass playing in the nineteenth century by enabling trumpets and cornets to play a chromatic scale in the lower octave of their range. (See appendix 2.)

Although valves revolutionized the artistic capabilities of brass instruments, the use of three valves created intonation problems because progressively complex **valve combinations** made the instrument play sharper. To solve this problem, moveable valve slides (with

thumb hooks, **triggers**, or **throw rings**) for the first and third valves were added in the late nineteenth century to enable pitch adjustments. Another intonation compromise was the invention of **compensating valves**, which automatically added auxiliary tubing when certain valves were used in combination.

valve button. A disc of metal or plastic on top of the valve stem on which the player places his or her fingers on the valves.

valve cap. The lid that screws onto the top of the **valve casing** to protect the inner workings of the valve. On a **piston valve** brass instrument, the valve cap includes a central hole through which the valve stem attaches to the **valve button**. On **rotary valve** instruments, the valve cap completely covers the valve mechanism. (See figure 43 under "rotary valve").

valve casing. The metal cylinder that surrounds the valve mechanism.

valve casing brush. A thick brush designed to fit inside the **valve casing** for periodic cleaning.

valve combination. A pattern of two or more **valves** that are engaged (pressed) to perform a specific pitch on a brass instrument. Such combinations are often referred to as **fingerings** and listed on a **fingering chart**.

valve guide. A small piece of metal connected to the side of a **piston valve** that fits into a slot inside the **valve casing** to stabilize the vertical movement of the valve.

valve slide. A piece of curved tubing in the body of a brass instrument through which the **airstream** travels when the attached valve is engaged (pressed). The third valve slide on the trumpet is usually fitted with a **throw ring** or **trigger** for making intonation adjustments while playing. The first valve slide is often fitted with a **thumb hook**, throw ring, or trigger for the same reason. Valve slides differ from **crooks** and **tuning slides** in that they are smaller and are designed for smooth and free movement rather than maintaining a fixed position during performance.

valve tremolo. A technique that simulates rapid tonguing on a single pitch by alternating an open note with a **valve combination** or an **alternate fingering**. (See figure 54.) Commonly used in jazz and **avant-garde** music, the technique resembles the sound of **doodle tonguing**.

Figure 54. Valve tremolo. *Elisa Koehler.*

Vanryne, Robert (b. 1963). English trumpeter and **period instrument** maker. He became a finalist at the age of fifteen in the BBC Young Musician of the Year competition. After completing a music degree at Royal Holloway College, he continued his studies on the trumpet as a postgraduate at the Royal College of Music with **Michael Laird**. Vanryne has both performed and recorded regularly with Europe's leading period-instrument ensembles as well as with modern orchestras throughout the United Kingdom. With the Kölner Akademie under the direction of Michael Alexander Willens, he has recorded previously unrecorded pieces for early **chromatic trumpet**, including works composed for various types of valved trumpet, **keyed trumpet**, and **cornet**. Also an instrument maker, he produced **Baroque trumpets** in the late twentieth century together with Stephen Keavy that employed Michael Laird's system of four **vent holes**.

Vejvanovský, Pavel Josef (ca. 1633–1693). Moravian trumpeter and composer. In 1681 he entered the service of Castelle, the administrator of the court of the prince-bishop of Olomouc at Kroměříž. In 1664 he was appointed first trumpeter and director of the court orchestra and remained in the post until his death. He succeeded **Heinrich Ignaz Franz von Biber** as *Kappelmeister* in 1670. An experienced music copyist, Vejvanovský amassed an impressive private music collection, which resides today in the archives at Kroměříž castle along with copies of all of his 127 surviving compositions. His instrumental works include several imaginative compositions for trumpet that frequently employ **nonharmonic tones** (notes not found in the **harmonic overtone series**) in minor keys, especially the *Sonata a 4*. Vejvanovský wrote for **cornett** as well as trumpet, and scored for both instruments together in his *Sonata Vespertina* and the *Sonata Ittalica a 12*. Some of his most virtuosic trumpet writing appears in *Tribus Quadrantibus* (ca. 1667).

Velvet tone mute. A type of **bucket mute** made by **Humes & Berg**. (See appendix 3.)

vent hole. A hole cut into the tubing of a brass instrument at a **nodal point** where sound waves rebound off the inner walls of the tube when the instrument is played. Vent holes appear on brass instruments including some nineteenth-century **posthorns** and modern **Baroque trumpets** to enable **nodal venting**. The **keyed bugle** and the **keyed trumpet** employ vent holes that are covered by keys or levers rather than a musician's fingers. When the holes are operated by a player's fingers, they are often called **finger holes**. The use of vent holes on a brass instrument was first suggested by **Marin Mersenne** in the early seventeenth century. The first surviving trumpet with vent holes was an eighteenth-century silver trumpet designed by **William Shaw** in 1787 with four vent holes, three of which are covered by an adjustable metal sleeve. The first trumpet in the twentieth century to employ vent holes was made by **Otto Steinkopf** and **Helmut Finke** in 1959 and played by **Walter Holy**. It was a coiled trumpet with three vent holes designed after the *Jägertrompete* held by **Gottfried Reiche** in the famous portrait by E. G. Haussman from 1727. Later twentieth-century Baroque trumpets used systems with either three vent holes (perfected by **Edward Tarr**) or four vent holes (developed by **Michael Laird**).

vented trumpet. A trumpet shaped like an eighteenth-century **natural trumpet** with **vent holes** strategically positioned at **nodal points** on the bottom **yard** to correct out-of-tune **partials** in the **harmonic overtone series**. Also called a **Baroque trumpet**, it should not be considered a genuine natural trumpet because of the modifications to its design, which sometimes include a tapered **leadpipe**, like that on a **modern trumpet**.

Ventil. (Ger.) **Valve.**

via sordino. (It.) Remove **mute**; open.

vibrato. An expressive ornament to the tone of an instrument that features a gentle wavering quality intended to simulate the natural expression of the human voice. Trumpeters produced this effect on the trumpet through a variety of means. They can either use variations in lip pressure, air pressure (sometimes called "diaphragm vibrato"), hand pressure (**hand vibrato**), or jaw movement for a wider vibrato used in some jazz styles.

vibrato linguale. (It.) **Flutter tonguing.**

Vienna valve. A **double piston valve** developed by **Christian Friedrich Sattler** in 1821 that was subsequently improved by **Josef Kail** and Joseph Riedel in 1823 in Vienna (hence the name) and later adapted by Leopold Uhlmann in 1830. The primary advantage of the mechanism is its right-angled **windways**, which produce a gentler tone than instruments with single piston valves. The valve was popular in central Europe in the nineteenth century and survives today on French horns favored by the Vienna Philharmonic Orchestra. (See appendix 2, figures A8 and A9.)

Vizzutti, Allen (b. 1952). American trumpeter and composer. Equally at home performing classical and jazz styles, Vizzutti studied with his father, Lido, until he entered college. During his high school years, he received advice from **Doc Severinsen** and became first chair of the World Youth Orchestra. He also attended the Interlochen Music Camp, where he was a concerto competition winner. Vizzutti earned a scholarship to attend the Eastman School of Music, where he studied with Sydney Mear and earned bachelor's and master's degrees in music. He went on to become the first and only wind player to date to earn an Artist's Diploma from Eastman. During his time at the school he performed with the Rochester Philharmonic as well as the Eastman Brass Quintet.

Vizzutti has performed as a classical soloist with numerous orchestras, bands, and brass ensembles worldwide, often in his own compositions. In addition to his solo appearances, Vizzutti worked as a studio musician while living in Los Angeles during the 1980s and performed on numerous film soundtracks and broadcasts, including *Star Trek*, *Back to the Future*, *Rocky II*, *Broadcast News*, and *1941*. As a jazz artist he has performed with **Chuck Mangione**, Frank Sinatra, Barbra Streisand, **Dizzy Gillespie**, Dave Brubeck, Stan Getz, Chick Corea, Woody Herman, **Doc Severinsen**, and many others. Vizzutti has presented hundreds of master classes and clinics around the world and has served as an artist in residence at numerous festivals and institutions, including the **Rafael Mendez** Brass Institute, the Banff Centre for the Arts, and the Bremen Trumpet Academy.

As a composer, Vizzutti has written a variety of works for trumpet and ensemble as well as unaccompanied solos and etudes. Some of his compositions include *The Rising Sun, Three Winter Scenes, The Emerald Concerto, Prism: Shards of Color for Brass* (commissioned by Summit Brass), *American Jazz Suite, Cascades* for unaccompanied trumpet, and three sonatas for trumpet and piano. His pedagogical works, which have become staples of the repertoire, include *The Allen Vizzutti Trumpet Method* (in three volumes, published by Alfred Music) and *New Concepts for Trumpet* (Alfred). Vizzutti wrote a series of works for student trumpeters published by DeHaske/Hal Leonard including duets, etudes, jazz play-along collections, and two volumes of solos with piano titled *Excursions and Explorations*. Vizzutti is a **Yamaha** performing artist and is currently an artist-in-residence at the University of South Carolina.

Voisin, Roger (1918–2008). French-American trumpeter. One of the most influential classical trumpeters of the twentieth century, Voisin settled in Boston with his family at the age of nine when his father, René Louis (1893–1952), joined the Boston Symphony Orchestra as fourth trumpet in 1928. He began studying the trumpet with his father and later became an American citizen on his eighteenth birthday. He continued trumpet studies with **Georges Mager**, the principal trumpet of the Boston Symphony, and Marcel LaFosse before joining the orchestra as third trumpet in 1935. He also studied

solfège with Boston Symphony contrabassist Gaston Dufresne. Voisin was promoted to principal trumpet when Mager retired in 1950, moved back to third trumpet in 1965, and retired in 1973.

As a teacher, Voisin served on the faculty of the New England Conservatory between 1946 and 1975, and taught at Boston University between 1969 and 1999, becoming full professor and chair of the Wind, Percussion, and Harp Department in 1975. He also taught at the Tanglewood Music Center from its inception in 1940 until his death in 2008, coaching ensembles and teaching solfège as well as trumpet. The New England Conservatory awarded him an honorary doctorate in 1991. Many of his students have gone on to illustrious careers including **Edward Tarr**, **James Thompson**, **Tim Morrison**, Edward Hoffman, Rodney Mack, and Anthony DiLorenzo.

As a pioneer classical trumpet soloist, he made five solo recordings for Kapp Records in the late 1950s and early 1960s of Baroque music and two brass ensemble recordings, and edited publications of the trumpet music he recorded for the International Music Company. He premiered **Paul Hindemith**'s *Trumpet Sonata* with the composer at the piano and Hovhaness's *Prayer to Saint Gregory* as well as Leroy Anderson's *A Trumpeter's Lullaby*, which was written for Voisin and the Boston Pops (he requested a lyrical solo to counter the trumpet's stereotypical martial repertoire). He also performed the North American premiere of the **Arutiunian** concerto. Voisin's unique playing style was influenced by his use of a small-bore, four-valve **Thibouville-Lamy** C/D trumpet. In addition to his many performances and recordings, he also edited the final five volumes of the ten-volume series *Orchestral Excerpts from the Symphonic Repertoire for Trumpet* published by the International Music Company between 1948 and 1970.

Voldyne. A plastic medical device used to determine a person's lung capacity by determining how much air can be moved in or out of the lungs in a single breath, measured in liters. The Voldyne has a capacity of five liters and features two chambers: one to measure the air volume and a smaller one to measure for air pressure.

vulgano. (It.) Common, ordinary. The second lowest part (usually a drone on G3) of the **natural trumpet** ensemble in the sixteenth century, as described by **Bendinelli** and **Fantini**.

vuvuzela. A short, straight trumpet made out of plastic approximately two feet in length (65 cm) that is traditionally played by football (soccer) fans in South Africa. It produces one pitch (B3), but can be manipulated to produce others with extra force. Many plastic vuvuzelas are made in two telescoping parts that fit inside of each other for easy transport. Inspired by organic trumpets made from the horn of a kudu antelope, the vuvuzela was developed in the 1960s and has been marketed at some U.S. sporting events since the mid-1960s as a "Stadium Horn." The precise origin of the instrument is a matter of dispute, but its name comes from the Zulu word *vuvu*, which roughly means "welcome" or "celebration." The vuvuzela gained worldwide attention at the 2010 FIFA World Cup in South Africa, after which its noisy din caused several sporting institutions to ban its use, including the 2011 Rugby World Cup and the 2012 Summer Olympic Games. Given this modern evidence of the power of the massed sound of numerous vuvuzelas, it is possible to imagine how ancient trumpets of similar dimensions were used as instruments of war.

wah-wah mute. Another term for a **Harmon mute**. (See appendix 3.)

walking stick trumpet. A novelty item made by John Augustus **Köhler** in 1833 that inserted a **coach horn** into the center of a gentleman's walking stick. The instrument's **mouthpiece** and **bell** were attached to the ends when the tips of the walking stick were removed to convert the device into a functioning coach horn.

Wallace, John (b. 1949). Scottish trumpeter. He attended King's College, Cambridge, and subsequently studied with Alan Bush at the Royal Academy of Music and with David Blake at York University. His début was in 1965 in Estoril with Haydn's Trumpet Concerto. Wallace was principal trumpeter with the Philharmonia Orchestra between 1976 and 1995, and in 1988 he joined the London Sinfonietta. In 1986 he founded the Wallace Collection, a brass ensemble of flexible instrumentation (including **period instruments**), with which he has toured and recorded extensively. In 1988 he gave the first performances of concertos by Tim Souster and Peter Maxwell Davies, both dedicated to him. An energetic advocate of new solo repertoire for the trumpet, Wallace's other premieres include Souster's *The Transistor Radio of St Narcissus* for flugelhorn and live electronics (1983), concertos by **Malcolm Arnold** (1982) and Dominic Muldowney (1993), Robert Saxton's *Psalm of Ascents* (1993), James Macmillan's *Epiclesis* (1993), and Turnage's *Dispelling the Fears* (1995). Wallace edited the *Companion to Brass Instruments* (Cambridge, 1997) with Trevor Herbert, as well as a series of brass music and educational collections, and has made many recordings. He was honored with an OBE in 1995. In January 2002 he became principal of the Royal Scottish Academy of Music and Drama, and in 2011 he coauthored *The Trumpet* (Yale University Press) with Alexander McGrattan.

Warburton. Canadian brass instrument manufacturer. The company was established in Toronto by trumpeter Terry Warburton (b. 1950) in 1974 as Warburton Music Industries to manufacture brass **mouthpieces**. The company moved to Florida in 1981 and became one of the world's leading makers of brass mouthpieces. Warburton specializes in a wide array of mouthpiece sizes that can be customized with removable **cups** and **backbores** that provide musicians with versatile options for different playing styles and equipment. In addition to mouthpieces, the company also markets several **practice aids** including the **P.E.T.E.** (Personal Embouchure Training Exerciser) and the Buzzard (a mouthpiece buzzing tool), as well as a line of wooden **mutes** and the **Tiger Trumpet** (a trumpet in B-flat made of plastic).

water key. A device on a trumpet or other brass instrument that allows accumulated condensation to be emptied from the instrument. The most common form operates through the mechanism of a lever with a spring that plugs an open hole in the instrument's tubing with a piece of cork or rubber. An alternative design, the Amado water key, employs a push-button mechanism with an internal spring intended to minimize disruption to the airflow through the instrument.

Weber, Bedřich Diviš [Friedrich Dionysus] (1766–1842). Bohemian composer. He studied philosophy and law in Prague before deciding on a musical career. Weber met **Mozart**, whose musical style he emulated, and studied harmony and composition with Georg Joseph Vogler (1749–1814). He became the first director of the Prague Conservatory in 1811 and had a particular interest in the development of **chromatic brass instruments**, especially the horn. Weber composed the first solo piece for valved trumpet and orchestra, *Variations in F* (ca. 1827). His student, **Joseph Kail**, the first professor of the valved trumpet at the Prague Conservatory, also wrote a *Variations in F* for the instrument. Bedřich Weber was not related to Carl Maria von Weber (1786–1826), whose music he disliked, or Mozart's wife, Constanze Weber Mozart (1762–1842).

Weidinger, Anton (1766–1852). Austrian trumpeter and virtuoso of the **keyed trumpet** for whom both the Haydn and Hummel concerti were composed. Weidinger studied under Vienna's chief court trumpeter, Johann Peter Neuhold (1724–1801), and progressed so quickly that his period of study was shortened, a rare distinction. He was released from his apprenticeship on September 18, 1785, and served as a military trumpeter until 1792, when he joined the orchestra of the Royal Imperial Theater (Hoftheater) in Vienna. Weidinger took up the new keyed trumpet shortly thereafter and demonstrated its new artistic possibilities for **Joseph Haydn**, who composed his *Concerto in E-flat Major* in 1796. The work received its premiere on March 28, 1800, in the Vienna's Burgtheater. Three years later, **Johann Nepomuk Hummel** composed his *Concerto in E Major* for Weidinger, who premiered the work on January 1, 1804, in Vienna on an improved keyed trumpet with five keys.

Other composers wrote works for Weidinger and his keyed trumpet including Leopold Kozeluch, Joseph Weigel, and Sigismund Neukomm. Tours throughout Germany, France, and England spread Weidinger's reputation, but the keyed trumpet failed to gain a wide acceptance, despite Weidinger's virtuosity. Contemporary audiences were not accustomed to hearing a trumpet perform melodies in the lower register and had trouble accepting the instrument outside of its traditional military role. By the 1820s, valved brass instruments supplanted the keyed trumpet, which fell out of use in the middle of the nineteenth century.

Weidinger's family ties included several trumpeters. His older brother Joseph (ca. 1755–1829) was an imperial court trumpeter (*kaiserlicher Hoftrompeter*) and his younger brother Franz (ca. 1770–1814) was a trumpeter at the imperial theater (*Hoftheater*). Anton Weidinger's son, Joseph, was a regional trumpeter (*landschaftstrompeter*) in Lower Austria (Niederösterreich), while another son, Ferdinand, became an imperial court timpanist (*kaiserlicher Hofpauker*). Weidinger married Susanna Zeiß, the daughter of Viennese court trumpeter Franz Zeiß (d. 1783).

Weinschenk, Christian Ferdinand (1831–1910). German trumpeter. Following studies with **Ernst Sachse**, he became the first professor of trumpet at the Leipzig Conservatory and served as the principal trumpeter of the Leipzig Gewandhaus Orchestra for thirty-two years (1867–1899). Many of his students went on to illustrious careers in European and American orchestras, no-

tably **Eduard Seifert** and Karl Heinrich (1882–1950). Weinschenk was also one of the first to perform the high trumpet parts of Bach and Handel on a small D trumpet in the late nineteenth century. The only trumpet concerto from the Romantic Era, **Oskar Böhme**'s *Concerto, Op. 18* (1899), was dedicated to Weinschenk.

weir trumpattis. A Scottish term for a military (war) trumpet from the early sixteenth century. The term was used to distinguish the instrument from the **dracht trumpet** (draught trumpattis), which was either a **slide trumpet** or a trombone.

Weissenfels. City in Germany known for its fine tradition of trumpet playing in the seventeenth and eighteenth centuries. During the tenure of court organist Johann Philipp Krieger (1684–1725) more than three hundred works were recorded as having trumpet parts, some calling for as many as twelve players. J. S. Bach's father-in-law, Johann Caspar Wilcke, served in Weissenfels, as did **Johann Caspar Altenburg**, the father of **Johann Ernst Altenburg**. **Gottfried Reiche** was born in Weissenfels as well.

West, Jeremy (b. 1953). English *cornetto* player and leading figure in the **period instrument** revival. His first musical studies were on the trumpet and West began playing the **cornett** in 1974 while a student at Durham University, where he was inspired by Jerome Roche. He went on to study with Philip Pickett at the Guildhall School of Music and subsequently embarked on a professional career. Regarded as one of the pioneers of modern cornett performance, West founded the period instrument ensemble His Majestys Sagbutts and Cornetts and serves as the Principal Wind Player with the Gabrieli Consort and Players. He has also performed with many of Europe's leading renaissance and early baroque ensembles and played on more than sixty recordings.

In addition to a playing career that has taken him to more than thirty countries, West became the director of the instrument-making workshops of **Christopher Monk** in 1991 at Monk's request. He wrote the first comprehensive method book for the cornett in modern times, *How to Play the Cornett*, with Susan Smith in 1995, which has sold more than one thousand copies worldwide. Having served as a professor of cornett at the Royal College of Music in London and as a consultant to the Royal Academy of Music, West is currently a professor at the Guildhall School of Music in London as well as Musician in Residence at Girton College, University of Cambridge.

Whitaker, Liesl (b. 1969). American jazz trumpeter. She studied trumpet with Bill Adam, Pat Harbison, and Joe Phelps and attended both Appalachian State University and the University of Cincinnati College-Conservatory of Music before beginning a career based out of New

York. In 1992 she became a charter member and lead trumpet of the world-renowned, all-female big band Diva. She has also performed frequently in Broadway pit orchestras, freelanced and recorded throughout New York, and taught trumpet for the New York Pops' Salute to Music Teaching Program. In 2000 she became the lead trumpet for the U.S. Army Blues Jazz Ensemble, the first woman to hold a lead chair in any of the major military jazz ensembles.

White, Edna (Richert) (ca. 1900–1969). American musical instrument manufacturer. Not to be confused with the trumpet soloist of the same name, she was the first female executive in the musical instrument industry in the United States. As the third wife of Henderson N. White (1873–1940), she became president and chief stockholder of the H. N. White Company (later known as **King Musical Instruments**) after her husband died in 1940. Her considerable business acumen acquired from previous work in real estate and retail led to increased sales and productivity for the company. Using the name Mrs. H. N. White for business purposes, she increased advertising and gained endorsements from noted musicians like **Harry James**, Tommy Dorsey, Woody Herman, and Stan Kenton, among others. When the company fell on hard times during the Second World War due to a shortage of brass, White successfully obtained lucrative government grants to manufacture radar equipment and silver proximity switches, which kept workers employed. In the 1950s she was renowned for entertaining celebrity musicians who played King instruments at her large home in Shaker Heights, Ohio. After selling the company to Nate Dolan in 1962, she built a new production plant in Eastlake, Ohio, near Cleveland in 1964, and retired the following year.

White, (Flora) Edna (1892–1992). American trumpeter. She began playing the **cornet** at the age of seven and gave her first public performance at the age of nine. Her first teachers were her father, John White, and **Anna Park**. At the age of eleven she entered the Institute of Musical Art (later known as the Juilliard School) on invitation from Frank Damrosch, where she studied with Adolphe Dubois and switched from the cornet to the trumpet, graduating in 1907 at the age of fourteen. White formed an all-female quartet of trumpets and cornets in 1908 known as the Aida Quartet. She married Myron H. Chandler in 1913, and although she divorced him two years later and married opera singer Torcom Bézazian in 1916, she continued to use the name Chandler in her later private life. In 1914 she formed the Edna White Trumpet Quartet, and in March 1915 she played "Silver Threads Among the Gold" at the opening ceremony of the first transcontinental telephone transmission between Brooklyn and San Francisco.

By 1916, White started recording for Columbia Records and Edison including a performance of **Herbert L. Clarke's** solo, "The Debutante." She formed a brass quartet (two trumpets and two trombones) called the Gloria Trumpeters in 1919, and during the 1920s toured on the Keith vaudeville circuit with Bézazian. She featured works by George Antheil and Virgil Thomson, performed with the Manhattan Symphony Orchestra and the Rochester Park Band. During the 1930s, she began to make regular appearances on radio, and also sang in musicals. In February 1949, she gave the first ever solo trumpet recital in Carnegie Hall, at which she premiered Virgil Thomson's solo, *At the Beach*, and Georges Enescu's *Légende*. She returned to Carnegie Hall to give her farewell concert in 1957.

White composed several works for the trumpet including *Suite for Solo Trumpet and Symphony Orchestra* (1980), which was recorded by Gaeton Berton with the Maryland Symphony Orchestra, and *On Taming the Devil's Tongue* (1982). She also wrote several books of poetry. In 1982 she published a cassette of recordings and reminiscences, *Life with My Trumpet*, and in 1990 published a memoir of her time in vaudeville, *The Night the Camel Sang*. White's personal papers reside in the Sibley Library of the Eastman School of Music.

Wick, Denis (b. 1931). English trombonist, brass **mouthpiece** manufacturer, and **mute** maker. He premiered Gordon Jacob's *Trombone Concerto* in 1955 and served as principal trombone of the London Symphony Orchestra between 1957 and 1988, performing with the orchestra on the soundtrack of *Star Wars* (1977) and numerous recordings, especially Mahler's Third Symphony. He taught at the Guildhall School of Music and Drama between 1967 and 1989, and began teaching at the Royal Academy of Music in 2000. Wick served as the president of the International Trombone Association between 2004 and 2006.

Denis Wick began crafting mouthpieces in 1968 and he later branched out to make mutes for all brass instruments and other instrumental accessories. The company makes a variety of aluminum **straight mutes** for trumpets of different sizes including **piccolo trumpet** and D trumpet as well as for **cornets** in E-flat and B-flat, and **flugelhorn**. Wick also makes straight mutes of fiber and wood to provide softer tone colors along with aluminum straight mutes with bottom sections made from copper (darker) and brass (more brilliant) for additional sound options. In addition to the full palette of color available in Wick straight mutes, the company also makes adjustable **cup mutes and practice mutes**. His full line of brass mouthpieces includes an extensive catalog of offerings for cornet and flugelhorn. Denis Wick Products was honored with the Queen's Award for Enterprise in International Trade in 2013.

Wiener Ventil. (Ger.) **Vienna valve.**

Williams, John (b. 1932). American composer, conductor, and pianist. The preeminent composer of film music since the 1970s, Williams was born in New York and later moved to Los Angeles with his family, where he studied composition with Mario Castelnuovo-Tedesco at the University of California at Los Angeles (UCLA). Following service in the U.S. Air Force, he studied piano at the Juilliard School with Madame Rosina Lhevinne while also performing as a jazz pianist in New York. He returned to Los Angeles in the 1950s and worked as a studio pianist and arranger, and began composing for television and films. Williams has composed scores for nearly eighty films, including *Jaws* (1975), *Close Encounters of the Third Kind* (1977), *Star Wars* (1977), *The Empire Strikes Back* (1980), *Return of the Jedi* (1983), *Raiders of the Lost Ark* (1981), *E.T.: the Extra Terrestrial* (1982), *Schindler's List*, (1993), and the first three *Harry Potter* films (2001–2004). Williams frequently featured trumpet solos in his scores—notably *Born on the Fourth of July* (1989) and the theme of the 1996 Olympic Games, *Summon the Heroes*, both written for trumpeter **Tim Morrison**. He composed a trumpet concerto for **Michael Sachs** and the Cleveland Orchestra in 1996. In addition to composing, Williams served as the conductor of the Boston Pops Orchestra between 1980 and 1993, and as conductor laureate thereafter. His music has earned numerous awards including five Academy Awards (with forty-nine nominations), seventeen Grammys, three Golden Globes, two Emmys, and five BAFTA Awards from the British Academy of Film and Television Arts.

windway. The complete path of tubing through which the **airstream** travels when a brass instrument is played, including **valve slides** for engaged (pressed) valves and **intervalve tubing** when valves are not used.

Wispa mute. A type of **practice mute** made by **Shastock**. Its full name was the "Charlie Spivak Wispa Mute." (See appendix 3.)

Wobisch, Helmut (1912–1980). Austrian trumpeter. He studied with Engelbert Lax and Franz Dengler and joined the orchestra of the Vienna Staatsoper as first trumpet in 1936. He became principal trumpet of the Vienna Philharmonic Orchestra in 1939. He later served as the manager of the Vienna Philharmonic between 1952 and 1969, and in 1970 he founded the Carinthian Summer Music Festival. Wobisch made several solo recordings in the 1950s including the Haydn concerto, Bach's *Brandenburg Concerto No. 2*, and several Bach cantatas. He has also performed with the Trompeterchor der Stadt Wien, for which Richard Strauss composed his expansive *Festmusik der Stadt Wien* (1942).

Wöggel, Michael (1748–1811). Court trumpeter in Karlsruhe, Germany, in the early 1770s who applied the technique of **hand-stopping** to the trumpet and developed the *Inventionstrompete.*

woodshed. Term used by jazz musicians to describe long periods of intense practice in seclusion (as in a woodshed); often shorted to **shed.**

wrap. The manner in which tubing of a brass instrument is bent, wound, or folded.

Wright, Elbridge G. (1811–1871). American brass instrument manufacturer. He established his business in Boston in 1841 and produced some of the finest **keyed bugles** and **ophicleides** in the United States. He also made brass instruments with string-operated **rotary valves.** His business merged with that of Graves & Co. in 1869 to form the **Boston Musical Instrument Manufactory.**

Wülcken, Johann Caspar (fl. 1718–1731). German trumpeter. A court trumpeter in **Weissenfels**, his daughter, Anna Magdalena, became the second wife of **Johann Sebastian Bach.**

Wurm, Wilhelm (1826–1904). German cornetist, composer, and bandmaster. Born in Bunswick, Germany, he immigrated to Russia at the age of twenty-one and became the "Soloist of the Imperial Theatre Orchestra" from 1847 to 1878 and director of bands of the Imperial Guards from 1869 to 1889. Wurm also served as musical adviser to Czar Aleksandr II and his son, Aleksandr III, who was an amateur cornet player and an enthusiastic supporter of brass chamber music, a new genre at the time. From 1867 until his death in 1904 Wurm taught cornet and brass chamber music at the St. Petersburg Conservatory, and served as chairman of the St. Petersburg Philharmonic Society for thirty-three years. In addition to performing and touring as popular cornet soloist, Wurm published several solo works for cornet piano and ensemble accompaniment as well as pedagogical works, including the first cornet method published in Russia. As a teacher, he was the first to advocate lip buzzing as a warm-up technique.

Yamaha. Musical Instrument Manufacturer. The corporation was started by Torakusu Yamaha (1851–1916), a Japanese entrepreneur who pioneered the production of Western musical instruments in Japan. What began with Yamaha's original reed organ design in 1887 grew into an international corporation that produces motorcycles and electronics as well as musical instruments. Yamaha began making wind instruments in the 1960s. The company produces a complete line of brass instruments including **trumpets, cornets,** and **flugelhorns** as well as **rotary valve** trumpets. Yamaha is particularly well known for their **high-pitched trumpets** and Xeno Artist series, as well as an electronic **practice mute** system called Silent Brass.

yard. Term used to describe the straight pipe on a **natural trumpet** that connects the **corpus** (bell section) to the first **bow**. On modern **Baroque trumpets** with **vent holes,** the yard contains the vent holes and is not soldered to the rest of the instrument to allow for positioning adjustments.

Zelenka, Jan Dismas (1679–1745). Czech composer. Born in Bohemia, Zelenka studied composition with Fux in Vienna and with Lotti in Venice, and settled in Dresden as a composer for the royal chapel and double bass player. The bulk of his output consists of church music, especially twenty mass settings, but he also composed several instrumental works including a set of six **fanfares** for four trumpets and timpani (ZWV 212, 1722).

Zink, Zinck. (Ger.) **Cornett.** The term stems from middle German origins and literally means an animal horn or, more generally, an item that protrudes, like a large tooth. It was sometimes used as a slang term for *horn* in the Renaissance to refer to a number of different wind instruments, but later became exclusively associated with the cornett.

Zug. (Ger.) **Slide.**

Zugtrompete. (Ger.) **Slide trumpet.** Also known as the **tromba da tirarsi**; the Baroque slide trumpet.

APPENDIX 1

Timeline of Trumpet History

ca. 1800 BC	Nordic **lur**
ca. 1480 BC	Ancient Israel: **chatzotzrah** (silver trumpet) and **shofar**
ca. 1323 BC	Ancient Egypt: two trumpets (**šnb**) buried in the tomb of King Tutankhamun
ca. 500 BC	Ancient Rome: **cornu**, **tuba**, **lituus**, **buccina**
ca. 396 BC	Ancient Greece: **Archias** wins three Olympic trumpet contests playing the **salpinx**
ca. 200 BC	Ancient Celts: **carnyx**
1090	*Chanson of Roland*: **oliphant**
ca. 1375	Medieval **buisine, Billingsgate trumpet**
1442	**Guitbert trumpet**
1511	Sebastian Virdung's *Musica getutscht*, is published, the first book about musical instruments. It includes woodcuts of a **natural trumpet** for **clarino** playing (*clareta*), a military trumpet (*Felttrummet*), and a **slide trumpet** (*Thurner horn*).
ca. 1600	**Magnus Thomsen** publishes a collection of military trumpet calls in a *Trompeterbuch*.
1607	Monteverdi writes for a **trumpet ensemble** in the opening "**Toccata**" for his opera *L'Orfeo*, but not as part of the opera orchestra.
1614	**Cesare Bendinelli** publishes the first known trumpet method, *Tutta l'arte della Trombetta*.
1638	**Girolamo Fantini** publishes *Modo imparare a sonare di tromba*, which includes the first sonatas for trumpet and keyboard.
ca. 1700	**Giuseppe Torelli** composes some of the first concerti and sinfonias for solo trumpet and orchestra in Bologna, Italy.
1721	**J. S. Bach** composes his ***Brandenburg Concerto No. 2*** in Cöthen.
ca. 1763	**Michael Haydn**'s *Concerto No. 2 in D* ascends to A6, the highest note yet written for the trumpet.
ca. 1770	**Michael Wöggel** applies the technique of **hand-stopping** to his new *Inventionstrompete*.
1784	**Charles Burney** criticizes trumpeter **John Sarjant**'s performance of "The Trumpet Shall Sound" at a performance of **Handel**'s *Messiah* in Westminster Abbey, which shows that the technique of **natural trumpet** playing is declining as public taste is changing.
1787	**William Shaw's** "**Harmonic Trumpet**"; the first trumpet with **vent holes**.

(continued)

1788	**Charles Clagget's "Cromatic** [*sic*] **Trumpet"**; the first attempt to apply a **valve** to a brass instrument.
1795	**Johann Ernst Altenburg** publishes his *Versuch einer Anleitung zur heroisch-musikalischen Trompeter und Pauker-Kunst.*
1799	**John Hyde** publishes his *New and Compleat Preceptor for the Trumpet and Bugle Horn.* Hyde is credited with inventing the **English slide trumpet.**
1800	**Anton Weidinger** premieres the *Concerto in E-flat Major* by **Joseph Haydn** on a **keyed trumpet** in Vienna's Burgtheater on March 28th. The concerto was composed in 1796.
1804	**Anton Weidinger** premieres the *Concerto in E Major* by **Johann Nepomuk Hummel** on a **keyed trumpet** in Vienna on New Year's Day. The concerto was composed in 1803.
1810	**Joseph Haliday** patents the **keyed bugle.**
1818	**Stölzel** and **Blühmel** jointly patent the concept of applying a **valve** mechanism to brass instruments.
ca. 1825	The first **cornet** with **Stölzel valves** (the **cornopean**).
1827	**Valved trumpets** debut in the orchestra of the Paris Opera.
1833	British trumpeter **John Distin** forms the Distin Family Quintet, one of the first brass chamber ensembles. **François Dauverné** is appointed the first professor of trumpet at the Paris Conservatory.
1835	The Boston Brass Band debuts under the leadership of **Edward (Ned) Kendall (keyed bugle** soloist).
1839	**Périnet** patents the **piston valve,** which is still widely used today.
1844	The **Distin** Family meets **Adolphe Sax** in Paris and begins playing **saxhorns.**
1857	**François Dauverné** publishes his *Méthode* in Paris.
1864	**J. B. Arban** publishes his *Grande méthode complète pour cornet à pistons et de saxhorn* in Paris.
1870	**Louis Saint-Jacome** publishes his *Grand Method for Cornet* in Paris.
1881	**Julius Kosleck** performs the first part to Bach's *Mass in B Minor* in Berlin on a long trumpet in A with two valves that became known as the "**Bach trumpet.**"
1894	**Hermann Ludwig Eichborn** publishes *Das alte Clarinblasen auf Trompeten,* claiming that the revival of **clarino** playing on **natural trumpets** was futile.
1898	**Théo Charlier** performs Bach's *Brandenburg Concerto No. 2* for the first time at pitch in the modern era on a trumpet in G in Antwerp.
1906	Georges Enesco composes *Legende* for **Merri Franquin,** who advocates using the **modern C trumpet** for solo and orchestral playing.
ca. 1920	The design of the **cornet** becomes more **cylindrical** and trumpet-like. The modern B-flat trumpet begins to usurp the role of the cornet.
ca. 1927	**Louis Armstrong** switches from the cornet to the trumpet.
1939	**George Eskdale** records the **Haydn** concerto for the first time (second and third movements) and edits a published version of the concerto.
1948	Three trumpet concertos are published by **Henri Tomasi** (*Concerto*), **André Jolivet** (*Concertino*), and **Vladimir Peskin** (*Concerto No. 1 in C Minor*).

(continued)

1951	**Philip Jones** Brass Ensemble formed.
1954	**Robert Nagel** and Harvey Phillips form the **New York Brass Quintet**.
1955	**Maurice André** wins first prize at the Geneva International Competition.
1959	**Miles Davis** releases his album, *Kind of Blue*.
1960	**American Brass Quintet** formed.
1964	**Walter Holy** records Bach's ***Brandenburg Concerto No. 2*** on a coiled **Baroque trumpet** with three **vent holes** and pioneers the revival of **clarino** playing. **Armando Ghitalla** records the **Hummel** concerto for the first time.
1970	**Canadian Brass** formed.
1975	**International Trumpet Guild** founded.
1983	**Wynton Marsalis** becomes the first musician to win Grammy Awards for both jazz and classical recordings.
1987	**Friedemann Immer** records the **Haydn** concerto on a **keyed trumpet** for the first time in the modern era.
1988	**Historic Brass Society** founded by Jeffrey Nussbaum.
2009	**Jean-François Madeuf** records Bach's ***Brandenburg Concerto No. 2*** on a **natural trumpet** without **vent holes**.

APPENDIX 2

Gallery of Valve Diagrams

Berlin Valve

Heinrich Stölzel, Wilhelm Wieprecht (Germany, 1835). See fig. A1.

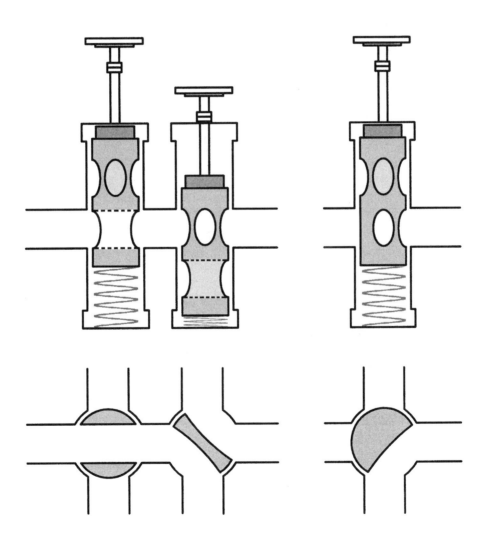

Figure A1. Berlin valve. *Drawing by T. M. Larsen.*

Box Valve

Friedrich Blühmel (Germany, 1814–1816), applied to brass instruments
by Friedrich Wilhelm Schuster. See fig. A2.

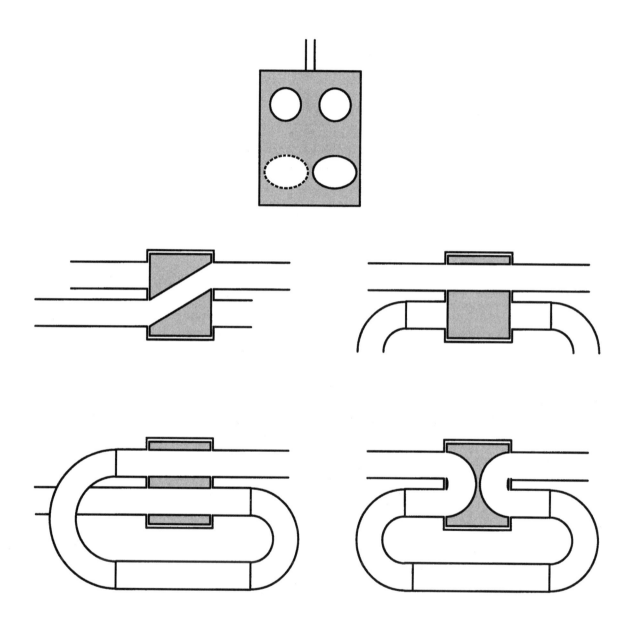

Figure A2. Box valve. *Drawing by T. M. Larsen.*

Disc Valve (Swivel Disc Valve, Axial Flow Valve)

John Shaw (England, 1838). See fig. A3.

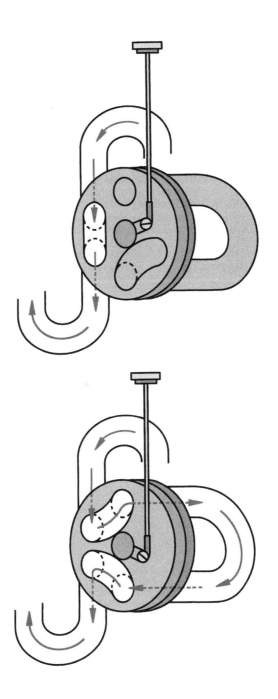

Figure A3. Disc valve or patent lever valve. *Drawing by T. M. Larsen.*

Périnet Piston Valve

François Périnet (France, 1839). See fig. A4.

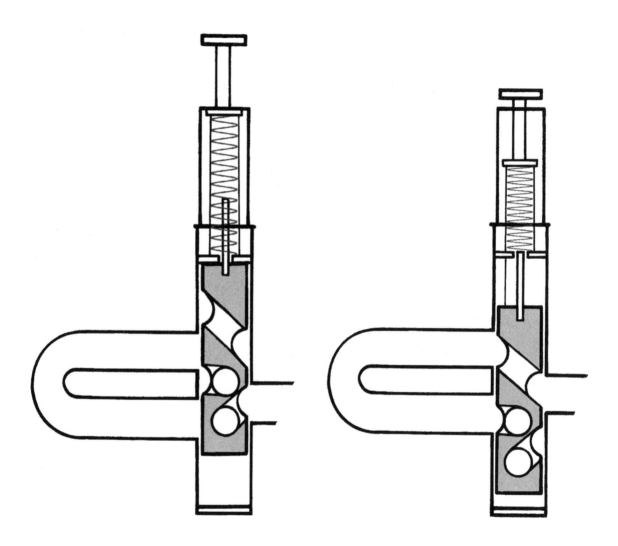

Figure A4. Périnet piston valve. *Drawing by T. M. Larsen.*

Rotary Valve

Side action rotary valve, Friedrich Blühmel (Germany, 1814–1816). See fig. A5.
Top action, string-operated rotary valve (Allen valve). See fig. A6.

Valve cap   Valve down   Valve up

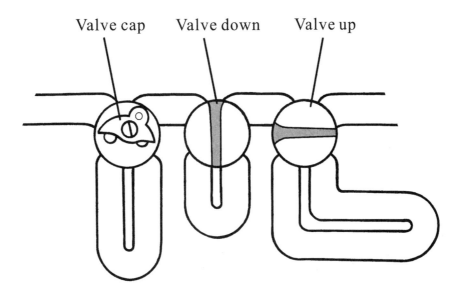

Figure A5. Side action rotary valve (levers omitted from diagram to show inner workings of the mechanism). *Drawing by T. M. Larsen.*

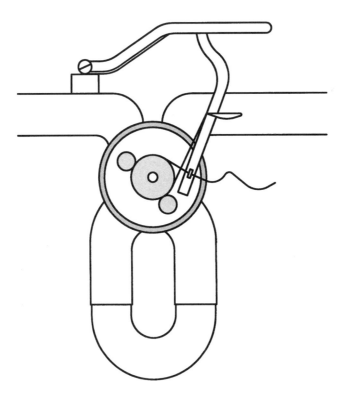

Figure A6. Top action rotary valve. *Drawing by T. M. Larsen.*

Stölzel Piston Valve

Heinrich Stölzel (Germany, 1814–1816). See fig. A7.

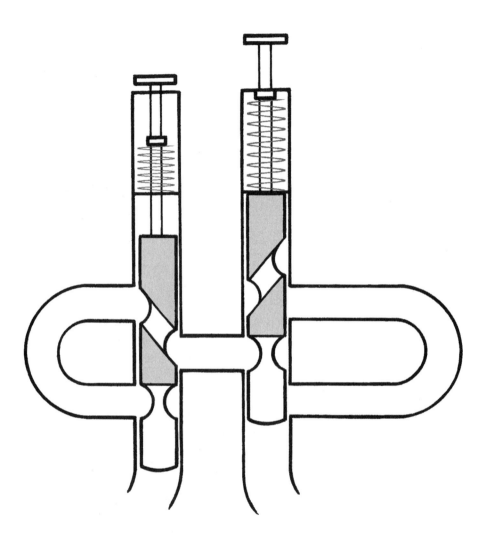

Figure A7. Stölzel piston valve. *Drawing by T. M. Larsen.*

Vienna Valve (Double Piston Valve)

Christian Friedrich Sattler, Friedrich Riedl, Joseph Kail (Germany, 1819, 1821–1830). See figs. A8 and A9.

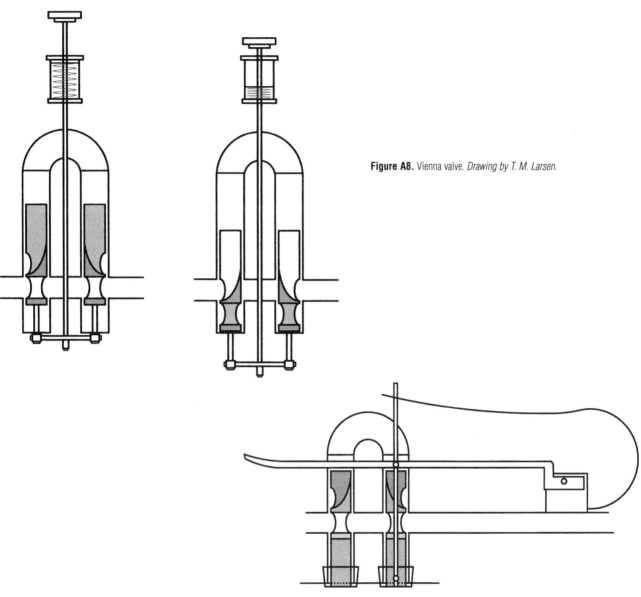

Figure A8. Vienna valve. *Drawing by T. M. Larsen.*

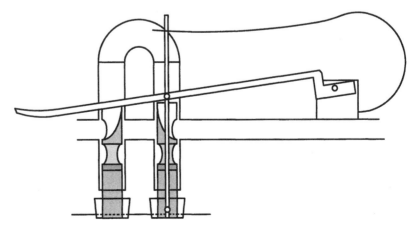

Figure A9. Double piston valve with lever action. *Drawing by T. M. Larsen.*

APPENDIX 3

Mute Classifications

The proliferation of mute designs in the twentieth century created new expressive sound possibilities for the trumpet, but it also created confusion as trade names and generic terminology blended together in a working trumpeter's vocabulary. Just as Kleenex, Puffs, and "facial tissue" refer to the same object, a similar relationship exists between terms like Harmon mute, wah-wah mute, and "The Zinger." To further complicate matters, composers sometimes created new names for unfamiliar mutes, or else they failed to specify what they wanted and simply indicated that a passage should be muted, leaving it up to the performers to decide what to use. The classification listed in this appendix (inspired by that of Dutch Uithoven at www.vintagemutes.com) attempts to group mutes of similar design together into functional categories.

Bucket	Bucket attached to the bell (Humes & Berg)
	EE-MO-YE mute (Shastock)
	Large straight mute design with chamber filled with cotton (Jo-Ral)
	Velvet tone mute (Humes & Berg)
Buzz	Buzz mute (Shastock)
	Buzz-Wow mute (Humes & Berg)
	Humes Jazzer (Guy Humes, 1920)
	Handful of kazoos in the bell (Joe "King" Oliver, ca. 1920)
Combination	Adjustable cup mute and straight mute (Denis Wick, TrumCor)
	Tonalcolor (Shastock, ca. 1930, adjustable cup mute)
Cup	Cup mute (generic term, used by several makers)
	Mica mute (Humes & Berg)
	Robinson mute (Robinson, ca. 1950)
Felt	Crown Royal bag
	Derby mute (a felt hat)
	Felt mute (generic term, draped over the bell)
Open Tube	Baroque mute (made of wood)
	Clear Tone mute (Humes & Berg)
	Double mute (generic term)
	Mega mute (Shastock)
	Solotone mute (Shastock)
Plunger	Plunger mute (generic name, used by several makers)
	Sink plunger (hardware store; toilet plunger is too large)
Practice	eBrass (Best Brass, electronic system with ear phones)
	Practice mute (generic name, used by several makers)
	Sh! Sh! Quiet! Mannie Klein (Humes & Berg)
	Silent Brass (Yamaha, electronic system with ear phones)
	Wispa mute (Shastock)
Stopped	*bouché*
	gestopft
	Hand in or over the bell
Straight	Fiber mute (generic term, indicates a softer type of straight mute)
	Lyric Mute (TrumCor, a type of softer mute)
	Mute (general indication, usually presumes the use of a straight mute)
	Pixie mute (Humes & Berg, small straight mute)
	Straight mute (generic name, used by several makers, different materials)
	Vocatone mute (Shastock)
Wah Wah	Bubble mute (Jo-Ral)
	Harmon mute (colloquial term)
	Wah-wah mute (generic term, used by several makers)
	Wow Wow mute (Harmon)
	Zinger (TrumCor)

APPENDIX 4

Orchestra and Opera Audition Excerpts

Adams	*Doctor Atomic Symphony*
	The Wound Dresser (piccolo trumpet solo)
Bach	*B Minor Mass* (Credo solo)
	Brandenburg Concerto No. 2 (Mvt. 3)
	Christmas Oratorio (Part VI, No. 64)
	Magnificat (Mvt.1)
Bartók	Concerto for Orchestra
Beethoven	*Leonore Overtures No. 2 and No. 3* (off stage calls)
Berg	*Wozzeck*
Berlioz	*Les Troyens*
Bizet	*Carmen* (Prelude and off stage calls)
Brahms	*Academic Festival Overture* (opening)
Britten	*Peter Grimes* ("Sunday Morning": Trumpet 3 in D)
	Midsummer Night's Dream
	Young Person's Guide to the Orchestra
Copland	*An Outdoor Overture*
Debussy	*Nocturnes* (Mvt. 2: Fêtes)
Donizetti	*Don Pasquale* (Act II prelude)
	Lucia di Lammermoor (opening)
Dvořák	Symphony No. 8 (Mvt. 2)
Gershwin	*An American in Paris*
	Concerto in F for Piano
Handel	*Messiah* ("The Trumpet Shall Sound")
Leoncavallo	*Pagliacci* (Coro d'introduzione)
Mahler	Symphony No. 3 (Mvt. 3: posthorn solo)
	Symphony No. 5 (Mvt. 1: opening)

(continued)

Mussorgsky/Ravel	*Pictures at an Exhibition* (Mvt. 1: Promenade, Mvt. 6: Samuel Goldenburg and Schmuyle)
Prokofiev	*Lieutenant Kijé*
	Romeo and Juliet
Ravel	*Alborada del Gracioso*
	Piano Concerto in G
Respighi	*Pines of Rome* (Mvt. 1: opening muted passages, Mvt. 2: offstage solo)
Rimsky-Korsakov	*Capriccio Espagnol* (Mvt. 4)
	Scheherazade
Schoenberg	*Moses und Aron*
Schumann	Symphony No. 2 (Mvt. 1: opening)
Shostakovich	Symphony No. 1 (Mvt. 3)
	Symphony No. 5
Strauss, R.	*Arabella*
	Ariadne auf Naxos
	Don Juan
	Don Quixote
	Ein Heldenleben (both B-flat and E-flat parts)
	Elektra
	Till Eulenspiegel
Stravinsky	*Firebird* (Danse Infernale)
	L'histoire du Soldat (Royal March)
	Petrouchka (1947 version: Ballerina's Dance and Waltz)
Tchaikovsky	*Capriccio Italien*
	Nutcracker (Act II: Spanish Dance "Chocolate")
	Symphony No. 4
Verdi	*Aida* (Act II)
	Nabucco (Overture)
	Rigoletto (Act I: Prelude, *banda* part)
	Stiffelio (Overture)
Wagner	*Götterdämmerung* (Act III: Siegfried's Funeral Music)
	Lohengrin
	Parsifal (Prelude)
	Tannhäuser (Overture)
	Die Walküre

Bibliography

This bibliography is divided into topical categories to facilitate the speedy location of specific resources. While a hierarchical organization from general to more specific topics would be logical, I have listed the categories in alphabetical order because they are too numerous. Some resources appear in more than one category for convenient access and maximum utility.

CONTENTS

BIOGRAPHIES AND AUTOBIOGRAPHIES

Bierley, Paul Edmund. *John Philip Sousa, American Phenomenon*. Westerville, OH: Integrity Press, 1973.

———. *The Incredible Band of John Philip Sousa*. Chicago: University of Illinois Press, 2006.

Birkemeier, Richard P. "The F Trumpet and Its Last Virtuoso, Walter Morrow (1850–1937)." *Brass Bulletin* 65 (1989): 34–45.

Bridges, Glenn. *Pioneers in Brass*. Originally published in 1965. Enumclaw, WA: Trescott Research, 2001. CD-ROM.

Catalano, Nick. *Clifford Brown: The Life and Art of the Legendary Jazz Trumpeter*. Oxford: Oxford University Press, 2000.

Cipolla, Frank J. "Dodworth." In *Grove Music Online. Oxford Music Online*, www.oxfordmusiconline.com/subscriber/article/grove/music/46755 (accessed August 6, 2012).

Clarke, Herbert L. *A Cornet-Playing Pilgrim's Progress: The Complete Autobiography of Herbert L. Clarke*. Originally published in 1930. Chandler, AZ: Hickman Music Editions, n.d.

Collins, Timothy. "Gottfried Reiche: A More Complete Biography." *International Trumpet Guild Journal* 15, no. 3 (1991): 4–28.

Conforzi, Igino. "Girolamo Fantini, 'Monarch of the Trumpet': Recent Additions to His Biography." *Historic Brass Society Journal* 5 (1993): 159–73.

———. "Girolamo Fantini, 'Monarch of the Trumpet': New Light on His Works." *Historic Brass Society Journal* 6 (1994): 32–60.

Dahlqvist, Reine. *The Keyed Trumpet and Its Greatest Virtuoso, Anton Weidinger*. Nashville: The Brass Press, 1975.

Davidson, Louis. *Trumpet Profiles*. Studio City, CA: Louis Davidson, 1975.

Dokshizer, Timofei. *The Memoirs of Timofei Dokshizer: An Autobiography*. Translated by Olga Braslavsky. Westfield, MA: International Trumpet Guild, 1997.

Dube, Steven. "Edward H. Tarr: Trumpet Scholar Extraordinaire." *International Trumpet Guild Journal* 36, no. 2 (January 2012): 6–11, 35.

Fleet, Susan. "The Richest Kind of Experience: Edna White (1892–1992)." *International Trumpet Guild Journal* 36, no. 2 (January 2012): 12–16.

Fleming, Renee. *The Inner Voice: The Making of a Singer*. New York: Viking, 2004.

Galloway, Michael. "Ernst Albert Couturier: American Cornet Virtuoso." *International Trumpet Guild Journal* 14, no. 4 (1990): 4–56.

Grano, John Baptist. *Handel's Trumpeter: The Diary of John Grano*. Edited by John Ginger. Bucina: Historic Brass Society Series, 3. Stuyvesant, NY: Pendragon Press, 1998.

Hammer, Rusty. *P.S. Gilmore: The Authorized Biography of America's First Superstar.* Gainesville, FL: Rusty Hammer, 2006.

Haynie, John, and Anne Hardin. *Inside John Haynie's Studio: A Master Teacher's Lessons on Trumpet and Life.* Denton: University of North Texas Press, 2007.

Hickman, David R. *Trumpet Greats: A Biographical Dictionary.* Edited by Michel Laplace and Edward H. Tarr. Chandler, AZ: Hickman Music Editions, 2013.

Hickman, Jane W., and Del Lyren. *Magnificent Méndez.* 2nd edition. Tempe, AZ: Summit Records, 2005.

Irish, John. "Crispian Steele-Perkins: The King's Trumpeter." *International Trumpet Guild Journal* 27, no. 4 (June 2003): 17–26.

Jakobsen Barth, Verena. *Die Trompete als Soloinstrument in der Kunstmusik Europas seit 1900 mit besonderer Berücksichtigung der Entwicklung ab 1980 am Beispiel der Solisten Håkan Hardenberger, Ole Edvard Antonsen und Reinhold Friedrich.* Gothenburg, Sweden: University of Gothenburg, 2007.

Jones, Charles K. *Francis Johnson, 1792–1844: Chronicle of a Black Musician in Early Nineteenth-Century Philadelphia.* Bethlehem, PA: Lehigh University Press, 2006.

Keim, Friedel. *Das Grosse Buch der Trompete.* Mainz, Germany: Schott Musik International, 2005.

———. *Das Grosse Buch der Trompete, Band 2.* Mainz, Germany: Schott Musik International, 2009.

Lindner, Andreas. *Die kaiserlichen Hoftrompeter und Hofpauker im 18. und 19. Jahrhundert.* Wiener Veröffentlichungen zur Musikwissenschaft, 36. Tutzing, Germany: Hans Schneider Verlag, 1999.

Macaluso, Rosario. "A Grand Master: Théo Charlier." Translated by Jeffrey Agrell. *International Trumpet Guild Journal* 25, no. 4 (June 2001): 30–36.

Mathez, Jean-Pierre. *Joseph Jean-Baptiste Laurent Arban (1825–1889).* Moudon, Switzerland: Editions BIM, 1977.

Meucci, Renato. "Cesare Bendinelli: Some Recent Biographical Discoveries." *Historic Brass Society Journal* 24 (2012): 37–60.

Miller, Betsy G. "Anna Teresa Berger, Cornet Virtuoso." *International Trumpet Guild Journal* 22, no. 3 (February 1998): 43–49.

Shamu, Geoffrey. "Merri Franquin and His Contribution to the Art of Trumpet Playing." PhD dissertation, Boston University, 2009.

Shook, Brian A. *Last Stop, Carnegie Hall: New York Philharmonic Trumpeter William Vacchiano.* Denton: University of North Texas Press, 2011.

Smith, Andre M. "Max Schlossberg: Founder of the American School of Trumpet Playing in the Twentieth Century." *International Trumpet Guild Journal* 21, no. 4 (May 1997): 23, 33.

Swafford, Jan. *Johannes Brahms: A Biography.* New York: Vintage Books, 1997.

Tarr, Edward H. "Ferdinand Weinschenk (1831–1910), Pivotal Figure in German Trumpet History." *Historic Brass Society Journal* 11 (1999): 10–36.

———. "Theodore Hoch, the 'Much Beloved Solo Cornetist of Bilse's Capelle'." *Historic Brass Society Journal* 19 (2007): 71–101.

Teachout, Terry. *Pops. A Life of Louis Armstrong.* New York: Houghton Mifflin Harcourt, 2009.

West, James. "In Memoriam: An Interview with Armando Ghitalla." *International Trumpet Guild Journal* 26, no. 3 (March 2002): 49–52.

CHAMBER MUSIC

Bosarge, Jonathan Todd. "An Overview of the Pedagogical Benefits of Trumpet Ensemble Playing." PhD dissertation, Ohio State University, 2010. ProQuest (AAT 3417848).

Burkhart, Raymond David. "Brass Chamber Music in Lyceum and Chautauqua." PhD dissertation, Claremont Graduate University, 2010.

Chumov, Leonid. "History of Russian Brass Ensembles." *International Trumpet Guild Journal* 19, no. 1 (1994): 23–43.

Dulin, Mark. "The Trumpets of the American Brass Quintet." *International Trumpet Guild Journal* 36, no. 1 (October 2011): 37–43.

Everett, Thomas G. "An Interview with Robert King." Updated and reprinted by the International Trumpet Guild from an article in *The Brass World* 2, no. 4 (November 2, 1974): 84–92. *International Trumpet Guild Journal* Resource Reprint (2000), www.trumpetguild.org/pdf/rareverettking.pdf (accessed August 17, 2012).

Gorman, Kurt. "The Trumpet in Mixed Chamber Ensembles." *International Trumpet Guild Journal* 32, no. 2 (January 2008): 26–29.

Hagarty, Scott. "Repertoire of the New York Brass Quintet." *International Trumpet Guild Journal* 35, no. 2 (January 2011): 6–16.

Lapie, Raymond. *Jean-François-Victor Bellon 1795–1869.* Vuarmarens, Switzerland: Editions BIM, 2000.

———. "A Sensational Discovery: 12 Original Brass Quintets by Jean Bellon (1850), Part I." *Brass Bulletin* 109 (2000): 32–43.

———. "A Sensational Discovery: 12 Original Brass Quintets by Jean Bellon (1850), Part II." *Brass Bulletin* 110 (2000): 58–71.

Lindahl, Robert Gordon. "Brass Quintet Instrumentation: Tuba Versus Bass Trombone." PhD dissertation, Arizona State University, 1988. ProQuest (AAT 8907717).

Mathez, Jean-Pierre. "Evolution of Trumpet Ensembles." *Brass Bulletin* 94 (1996): 11–25.

McDonald, Donna. *The Odyssey of the Philip Jones Brass Ensemble.* Bulle, Switzerland: Editions BIM, 1986.

Metcalf, Owen Wells. "The New York Brass Quintet: Its History and Influence on Brass Literature and Performance." PhD dissertation, Indiana University, 1978.

Nilsson, Ann-Marie. "Brass Instruments in Small Swedish Wind Ensembles During the Late Nineteenth Century." *Historic Brass Society Journal* 13 (2001): 176–209.

Shakespeare, Margaret. "40 Years of the ABQ." *American Brass Quintet Newsletter* 8, no. 1 (November 2000): 1–7.

Sherry, James. "The New York Brass Quintet (1954–1985): Pioneers of Brass Chamber Music." PhD dissertation, Peabody Institute of the Johns Hopkins University, 2002.

Smith, Andre M. "The History of the Four Quintets for Brass by Victor Ewald." *International Trumpet Guild Journal* 18, no. 4 (May 1994): 4–33.

Tunnell, Michael H. "An Essay on Selected Trumpet Excerpts from Brass Quintets by Ingolf Dahl, Gunther Schuller, Alvin Etler, and Jan Bach." *International Trumpet Guild Journal* 8, no. 3 (February 1984): 14–38.

Walters, Rick. *The Canadian Brass Book: The Story of the World's Favorite Brass Ensemble*. Milwaukee, WI: Hal Leonard, 1992.

GENERAL MUSICAL TOPICS

Baines, Anthony. *Brass Instruments: Their History and Development*. London: Faber & Faber, 1980.

———. *Woodwind Instruments: Their History and Development*. Mineola, NY: Dover, 1991.

Berlioz, Hector, and Richard Strauss. *Treatise on Instrumentation*. Translated by Theodore Front. New York: Dover Publications, 1991.

Bevan, Clifford. *The Tuba Family*. 2nd edition, revised, enlarged, and updated. Hampshire, England: Piccolo Press, 2000.

Braun, Joachim. *Music in Ancient Israel/Palestine: Archaeological, Written, and Comparative Sources*. Grand Rapids: William B. Eerdmans, 2002.

Bridges, Glenn. *Pioneers in Brass*. Originally published in 1965. Enumclaw, WA: Trescott Research, 2001. CD-ROM.

Burns, Ken. *Jazz: A Film by Ken Burns*. PBS Home Video, 2001. 10-DVD set. 1,140 min.

Campbell, Murray, Clive Greated, and Arnold Myers. *Musical Instruments: History, Technology, and Performance of Instruments of Western Music*. Oxford: Oxford University Press, 2004.

Dickreiter, Michael. *Score Reading: A Key to the Music Experience*. Translated by Reinhard G. Pauly. Portland, OR: Amadeus Press, 2003.

Fennell, Frederick. *Time and the Winds: A Short History of the Use of Wind Instruments in the Orchestra, Band and the Wind Ensemble*. Kenosha: Leblanc Educational Publications, 1954.

Grun, Bernard. *The Timetables of History: A Horizontal Linkage of People and Events*. 4th revised edition. New York: Touchstone Books, 2005.

Hansen, Richard K. *The American Wind Band: A Cultural History*. Chicago: GIA Publications, 2005.

Hazen, Robert, and Margaret Hindle Hazen. *The Music Men: An Illustrated History of Brass Bands in America, 1800–1920*. Washington, DC: Smithsonian Institution Press, 1987.

Helmholtz, Hermann. *On the Sensations of Tone as a Physiological Basis for the Theory of Music*. Translated by Alexander J. Ellis. New York: Dover, 1954.

Herbert, Trevor. "Brass Bands and Other Vernacular Brass Traditions." In *The Cambridge Companion to Brass Instruments*, edited by Trevor Herbert and John Wallace, 177–92. Cambridge: Cambridge University Press, 1997.

———. *The Trombone*. Yale Musical Instruments Series. New Haven and London: Yale University Press, 2006.

———. "Brass Playing in the Early Twentieth Century: Idioms and Cultures of Performance." In *Early Twentieth-Century Brass Idioms: Art, Jazz, and Other Popular Traditions*, edited by Howard Weiner, xi–xvii. Lanham, MD: Scarecrow Press, 2009.

Herbert, Trevor, and Helen Barlow. *Music and the British Military in the Long Nineteenth Century*. Oxford: Oxford University Press, 2013.

Herbert, Trevor, and John Wallace, eds. *The Cambridge Companion to Brass Instruments*. Cambridge Companions to Music. Cambridge, UK: Cambridge University Press, 1997.

Koehler, Elisa. "Banda Minichini: An Italian Band in America." PhD dissertation, Peabody Institute of Johns Hopkins University, 1996. ProQuest (AAT 9639459).

———. "The Italian Wind Band: Its Heritage and Legacy." *Journal of the Conductors Guild* 16, no. 2 (Fall 1997): 96–105.

Landels, John G. *Music in Ancient Greece and Rome*. New York: Routledge, 2001.

Nelson, David P. *Solkaṭṭu Manual: An Introduction to the Rhythmic Language of South Indian Music*. Middletown, CT: Weslyan University Press, 2008.

Nevin, Jeff. *Virtuoso Mariachi*. Lanham, MD: University Press of America, 2002.

Rees, Jasper. *A Devil to Play: One Man's Year-Long Quest to Master the Orchestra's Most Difficult Instrument*. New York: Harper Collins, 2008.

Rehrig, William H. *The Heritage Encyclopedia of Band Music*. Westerville, OH: Integrity Press, 1996.

Rimsky-Korsakov, Nicolay. *Principles of Orchestration*. Translated by Edward Agate. Edited by Maximilian Steinberg. First published in 1891. New York: Dover, 1964.

Sadie, Stanley, and John Tyrrell, eds. *The New Grove Dictionary of Music and Musicians*. Oxford: Oxford

University Press, 2004. Available online at www.oxford musiconline.com.

Schwartz, H. W. *Bands of America*. New York: Doubleday, 1957.

Smith, Brian. *Bandstands to Battlefields: Brass Bands in 19th-Century America*. Gansevoort, NY: Corner House Historical Publications, 2004.

Spitzer, John, and Neal Zaslaw. *The Birth of the Orchestra*. New York: Oxford University Press, 2004.

VanderCook, Hale A. *Expression in Music*. Milwaukee, WI: Rubank, 1942.

Vessella, Alessandro. *Instrumentation Studies for Band*. Translated by Thomas V. Fraschillo. Originally published in 1955. Milan: Ricordi, 2001.

West, Martin Litchfield. *Ancient Greek Music*. New York: Oxford University Press, 1992.

Whitener, Scott. *A Complete Guide to Brass: Instruments and Technique*. 3rd edition. New York: Schirmer, 2006.

Widor, Charles-Marie. *The Technique of the Modern Orchestra: A Manual of Practical Instrumentation*. Translated by Edward Suddard. Originally published in 1904 and revised in 1946. New York: Dover, 2005.

Woolf, Adam. *Sackbut Solutions: A Practical Guide to Playing the Sackbut*. Mechelen, Belgium: Adam Woolf, 2009.

Yeo, Douglas. *Approaching the Serpent: An Historical and Pedagogical Overview*. Berlioz Historical Brass, 2010. BHB DVD 001.

HISTORICALLY INFORMED PERFORMANCE

Butt, John. *Playing with History: The Historical Approach to Musical Performance*. Cambridge: Cambridge University Press, 2002.

Carter, Stewart. *A Performer's Guide to Seventeenth-Century Music*. 2nd edition, revised and expanded by Jeffrey Kite-Powell. Bloomington: Indiana University Press, 2012.

Dahlqvist, Reine. "Pitches of German, French, and English Trumpets in the 17th and 18th Centuries." *Historic Brass Society Journal* 5 (1993): 42–74.

Dickey, Bruce. "L'accento: In Search of a Forgotten Ornament." *Historic Brass Society Journal* 3 (1991): 98–121.

———. "Ornamentation in Sixteenth-Century Music." In *A Performer's Guide to Renaissance Music*, edited by Jeffrey Kite-Powell, 300–324. Bloomington: Indiana University Press, 2007.

———. "Ornamentation in Early Seventeenth-Century Italian Music." In *A Performer's Guide to Seventeenth-Century Music*, edited by Stewart Carter, 293–316. Bloomington: Indiana University Press, 2012.

Donnington, Robert. *Baroque Music, Style and Performance: A Handbook*. New York: Norton, 1982.

———. *The Interpretation of Early Music, New Revised Edition*. New York: W. W. Norton, 1992.

Duffin, Ross W. *How Equal Temperament Ruined Harmony (and Why You Should Care)*. New York: W. W. Norton, 2007.

Haskell, Harry. *The Early Music Revival: A History*. Mineola: Dover, 1996.

Haynes, Bruce. "Cornetts and Historical Pitch Standards." *Historic Brass Society Journal* 6 (1994): 84–109.

———. *A History of Performing Pitch: The Story of "A."* Lanham, MD: Scarecrow Press, 2002.

———. *The End of Early Music: A Period Performer's History of Music for the Twenty-First Century*. Oxford: Oxford University Press, 2007.

Hunsaker, Leigh Anne. "Baroque Trumpet Study in the United States." *International Trumpet Guild Journal* 31, no. 4 (June 2005): 37–43.

———. "Edward H. Tarr and the Historic Brass Revival." *International Trumpet Guild Journal* 35, no. 2 (January 2007): 35–39.

Kite-Powell, Jeffrey, ed. *A Performer's Guide to Renaissance Music*. 2nd edition. Bloomington: Indiana University Press, 2007.

Kivy, Peter. *Authenticities: Philosophical Reflections on Musical Performance*. Ithaca: Cornell University Press, 1995.

Lawson, Colin, and Robin Stowell. *The Historical Performance of Music: An Introduction*. Cambridge: Cambridge University Press, 1999.

Leonards, Petra. "Historische Quellen zur Spielweise des Zinke." *Basler Jahrbuch für Musikpraxis* 5 (1981): 315–46.

Little, Meredith, and Natalie Jenne. *Dance and the Music of J. S. Bach*. Bloomington: Indiana University Press, 2001.

MacCracken, Thomas G. "Die Verwendung der Blechblasinstrumente bei J.S. Bach unter besonderer Berücksichtigung der *Tromba da tirarsi*." *Bach-Jahrbuch* 70 (1984): 59–89.

Madeuf, Jean-Francois. "The Revival of the Natural Trumpet in the Baroque Repertory." *Early Music* 38, no. 2 (2010): 203–4.

Mather, Betty Bang. *Dance Rhythms of the French Baroque: A Handbook for Performance*. Bloomington: Indiana University Press, 1988.

Neumann, Frederick. *Ornamentation in Baroque and Post-Baroque Music, with Special Emphasis on J. S. Bach*. Princeton: Princeton University Press, 1983.

Nicholson, Graham. "The Unnatural Trumpet." *Early Music* 38, no. 2 (2010): 193–202.

Steele-Perkins, Crispian. "Practical Observations on Natural, Slide and Flat Trumpets." *The Galpin Society Journal* 42 (August 1989): 122–27.

Tarr, Edward H., and Bruce Dickey. *Articulation in Early Wind Music: A Source Book with Commentary*. Practica

Musicale, 8. Winterthur, Switzerland: Amadeus Verlag, 2007.

Tarushkin, Richard. *Text and Act.* Oxford: Oxford University Press, 1995.

Terry, Charles Sanford. *Bach's Orchestra.* London: Oxford University Press, 1932.

HISTORIC SOURCES

Altenburg, Johann Ernst. *Essay on an Introduction to the Heroic and Musical Trumpeters' and Kettledrummers' Art: For the Sake of a Wider Acceptance of the Same, Described Historically, Theoretically, and Practically and Illustrated with Examples.* Translated by Edward H. Tarr. Originally published in 1795. Nashville: The Brass Press, 1974.

Anzenberger, Friedrich. "Method Books for Natural Trumpet in the 19th Century: An Annotated Bibliography." *Historic Brass Society Journal* 5 (1993): 1–21.

———. "Method Books for Keyed Trumpet in the 19th Century: An Annotated Bibliography." *Historic Brass Society Journal* 6 (1994): 1–10.

Arban, Jean-Baptiste. *Complete Celebrated Method for the Trumpet.* Dr. Charles Colin edition. New York: Charles Colin, n.d.

Baldwin, David. "Arbuckle's Complete Cornet Method (1866)." *International Trumpet Guild Journal* 14, no. 3 (February 1990): 31–37.

Bassano, Giovanni. *Ricercate/passage et cadentie, Venice, 1585.* Edited by Richard Erig. Zürich: Musikverlag zum Pelikan, 1976.

Bendinelli, Cesare. *Tutta L'arte Della Trombetta (1614).* Edited by Edward H. Tarr. Facsimile edition. Vuarmarens, Switzerland: Editions BIM, 2011.

Bovicelli, Giovanni Battista. *Regole, passaggi di musica, madrigal et motetti passegiati, Venice, 1594.* Edited by Nanie Bridgman. Kassel: Bärenreiter, 1957.

Briney, Bruce C. "The Methods and Etudes of Wilhelm Wurm." *International Trumpet Guild Journal* 21, no. 3 (February 1997): 51–64.

Brunelli, Antonio. *Varii esercitii, Firenze, 1614.* Edited by Richard Erig. Zürich: Musikverlag zum Pelikan, 1977.

Burney, Charles. *An Account of the Musical Performances in Westminster Abbey and the Pantheon May 26th, 27th, 29th and June 3rd and 5th, 1784 in Commemoration of Handel.* Facsimile of the 1785 edition. London: Travis and Emery, 2008.

Dalla Casa, Girolamo. *Il Vero Modo di Diminuir con tutte le sorti di stromenti, Venice, 1584.* Edited by Arnaldo Forni. Bologna: Sala Bolognese, 1970.

Dana, William H. *J. W. Pepper's Practical Guide and Study to the Secret of Arranging Band Music, or the Amateur's Guide.* Philadelphia: J. W. Pepper, 1878.

Dauverné, François Georges Auguste. "Méthode pour la trompette." Translated by Chenier, Gaetan, Ruby Miller, Rebecca Pike Orval, and Jeffrey Snedeker. *Historic Brass Society Journal* 3 (1991): 179–261.

———. *Méthode pour la trompette, précédée d'un précis historique sur cet instrument en usage chez les différents peuples depuis l'antiquité jusqu'à nos jours: ouvrage approuvé et adopté par la Section de Musique de l'Académie des Beaux Arts (Institute de France) et par le Conservatoire National de Musique.* G. Brandus, Dufour, 1857. Facsimile edition. Paris: Edition I.M.D. Diffusion Apreges, 1991.

Dodworth, Allen. *Dodworth's Brass Band School.* New York: H. B. Dodworth, 1853.

Fantini, Girolamo. *Modo per imparare a sonare di tromba tanto di guerra quanto musicalmente, 1638.* Facsimile reprint with English translation and critical commentary by Edward H. Tarr. Nashville: The Brass Press, 1978.

———. *Modo per imparare a sonare di tromba (1638).* Urtext edition by Igino Conforzi. Bologna: UT Orpheus Edizioni, 1998.

Forestier, Joseph. *Grande Méthode de cornet à pistons.* Revised by E. Guilbaut (1932). In three volumes. Paris: International Music Diffusion, 2004.

Franquin, Merri. *Méthode complète de trompette modern, de cornet et de bugle [flugelhorn], théorique et pratique.* Paris: Enoch, 1908.

Harper, Thomas. *Instructions for the Trumpet.* Facsimile of the 1837 edition. Homer, NY: Spring Tree Enterprises, 1998.

Hotteterre, Jacques Martin. *Principles of the Flute, Recorder, and Oboe.* Translated by Paul Marshall Douglass. Originally published in Paris in 1707. Mineola, NY: Dover, 1968.

Kenyon de Pascual, Beryl. "Jose de Juan Martinez' *Método de Clarin* (1830): Introduction and Translation." *Historic Brass Society Journal* 5 (1993): 92–106.

Kosleck, Julius. *Julius Kosleck's School for the Trumpet.* Revised and adapted to the study of the "Trumpet-a-Pistons in F" by Walter Morrow. London: Breitkopf & Haertel, 1907.

Morrow, Walter. "The Trumpet as an Orchestral Instrument." *Proceedings of the Musical Association* 21 (1895): 133–47.

Praetorius, Michael. *Syntagma Musicum III, Wolfenbüttel, 1619.* Translated and edited by Jeffrey Kite-Powell. Oxford: Oxford University Press, 2004.

Quantz, Johann Joachim. *Versuch einer Anweisung die Flöte Traversiere zu Spielen [On Playing the Flute, Berlin, 1752].* Translated by Edward R. Reilley. 2nd edition. Boston: Northeastern University Press, 2001.

Rognoni, Francesco. *Selva de Varii Passaggi, Milan, 1620.* Edited by Arnaldo Forni. Bologna: Sala Bolognese, 2001.

Rostirolla, Giancarlo. "Regole, Passaggi Di Musica (1594) by Gio. Battista Bovicelli (Preface)." Translated by

Jesse Rosenberg. *Historic Brass Society Journal* 4 (1992): 27–44.

Roy, C. Eugène. *Tutor for the Natural Trumpet and the Keyed Trumpet/Keyed Bugle (1824 Facsimile)*. HKB—Historic Brass Series. Vuarmarens, Switzerland: Editions BIM, 2009.

HISTORY OF THE TRUMPET FAMILY

Ahrens, Christian. *Valved Brass: The History of an Invention*. Translated by Steven E. Plank. Bucina: The Historic Brass Society Series. Edited by Stewart Carter. Hillsdale, NY: Pendragon Press, 2008.

Albrecht, Theodore. "Beethoven's Brass Players: New Discoveries in Composer-Performer Relations." *Historic Brass Society Journal* 18 (2006): 47–72.

Barclay, Robert. *The Art of the Trumpet-Maker*. Early Music Series. Oxford: Clarendon Press, 1992.

Bate, Philip. *The Trumpet and Trombone. An Outline of Their History, Development and Construction*. New York: W. W. Norton, 1966.

Beck, Frederick A. "The Flugelhorn: Its History and Development." *International Trumpet Guild Journal* 5 (October 1980): 2–13.

Brownlow, Art. *The Last Trumpet. A History of the English Slide Trumpet*. Bucina: The Historic Brass Society Series. Edited by Stewart Carter. New York: Pendragon Press, 1996.

Burrows, Donald. "Of Handel, London Trumpeters, and Trumpet Music." *Historic Brass Society Journal* 11 (1999): 1–10.

Carse, Adam. "Adolphe Sax and the Distin Family." *The Music Review* 6 (1945): 193–201.

Cassone, Gabriele. *The Trumpet Book*. Translated by Tom Dambly. Varese, Italy: Zecchini Editore, 2009.

Collins, Timothy. "'Of the Differences Between Trumpeters and City Tower Musicians.' The Relationship of Stadtpfeifer and Kammeradschaft Trumpeters." *The Galpin Society Journal* 53 (April 2000): 51–59.

———. "Mr. Clarke on the Trumpet: Herbert L. Clarke's Famous Letter in Context." *International Trumpet Guild Journal* 33, no. 4 (June 2009): 6–21, 40.

Csiba, Gisela, and Jozsef Csiba. *Die Blechbasinstrumente in J. S. Bach's Werken*. Berlin: Edition Merseburger, 1994.

Dahlqvist, Reine. *The Keyed Trumpet and Its Greatest Virtuoso, Anton Weidinger*. Nashville: The Brass Press, 1975.

Downey, Peter. "The Renaissance Slide Trumpet: Fact or Fiction?" *Early Music* 12, no. 1 (February 1984): 26–33.

Dunnick, D. Kim. "Twenty Years of the International Trumpet Guild." *International Trumpet Guild Journal* 21, no. 2 (February 1996): 42–47.

Eichborn, Hermann Ludwig. *The Old Art of Clarino Playing on Trumpets*. Translated by Bryan R. Simms. Denver, CO: Tromba Publications, 1976.

Eldredge, Niles. "A Brief History of Piston-Valved Cornets." *Historic Brass Society Journal* 14 (2002): 337–90.

Eliason, Robert E. *Keyed Bugles in the United States*. Washington, DC: Smithsonian Institution Press, 1972.

———. *Early American Brass Makers*. Nashville: Brass Press, 1979.

Franquin, Merri. "La Trompette et le Cornet." In *Encyclopédie de la Musique et Dictionnaire du Conservatoire*, part 2, vol. 3, pp. 1597–1637. Paris: Delagrave, 1927.

Gosch, Werner. "Trumpet and Horn Music in 18th Century Weissenfels." Translated by Edward H. Tarr. *International Trumpet Guild Journal* 17, no. 1 (1992): 24–30.

Hall, Jack. "The Saga of the Cornet and Six of Its Outstanding Artists." *Brass Bulletin* 12 (1975): 19–27.

Hedwig, Douglas. "Bugle Calls and Bel Canto: The Yang & Yin of Trumpet Playing." *International Trumpet Guild Journal* 30, no. 4 (June 2006): 13–17.

Henssen, Ralph. "The Use of Trumpet on Board Ships of the Dutch East India Company." *International Trumpet Guild Journal* 35, no. 2 (January 2011): 27–37.

Herbert, Trevor. "'Men of Great Perfection in Their Science': The Trumpeter as Musician and Diplomat in England in the Later Fifteenth and Sixteenth Centuries." *Historic Brass Society Journal* 23 (2011): 1–23.

Heyde, Herbert. "On the Early History of Valves and Valve Instruments in Germany (1814–1833)." *Brass Bulletin* 24 (1978): 9–33; 25 (1979): 41–50; 26 (1979): 69–82; 27 (1979): 51–61.

Hoover, Cynthia. "A Trumpet Battle at Niblo's Pleasure Garden." *The Musical Quarterly* 55, no. 3 (July 1969): 384–95.

Howey, Henry. "The Lives of Hoftrompeter and Stadtpfeiffer as Portrayed in Three Novels of Daniel Speer." *Historic Brass Society Journal* 3 (1991): 65–78.

Keim, Friedel. *Das Grosse Buch der Trompete*. Mainz, Germany: Schott Musik International, 2005.

———. *Das Grosse Buch der Trompete, Band 2*. Mainz, Germany: Schott Musik International, 2009.

Klaus, Sabine K. *Trumpets and Other High Brass, Vol. 1: Instruments of the Single Harmonic Series*. Vermillion, SD: National Music Museum, 2012.

Knudsvig, Peter. "Louis Klöpfel, Gustav Heim, and the Legacy of American Classical Trumpeting." *International Trumpet Guild Journal* 36, no. 4 (June 2012): 39–43.

Koehler, Elisa. *Fanfares & Finesse: A Performer's Guide to Trumpet History and Literature*. Bloomington: Indiana University Press, 2014.

Kurtzman, Jeffrey, and Linda Maria Koldau. "*Trombe, Trombe D'argento, Trombe Squarciate, Trombone*, and *Pifferi* in Venetian Processions and Ceremonies of the Sixteenth and Seventeenth Centuries." *Journal of Seventeenth-Century Music* 8, no. 1 (2002). Available online at www.sscm-jscm.org/v8/no1/kurtzman_v.html (accessed May 29, 2013).

Lowrey, Alvin. *Lowrey's International Trumpet Discography*. 2 vols. Columbia, SC: Camden House, 1990.

Menke, Werner. *History of the Trumpet of Bach and Handel*. Translated by Gerald Abraham. Brass Research Series. Nashville: The Brass Press, 1985.

Proksch, Bryan. "Buhl, Dauverne, Kresser, and the Trumpet in Paris Ca. 1800–1840." *Historic Brass Society Journal* 20 (2008): 69–91.

Rose, Stephen. "Trumpeters and Diplomacy on the Eve of the Thirty Years' War: The *album amicorum* of Jonas Kröschel." *Early Music* 40, no. 3 (2012): 379–92.

Savan, Jamie. "From Hornet to Cornett: In Search of the 'Missing Link.'" *Historic Brass Society Journal* 24 (2012): 1–23.

Schwartz, Richard I. *The Cornet Compendium: The History and Development of the Nineteenth-Century Cornet*. Privately published, 2002. Available online at www .angelfire.com/music2/thecornetcompendium (accessed September 29, 2014).

Schwartz, Richard, and Iris Schwartz. "Bands and Cornet Soloists at the St. Louis World's Fair of 1904." *Historic Brass Society Journal* 20 (2008): 175–204.

Shamu, Geoffrey. "Inventing the Warm-Up: Merri Franquin's 'Principles of Study'." *Historic Brass Society Journal* 24 (2012): 129–57.

Smithers, Don. "The Hapsburg Imperial *Trompeter* and *Heerpaucker* Privileges of 1653." *The Galpin Society Journal* 24 (1971): 84–95.

———. "The Baroque Trumpet after 1721: Some Preliminary Observations. Part One: Science and Practice." *Early Music* 5, no. 2 (April 1977): 176–79.

———. "The Baroque Trumpet after 1721: Some Preliminary Observations. Part Two: Function and Use." *Early Music* 6, no. 3 (July 1978): 356–61.

———. *The Music and History of the Baroque Trumpet before 1721*. 2nd edition. Carbondale: Southern Illinois University Press, 1988.

———. "Bach, Reiche and the Leipzig Collegia Musica." *Historic Brass Society Journal* 2 (1990): 1–51.

Sorenson, Scott, and John Webb. "The Harpers and the Trumpet." *The Galpin Society Journal* 39 (September 1986): 35–57.

Steele-Perkins, Crispian. *Trumpet*. Yehudi Menuhin Music Guides. London: Kahn & Averill, 2001.

Tarr, Edward H. "Mandate Against the Unauthorized Playing of Trumpets and Beating of Military Kettledrums. Dated the 23rd of July in the Year 1711. (English Translation and Commentary)." *International Trumpet Guild Journal* special supplement (1991).

———. "The Romantic Trumpet." *Historic Brass Society Journal* 5 (1993): 262–79.

———. "The Romantic Trumpet: Part Two." *Historic Brass Society Journal* 6 (1994): 110–215.

———. "Further Mandate Against the Unauthorized Playing of Trumpets (Dresden, 1736): Introduction and Translation." *Historic Brass Society Journal* 13 (2001): 67–89.

———. *East Meets West: The Russian Trumpet Tradition from the Time of Peter the Great to the October Revolution, with a Lexicon of Trumpeters Active in Russia from the Seventeenth Century to the Twentieth*. Bucina: The Historic Brass Society Series, 4. Hillsdale, NY: Pendragon Press, 2003.

———. "'The Bach Trumpet' in the Nineteenth and Twentieth Centuries." In *Musique Ancienne—Instruments et Imagination: Actes des Rencontres Internationales Harmoniques, Lausanne 2004 [Music of the Past—Instruments and Imagination: Proceedings of the Harmoniques International Congress, Lausanne 2004]*, edited by M. Latchmam, 17–48. Bern: Peter Lang, 2006.

———. *The Trumpet*. 3rd edition, revised and enlarged. Translated by S. E. Plank and Edward H. Tarr. Chandler, AZ: Hickman Music Editions, 2008.

———. *Bendinelli: Tutta l'arte della Trombetta (1614)*. Complete English Translation, Biography, and Critical Commentary. Revised, augmented edition. Vuarmarens, Switzerland: The Brass Press/Editions BIM, 2011.

Wallace, John, and Alexander McGrattan. *The Trumpet*. Yale Musical Instrument Series. New Haven and London: Yale University Press, 2011.

INSTRUMENTS AND EQUIPMENT

Barclay, Robert. *The Art of the Trumpet-Maker*. Early Music Series. Oxford: Clarendon Press, 1992.

Beck, Frederick A. "The Flugelhorn: Its History and Development." *International Trumpet Guild Journal* 5 (October 1980): 2–13.

Beißwenger, Kirsten, and Uwe Wolf. "Tromba, Tromba Da Tirarsi Oder Corno? Zur Clarinostimme der Kantata 'Ein ungefärbt Gemüte'." *Bach-Jahrbuch* 79 (1993): 91–101.

Bennett, Conte Jay. "Selection of Trumpets and Mouthpieces by Classically-Trained Players for Commercial Music Performance." PhD dissertation, University of Miami, 2006. ProQuest (AAT 3243101).

Birkemeier, Richard P. "The F Trumpet and Its Last Virtuoso, Walter Morrow (1850–1937)." *Brass Bulletin* 65 (1989): 34–45.

Brownlow, Art. *The Last Trumpet: A History of the English Slide Trumpet*. Bucina: The Historic Brass Society Series. Edited by Stewart Carter. New York: Pendragon Press, 1996.

Burt, Jack. "The Rotary Trumpet: An Introduction." *International Trumpet Guild Journal* 28, no. 3 (March 2004): 52–55.

Carter, Stewart. "The Salem Cornetts." *Historic Brass Society Journal* 14 (2002): 279–308.

Cassone, Gabriele. *The Trumpet Book*. Translated by Tom Dambly. Varese, Italy: Zecchini Editore, 2009.

Crown, Tom. "Mostly Mozart's Mutes." *International Trumpet Guild Journal* 8, no. 3 (February 1984): 9–13.

———. "Mutes from Monteverdi to Miles: Brass Instrument Mutes Through the Ages." Paper presented at the 23rd Annual Historic Brass Society Early Brass Festival. Spartanburg, SC, August 3, 2007. Available in video format online at www.tomcrownmutes.com/learn_history.html (accessed January 1, 2013).

Dahlqvist, Reine. *The Keyed Trumpet and Its Greatest Virtuoso, Anton Weidinger*. Nashville: The Brass Press, 1975.

———. "Gottfried Reiche's Instrument: A Problem of Classification." *Historic Brass Society Journal* 5 (1993): 174–91.

———. "Pitches of German, French, and English Trumpets in the 17th and 18th Centuries." *Historic Brass Society Journal* 5 (1993): 42–74.

DeCarlis, Nick. *Pocket Cornets: Actual Size*. Blurb.com, 2009.

Dickey, Bruce. "The Cornett." In *The Cambridge Companion to Brass Instruments*, edited by Trevor Herbert and John Wallace, 51–67. Cambridge: Cambridge University Press, 1997.

———. "Cornett and Sackbut." In *A Performer's Guide to Seventeenth-Century Music*, edited by Stewart Carter, 100–18. Bloomington: Indiana University Press, 2012.

Dudgeon, Ralph T. *The Keyed Bugle*. 2nd edition. Lanham, MD: Scarecrow Press, 2004.

Dudgeon, Ralph T., and Franz X. Streitwieser. *The Flügelhorn* [in German and English] [Das Flügelhorn]. Bergkirchen: Edition Bochinsky, 2004.

Duffin, Ross W. "The *trompette des menestrels* in the 15th-Century *alta cappella*." *Early Music* 17, no. 3 (August 1989): 397–402.

Eldredge, Niles. "A Brief History of Piston-Valved Cornets." *Historic Brass Society Journal* 14 (2002): 337–90.

Foster, John. *The Natural Trumpet and Other Related Instruments*. Sydney: Kookaburra Music, 2010.

Frederick, Matthew. "Instruments of Transition: The Keyed Bugles of the Smithsonian Institute." *International Trumpet Guild Journal* 36, no. 1 (October 2011): 10–51, 65.

Gekker, Chris. *Fifteen Studies for Piccolo Trumpet Plus Text on Repertoire, Style & Equipment*. New York: Charles Colin Music, 2005.

Güttler, Ludwig. "The Corno da Caccia in the Music of J. S. Bach." *Brass Bulletin* 91 (1995): 36–45.

Halfpenny, Eric. "William Shaw's 'Harmonic Trumpet'." *The Galpin Society Journal* 13 (July 1960): 7–13.

———. "William Bull and the English Baroque Trumpet." *The Galpin Society Journal* 15 (March 1962): 18–24.

———. "Early British Trumpet Mouthpieces." *The Galpin Society Journal* 20 (March 1967): 76–88.

———. "British Trumpet Mouthpieces: Addendum." *The Galpin Society Journal* 21 (March 1968): 185.

Hickman, David. *The Piccolo Trumpet Big Book*. Denver, CO: Tromba, 1991.

Hiller, Albert. *Das Grosse Buch vom Posthorn*. Wilhelmshaven: Heinrichshofen, 1985.

———. "The Posthorn of the 19th Century Royal Post Office in the Service of Folk Music." *Brass Bulletin* 50 (1985).

———. "Finger-Holes in Post Horns: An Explanation." *The Galpin Society Journal* 43 (March 1990): 161–64.

Kaminsky, Joseph. "Asante Ivory Trumpets in Time, Place, and Context: An Analysis of a Field Study." *Historic Brass Society Journal* 15 (2003): 259–90.

Kirk, Douglas. "Cornett." In *A Performer's Guide to Renaissance Music*, edited by Jeffrey Kite-Powell, 106–25. Bloomington: Indiana University Press, 2007.

Klaus, Sabine K. "More Thoughts on the Discipline of Organology." *Historic Brass Society Journal* 14 (2002): 1–10.

———. "A Fresh Look at 'Some Ingenious Mechanical Contrivance'—the Rodenbostel/Woodham Slide Trumpet." *Historic Brass Society Journal* 20 (2008): 37–67.

———. *Trumpets and Other High Brass, Vol. 1: Instruments of the Single Harmonic Series*. Vermillion, SD: National Music Museum, 2012.

Koehler, Elisa. *Fanfares & Finesse: A Performer's Guide to Trumpet History and Literature*. Bloomington: Indiana University Press, 2014.

Lasocki, David. "New Light on the Early History of the Keyed Bugle—Part I: The Astor Advertisement and Collins V. Green." *Historic Brass Society Journal* 21 (2009): 11–50.

Lessen, Martin, and Andre M. Smith. "A New Compensating Valve System for Brass Instruments." *International Trumpet Guild Journal* 19, no. 4 (May 1995): 47–56.

Lewis, H. M. "How the Cornet Became a Trumpet—the Instruments and Music of a Traditional Period in American Music: 1880–1925." *International Trumpet Guild Journal* 17, no. 1 (September 1991): 17–23, 26.

———. "Antique Cornets and Other Frustrations: A Performer's Guide to Cornets by the C.G. Conn Company, 1888–1911." *International Trumpet Guild Journal* 19, no. 4 (May 1995): 39–46.

———. "An Early Bach Cornet and Trumpet." *International Trumpet Guild Journal* 26, no. 3 (March 2002): 52–54.

Madeuf, Pierre-Yves, Jean-Francois Madeuf, and Graham Nicholson. "The Guitbert Trumpet: A Remarkable Discovery." *Historic Brass Society Journal* (1999): 181–86.

Malek, Jaromir. "Trumpets and Kohl-Tubes." *The Journal of Egyptian Archaeology* 77 (1991): 185–86.

Meucci, Renato. "The Pelitti Firm: Makers of Brass Instruments in Nineteenth-Century Milan." *Historic Brass Society Journal* 6 (1994): 304–33.

Mitroulia, Eugenia, and Arnold Myers. "Adolphe Sax: Visionary or Plagiarist?" *Historic Brass Society Journal* 20 (2008): 93–141.

———. "The Distin Family as Instrument Makers and Dealers 1845–1874." *Scottish Music Review* 2, no. 1 (2011): 1–20.

Myers, Arnold. "Brasswind Manufacturing at Boosey & Hawkes, 1930–1959." *Historic Brass Society Journal* 15 (2003): 55–72.

———. "How Different Are Cornets and Trumpets?" *Historic Brass Society Journal* 24 (2012): 113–28.

Myers, Arnold, and Niles Eldredge. "The Brasswind Production of Marthe Besson's London Factory." *The Galpin Society Journal* 59 (2006): 43–75.

Nussbaum, Jeffrey. "A Survey of Trumpet Makers World-Wide." *Historic Brass Society Newsletter*, no. 14 (Summer 2001): 12–19.

Nussbaum, Jeffrey, Niles Eldredge, and Robb Stewart. "Louis Armstrong's First Cornet?" *Historic Brass Society Journal* 15 (2003): 355–58.

Overton, Friend Robert. *Der Zink: Geschichte, Bauweise Und Spieltechnik Eines Historischen Musikinstruments.* Mainz: Schott, 1981.

Phillips, Edward. "The Keyed Trumpet and the Concerti of Haydn and Hummel: Products of the Enlightenment." *International Trumpet Guild Journal* 32, no. 4 (June 2008): 22–28.

Picon, Olivier. "The Corno da Tirarsi." Diploma Thesis, Schola Cantorum Basiliensis, 2010.

Pirtle, Scooter. "Evolution of the Bugle." In *A History of Drum and Bugle Corps. Volume 1*, edited by Steve Vickers, 63–90. Madison, WI: Drum Corps Sights and Sounds, 2002.

Plank, Steven E. "'Knowledge in the Making': Recent Discourse on Bach and the Slide Trumpet." *Historic Brass Society Journal* 8 (1996): 1–5.

———. "Trumpet and Horn." In *A Performer's Guide to Seventeenth-Century Music*, edited by Stewart Carter, 133–49. Bloomington: Indiana University Press, 2012.

Polk, Keith. "Augustein Schubinger and the Zinck: Innovation in Performance Practice." *Historic Brass Society Journal* 1 (1989): 83–92.

———. "The Trombone, the Slide Trumpet and the Ensemble Tradition of the Early Renaissance." *Early Music* 17, no. 3 (August 1989): 389–97.

Rice, Albert R. "Curtis Janssen and a Selection of Outstanding Brasses at the Fiske Museum, the Claremont College, California." *Historic Brass Society Journal* 17 (2005): 85–113.

Schwartz, Richard I. *The Cornet Compendium: The History and Development of the Nineteenth-Century Cornet.* Privately published, 2002. Available online at www.angelfire.com/music2/thecornetcompendium (accessed September 29, 2014).

Shamu, Geoffrey. "Inventing the Warm-Up: Merri Franquin's 'Principles of Study'." *Historic Brass Society Journal* 24 (2012): 129–57.

Smithers, Don. "The Trumpets of J. W. Haas: A Survey of Four Generations of Nuremberg Brass Instrument Makers." *The Galpin Society Journal* 18 (March 1965): 23–41.

Stewart, Robb. "The History of the Modern Trumpet or 'Get that #@$%&! Cornet out of my Orchestra'." http://robbstewart.com/Essays/HistoryModernTrumpet.html.

———. "Trumpet Schmumpet: Some Facts and Observations on the Difference between Trumpets and Cornets." http://robbstewart.com/Essays/TrumpetSchmumpet.html.

Strange, Richard. "Cornet vs. Trumpet: Is There a Valid Distinction in Today's Bands?" *Bandmasters Review* (Texas Bandmasters Association) (December 2004): 25–27.

Tarr, Edward H. "Why Do I—a Trumpeter—Play the Horn?" *International Trumpet Guild Newsletter* 3, no. 2 (February 1977): 6.

Utley, Joe R., and Sabine K. Klaus. "The "Catholic" Fingering—First Valve Semitone: Reversed Valve Order in Brass Instruments and Related Valve Constructions." *Historic Brass Society Journal* 15 (2003): 73–162.

Waterhouse, William. *The New Langwill Index: A Dictionary of Musical Wind-Instrument Makers and Inventors* London: Tony Bingham, 1993.

Webb, John. "The Billingsgate Trumpet." *The Galpin Society Journal* 41 (October 1988): 59–62.

———. "The English Slide Trumpet." *Historic Brass Society Journal* (1993): 280–87.

———. "The Flat Trumpet in Perspective." *The Galpin Society Journal* 46 (March 1993): 154–60.

Weiner, Howard. "Trombone Slide Lubrication and Other Practical Information for Brass Players in Joseph Froehlich's *Musikschule* (1813)." *Historic Brass Society Journal* 21 (2009): 51–67.

Wheeler, Joseph. "New Light on the Regent's Bugle with Some Notes on the Keyed Bugle." *The Galpin Society Journal* 19 (April 1966): 63–70.

Wulstan, David. "The Sounding of the Shofar." *The Galpin Society Journal* 26 (May 1973): 29–46.

Xanthoulis, Nikos. "The Salpinx in Greek Antiquity." *International Trumpet Guild Journal* 31, no. 1 (October 2006): 39–45.

Ziolkowski, John. "The Roman *Bucina*: A Distinct Musical Instrument?" *Historic Brass Society Journal* 14 (2002): 31–58.

JAZZ TRUMPET

Aebersold, Jamey. *How to Play Jazz and Improvise, Volume 1*. 6th edition. Book and CD set. New Albany, IN: Jamey Aebersold Jazz, 2000.

Barnhart, Scotty. *The World of Jazz Trumpet: A Comprehensive History and Practical Philosophy*. Milwaukee, WI: Hal Leonard, 2005.

Ecklund, Peter. *Great Cornet Solos of Bix Beiderbecke*. New York: Charles Colin, 1998.

———. "'Louis Licks' and Nineteenth-Century Cornet Etudes: The Roots of Melodic Improvisation as Seen in the Jazz Style of Louis Armstrong." *Historic Brass Society Journal* 13 (2001): 90–101.

Gabbard, Krin. *Hotter Than That: The Trumpet, Jazz, and American Culture*. New York: Faber and Faber, 2008.

Leach, Catherine F. "Confronting the Fear Factor." *International Trumpet Guild Journal* 36, no. 3 (March 2012): 46–47.

Levine, Mark. *The Jazz Theory Book*. Petaluma, CA: Sher Music, 1995.

Lynch, John H. *A New Approach to Altissimo Trumpet Playing*. Oskaloosa, IA: C. L. Barnhouse, 1984.

Mauleon, Rebecca. *Salsa Guidebook for Piano and Ensemble*. Petaluma, CA: Sher Music, 2005.

McNeil, John. *The Art of Jazz Trumpet*. Brooklyn, NY: Gerard & Sarzin, 1999.

Parker, Charlie. *Charlie Parker Ominibook for B-Flat Instruments*. Milwaukee, WI: Hal Leonard, 2009.

Raph, Alan. *Dance Band Reading and Interpretation*. Van Nuys, CA: Alfred, 1962.

The Real Book (B-Flat Edition). 6th edition. Milwaukee, WI: Hal Leonard, 2005.

Rubin, Joel E. "'Like a String of Pearls': Reflections on the Role of Brass Instrumentalists in Jewish Instrumental Klezmer Music and the Trope of 'Jewish Jazz'." In *Early Twentieth-Century Brass Idioms: Art, Jazz, and Other Popular Traditions*, edited by Howard Weiner, 77–102. Lanham, MD: Scarecrow Press, 2009.

Sanborn, Chase. *Jazz Tactics*. Toronto: Brass Tactics, 2002.

Shaw, Brian. *How to Play Lead Trumpet in a Big Band*. Tübingen, Germany: Advance Music, 2007.

Slone, Ken. *28 Modern Jazz Trumpet Solos*. Miami: Warner Brothers, 1983.

———. *28 Modern Jazz Trumpet Solos, Book 2*. Miami: Warner Brothers, 1995.

Tauber, Philip. *Solo Fluency: The Language of Modern Jazz Improvisation for Trumpet*. Carson City, NV: Seedling Music, 2009.

ORCHESTRAL PLAYING

Birkemeier, Richard P. "The History and Music of the Orchestral Trumpet of the Nineteenth Century, Part 1." *International Trumpet Guild Journal* 9, no. 3 (February 1985): 23–39.

———. "The History and Music of the Orchestral Trumpet of the Nineteenth Century, Part 2." *International Trumpet Guild Journal* 9, no. 4 (May 1985): 13–27.

Crown, Tom. "The Chicago Symphony Orchestra Trumpet Section 1902–1932." *International Trumpet Guild Journal* 35, no. 4 (June 2011): 38–47.

Daniels, David. *Orchestral Music: A Handbook*. Fourth edition. Lanham, MD: Scarecrow Press, 2005.

Dickreiter, Michael. *Score Reading: A Key to the Music Experience*. Translated by Reinhard G. Pauly. Portland, OR: Amadeus Press, 2003.

Hardin, Anne F. *A Trumpeter's Guide to Orchestral Excerpts*. 2nd edition, revised and enlarged. Columbia, SC: Camden House, 1986.

Hunsicker, J. David. "Surveys of Orchestral Audition Lists." *International Trumpet Guild Journal* 35, no. 3 (2011): 66–68.

Lewis, H. M. "Roger Voisin: An Orchestral Legend." *International Trumpet Guild Newsletter* 6, no. 2 (February 1980): 5–7.

Norris, Philip. *Top 50 Orchestral Audition Excerpts for Trumpet*. Libertyville, IL: Crown Music Press, 1997.

Sachs, Michael. "Using Different Keyed Instruments in the Orchestra: When, How, and Why." *International Trumpet Guild Journal* 35, no. 4 (June 2011): 84–87.

———. *The Orchestral Trumpet*. Tricordia, 2012.

Sachs, Michael, and Paul Yancich. "The Partnership of Trumpets and Timpani in Classical Repertoire." *International Trumpet Guild Journal* 36, no. 1 (October 2011): 80–86.

Schuller, Gunther. "Trumpet Transposition and Key Changes in Late 19th-Century Romantic Compositions." *International Trumpet Guild Journal* 13, no. 3 (February 1989): 19–24.

PEDAGOGY

Agrell, Jeffrey. *Improvisation Games for Classical Musicians: A Collection of Musical Games with Suggestions for Use*. Chicago: G.I.A. Publications, 2008.

Bachelder, Dan, and Norman Hunt. *Guide to Teaching Brass*. 6th edition. New York: McGraw Hill, 2002.

Baldwin, David. "J. B. Arban: Teaching Us for 134 Years." *International Trumpet Guild Journal* 33, no. 1 (October 2008): 37, 57.

Bosarge, Jonathan Todd. "An Overview of the Pedagogical Benefits of Trumpet Ensemble Playing." PhD dissertation, Ohio State University, 2010. ProQuest (AAT 3417848).

Brockmann, Nicole M. *From Sight to Sound: Improvisational Games for Classical Musicians*. Bloomington: Indiana University Press, 2009.

Callet, Jerome, and Bahb Civiletti. *Trumpet Secrets. Volume 1*. Staten Island, NY: Royal Press Printing, 2002.

Campos, Frank Gabriel. *Trumpet Technique*. New York: Oxford University Press, 2005.

Cassone, Gabriele. *The Trumpet Book*. Translated by Tom Dambly. Varese, Italy: Zecchini Editore, 2009.

Colin, Charles. *Advanced Lip Flexibilities*. New York: Charles Colin, 1972.

Collver, Michael. *222 Chop-Busters for the Cornetto*. Bedford, MA: Michael Collver, 1999.

Farley, Robert, and John Hutchins. *Natural Trumpet Studies*. Manton UK: Brass Wind Publications, 2003.

Foster, John. *The Natural Trumpet and Other Related Instruments*. Sydney: Kookaburra Music, 2010.

Gekker, Chris. *Fifteen Studies for Piccolo Trumpet Plus Text on Repertoire, Style & Equipment*. New York: Charles Colin Music, 2005.

———. "Performance Suggestions for J. S. Bach's 2nd Brandenburg Concerto." *International Trumpet Guild Journal* 31, no. 3 (March 2007): 69–70.

Gordon, Claude. *Brass Playing Is No Harder Than Deep Breathing*. New York: Carl Fischer, 1987.

Harnum, Johnathan. *Sound the Trumpet: How to Blow Your Own Horn*. Chicago: Sol Ut Press, 2006.

Haynie, John, and Anne Hardin. *Inside John Haynie's Studio: A Master Teacher's Lessons on Trumpet and Life*. Denton: University of North Texas Press, 2007.

Hickman, David. *Trumpet Pedagogy: A Compendium of Modern Teaching Techniques*. Edited by Amanda Pepping. Chandler, AZ: Hickman Music Editions, 2006.

Irons, Earl D. *Twenty-Seven Groups of Exercises for Cornet and Trumpet*. Revised edition. Originally published in 1938. San Antonio, TX: Southern Music Company, 1966.

Johnson, Keith. *The Art of Trumpet Playing*. Ames: Iowa State University Press, 1983.

Klickstein, Gerald. *The Musician's Way: A Guide to Practice, Performance, and Wellness*. Oxford: Oxford University Press, 2009.

Koehler, Elisa. "A Beginner's Guide to the Baroque Natural Trumpet." *International Trumpet Guild Journal* 26, no. 3 (March 2002): 16–24.

———. "A Trumpeter's Guide to the Cornett." *International Trumpet Guild Journal* 30, no. 2 (January 2006). 14–25, 31.

Laird, Michael. *Brassworkbook for Natural Trumpet*. Essex, UK: BrassWorks, 1999.

Shamu, Geoffrey. "Inventing the Warm-Up: Merri Franquin's 'Principles of Study'." *Historic Brass Society Journal* 24 (2012): 129–57.

Sherman, Roger. *The Trumpeter's Handbook. A Comprehensive Guide to Playing and Teaching the Trumpet*. Athens, OH: Accura Music, 1979.

Stamp, James. *Warm-Ups + Studies for Trumpet or Cornet/Flugelhorn*. Bulle, Switzerland: Editions BIM, 1982.

Tarr, Edward H. *The Art of Baroque Trumpet Playing, Vol. 1: Basic Exercises*. Mainz, Germany: Schott, 1999.

———. *The Art of Baroque Trumpet Playing, Vol. 2: Method of Ensemble Playing*. Mainz, Germany: Schott, 2000.

———. *The Art of Baroque Trumpet Playing, Vol. 3: A Beautiful Bouquet of the Finest Fanfares*. Mainz, Germany: Schott, 2000.

Thompson, James. *The Buzzing Book. Complete Method for Trumpet or Other Treble Clef Brass Instruments (Bb or C)*. Vuarmarens, Switzerland: Editions BIM, 2001.

West, Jeremy, and Susan Smith. *How to Play the Cornett*. London: JW Publications, 1995.

PERIODICALS

Brass Herald
Early Music
Early Music America
Galpin Society Journal
Historic Brass Society Journal
International Trumpet Guild Journal
The Instrumentalist

REPERTOIRE

Bach, Johann Sebastian *Bach for Brass, Vol. 1: Cantatas BWV 1–100*. Edited by Edward H. Tarr and Uwe Wolf. Stuttgart, Germany: Carus Verlag, 2007.

———. *Bach for Brass, Vol. 2: Cantatas BWV 101–200*. Edited by Edward H. Tarr and Uwe Wolf. Stuttgart, Germany: Carus Verlag, 2009.

———. *Bach for Brass, Vol. 3: Latin Sacred Music and Oratorios*. Edited by Edward H. Tarr and Uwe Wolf. Stuttgart, Germany: Carus Verlag, 2002.

———. *Bach for Brass, Vol. 4: Orchestral Works*. Edited by Edward H. Tarr and Uwe Wolf. Stuttgart, Germany: Carus Verlag, 2004.

Bickley, Diana. "The Trumpet Shall Sound: Some Reasons That Suggest Why Berlioz Altered the Part for *Trompette a Pistons* in His Overture *Waverley*." *Historic Brass Society Journal* 6 (1994): 61–83.

Biermann, Joanna Cobb. "Trumpets in 18th Century Darmstadt Symphonies." *International Trumpet Guild Journal* 35, no. 2 (January 2011): 75–76.

Boyd, Malcolm. *Bach: The Brandenburg Concertos*. Cambridge: Cambridge University Press, 1993.

Burrows, Donald. *Handel: Messiah*. Cambridge Music Handbooks. Cambridge: Cambridge University Press, 1991.

Carnovale, Norbert A., and Paul F. Doerksen. *Twentieth-Century Music for Trumpet and Orchestra: An Annotated Bibliography*. 2nd revised edition. Nashville, TN: The Brass Press, 1994.

Cipolla, Frank J., and Donald Hunsberger, eds. *The Wind Ensemble and Its Repertoire: Essays on the Fortieth Anniversary of the Eastman Wind Ensemble*. Rochester, NY: University of Rochester Press, 1994.

Collver, Michael, and Bruce Dickey. *A Catalog of Music for the Cornett*. Bloomington: Indiana University Press, 1996.

Cord, John T. "Francis Poulenc's *Sonata for Horn, Trumpet, and Trombone.*" *International Trumpet Guild Journal* 36, no. 3 (March 2012): 60–62.

Cron, Matthew, and Don Smithers. "A Calendar and Comprehensive Source Catalogue of Georg Philipp Telemann's Vocal and Instrumental Music with Brass." *International Trumpet Guild Journal* special supplement (December 1995): 120.

Dürr, Alfred. *The Cantatas of J. S. Bach.* Revised and translated by Richard D. P. Jones. Oxford: Oxford University Press, 2005.

Ehmann, Wilhelm. "100 Years of Kuhlo's *Posaunenchor* Book." *Brass Bulletin* 38 (1982): 33–53.

Eisensmith, Kevin. "Joseph Riepel's Concerto in D a Clarino Principale." *International Trumpet Guild Journal* 27, no. 4 (June 2003): 8–16.

Franklin, Peter. *Mahler: Symphony No. 3.* Cambridge Music Handbooks. Cambridge: Cambridge University Press, 1991.

Gekker, Chris. "Performance Suggestions for J. S. Bach's 2nd Brandenburg Concerto." *International Trumpet Guild Journal* 31, no. 3 (March 2007): 69–70.

Hazen, Robert M. "Parisian Cornet Solos of the 1830s and 1840s: The Earliest Solo Literature for Valved Brass and Piano." *International Trumpet Guild Journal* 19, no. 4 (May 1995): 35–38.

Hummel, Johann Nepomuk. *Concerto a Tromba Principale (1803): Introduction, Historical Consideration, Analysis, Critical Commentary, Original Solo Part.* Edited by Edward H. Tarr. HKB Historic Brass Series. Vuarmarens, Switzerland: The Brass Press/Editions BIM, 2011.

Jakobsen Barth, Verena. *Die Trompete als Soloinstrument in der Kunstmusik Europas seit 1900 mit besonderer Berücksichtigung der Entwicklung ab 1980 am Beispiel der Solisten Håkan Hardenberger, Ole Edvard Antonsen und Reinhold Friedrich.* Gothenburg, Sweden: University of Gothenburg, 2007.

Kelly, Daniel. "The Competition Solos of J. B. Arban." *International Trumpet Guild Journal* 30, no. 3 (March 2006): 17–28.

Koehler, Elisa. "In Search of Hummel: Perspectives on the Trumpet Concerto of 1803." *International Trumpet Guild Journal* 27, no. 2 (January 2003): 7–17.

———. "Bach Cantata Trumpet Parts: A Compendium." *International Trumpet Guild Journal* 32, no. 2 (January 2008): 17–23.

———. *Fanfares & Finesse: A Performer's Guide to Trumpet History and Literature.* Bloomington: Indiana University Press, 2014.

MacKay, M. Gillian. "Trumpet and Cornet *Concours* Music at the Paris Conservatoire, 1835–1925: The Development of Styles and Roles." PhD dissertation, Northwestern University, 1996.

Monelle, Raymond. *The Musical Topic: Hunt, Military and Pastoral.* Bloomington: Indiana University Press, 2006.

Moore, Brian. "The Rebirth of Haydn's Trumpet Concerto in England: Ernest Hall, George Eskdale, and the BBC." *International Trumpet Guild Journal* 30, no. 4 (June 2006): 26–29.

Mortenson, Gary. "Historical Perspectives and Analytical Observations on Francis Poulenc's Sonata (1922)." *International Trumpet Guild Journal* 10, no. 3 (February 1986): 10–13.

Olcott, James. "A Hoffnung Fanfare—No Joke! Reminiscences on *a Hoffnung Fanfare* on the Occasion of the 50th Anniversary of Its Composition." *The Brass Herald*, no. 34 (August 2010): 62–64.

Pearson, Ian. "Johann Nepomuk Hummel's 'Rescue' Concerto: Cherubini's Influence on Hummel's Trumpet Concerto." *International Trumpet Guild Journal* 16, no. 4 (May 1992): 14–20.

Phillips, Edward. "The Keyed Trumpet and the Concerti of Haydn and Hummel: Products of the Enlightenment." *International Trumpet Guild Journal* 32, no. 4 (June 2008): 22–28.

Proksch, Bryan. "The Context of the Tromba in F in J. S. Bach's Second Brandenburg Concerto, BWV 1047." *Historic Brass Society Journal* 23 (2011): 43–66.

———. "Excavating the Trumpet's Earliest Repertoire." *International Trumpet Guild Journal* 35, no. 3 (March 2011): 64–65.

Rabbai, George. *Infantry Bugle Calls of the American Civil War.* Pacific, MO: Mel Bay, 1997. Booklet with CD.

Rettelbach, Simon. *Trompeten, Hörner und Klarinetten in der in Frankfurt am Main überlieferten "Ordentlichen Kirchenmusik" Georg Philipp Telemanns.* Frankfuerter Beitraege Zur Musikwissenschaft, vol. 35, Tutzing, Germany: Hans Schneider, 2008.

Rice, John A. "The Musical Bee: References to Mozart and Cherubini in Hummel's 'New Year' Concerto." *Music & Letters* 77, no. 3 (August 1996): 401–24.

Schünemann, Georg, ed. "Trompeterfanfaren, Sonaten und Feldstücke. Nach Aufzeichnungen deutscher Hoftrompeter des 16./17. Jahrhunderts." In *Das Erbe deutscher Musik*, Erste Reihe, Reichsdenkmale, Band 7, Erster Band der Abteilung Einstimmige Musik, 3–71. Kassel, Germany: Bärenreiter, 1936.

Tarr, Edward H. "Haydn's Trumpet Concerto (1796–1996) and Its Origins." *International Trumpet Guild Journal* 21, no. 1 (September 1996): 30–34, 43.

Treybig, Joel. "A Cornetist's Perspective on Stravinsky's *Histoire Du Soldat.*" *International Trumpet Guild Journal* 27, no. 1 (October 2002): 49–56.

———. "J.S. Bach's Obbligatos: Beautiful and Significant Curiosities from BWV 5, 46, & 90." *International Trumpet Guild Journal* 35, no. 3 (March 2011): 13–28.

Villanueva, Jari. *Twenty-Four Notes That Tap Deep Emotions: The Story of America's Most Famous Bugle Call.* Baltimore, MD: JV Music, 2001.

West, Ann M. "The Cornet Obligato [*sic*] in Hector Berlioz's 'Un Bal' of *Symphonie Fantastique.*" *International Trumpet Guild Journal* 17, no. 3 (February 1993): 12–15.

Winegardner, Brian J. "A Performer's Guide to Concertos for Trumpet and Orchestra by Lowell Liebermann and John Williams." PhD dissertation, University of Miami, 2011. Open Access Dissertations (Paper 520).

Wood, Peter Joseph. "Gunther Schuller's Concerto for Trumpet and Chamber Orchestra: A Performance Analysis." PhD dissertation, Indiana University, 2000. ProQuest (AAT 3056814).

Zaslaw, Neal. *Mozart's Symphonies: Context, Performance Practice, Reception.* Oxford: Clarendon Press, 1991.

WEBSITES

Baroque Trumpet Shop (www.baroquetrumpet.com)

Grove Music Online (www.oxfordmusiconline.com)

Historic Brass Society (www.historicbrass.org)

Horn-u-Copia (http://horn-u-copia.net)

International Music Score Library Project (http://imslp.org)

International Trumpet Guild (www.trumpetguild.org)

Musical Instrument Museums Online (www.mimo-international.com)

O. J.'s Trumpet Page (http://abel.hive.no/trumpet)

Rafael Mendez Online Library (http://mendezlibrary.asu.edu)

Robb Stewart Brass Instruments (www.robbstewart.com)

Vintage Cornets (www.vintagecornets.com)

Vintage Mutes (www.vintagemutes.com)

About the Author

Elisa Koehler is an associate professor of music and department chair at Goucher College as well as an active professional trumpeter. She has performed on trumpets both old and new with groups as diverse as the Baltimore Chamber Orchestra, the Knoxville Symphony, the Handel Choir of Baltimore, the Orchestra of the 17th Century, the Washington Cornett and Sackbut Ensemble, and Newberry's Victorian Cornet Band. She is the author of *Fanfares & Finesse:* *A Performer's Guide to Trumpet History and Literature* and was the music director and conductor of the Frederick Symphony Orchestra for seventeen years. A member of the editorial staff of the *International Trumpet Guild Journal* since 2002, she has written widely about historic brass for the ITG. Dr. Koehler earned degrees from the Peabody Conservatory (DMA, conducting; BM, trumpet; BM, music education) and the University of Tennessee–Knoxville (MM, trumpet).